MUSSOLINI

" I am turning Foarty"
by Judith

趙月窗，

Mussolini

BY

Laura Fermi

THE UNIVERSITY OF CHICAGO PRESS
CHICAGO & LONDON

THE UNIVERSITY OF CHICAGO PRESS, CHICAGO 60637

The University of Chicago Press, Ltd., London

© 1961 by The University of Chicago. All rights
reserved. Published 1961. First Phoenix Edition 1974
Printed in the United States of America

82 81 80 79 78   11 10 9 8 7

ISBN: 0-226-24374-5 (clothbound); 0-226-24375-3 (paperbound)
Library of Congress Catalog Card Number: 61-17075

PREFACE

THE urge to write this book grew in me out of the bewilderment I experienced several years ago when in the course of checking dates and events for another book I began to discover the "true" Mussolini. I thought I knew what he had been like, for I had lived in Rome until 1938, when I came to the United States with my family, and Mussolini had been in power sixteen years. Although I had seen him but seldom in the flesh, his physical aspect, his mannerisms and voice, his actions and feats, all were familiar to me. I had formed a well-defined picture of the man in my mind, a picture which I have reason to believe many people, both in Italy and abroad, shared and accepted.

It was then with an acute shock that, having chanced on biographical material published after Mussolini's death, I came to realize how incredibly distorted my mental picture had been. And not only distorted, but incomplete as well, because in the mild political apathy common to large sections of the Italian middle class of that time, I had never asked myself, let alone taken the trouble to find out, what Mussolini had been and had stood for before he came into the limelight. But now, in the nineteen fifties, I could easily read about him from his origins to his death: I had at my disposal, along with the biographical, much documentary material and an exceedingly vast literature on fascism. As I read further and further my whole perspective changed, historical events acquired new values, different reasons for their being, and different correlations. But the greatest transformation occurred in my view of Mussolini himself: the man who had committed, to be sure, errors and sins, but who had been all of one piece, monolithic to use a word popular in Fascist times, strong, self-assured, intelligent to the point of being almost a genius, gave way to a far more complex personality, full of contradictions, of unanswered and probably unanswerable questions.

None of the existing biographies exactly drew the picture that was shaping before me, and I thought it relevant for me to let other people see the Mussolini whom I was discovering. Many of us are forgetting what fascism and nazism, indeed what Mussolini and Hitler, have done to our generation; we are forgetting that without them World War II would not have been fought and our lives would have taken entirely different courses. Why should we not re-examine, with the cool objectivity which we may apply to the past, the traits that make a dictator and the forces that mold him and allow him to rise? Thus I undertook to write this book.

Strictly speaking it is not a biography, and certainly it is not definitive. Out of all the incidents and details of Mussolini's life I have picked only a limited number and built up the episodes that best lend themselves to illustrate his character, his achievements and failures, the interrelations between the society of his times and his own career. Here and there, in the chapters on his youth before he came to power, I let my imagination help me reconstruct a scene or a piece of conversation, but I have always adhered strictly to facts and have not tampered with history.

I am not a scholar and make no claim to historical contributions. In writing this book I have relied almost entirely on published material: books, documents, magazines, and newspaper files. I was fortunate in that thirty-two of the thirty-four planned volumes of Mussolini's *Opera omnia (Collected Works)*, edited by Edoardo and Duilio Susmel, have been published to date. They contain, besides Mussolini's writings and speeches, documents, letters from and to him, telegrams, official orders and directives, and so forth. More documents are locked up in Italian archives and when they are released, probably in a matter of decades, they may shed new light and further modify the picture of the "true" Mussolini.

¶

This work has been made possible by a grant from the John Simon Guggenheim Memorial Foundation, for which I wish to express my gratitude.

I wish also to extend my thanks to the many people who have assisted me in the course of my work, and especially: to Angelica Balabanoff and Margherita Sarfatti for their personal recollections; to Denis Mack Smith, of Cambridge University, for his thorough and constructive criticism; to Luigi Salvatorelli for his kind advice; to Annalena Iona-Lasinio for helping in the preparation of the manuscript and for her numerous suggestions; to Ruth Grodzins, Alice Marcus, Max Ascoli, of the *Reporter*, and Samuel K. Allison, of the University of Chicago, for reading all or parts of the manuscript and giving me the benefit of their opinions; to Anna Capon and Anna Vannini for their help in gathering information in Italy; to the staffs of Harper Library, the University of Chicago, and of other libraries both in the United States and in Italy for having facilitated the task of research for me.

The photographs of Predappio, the birthplace of Mussolini, and the Mussolini family are reproduced by kind permission of Edizioni Flamigni Olindo, Predappio. The photographs of the Rocca of Caterina Sforza and of Mussolini as soldier are taken from the first volume of *Mussolini, l'uomo e l'opera*, by Giorgio Pini and Duilio Susmel, and are reproduced by kind permission of the publisher, La Fenice, Florence. The remaining photographs appear by kind permission of *Epoca* of Milan.

CONTENTS

ILLUSTRATIONS

INTRODUCTION

"Bullet shots pass by and Mussolini remains
— long live the Fascist Revolution!"
MUSSOLINI, April, 1926

THE trees that grow in Piazzale Loreto in Milan are young
and tender and they murmur softly when the breeze plays
among them. The buildings that inclose the square are modern and attractive with polished walls and sparkling shop-
windows. But Piazzale Loreto is old and lies in an old, poor
section of the city. It wears this new make-up to hide wartime
wounds, to forget the tragedies that it witnessed, bombings
and open fights, and acts of terror: Italian partisans throwing
a bomb at a German truck and the German retaliation — fifteen Italian hostages shot by Italian soldiers under German
orders — and, last, the morning of April 29, 1945.

April 29, 9:30 A.M. — a crowd had gathered in Piazzale
Loreto, a grim crowd, almost all of men, tense and haggard.
Along the many streets that converge upon Piazzale Loreto
from all directions more men were flowing in steadily, and as
they arrived pressing and pushing, the vast square heaved in
concentric waves. They pressed and pushed, trying to reach a
small area that appeared empty to them, seen as it was over
many shoulders, between many heads. A few armed men
guarded that little space and held back the crowd.

"We want to see them," shouted an exasperated voice far
from the small area. "Let us see them!" roared the mob. "We
have a right to see them!" The armed men looked at each

other, then at the heap of bodies in the space that from a distance seemed empty, and they decided that the mob should see them.

10:00 A.M. — six bodies hung by their feet from a steel beam in the roof of a gas station, a station that had no gasoline to sell. Six rigid bodies with arms stretched downward, dancing an upside-down macabre dance at each gust of wind.

The eyes of the crowd were on the two bodies hanging in the center of the row, the body of a man past the prime of life and that of a young woman. The man wore the black boots and black riding pants of the Fascist uniform and only a T-shirt on his sturdy chest. His neck was short and thick, his head clean-shaven; his big, square jaw hung down and his mouth was open wide; his face was disfigured by bullet wounds and the marks of kicks.

The girl had short, curly hair and appeared dainty even in death: she wore blue high-heeled shoes and a lacy blouse under a prim gray suit. A rope between her legs held her skirt in place. In life they had been lovers: Benito Mussolini, for over twenty-two years dictator of Italy, fed on a steady diet of applause in all the squares of Italy, for which Piazzale Loreto now took revenge, and Claretta Petacci, who of her own volition had shared his fate in the hours of judgment.

On each side of the central couple hung the bodies of two high Fascist officials, the most gruesome guard of honor lovers ever had.

Italians are not bloodthirsty. The people of Milan are usually quiet and law-abiding. If they behaved like barbarians on the morning of April 29, 1945, it was because they were under extreme provocation, because they had reached the limit of endurance. Almost five years of war had brought devastation to their country, had left Italy a physical and moral wreck the full extent of which not even the Italians could at once realize, busy as they were with their own problems, mourning their dead, reuniting families, rebuilding homes, fighting against starvation.

In the last two years the war had taken a tragic and un-expected turn. It was fought by foreign armies over the entire length of the Italian peninsula, from the shores of Sicily, where the Allies had made their first landing, to the northern frontiers, out of which the last German troops were just being chased. The conquering armies had invaded Italy from south to north. Their front line, stretching across the width of the peninsula, moved slowly, laboriously, against stubborn German resistance, dividing the Italians in two fluid groups, separate yet occasionally joining during clandestine migration around battlefields. Thus divided the Italians fought an ideological war, the war between democracy and totalitarianism, some on the Allies' side, some along with the Germans; and here and there in the sunny peninsula Italian partisans fought Italian Fascists in sporadic acts of civil war.

By April 29, 1945, the date that virtually marked the end of the Italian war, Italy was covered with scars: there were ruins everywhere, in towns, villages, and in the countryside; rubble, buildings half standing; works of art damaged or destroyed; churches torn apart, no longer able to give shelter or sanctuary. To the devastation of direct fighting and bombing there was added the systematic vandalism of the withdrawing Germans, who took bitter revenge on the Italians for their "unconditional surrender" to the Allies: the blowing up of bridges, of port works; the severing of sewers and water mains with the consequent spread of disease; the destruction of power plants that left cities in the dark and paralyzed industries; the scuttling of battleships to obstruct ports and block their approaches; the disruption of railroads and other means of communication.

Much worse were the moral scars. The people were tired of a war they had never wanted, for which they were not prepared; they were disgusted with themselves and with others, hoping to regain their spiritual values and yet knowing themselves corrupted. The disastrous conditions of the last two years, years of total war, had brought forth unbelievable generosity, self-sacrifice, and human solidarity, but also callousness and the worst egoism. The protective feelings of mothers who sought food and shelter for their families, the greed of

a few, the indifference of many, and the connivance of conquering armies had encouraged prostitution and a black
market on which almost anything could be had for money in
that Italy where there was nothing to be had — a black market
that in the long run was to save the country from starvation
even while it encouraged unscrupulous speculation.

This confusion of values had its roots not only in the very
nature of war, which always sharpens both the best and the
worst in men, in which good and evil are always mixed and
the same actions can be interpreted both as treason and as
heroism, as murder and as victory over tyranny; but also in
more than twenty years of dictatorship. This system, in which
lies and arbitrariness had consciously or unconsciously been
the norm, in which criticism and independent thinking had
been suppressed, to be replaced by submission and hypocrisy,
had left men disoriented, incapable of finding in themselves
moral directives that would guide their actions. The young
had known nothing but servitude, the old had slowly adapted
to servitude. All had followed the will of one man who had
dragged them along in the wild adventure that was his life.

PART 1

THE
SOCIALIST

1

CHILDHOOD IN ROMAGNA

"To us violence is not a system, not an aestheti-
cism, and even less a sport: it is a hard necessity to which we have submitted."
                                    MUSSOLINI, June, 1921

BENITO Mussolini, the oldest of Alessandro Mussolini's
and Rosa Maltoni's three children, was born on July 29,
1883, in Predappio, a village about ten miles from the city
of Forlì in that region of east-central Italy called Romagna.
Predappio was divided into several scattered groups of houses,
and each group had its name. The Mussolinis lived in the one
that was then called Dovia.

In the early formation of Benito's character four factors
are outstanding: the influence of his native Romagna, a land
of restlessness and rebellion, once called the Sicily of con-
tinental Italy; the ideology of his father, a village blacksmith,
atheist, and convinced revolutionary; the middle-class heritage and devout Catholicism of his mother, a gentle, somewhat
unbending elementary school teacher; and the distressing
poverty of the people around him, shared from time to time
by his own family.

Romagna, which extends from the crest of the Apennines
to the Adriatic Sea, is barren in its highest, most mountainous
parts, gray with craggy rocks, only sparsely covered with
sand and soil. It gradually changes into sunny hills where the
wheat fields are cut by rows of grapevines that stretch their
long branches to one another, like long lines of motionless
girls holding hands. Ruins of medieval castles stand on small,

rounded hilltops, and here and there patches of cherry trees provide an element of surprise in the quiet landscape. The hills give way to low, intensively cultivated plains which almost immediately turn into sandy shores and disappear into the sea. Rivers with the unreliable nature of torrents carve their parallel beds from mountain to sea, and on the river that bears the name of Rabbi, in a wide basin blandished by sunshine, is the village of Predappio.

The historical vicissitudes of Romagna shaped the character of its people. Invaded by barbarian hordes, conquered first by the Lombards, then by the Byzantines, contended by emperors and popes, torn by international rivalries and strife, overrun by foreign armies fighting their battles on its soil, poorly administered under a protracted ecclesiastical government, repeatedly occupied by foreign countries — over the centuries Romagna knew neither peace nor wealth. Over the centuries it bred a tough, wilful population from which sprang the most famous *condottieri*, some of the long-remembered rulers, and a hard-working common people. Over the centuries the sons of Romagna became violent and proud, accustomed to fighting and quick to revolt against established law. Their hands ran swiftly to a knife or a gun if their passions were aroused, and they did not mind the splash of blood on themselves or on others. The Romagnoli were loyal and generous men who could at once be brigands and rescuers of the weak, to whom politics was as necessary as the air they breathed, and who conceived of politics as one of the many hues of red.

In Romagna, among these proud and restless Romagnoli, in the second half of the nineteenth century, anarchism and socialism found fertile soil. The laborers of Romagna were in a chronic state of discontent, of poverty and want. They did not always find work, and when they did, it was invariably poorly paid. The luckiest laborers were hired for public works; others did seasonal work by the day, helping farmers in their chores. The farmers fared better than the laborers, especially the farmers of the fertile lower hills. But they were mostly sharecroppers, at the mercy of not-always-fair landowners, and so they too were often dissatisfied.

When the Russian anarchist Bakunin traveled through Romagna, he received a warm welcome and left a trail of enthusiastic followers who were aroused by his words although they did not fully share and perhaps did not understand his political views. Under his influence they organized colorful political groups with heroic, sentimental ideals of a revolution and a new social order. They adhered to the First International and were hopeful it would prove to be *"il sole dell'avvenire"* ("the sun of times to come") as Garibaldi had called it. They were not deterred by the opposition of conservative citizens and the label of "subversives" that they soon acquired but went on fighting for their cause in their peculiar, boastful way. They became forerunners of the Italian Socialist Party that did not yet exist in the kingdom of Italy, which was still very young.*

Prominent among Bakunin's admirers and followers was Alessandro Mussolini, Benito's father. Alessandro came from a family of peasants who for generations had lived and toiled on their own bit of land until Alessandro's father, who did not like hard work, sold his property and wasted its proceeds after settling in Predappio. From his father Alessandro inherited the soul, looks, and manner of a peasant, but he was not one; he did not return to the land and, instead, became an apprentice to a smith. This young village artisan, dissatisfied with his lot, unwilling or perhaps unable to try the traditional occupation of his ancestors, was a perfect target for "subversive" propaganda, and at eighteen he embraced the revolutionary socialism of that minority of workers in Romagna who had been aroused by Bakunin's words and writings. A few years later he asserted himself in his village both by opening his own smithy and by promoting a local branch of the International.

Alessandro the atheist was stocky, dark-haired, and dark-complexioned, with a friendly face cut by a pair of soldierly mustaches, and short, square hands. He spoke easily and persuasively, and many who loved him in Predappio came to share his ardent faith which mixed anarchism, revolutionism,

* The kingdom of Italy was proclaimed in 1861, and Bakunin first visited Italy in 1864. The Socialist Party was founded in 1892.

and a violent anticlericalism. He kept his ideals fresh and dynamic by frequent contact with other Internationalists and revolutionists, whom he met at rallies in neighboring villages and towns. He was honest and generous and always ready to help a political friend in trouble with the authorities. His most constructive achievement — apart from the less easily measurable results of his propaganda and his influence in local elections — was the introduction of the first threshing machine in Predappio, purchased by some sort of co-operative he had organized for that purpose.

The local police, who, like the police everywhere, were suspicious of leftist activities, soon found a pretext to arrest him. He was held in jail for six months and thereafter kept under watchful eyes. The police record of his arrest states that he had a "bent for blood-crimes and banditry, had been accused by popular voice, and was therefore believed dangerous to society and public order." The "popular voice," the reactionary element in the village, suspected him of hiding bombs and weapons, of preparing to become one of the leaders when the revolution broke out. In fact, the only evidence the police found against him was a few pamphlets by Bakunin and a few letters from Italian Internationalists.

His prison term and his skirmishes with the police inflamed rather than damped Alessandro's fighting spirit. He was courageous and loved argument. (He loved political argument especially when he could help it with large amounts of the strong wine from the hills of Romagna which fortified Romagna's sons.)

Alessandro had no formal schooling and yet he was more inclined to write political articles for local weekly papers or to harangue his fellow villagers than to wield a hammer at the anvil. His articles were not particularly good, nor did they contain original thought, but they helped him gain some ascendancy in local affairs and in later years earned him posts in the administration of Predappio. Before this happened, however, he married and got himself a family.

Rosa Maltoni came from a family of the lower middle class. Her father had been the veterinary of a village a few miles from Predappio. She had gone through normal school and had obtained the diploma of elementary school teacher. In 1877, at nineteen, she was appointed to teach the only two elementary grades offered at the small school of Dovia.* With her elderly parents, who adored her, she settled in Predappio. Everyone in the village, children and grownups, at once took a liking to the kind and well-mannered *maestrina*.

Physically, Rosa Maltoni was not dissimilar to Alessandro, for she too was stocky, with black hair and a dark complexion; but the square and prominent jaw that her son Benito was to inherit gave her a more determined look, which was softened somewhat by the gentle expression of her deep-set eyes. Altogether, she gave the impression of strength, balance, self-reliance, and modesty. The village passed the common judgment that she was a "good woman," and for many years after her death the villagers went on speaking of her, recalling what a good woman she had been.

Young men did not dare approach her, since in the streets she walked quickly, looking straight ahead and without turning to glance around, and when she was not headed toward school she was almost certainly on her way to church. It was as if she wanted to let others know that teaching and religion were her only interests. She was then much surprised when one day, in the notebook of one of her pupils, a little girl, she discovered a love letter from the smith Alessandro Mussolini. Shyly she answered, and soon the exchange of letters hidden in schoolbooks became their practice. Alessandro's literary courtship must have been persuasive, for Rosa, though not interested in politics and attached to her bourgeois traditions, fell deeply in love. Her religion was strongly rooted, yet her love for the atheist became as unshakable as her faith. Her parents, firmly intrenched in their middle-class conservatism, were alarmed and grieved at the prospect of their only daughter marrying the good-for-nothing smith who was known to have a prison record. For a long time they refused their consent, but in the end they gave in to Rosa's plea that they have faith in her, her choice, and God's will.

Rosa and Alessandro were married in the little Church of

* That year, an Education Act introduced compulsory elementary education, at least on paper.

San Cassiano in January, 1882. She was twenty-three years old and he was twenty-seven. They settled in a small rustic house in which Alessandro hung a portrait of Garibaldi, in recognition of the hero's enthusiastic revolutionary views, and Rosa hung a picture of the Virgin. Thus they started life together, and they were to travel together to the end of Rosa's days. The sweet *maestrina* proved to be the stronger, the one of firmer will, the sturdier supporter of the family. With the forthright loyalty of the women of Romagna, she stood by her man even when he went against her traditions; she tolerated and often helped his "subversive" trends, and she opened her home to his comrades who sought refuge from the police. Thus her role was less obvious than her husband's, as is so often the case of women's roles. Yet it was important, and without her constant support the good-for-nothing Alessandro would have achieved less than he did.

When their first son was born, Alessandro gave him three names, Benito Amilcare Andrea, in honor of three revolutionists: the Mexican Benito Juárez who led the revolt against the emperor Maximilian, and the Italians Amilcare Cipriani and Andrea Costa, both picturesque exponents and early heroes of socialism in Italy. Alessandro had known these two — or at least had seen them both at meetings — and with Andrea Costa, a son of Romagna like himself and a deputy in Parliament, he had also corresponded. Rosa accepted the political names, but with typical stubbornness she overcame her husband's objections and had the baby baptized in the Catholic faith, in the same Church of San Cassiano where she and Alessandro had been married.

The Mussolinis were poor. The role of Socialist propagandist left the smith little time or inclination for work, and his earnings were always uncertain. Rosa's salary was steady but meager. After another boy, Arnaldo, was born in 1885, and a girl, Edvige, in 1888, husband's and wife's combined earnings were only sufficient to provide the family with necessities. In later years Benito could remember the family living in three rooms of a gloomy old house with crumbling walls damp with moss, a house which had seen better times and was still called Palazzo Varano. In one of the rooms was Rosa's school, and in the morning her little pupils flocked there from the thinly scattered houses of the neighboring countryside. During summer vacation the schoolroom was turned into a granary. Winters were cold, and there was not always a fire in the kitchen, which served also as the boys' bedroom; nor was there always nourishing food on the table. The only sign of wealth were nine bolts of linen, stored on top of a large, dark wardrobe, bolts that Rosa had taken along as a bride and of which she was very proud. For many years grandmother Marianna, Rosa's mother, lived with the Mussolinis. She looked after the children while Rosa taught school, she gathered greens for salad in the fields and driftwood to cook with on the banks of the Rabbi River. When money was scarce, she went to her neighbors to borrow cooking oil, bread, or salt — salt is always expensive in Italy, where it is a state monopoly.

This poverty, fluctuating with the yield of the land as reflected in the price of food, as well as with Alessandro's earnings, and sometimes increased by the financial help which he never refused to political friends in need, was by no means distinctive of the Mussolinis. They were not worse off than many villagers and in years of poor crops certainly better off than most farm laborers. Italy has always been a poor country with few natural resources, where much toil very rarely produces much wealth, and during Benito's childhood Italy was going through one of her severest economic crises. Among the most important factors of this crisis were the loss of help and protection from the more powerful and richer nations that before Italy's unification had occupied much of the Italian territory; the inexperience and inefficiency of the men in power, who were not prepared to govern a nation whose independence had been so recently achieved; and the building of railroads over the Alps, which had opened Italy to the competition of the large European markets.

Poverty, if not characteristic of the Mussolinis, hit them in the peculiar way in which it hits that lowest echelon of the middle class to which Rosa belonged, the low-waged white-collar workers and teachers. Because of her position, education, and bourgeois traditions, Rosa was always respected in Predappio. Although occasionally, when Alessandro's political activities made him too conspicuous, some of the more conservative families withdrew their children from school, Rosa personally was always in good standing. Her family, she felt, had the moral obligation to behave accordingly and keep up that measure of decorum that her own position demanded. Like other intelligent mothers of the lower middle class, she hoped that her children would rise above her own condition, receive a better education, and attain a higher standing in society. Poverty not only dimmed her hopes of bettering her children's status but also made it very difficult for her to maintain them on her own social level; it threatened to push them down to her husband's.

Rosa loved Alessandro, the penniless smith, but in him she admired the propagandist of ideas rather than the wielder of hammers. She had encouraged her husband to enter her middle-class world, but she had not identified herself with the proletariat to which he belonged and for which she felt some sympathy and an indirect allegiance. For her children, she decidedly rejected a return to the proletariat.

The disparity between Rosa's ambitions and means, her ambivalence toward the working class, her constant endeavor to have her children rise above their status and reach higher strata of society were to be reflected in her oldest son's temperament and behavior.

Benito lacked the qualities that make the majority of children attractive. He was stubborn and sullen, incapable of true affection even toward his parents and younger brother and sister. Although he early taught himself to read, he did not talk much, preferring the use of fists. He was violent and vindictive and once spent hours sharpening a stone with which he then struck repeatedly a boy who had provoked him, until he saw blood. His was a conscious cruelty of which he liked to boast later in life.

During his early childhood, his mother took him regularly to the Church of San Cassiano; his father took him to his smithy or to the tavern where Socialists were likely to gather.

In church the boy loved the mystic rites, the symbolic decorations, the all-pervading awe, but he was restless, and the strong scent of incense upset him, made him faint once, it is said. When his mother sent him to wait outdoors, he climbed to the top of the old oak tree at the side of the church and threw acorns and stones at the faithful as they came from the church.

In his father's shop he helped work the bellows and absorbed revolutionary ideas. "Socialism," his father would say, "is open and violent rebellion against our inhuman state of things. It is the knowledge and the light of the world. It is justice coming to an unjust world, a free pact among all men. . . . Do not believe the priest and the bourgeois when they say that Socialists are visionaries who want to steal the possessions of others and should be put in jail or hung. . . ."

Occasionally Alessandro took his small son to see caravans of gaunt, lean men, worn out by malaria or pellagra, going through Predappio. They were unemployed laborers from the plains of Romagna on a journey toward more promising lands, in search of work and means of support for the families they had left behind. The blacksmith talked to them, explaining that workers everywhere should unite, give up religious and political prejudice, and embrace socialism, for only then would peace and love reign on earth. But the men on the road who needed bread more than words did not understand him. Nor did the child Benito understand. Yet the boy stored his father's words in his strong memory, and the smith's eloquence was not lost on him. It increased his rebelliousness and prepared him for the role of revolutionary Socialist agitator which he assumed during the first part of his life.

To the religious ceremonies that he attended with his mother and to his father's lessons in socialism the boy preferred action and fighting. Often alone, or isolated among playmates, he roamed the country, climbing trees and stealing fruit or nests. He had tamed an owl which he kept by his bed, and in writing he recalled that when he woke at night he felt reassured by the fixed gaze of the golden disks. He liked to play on the banks of the river — sometimes with his younger brother Arnaldo, whom he had turned into an obedient slave and willing victim. With other children he felt at ease only when he could lead them into acts of vandalism and provoke the anger of farmers.

The child's increasing wildness deeply worried his mother. Rosa was too busy with family and school chores to give sufficient attention to her unmanageable son, but she had faith in his intelligence and would not let him grow up a savage. Perhaps the little boy sensed that he was causing sorrow to her, for occasionally he would try to hide a wound or a bruise that he had got in a fight; but fight he must, for his affection for her was not sufficiently deep to cause him to reform. When he was nine years of age, she decided to send him to a boarding school run by the monks of the Society of St. Francis de Sales in the nearby town of Faenza. The excellent discipline of the Salesian Institute, she trusted, would transform her unruly child into a well-behaved and accomplished youth.

Alessandro the atheist was opposed to education in a parochial school, but Rosa could handle her husband as firmly as she dealt with school children. Alessandro gave in. By the time the school was to open in mid-October, 1892, the boarding fee had been set aside and a few new clothes were in a suitcase. After a cool goodbye to the rest of his family, Benito left with his father.

Father and son were quiet and long-faced during the lengthy trip. A small cart pulled by a donkey took them slowly along the dusty road between fields that had started to shed their green and turn yellow and red. They jogged along the range that prevents Predappio from seeing the sea, followed the valley of the Rabbi, then entered the plains. And all the time they could see on the highest part of the range the old ruin of the Rocca delle Caminate where Benito had often played and which many years later was to be rebuilt and offered to him by the people of Italy.

At last they reached Faenza, and through its narrow streets they arrived in front of the long, low building of the Salesian school. They had taken six hours to cover the less than twenty miles from Predappio. Having duly presented the boy to the school director, Alessandro left. The heavy gate closed behind him, and a new chapter opened in Benito's life.

The Society of St. Francis de Sales and its schools were founded a decade or so before Mussolini's birth by a diocesan priest and progressive educator, the blessed Giovanni Bosco. In order to put his ideas into practice, he gathered about him a group of men, chosen for their natural ability as educators, who became the first Salesians. He taught them to observe children and to study their souls with love, through reason and religion; to gain their friendship; to refrain from punishment as far as possible; to refrain from any physical violence and moral coercion; to encourage physical exercise; in short, to practice those principles that are now considered essential in education.

It is not easy to ascertain whether all Salesian schools were run according to theory some twenty years after Don Bosco's enlightened teaching. However this may be, the two years that Benito Mussolini spent in the institute at Faenza, far from bringing the beneficial effects for which his mother had hoped, ended in his expulsion from that school. In his rebellious state of mind he did not adapt to routine and discipline and went through experiences that must have had a marked influence on his later development.

The Salesian Institute at Faenza, being both a vocational school and a preparatory school leading to further study for the liberal professions, gathered children from all walks of life. The Salesians followed current practice, and at mealtimes the pupils were seated at three tables, according to the size of the fees they paid. The same food was not served to all tables. Benito was made to share the most frugal fare at the table of the poorest children and was thus separated from most of his classmates. The pupils at the Salesian Institute came from all walks of life, but Benito's companions at table were children from the lower class who were learning a trade by working in the school shops. In adult life Benito neither forgot nor forgave what at nine, with the awareness coming from his father's teaching, he felt was a great social injustice. It stressed the rift between his mother's ambition of a good education for him and his own realization that he was only a blacksmith's son and of peasant stock, not fit to eat with those with whom he studied. Poverty at home had not disturbed him because others in the village were as poor or poorer than his own family. Now it slapped him in the face and left its stinging mark. By one of those twists of the mind so common to human beings, he later embraced poverty as something of which he must pretend he had always been proud, a prop which won him favor in his histrionic career.

Other reasons for unhappiness were in the boy's nature, too wild, nomadic, and defiant to adjust to school life. Classrooms and halls were wide and spacious. The courtyard where children played and Salesian monks walked while saying their prayers was vast and pleasant, closed on one side by the institute's own church. Ancient oaks changed the glare of the sun into restful light, and a covered portico offered protection on rainy days. There was a roominess in the whole school, a moderate well-being that was lacking in Mussolini's home, but there was not the unlimited space of the open countryside, offering infinite possibilities to a child of imagination and few scruples. And within the walls of the institute there were eyes everywhere, the indifferent eyes of children and the watchful eyes of adults. "Study the young," Don Bosco had said; "be kind to them; never leave them alone." So the Salesians followed their pupils everywhere. The little children, always accompanied by the black gowns of the Salesians, moved to the peremptory sound of the bell. Up in the morning, and then in file from place to place: to mass, to classrooms, to meals, to play, and, before retiring, to kiss the long bony hand of the director. Even during periods of exceptional entertainment, black-robed priests or lay teachers were always along — on excursions in the country, at rehearsals and shows in the school theater.

The boy who did not feel affection, who had no use for other boys unless they were a gang and he their leader, lacked

isolation and solitude and, lonely among so many people, re-
volted against the inescapable togetherness of the institute's
life. His unruliness often earned him that punishment that
Don Bosco had hoped it would be possible to avoid. Alert and
prompt in school, he learned what he cared to learn, not what
he was asked to study. His preference was the history of ancient Rome, the glorification of the great Roman past which
has always been a prominent part of the school curriculum in
Italy and which has often produced a wrong perspective of
the present. On the margins of his books he often scribbled
"Roma-Dovia," and perhaps he had dreams, or a premoni-
tion, of the time when he would rule in the Italian capital.

Deaf to reason and admonition, he was at odds with children and adults and kept his fists and feet ready for action.
His first year at the Salesian school was a constant state of
war with the third-grade teacher: "He loathed me and I hated
him," Mussolini later recalled. The feud ended with the
teacher hitting the boy with a ruler and the boy throwing an
inkpot at the teacher in retaliation. In his second year, during
a scuffle, he stabbed a schoolmate with his pocketknife.

The daily mass, the religious exercises in connection with
Easter and First Communion, appealed to him and kept him
in terror of sin and God. The strong impression they made on
him was to persist during his entire life but did not reduce
his insubordination. He remained the black sheep of the
school. His standing with school authorities was not improved
by his father's being an atheist and a Socialist, a "leader of
mobs," who wrote articles inviting priests to burn their gowns
and wear worker's clothes, and who was not even able to pay
his son's school bills in full. At the end of his second year
Benito was expelled for good from the Salesian Institute — he
had been expelled before, but his mother's pleas had earned
him temporary forgiveness.

The expulsion from the school in Faenza took place in the
summer of 1894. Seven years later, at eighteen, Mussolini ob-

tained the diploma of elementary school teacher with honors from a lay school in Forlimpopoli, a small town near Predappio and Forlì.

The atmosphere in this school was less repressive than in the Salesian Institute. Still, Mussolini's stay was punctuated with acts of rebellion, with frequent punishment and brief expulsions. Again he became known in the school for his promptness in learning what he liked, for his refusal to follow requirements and rules, for his strong fists, and his violence. Again, in a fight, he wounded a boy with a knife. He still preferred isolation to company, unless he could assume the role of leader in some act of rebellion, such as organizing a students' strike for better food.

The expenses involved in keeping Benito — and later Arnaldo — in school were hardships for the parents. Mussolini's mother, always the one to struggle against financial difficulties, once wrote a letter to the prefect of Forlì who had promised to propose her for an award in recognition of her good teaching. It is evident that writing this letter was not a light or easy task: "Ever mindful of that auspicious day for me when Your Excellence deigned to visit my humble school . . . and expressed too-flattering words on my behalf despite my [small] merits. . . . " She went on: "Your Excellency may see for yourself that this year the economic hardship in this little village is at its height, owing to the reduced yield of the crops and the total failure of the grape harvest, the only produce of these places. And it is precisely for the above-mentioned reasons that my poor family [which had meanwhile got a vineyard on a nine-year lease] is in such strained financial circumstances that we are forced to cut off the studies of a poor little boy of ours, twelve years old, who is now at the Royal Normal School in Forlimpopoli, and who according to his teachers promises to amount to something." She concluded by asking the prefect to speak to the proper authorities on her behalf, according to his promise. The award was never granted, but Benito, the boy whom his mother pathetically and shyly described as promising, went on with school.

At the end of this period his tendencies to leadership were focused and directed toward socialism. The nearness of his

school to Predappio made it possible for him to spend vacations, holidays, and Sundays at home, thus coming again
under the influence of his father's ideas at an age when he
could better understand them. His father had meanwhile acquired stature in the eyes of his fellow villagers: he had created
a producers' and consumers' co-operative and had occupied the
posts of vice-mayor and town counselor (*consigliere comu-
nale*). Even so, he had not given up his subversive activities
both in the open and underground. On May Day, Benito, of
whom his father was growing increasingly proud, could now
be trusted to help dig up the metal box hidden in the earth of
the cellar and containing the large red-satin flag which the
police had often looked for and never found. He could now
participate in political discussions with his father's comrades
and appreciate the propaganda leaflets his father's friends
brought along as well as the fragments of Marxian doctrine that
they had learned and were willing to teach. This was a crude
political education. Neither his father nor his father's friends
had original views to offer, and they spoke in platitudes
picked up here and there in the Socialist press. Yet even platitudes acquired vividness in the mouths of true sons of
Romagna who warmed up in their friendly companionship
under the effects of several glasses of wine. Benito absorbed
these platitudes and passed them on to his schoolmates at
"political rallies" that he organized in secluded corners of
the schoolyard. He improved his father's picturesque presentation with his own coloring, his own strong sense of drama,
and as his fellow students listened to him attentively he had
his first audiences and his first practice in public speaking.

A few months before he was to get his diploma, he received
his first public recognition: his name appeared in a daily
paper. The occasion was modest. The director of his school
had asked him to commemorate, before the entire school, the
very recent death of the great composer Giuseppe Verdi, "the
Swan of Busseto," who was mourned all over Italy. Benito
accepted but did not submit a copy of his speech for approval.
When the time came, he stressed Verdi's political activity and
participation in the first government of the new kingdom of
Italy. Using the fact that the composer had been a philanthro-

pist who spoke out against the poor conditions under which the lower classes lived, Benito turned the commemoration into a political speech.

The next day the official newspaper of the Socialist Party, *Avanti!* published a brief item:

VERDI'S COMMEMORATION
Forlimpopoli, February 2, 1901. — Last night,
in the Civic Theater, the comrade student Mussolini commemorated the Swan of Busseto, delivering
a much applauded speech.

This was the first time Mussolini's name appeared in print.

2

SWITZERLAND

"We have torn to shreds all revealed truths,
we have spit on all dogmas, rejected all
heavens, derided all charlatans — white, red,
or black — who peddle on the market the
miraculous drugs that give 'happiness' to
mankind."

MUSSOLINI, January, 1920

T HE train that on the night of July 9, 1902, left Chiasso
on the Italian-Swiss border for Lausanne carried among
many Italian passengers a young man, Benito Mussolini.
While most of the passengers in the third-class car were sleep-
ing or dozing on the hard wooden benches, he stood alone by
a window in the corridor. The wide-brimmed hat, bandit-style,
the large black tie, and the square chin pushed forward gave
him a certain air of defiance. His erect posture that made him
seem taller than his five feet, six inches, the fiery glance of
his dark eyes, the bit of mustache that did not manage to
cover his lip, all indicated assertiveness and the wish to appear older than his true age: in twenty days he would be
nineteen.

He watched through the train windows the dim scenery, the
majestic peaks of the Alps. "The moon rose behind very high
mountains, white with snow, amid a silvery smile of stars,"
he wrote early the following September in a letter to a friend,
a highly dramatic account of his first Swiss experiences.
"Lake Lugano gave out magic reflections like a polished sheet
of metal on which beat unknown, enchanting lights."

Were his thoughts running ahead of train and time into the

unknown future, or did they stay behind with the things and people to whom he had said goodbye? He was starting on a new venture with no purpose, for no good reason. While most of his companions in the train were laborers who were emigrating because they could not find work at home, he had given up a small position which could have been the beginning of a modest career. After getting his diploma as an elementary school teacher he had spent months in fruitless search of a teaching or other white-collar position. When discouragement and frustration had fast hold, he was named substitute teacher in Gualtieri Emilia, a small town on the Po River. From February until the beginning of the summer vacation he taught quietly and conscientiously, drawing little satisfaction from it. Then, on a sudden impulse, as if following the whim of the moment, he decided to try his luck in Switzerland. He lied to his parents and, letting them believe that he had been promised a job, wired asking them to send the train fare. But he had no job in view and no idea where he would go in Switzerland. Train and time, moving along together, gave finality to his rash decision. When morning came and the "serpent of steel" that took him toward "new people" went through German Switzerland under a cold rain, he recalled "the green countryside of Italy kissed by a sun of fire. . . . Was this a first touch of nostalgia?"

It may not have been nostalgia: The youth had learned to watch the sound of his own words and was developing that strong sense of drama which was to give him an almost uncanny intuition of the role in which he made the best impression on others — and, quite likely, on himself. Perhaps it was nostalgia; but in the apparently romantic adolescent the self-centered aloofness and lack of true affection that had characterized his childhood still prevailed. At Chiasso, while waiting for the train, he had bought a newspaper and learned that in Predappio his father had been arrested and jailed for his part in electoral disorders. Benito hesitated only a moment. He considered the possibility of changing his plans and going home, but dismissed it promptly and lightly, telling himself that the news was of little importance. (Alessandro Mussolini was in jail five months awaiting trial. He was then absolved and released, but this last imprisonment broke his health and his spirit, and he was never again the active political fighter he had been.)

Violence was still one of Benito's most prominent traits. On the trip to Switzerland he had taken along among his few belongings an "Arabian-style" knife with which, a few weeks earlier, in a fit of passion, love or jealousy, he had wounded a young married woman — the third person Mussolini admits stabbing with a knife. The young woman, whose husband was in the army, had been his mistress while he was teaching in Gualtieri and had accepted the wound as she had accepted all that the relation with Benito brought her. On the night before he left for Switzerland they had exchanged kisses and solemn promises, and that was the last she was to see of him.

It would be futile to look for a set pattern or a directing line in the actions of young Mussolini during the two years he spent in Switzerland. He was at an age when most young people who have not yet found a driving interest to which to dedicate their lives are investigating possibilities and opportunities, shifting from one set of values to another in an effort to find and assert themselves. Mussolini, in whom the spirit of adventure and ambition were stronger than in the average young man, could not escape the restlessness, disappointments, and frustrations of his difficult age. He lived from day to day, moving from place to place on the spur of the moment or on the advice of a casual friend. He sought experiences for their own sake, making no effort to channel them and give them purpose, letting himself drift with circumstance as a piece of wood is carried along by a tortuous stream. In these aimless wanderings and through the difficulties that he had to face, he discovered his likings and abilities and set the foundations of his future career. His first three weeks in Switzerland were especially difficult, if the dramatic letter in which he related his early experiences can be regarded as a reliable source of information.

On the advice of an acquaintance made on the train, young Mussolini got off at Yverdon near Lucerne. To provide for his first needs he sold his Arabian knife and discarded the memory of the young woman he had passionately loved and the wound he had inflicted. Within a few days he obtained work in a nearby village as an unskilled laborer in the construction of a chocolate factory. On his first Monday in Switzerland, clad in his dark teacher's suit, the young man who knew only desk work grabbed the handles of a wheelbarrow loaded with stones and started his trips to the second story of the building. At the end of eleven hours, the regular working day, he had made 121 trips, his white hands were cracked and blistered, his muscles swollen, and his back felt as if in a thousand pieces. The following Saturday he quit, appalled at the meagerness of the wages he received (20 lire, about four dollars of those times, for the full week). Like other Italian workers in Switzerland, Mussolini was at the mercy of his boss. There was no possible appeal, no organization to which workers could turn for protection, and most of the diplomatic representatives in charge of the interests of Italian citizens abroad were unwilling to intervene. Mussolini's boss dismissed him, saying that he was too well dressed to be a worker and had not really earned his money. A boss in Switzerland had an advantage over the men he hired, since he was always able to find another immigrant in desperate need of money and willing to accept any wage, however low.

Mussolini bought a pair of sturdy shoes to replace the lightweight "teacher's shoes" that had gone to shreds in a week of heavy labor and then took a train for Lausanne. The mere idea of Lausanne could not fail to exert on him the attraction that cities have for those who come from small towns and believe that cities are bursting with opportunities, offering everything just for the asking. Moreover, in Lausanne he would find many Italians tied by strong bonds of solidarity and generous to one another. Young Mussolini could hope that they would go out of their way to help a newcomer. Life is often filled with disappointments for a young man out in the world on his own, with a dislike for manual labor and hopes set too high. An unknown city is at first overwhelming even under the best of circumstances, and in Lausanne Musso-lini could not understand what people said, for although he had studied French, his ears were not yet used to the sound of it. The little money he had saved was soon completely gone, and the only coin he had in his pocket was a medal honoring Karl Marx. After an unsuccessful attempt to get help from one Italian, he was too shy, or too proud, or too deeply wounded, to look to anyone else.

He went hungry, had a try at begging, and while walking along the shore of the lake asked himself whether it was worth living another day. But instead of plunging into the water, he made himself a bed in an abandoned crate under one of the arches of the Grand Pont, the long bridge that connects two hills of Lausanne. Early one morning, wakened by the chill of dawn, he had the misfortune to be seen by two policemen as he was crawling out of his crate. They arrested him for vagrancy, and he went to jail. Upon his release three days later, he set aside previous hesitation and sought the help of a group of Italian Socialists. His first contact with them marked the end of the most difficult period of his life. It had lasted less than three weeks and ended, with good approxima-tion, on his nineteenth birthday. Four days later an article of his was published in the Italian language Socialist weekly of Lausanne, the *Avvenire del Lavoratore* — his third published article, for twice before a piece of writing by Benito Mussolini had appeared in a weekly for Italian schoolteachers.

The Italian comrades used to meet in a café near the Grand Pont, and it was there that Mussolini got in touch with them. He was reluctant at first to talk about his predicament, ashamed to have to confess his hunger and his need. But the comrades assured him that his experiences were by no means unique and that many Italians before him, especially seasonal workers, had gone without food as he had. (The *hours* he had gone without food were twenty-six in the highly dramatic let-ter he wrote early in September and became forty-eight in a later version of the story.)

The young man relaxed, accepted a dish of spaghetti from the librarian of the Italian Socialist section and hospitality in the attic of a woodcarver, a political refugee who was also assistant editor of the *Avvenire del Lavoratore*; he shared the bed of a tailor, received advice from many, and from a few had the promise of assistance in his search for work. This was not going to be easy, all agreed, because the only jobs available to Italian immigrants were those that the Swiss disliked, heavy outdoor work constructing buildings and roads, or opening railway tunnels through the mountains. (Italian laborers had built the St. Gotthard Tunnel through which Mussolini had come to Switzerland, and while he was there Italian laborers were opening the Simplon Tunnel with much hardship and loss of life.)

Regardless of the kind of job he might find, the Socialists encouraged him to help them in their work among Italian immigrants, whose low status they were striving to raise. The great majority of the immigrants were poor, ignorant, often altogether illiterate, and the usual plagues of poverty, disease, dirt, and crime were widespread among them. "In Italy," Mussolini himself was to write from Lausanne, "one can be a poet; not in Switzerland. There is something prosaic in the Italian element; poverty and daily cares do not let one admire the most pure line that Lac Leman draws with its blue waters at the feet of the very high mountains of Savoy and the snowy peaks of the Dent du Midi."

Because of their poverty and ignorance, Italian workers, not solely in Switzerland but wherever they went, acquired the reputation of being the cheapest labor, willing to accept almost any wage. Their competition was unfair to local workers, for they broke the rule of solidarity by going to work when others were on strike. The Socialists were trying to educate and organize this uneducated mass, to arouse a social conscience and a sense of human dignity. A young man like Mussolini, who had an education much above average and was aware of the workers' problems, who could talk their language and speak effectively, was a good instrument for the dissemination of Socialist propaganda.

Helped by the comrades he met at the café, Benito started

his Swiss activities on two different levels. On the one there was a succession of unsatisfactory jobs in Lausanne, in Bern, and other cities, jobs that he disliked and that he did not keep long enough to enable him to learn any trade: he was clerk in a wholesale wine store, assistant to a painter-sculptor, errand boy in a grocery store; he tried construction work again and specialized in window moldings; and he went on shifting from one job to another until he gave up manual work for good. Simultaneously, on another level, he was engaged in Socialist propaganda, and in this work he was sufficiently successful to become a link between the Socialist organizers and the masses they wished to organize. He wrote articles for *Avvenire del Lavoratore* and for other Socialist papers both in Italy and abroad, among which was the Italian *Proletario* of Philadelphia and New York. (At one time there was talk of his going to the United States to become editor of *Proletario*.) As secretary, he took the minutes for the Italian union of masons and mason helpers in Lausanne. He spoke almost every Sunday to groups of workers in Lausanne and in other Swiss cities and towns.

One of Mussolini's striking characteristics was the extreme position he took in his writings and speeches. The ideals he embraced, following his father's example, were radical, expressions of rebellion, violence, class warfare, and atheism; in expounding them he avoided the middle of the road and adopted the most intransigent, unrestrained, often paradoxical point of view. He seemed to know by intuition that in this way he placed himself in a conspicuous position that singled him out and made a deeper and longer-lasting impression on his listeners than if he were to take a more moderate stand. He was the actor who perfects a mannerism and dramatizes his performance in order to excite a strong reaction in his audience. For the art of acting Mussolini was developing an extraordinary ability.

His speeches were well liked. He had one great gift: he could speak feelingly, whether or not he felt at all, and sound sincere, whether or not he believed in the ideas he was propounding. His romantic appearance, his dramatic gestures, the bits of knowledge that he learned to absorb and use when needed, his dry, direct way of presenting facts, appealed to simple people. The dark young man in the threadbare suit, with the white hands of one who loathes manual work, the retiring young man who knew how to appear fierce at times and at other times lonely, who never mixed with others — this intent young man became a well-known figure among certain groups of Italian immigrants. When he entered a meeting place and when he ended a speech he was often cheered. Thus, the applause of the masses, which was later to become one of his basic necessities, was a commonplace experience when he was nineteen.

The ideas that young Mussolini developed in the course of his stay in Switzerland form an interesting background for his later career. In many respects this background is in contrast with all he was to stand for while ruling over Italy, and it is therefore important to differentiate between the intrinsic traits of his temperament and the ideas that he temporarily embraced, partly because his education and environment bent him toward them, partly because, at this early stage, he knew (intuitively, perhaps subconsciously) that he was meant for extreme roles and had the ability to perform them.

Throughout his life Benito Mussolini was a theoretician of action. He considered action more important than anything else, certainly far more important than thinking. "I could not understand," he was to write in recalling his childhood, "why one had to think so much before acting. . . . In those youthful years, as indeed now, my day used to begin and end with an act of will translated into action." The need for action was intrinsic in his nature, and to him action was a synonym of violence. It was the mystic expression of the undefined rebelliousness inherited from his father, of his rancors and restlessness, and the instrument with which he might fulfil his ambitions. His cult of action helped create the legend of Mussolini the man of action, a legend which outlasted his death. Yet, throughout his life, his need for action seemed to find a satisfactory outlet in his words rather than in his deeds, and when he was faced with an opportunity for action, he almost invariably hesitated, pulled back, and let the moment pass. He was to be called "the man of the barricades," but to the barricades he was to send others more often than go himself, and in his whole life there is hardly an act that can be ascribed to genuine courage. In Switzerland the outlet of his need for action was the Socialist propaganda, the incitement to class warfare and the use of violent means, the attacks on all symbols of vested authority, from kings to police. A good example of his central theme is provided by words that he wrote as early as August, 1902: "We have no formulas. We only hope that our party will go back to its ancient methods of struggle, that it will attack, with implacable combativeness, constituted power, without ever descending . . . to pacts and bargains."

A violent and intransigent class warfare was among the ideals that Mussolini was to retain as long as he was a Socialist. Longer lasting was his antimonarchism. His first antimonarchic article, written in 1903 for the *Proletario* of New York, was titled "The Sport of Kings." A series of visits that Victor Emmanuel III of Italy paid to several European capitals and of which young Mussolini disapproved, feeling that it was a form of exhibitionism, gave him an excuse to criticize all monarchs. The kings of Greece, England, and Italy, the emperor of Germany, the czar of Russia, all were intellectual nonentities, he wrote. "Their mentality is barely sufficient to sign decrees. Their military career, the education they usually receive from Jesuits, the stupid court etiquette, in the long run crush their brains and deprive them of their thinking power. They hate progress — because they are obliged to suffer it. If a decree were sufficient, they would chase humanity back into absolutism and barbarism." He was especially bitter against the House of Savoy, which he called reactionary and bigoted. He accused the kings of Italy of having bled the country to exhaustion for military expenses at a time when she needed bread and of having allowed troops to shed the people's blood. He was here alluding to the famous riots that had taken place five years before, in 1898, following an increase in the price of bread. Indeed, these

riots and the large-scale repression that ensued were still
fresh in the minds of the Socialists in Switzerland, many of
whom were refugees of the political persecution in 1898, as
was the woodcarver who had given Mussolini hospitality in
his attic. In Milan alone, which had been hit harder than any
other city, there had been some four hundred dead, and almost seven hundred men were sent to jail. From what his
comrades in Lausanne told him, Mussolini had come to the
conclusion that King Humbert had been responsible for this
cruel repressive action, and in his article he wrote: "The dawn
of the new kingdom is red with workers' blood."

Along with his antimonarchism, Mussolini professed an
antimilitarism that appeared deeply felt. He deprecated "the
bestial and blind coercion" which he considered "the moral
basis of the army." He deplored the people's acquiescence in
militaristic systems. In February, 1904, in *Avvenire del
Lavoratore*, he wrote of the army: "It is ourselves who fatten
the beast when, with stupid resignation, we pay the taxes
destined to maintain it; it is the sons of the proletarians who
people the army barracks, and it is our sense of conceit that
fortifies patriotism. Instead of scratching the velvety skin of
professional armymen, there is one infallible means of destroying infamous militarism: desertion." But in this stand
Mussolini was very soon to show great inconsistency.

Among Benito's most radical opinions at this time, the
most intolerant were those that concerned religion. The boy,
raised according to the dogmas of his atheist father, bitter
against priests who had troubled his elementary school days,
now pushed anticlericalism and atheism to a degree exceeding
the limits of all reason. His first printed expression of anticlericalism appeared in November, 1902, when, commenting
on socialism in Switzerland and on the "incoherent elasticity"
of "the chiefs of local socialism," he wrote: "There are deputies who affirm that religion is necessary to the people and
thus help all pastors of all cults in an efficient, unhoped for,
gratuitous way." His anticlericalism is still hesitant. His
bland disapproval of the help given "all pastors of all cults"
is further tempered by the effect of his next article, "The
Human Christmas," a strangely mystic piece of writing:

"Since your appearance, Messiah, 1,902 years have gone by. Humanity was waiting then as it is now. Was perhaps your word thrown in vain to the crowds that followed you, Apostle, over the green-blue lands of Galilee? . . . That cross which you carried up the strenuous ascent of Golgotha the prole-tarians of today carry throughout their lives." The masses, Mussolini wrote, do not celebrate Christmas as the rich people do ("The traditional log does not burn in the thousands huts that have no fireplaces"), but they wait, fighting, for the com-ing of the human Christmas. ~religious~ ~writing~

Soon his writings about religion became more violent, more assured. In "The Horrors of the Cloisters," he commented on the trials, which were being held in Paris, of nuns accused of cruelty toward the young girls entrusted to them: "The walls of convents hide a gangrenous sore. They defend the *Bastilles* of religion. And as such they must be torn down." He denounced the nuns' "ritual bigotism and divine erotism. . . . In the innermost spirit of religion torture is hiding. . . . Re-ligion . . . today has revealed itself as an institution that tends toward political power in order to perpetuate ignorance and economic exploitation: Today's priests and nuns . . . will appear to the 'new peoples' as black pages of human pre-history."

In 1904 Mussolini went on tour, giving lectures that at-tacked religion, and held two public debates about the existence of God with a Protestant evangelical pastor. The debates were successful, and Mussolini thought that his "scien-tific" arguments had silenced his opponent and were worth publishing. The small booklet called *"L'uomo e la divinità"* ("Man and Divinity") which he then wrote became the first publication of the "International Library of Rationalistic Propaganda" founded in Lausanne by Mussolini and other Italian Socialists. "Man and Divinity" is interesting for sev-eral reasons. The specific theme of his debates and of his book was that God does not exist: "Religion in science is an ab-surdity, in practice an immorality, in men a disease." To prove his point he invoked the authority of all sorts of authors and philosophers, from Epicurus to Galileo, from Plato to Spencer, from St. Augustine to Bakunin. In a style as muddled as the arguments he proposed he gave sweeping "scientific" explanations of facts that are still great problems to modern scientists and far from a solution. He said, for instance: "After Locke with his method of introspection initiated experimental psychology it was recognized that the soul is the product . . . of the central organs in our nervous system — a simple result of the laborious work of the cerebral cells — as the result of the internal motion of a clock is the marking of hours, the measurement of time. The excitation of these cells . . . leads to their chemical modification in a process of which the laws are known. . . . The soul, 'product of the brain,' explains many phenomena not understandable through the soul, 'particle of the divine essence.' " Having thus "proved" that the soul is not of divine essence, Mussolini went on to prove that God does not exist and is not needed, that religious morality is immoral, authoritarian, legislative, that it debases man and drives him back toward animality, and that it atrophies his powers of reason.

This is Mussolini's first published book, a pamphlet of about sixty pages, written when he was barely twenty-one years old. In Fascist times all copies of "Man and Divinity" were to disappear in Italy and the memory of it to be blotted out. None of Mussolini's Fascist biographers mention it. Yet, fortunately for serious historians like Gaudens Megaro, who was to study it, the pamphlet survived these attempts at obliteration, and in 1924, twenty years after its first publication, it was republished, strangely enough, in the United States, by the Italian Social Library of New York. The editors stated that their aim in issuing a new edition of this pamphlet was to show the dictator of Italy as a turncoat. Five years later the reasons for calling him a turncoat would have been much stronger: in 1929, with much fanfare and the praise of the Catholic world, he achieved a long-awaited reconciliation between Church and State.

The information gathered for his debates and booklet and easily "sold" to his uneducated audiences gave him the feeling that he was expert on the subject of religion and could hold his ground against any adversary. At the end of a lecture on religion he attended one day in the Maison du Peuple in Lausanne, Mussolini got up and asked to debate. The speaker was Emile Vandervelde, the future foreign minister of Belgium, then thirty years old, a Socialist member of the Belgian Parliament and a brilliant speaker. He lectured often in Lausanne at the Maison du Peuple, which had been inspired by the Belgian Maison du Peuple founded by Vandervelde himself.

In June, 1904, Vandervelde held a series of three lectures dealing with socialism and religion and maintained the old Socialist formula that religion is a private affair, an affair of conscience. He concluded that proletarians ought to unite in the class struggle, setting aside any differences in their philosophical and religious convictions. When a young man whom he did not know asked to debate, he willingly agreed. Mussolini, who did not consider Vandervelde's speech in line with the views of revolutionary Socialists, contended that anyone trying to cajole the powers of reaction, the Catholic Church first among them, was a traitor to the Socialist cause. Against religion he brought forth some of the proofs published in his booklet: he compared Jesus' doctrine with Buddha's, and went on to say that in India, seven hundred years before Christ, Buddha spent some forty-five years preaching fraternity, benevolence, and love of others. Before this colossus of charity how small and insignificant Christ appears to us, Christ who preached for two years only, in small villages, and succeeded in convincing a mere dozen of ignorant vagabonds! This comparison between Buddha and Christ was included in his pamphlet; he had used it before, and no one had pointed out weaknesses in it. Mussolini must have thought it sound and impressive, but Vandervelde quietly reminded him that if Christ had not preached forty-five years as Buddha had, this was due to a "little professional accident" which put an end to his career in his thirtieth year. After this rebuke Mussolini's pride must have been badly smarting, for he called the debate with Vandervelde "unfortunate."

¶

Mussolini's imprisonment for vagrancy shortly after he arrived in Lausanne was not his only imprisonment in Switzerland. His growing fame as political agitator inevitably

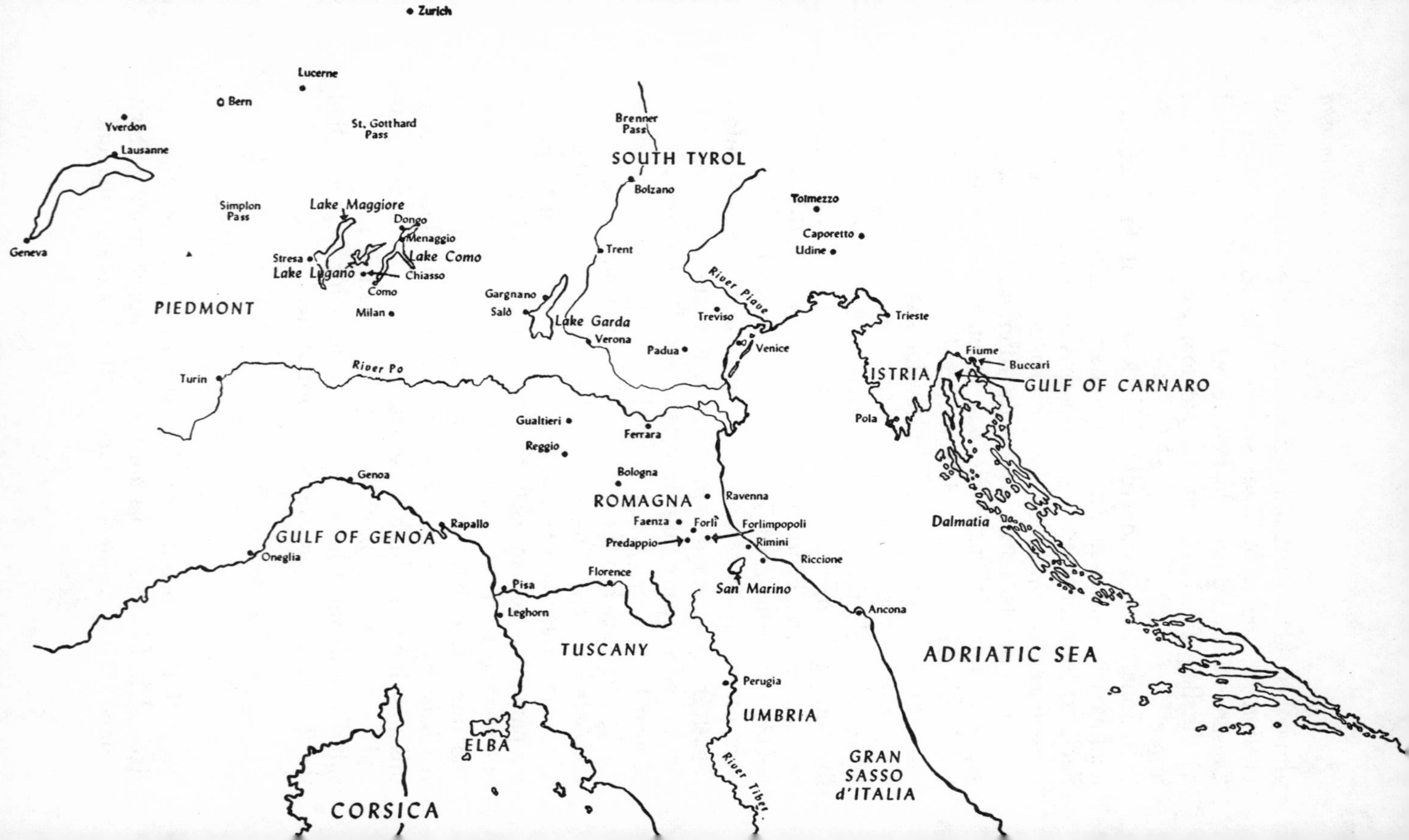
Zurich
Lucerne
Bern
Yverdon
St. Gotthard Pass
Lausanne
Geneva
Simplon Pass
Lake Maggiore
Dongo
Menaggio
Lake Como
Stresa
Lake Lugano
Chiasso
Como
Milan
PIEDMONT
Turin
River Po
Brenner Pass
SOUTH TYROL
Bolzano
Trent
Gargnano
Salò
Lake Garda
Verona
Tolmezzo
Caporetto
Udine
River Piave
Treviso
Padua
Venice
Trieste
Fiume
Buccari
ISTRIA
GULF OF CARNARO
Pola
Gualtieri
Ferrara
Reggio
Bologna
ROMAGNA
Ravenna
Faenza
Forlì
Forlimpopoli
Predappio
Rimini
Riccione
San Marino
Dalmatia
Genoa
Rapallo
GULF OF GENOA
Oneglia
Pisa
Florence
Leghorn
Ancona
TUSCANY
ADRIATIC SEA
Perugia
UMBRIA
ELBA
GRAN SASSO d'ITALIA
River Tiber
CORSICA

caused him other entanglements with the Swiss police, who
threw him into jail twice more, in 1903 and in 1904.

In the early years of the twentieth century, Switzerland,
which Benito Mussolini called the "republic of sausages" and
accused of being reactionary and bigoted, was a home for
political exiles from many countries, a center of international
socialism and more extreme political currents. There were
few well-known exponents of anarchism, Marxism, or revolutionary syndicalism who did not spend at least some time in
Switzerland, either of their own free will or as a result of
persecution in their native countries. Lenin himself founded
a Russian language revolutionary paper, *Iskra*, in Switzerland and spent some time writing for it in the years of Mussolini's stay in that country — but there is no evidence that the
two ever met.

Police authorities were trying to curb the activities of the
extreme revolutionists, and especially of the anarchists. The
end of the nineteenth and the beginning of the twentieth century had seen a wave of terrorist acts and the assassination of
rulers at the hands of men accused of being anarchists: the
president of the French Republic, M. F. Sadi Carnot; Elizabeth, empress of Austria; King Humbert I of Italy; and
President William McKinley of the United States were
assassinated between 1894 and 1901. Foreigners in Switzerland were involved in some of these deeds: Elizabeth of Austria was killed in Geneva by an Italian; conspiratorial
meetings in Geneva preceded the military revolt in Serbia in
which King Alexander and Queen Draga were killed. Alexander's successor, Peter Karageorgevic, accused of having
incited the revolt, was living in Switzerland at the time.

The Swiss police kept a close watch on nationalist groups,
especially if they had reason to suspect them of anarchism.
When Mussolini spoke in 1903 in favor of a general strike
and advocated the use of violence, the police arrested him,
held him for twelve days, and then expelled him from the
canton of Bern. He made the trip to the Italian frontier in a
"narrow prison cell in a freight car, together with four other
men who were being expelled." At the border the Swiss police
handed him over to Italian authorities, who released him

shortly afterward. Within a matter of days he was back in Switzerland, spent a few weeks in the canton of Ticino, and then returned to Lausanne. (Expulsion from one Swiss canton did not prohibit residence in another.) News of his arrest and expulsion caused "a certain sensation" in Italy and in Italian circles in Switzerland, as did all expulsions which were considered unfair and for insufficient reason. Greater excitement arose over his next arrest and expulsion.

On March 18, 1904, Mussolini commemorated the Paris Commune in Geneva. The brief dictatorship of the Parisian proletariat, which followed the fall of Napoleon III at the end of the Franco-Prussian War and lasted from March 18 to May 29, 1871, was a subject dear to Mussolini. He was to speak of it often, and always with fresh enthusiasm, in his Socialist years. He saw in it a glorious instance of that Marxian revolution which he strenuously advocated. He admired the gallant people of Paris who, inspired by Louis Blanqui's thought, had defied Louis Adolphe Thiers and the French army and, in the name of the Commune they had proclaimed, fought and died by the thousands — the number of dead was estimated at 36,000 — before they were forced to surrender. In the Commune had fought Amilcare Cipriani, the Italian revolutionist, one of the three men for whom Mussolini had been named. After the arrest of Blanqui, the leadership of the Commune was offered to the Italian hero Garibaldi, who appreciated the honor but felt too old to accept it. When the Commune fell, Karl Marx exclaimed: "The revolution is dead, long live the revolution!"

All this greatly appealed to Mussolini's youthful romanticism and his cult of action. He willingly accepted the invitation to commemorate the Commune at an international gathering in the Salle Handwerk. "There was the usual cosmopolitan crowd," he reported in *Avanguardia Socialista*. The Commune was celebrated by three speakers in German, French, and Italian. "Several associations sang revolutionary hymns. . . . We fraternized with the Russians, who answered our songs with the cry 'Long live the Italian proletariat, long live socialism!' "

The police could not approve of this activity. Neither did

they like the fact that since early March Mussolini had been residing in Geneva; they were anxious to get rid of him. And a pretext came very soon. He had applied for a permit to stay in Geneva and had been asked to show his passport. It then became evident that the expiration date had been altered to read 1905 rather than 1903. He received a temporary permit, but when he returned for his passport, he was arrested and sent to jail. He denied having altered the date himself, but facts put his sincerity in doubt. The passport was the same with which he had first entered Switzerland in the summer of 1902. It was good only until the end of 1903, for in the following year he was expected to return to Italy for his compulsory military service. In October, 1903, his father had called him back home because of his mother's serious illness. He returned to Switzerland at the end of December, 1903, or the beginning of 1904 when his passport had either already expired or the expiration date was so close that he would not have been able to use it.

Although no more drastic legal proceedings followed, his expulsion from the canton of Geneva was decreed, and once more he was to be taken to the Italian border. But now he was a draft dodger, sentenced *in absentia* to a year in prison by the Italian military court. If the Swiss authorities were to deport him to Italy, he would be arrested at once, and the Swiss would violate the right of sanctuary that international practice, though not international law, grants in such cases. Italian Socialists, always on the alert to spot instances of social and political injustice, were aroused by the predicament in which the decree of expulsion placed Mussolini. While he was still in jail, first in Geneva, then in Lucerne, the Italian Socialist press took up his case. Socialists in Geneva wired to their comrades in the canton of Ticino, who applied pressure on the cantonal government. As a result, Mussolini started the trip to Chiasso but was set free in Bellinzona.

The fuss over Mussolini's case did not stop here. The Swiss Socialist representative Adrien Wyss sent to the Grand Conseil of the canton of Geneva a formal protest at Mussolini's expulsion. Meanwhile, Mussolini, who had gone to the

French town of Annemasse, sent Wyss "some information which you may need. . . . People will tell you that I am an 'anarchist.' Well comrade, nothing could be more false. . . . I defy any authority to find in a single article [of mine] a single line or argument that could classify me among the anarchists. I have always been registered, both in Italy and Switzerland, in the Socialist Party. . . . I am very glad that you are bringing the question before the Grand Conseil because my expulsion might cover with shame a democracy that wants to keep intact the holy traditions of Helvetic liberties and yet does not raise a protest against these proceedings, unworthy of a monarchy. . . . "

The distinction between a revolutionary Socialist, as Mussolini called himself, and an anarchist was an important and subtle one. It was important because the program of the anarchists, openly divulged in the press, contemplated the "abolition of government and of any power making a law and imposing it upon others: consequently, of all monarchies, republics, parliaments, armies, policies, magistracies, and all institutions armed with coercive means." Active anarchists were thus in opposition to Swiss law and could be expelled because of their political affiliation.

Mussolini claimed that he was not an anarchist, which, strictly speaking, was true. But for Mussolini, as for his father and for most of the Socialists of Romagna, socialism was strongly tinged with anarchic ideals. In his speeches he asserted that socialism must be revolutionary and fight the state; he praised articles and lectures by anarchists like Sébastien Faure and Peter Alexeivich Kropotkin; he translated one of Kropotkin's booklets and wrote an enthusiastic comment on it for an "anarchic-Socialist" paper, *Le Reveil*, to which he contributed articles now and then; and he had friends among the anarchists in Switzerland. It is easy to understand why the Swiss government would point out Mussolini as an "anarchist" to the police of Geneva and why the head of the police and justice department in Geneva in answering Wyss should state that Mussolini was "a man whose presence is dangerous because of the ideas which he professes and, above all, because of the means he preaches and the activity he tries to arouse among Italian co-religionists and compatriots."

The fact that newspapers kept talking about his expulsion could not but flatter Mussolini's ego. One Italian conservative paper, the *Tribuna*, went so far as to call him the "great duce" of the local Italian Socialist section. Mussolini was twenty. What are a few days in prison to a twenty-year-old if they bring forth such praise? But there is no evidence that the young man who for so long was to be called duce ever read those prophetic words.

Pareto

In May, 1904, Mussolini was back in Lausanne, and this time he registered at the university for the summer session in the school of social sciences. The session, which had begun in April, lasted until July 25, and Benito would have been able to attend courses for almost two months. The courses he wished to follow were those of the great Italian economist Vilfredo Pareto and in later life he was to give strong hints that he had: he was to call Pareto "the most illustrious" of his teachers and, in some sort of act of gratitude, made Pareto a senator. In 1937, however, when a Fascist historian in search of evidence of the relationship between Mussolini and Pareto interviewed Pareto's assistant in Lausanne, the assistant denied categorically that the two had met or that Mussolini had ever been in one of Pareto's classes.

Four years after he left Switzerland, Mussolini was to show that he was acquainted with at least the best known of Pareto's theories, the theory of *élites*, of which he then wrote: "It is perhaps the most inspired sociological concept of our times. History is nothing but a succession of dominant *élites*. In the same way as the *bourgeoisie* has taken the place of clergy and nobility — in the ownership of wealth and political supremacy — so the *bourgeoisie* will be replaced by the proletariat, the new social *élite*, which in its syndicates, its unions, its chambers of labor, is today forming the nucleus of the future economic organization on a Communist basis.

While the bourgeois revolution has maintained classes, the proletarian revolution will suppress them." It has been stated that Pareto's theory of *élites* greatly influenced Hitler and the advent of nazism. There is no evidence that Mussolini got from Pareto any more than this sketchy and superficial idea.

The legend of a Mussolini seriously studying social theories in Lausanne and attending Pareto's classes is not the only one that Mussolini was to create out of his Swiss experiences. Another, much more widespread and readily accepted in the Fascist period, was that of Mussolini the *manovale*, or unskilled construction worker. While he was in power he liked to stress his humble origins, his peasant ancestors, and the hard work he had done in his youth. Often he would stop by a building under construction to talk with the workers, reminding them that at heart he was one of them, describing to them, in nostalgic tones, the days when he was a *manovale* and how wonderful was the feeling of the mastery of matter. He thus created the impression that he had been a laborer over a long period of time and had enjoyed being one, while in fact his experience of manual labor was limited to the fall of 1902, when in the first instance he had spent six days at it and in the second at most a few weeks, and had given no signs of liking it.

Of the numerous persons, both from Italy and other countries, whom Mussolini met in Switzerland, only two were to keep in touch with him later and have important roles in his life: Giacinto Menotti Serrati and Angelica Balabanoff.

Some eight years older than Mussolini, Giacinto Menotti Serrati, a colorful Socialist with a long black beard, had had a most adventurous past. Condemned for subversive activities at a very early age, he left Italy and roamed the world. He had been twice expelled from France and lived by the humblest means, sometimes as a laborer, once helping on a small boat that traded along the Madagascar coast. In Switzerland in the past he had founded a Socialist federation among Italian immigrants. From Switzerland he had gone to New

York to become the editor of the Socialist paper *Proletario* in which he had published some of Mussolini's early articles.

Toward the end of 1903, on a tour of the United States to spread Socialist propaganda, Serrati found himself involved in riots between Socialists and anarchists in Barre, Vermont, in which an anarchist was killed. He was arrested and later tried and acquitted. But either because he felt his reputation undermined or because the *Proletario* was about to cease publication, Serrati left New York. He could not go to Italy, where he would still have to serve time in jail, and so returned to Switzerland.

Upon his arrival, early in 1904, he met Benito Mussolini in a "peoples' kitchen" in Lausanne, where a meal could be had for practically nothing. The two became friends. In the summer after Mussolini's expulsion and return to Lausanne, they shared a bohemian existence. Benito had given up manual work and was living on money his mother sent from home, on meager earnings derived from Italian lessons, and on the help of friends. Part of this help came from an odd division of work between Serrati and himself. Serrati, almost as short of money as his younger friend, felt a certain embarrassment in entering a pawnshop, and Benito, who was not so sensitive, went to pawn Serrati's suits and other belongings. The proceeds were spent to feed the two men. Together Serrati and Mussolini founded the "International Library of Rationalist Propaganda," the first publication of which was Mussolini's pamphlet "Man and Divinity." In later years their friendship turned to enmity, but this was the fate of most of the relations that Mussolini established before 1914, and of many of his later ones.

More details are known of Mussolini's first encounter and friendship with Angelica Balabanoff. She was to relate this encounter and friendship at length in her book *My Life as a Rebel* and in other writings. The occasion for their first acquaintance was the international celebration of the Paris Commune in Geneva at which Mussolini was one of the speakers and which caused his imprisonment. While waiting his turn to speak he sat tense and pale, nervously twisting his fingers, absorbed in himself and isolated from the crowd. He was more shabbily dressed than anyone else, and, according to Angelica Balabanoff, more unkempt and dirty. But when he spoke he acquired assurance, his eyes shone dark and fiery, and his square jaw pushed forward, adding power to his words. At the end of the meeting a comrade introduced him to Angelica Balabanoff, a short, plump young woman with heavy blonde braids. Struck by the looks of the strange youth, she had expressed a wish to meet him. In correct Italian, but with a strong accent, she offered to help him, explaining that although Russian born she was a member of the Italian Socialist Party.

Shortly afterward they met at a gathering in Zurich, at which Angelica was the main speaker. In *Avvenire del Lavoratore* Mussolini summarized her "most interesting report" on the exploitation of girls in religious institutions attached to industrial plants, especially textile mills. In two of these institutions in German-speaking cantons, girls recruited in the Italian province of Veneto were exploited "in a most infamous way." (The meeting resolved to have Angelica Balabanoff's report published by the International Library of Rationalist Propaganda. The pamphlet was to arouse public opinion and eventually bring government intervention.)

The acquaintance between Benito Mussolini and Angelica Balabanoff soon developed into a close intellectual relationship. They had one trait in common, rebelliousness against society. Benito's rebelliousness was a sort of personal revenge, but Angelica's was a revolt against her own privileged origin. She had spent her childhood in the town of Chernigov, near Kiev, in a twenty-two-room house surrounded by a large park. At an early age her sense of human dignity had made her rebel at the sight of servants harshly treated by her mother and of peasants kissing her father's coat. At seventeen she had given up family, country, and wealth to lead the life of a poor student in Belgium and Germany, and, attracted by the warmth of the Latin people, in Rome. There she had joined the Italian Socialist Party, and as a member of it she eventually went to work among Italian immigrants in Switzerland.

Although Benito was only a few years younger than she, their relation was one of pupil and teacher. Of Socialist theories he had only the spotty knowledge acquired during his brief career as journalist and agitator, and her university studies and the many languages she knew placed her well above him. Perhaps, as Angelica later wrote, he felt "a snobbish pride in association with a member of a class he affected to despise." To her he revealed sides of his character that he hid from men. She was receptive. His somber description of conditions in his home, of his childhood, so destitute by comparison with hers, easily aroused the pity and compassion which she was prepared to shed on those who had not known the privileges she had had. And she was at an age when in all women motherly instincts are unconsciously blooming, perhaps seeking a weak being on whom to expand. He let her see that he was discouraged, frustrated; that he despised manual labor; that in spite of his radicalism he did not want to be a proletarian. He made her realize that he was ambitious and self-centered, that the contrast between his conception of himself and the modest life that he was leading gave him an exaggerated self-pity and will toward revenge. She came to feel that his boisterousness, his glorification of strength and violence were a cover for weakness and fear; that his socialism was not based on sympathy for the proletariat but on his individualism and need to acquire leadership. She recognized his sincere wish to learn and his amazing power to work intensely at any intellectual task — to write feverishly, to be always willing to speak to Socialist groups no matter how inconvenient the place might be. Perhaps she hoped to remold him. She lent him books and encouraged and directed his study. She taught him German and helped him translate German Socialist pamphlets.

In November, 1904, Mussolini abruptly ended his status as draft dodger and his sojourn in Switzerland: in September the king of Italy had celebrated the birth of his first son after two daughters with an amnesty which applied to simple deserters provided they would serve their army term. The young man who in February had written "There is indeed an infallible means of destroying infamous militarism: desertion," in November yielded to the call of a monarchy which he despised, returned to Italy, and joined an army whose "moral basis" was discipline through "blind and bestial obedience."

His two years in the "republic of sausages" were far from useless: he had learned to speak French, to "babble" and read in German, to write easily for newspapers and collaborate in their publication; he had gained an understanding of the crowd and the sort of speeches to which they responded, and he had established the basis of a possible political career.

3

A SPELL OF SILENCE

"Does it matter if the first illusions vanish?
Nevertheless, their brief smile has lit our
early youth. To die, better, to pass, is the
fate of human things. What an old and deep
truth!"

MUSSOLINI, April, 1906

In early January, 1905, Benito Mussolini became a soldier
in a regiment of *bersaglieri* stationed in Verona, but his active
service was soon interrupted for a time when he was called to
the bedside of his mother. She died on February 19, 1905,
and Benito showed deep grief. A local newspaper, reporting
on the "imposing funeral," attended by "about a thousand
people" stated that "young Benito Mussolini . . . seemed
to wish to give her a last farewell, but in the anguished effort
he broke into tears and was able only to throw a few flowers
on the grave."

His grief was probably sincere, and if so, his affection for
his mother was a rare exception to his inability to feel for
others. Yet the consciousness of this affection, if not simulated,
came late to him. When in 1903 she had been seriously ill
and seemingly on the point of death, he had returned from
Switzerland, as a good son would, but he had written a much-
too-casual note to a friend: "I am home because of my
mother's health. As soon as the crisis will be resolved, for the
good, as I hope and wish, or for the worse, I shall go back to
wander in the world. . . . "

Immediately after her death, having asked and obtained an

extension of leave from his commanding officer, he wrote to him this florid letter:

"Most honorable Captain:

". . . of the tens of letters that I received these days, many will go into the fire, because they only repeat the usual, conventional sentences for such occasions, but I shall keep yours instead, my Captain, among the dearest memories of my life. Now as you say, I can but follow my mother's counsel and honor her memory by fulfilling all my duties as soldier and citizen.

"Much moaning and weeping are proper in women, [but it is better for] strong men to suffer and die in silence rather than to weep: to toil and toil up the path toward virtue, to honor domestic memories and those, more sacred, of the Fatherland, not with sterile lamentations but with great deeds. It is well to remember, to commemorate the heroes who cemented the unity of our Fatherland with their blood, but it is even better that we prepare ourselves so as not to be their cowardly descendants and to oppose instead a valiant bulwark of breasts in case the barbarians of the North should try to reduce Italy to a 'geographical expression.' These are my sentiments. Please accept, my Captain, my respectful regards."

It was only six years later, in a short autobiography, that he described his mother's death in dramatic tones. He then wrote that when he arrived in Predappio "her chest was shaken by a slow and deep sob, her waxy forehead dripped a cold sweat of death. Those who were present were crying. . . . The next day her condition became critical. The priest came and started to mumble his prayers. . . . The priest came to us and said 'She is at the end of her life.' We all rushed in [her room]. I knelt near her pillow and covering that already cold hand with kisses I asked my mother's forgiveness. Little by little her sobs became weaker, her heart slowed its rhythm. Then a great silence. My mother was dead. . . . They closed her in her coffin. . . . Oh! how the blows of the hammer on the nails resounded, sinister, in the deserted house. It was as if the sharp points were penetrating my bleeding heart! My mother was only forty-six."

It seems impossible that the same man wrote this description and the letter to his captain. In fact, the authenticity of the letter was questioned by one of Mussolini's most reliable biographers, Gaudens Megaro, on the ground that it belongs to a period of Mussolini's life sandwiched, so to say, between two longer periods of violent antimilitarism. And Megaro could not believe that Mussolini was a hypocrite as early as 1905. Mussolini was not so much a hypocrite as a person with an almost unbelievable sense of what was "befitting" at any particular moment, of the attitude or impression he would give that would put him in the best light. The letter to his captain is certainly "befitting" a good soldier, and at the time of his mother's death he was undoubtedly impersonating the good soldier and the dutiful son.

While still on leave at home he gave further evidence of his new loyalty to the army. To a friend of his Swiss days who urged him to spread antimilitarist propaganda among his fellow soldiers, Mussolini answered with an evasive letter, full of hesitation and contradiction: "I am in a very delicate position," he wrote. "I find myself in a period of moral and material uneasiness. . . . I'll tell you my thought frankly, with the frankness of one who has gone through a hard intellectual chastening, leaving behind the largest part of the old traditional Socialist ideology. . . . I fully subscribe to your general ideas. Psychological preparation is necessary, but so is material preparation. If the 140,000 demonstrators in St. Petersburg had had guns, perhaps by now the throne of the czar would have crumbled. You believe that once the army were won to our side the problem of material organization would also be solved. . . . True, there are men of subversive tendencies among soldiers and officers, but their subversive faith is so weak that they would not be capable of an act of rebellion. . . . The army will revolt — because discontent is deep — but only when it sees an attempt at armed resistance on the part of the people, a beginning of civil war. It seems to me that before winning the army we must arm the people. . . . On the other hand, believe me, if decisive popular commotions occur, my gun will never be able to betray the cause of the Revolution. . . . "

In April, his leave being over, Mussolini went back to

Verona and his regiment. Perhaps he was not an outstandingly good soldier, for there is no record of promotions or citations. He entered the army as a private and as a private he left. When he became the leader of Italy, among the many voices of acquaintances and opponents turned suddenly into friends, none arose to exalt the period of his military service. But neither is there a record of punishment or criticism, although he started his term in the army against great odds: he had been a deserter sentenced to a year in jail and was a "red conscript"; very likely the police of Forlì had sent on to the army his "biographical notes," which had been kept since 1903. There is no doubt that he was closely watched. Yet he gave no cause for reprimand or punishment.

When he joined the army, Benito willingly exchanged his black bandit-style hat for the popular plumed hat of the *bersaglieri* and gave up all Socialist propaganda in favor of less intellectual military chores. He enjoyed the long "marches," at running pace, along the banks of the Adige River which were part of his training in the *bersaglieri*, a fast running corps of infantry. These daily races made "his lungs expand and strengthened his leg muscles."

In this period there is total silence from one of the most vocal of self-publicizers, there is a gap in Mussolini's story, as if nothing remained of his military service but expanded lungs and strengthened legs. With these for patrimony, upon his release from the army in September, 1906, the man who had learned to forget his previous opinions forgot his good behavior as a soldier, his obedience and his patriotic expressions, and resumed, with renewed ardor, his career of wanderer, of pourer of words and rebel against the order that he had just served.

4

IN THE ROCCA OF CATERINA SFORZA

"Life would be too beautiful, and too comfortable and too contemptible, if now and then great difficulties did not come up."
MUSSOLINI, March, 1926

THE city of Forlì, the *Forum Livii* of the Romans, at the foot of the Apennines in the plains of Romagna, has its share of old churches and slender bell towers, of palaces and works of art. It has also a medieval citadel, yellow, massive, and squat. The broad bulk of the corner towers, low and round, without windows or battlements, adds to its might and its lack of elegance. In the bright light of the sunny plains, among the trees growing along its walls, the fortress is neither gloomy nor unfriendly, and the *carabinieri* who steadily pace its bulwarks seem no more than puppets in some side show. Yet the *Rocca* of Caterina Sforza, as it is called in Forlì, has long been the jail for the entire province. There in the fifteenth century the gallant Caterina Sforza fought against her enemies. There, within the fortress, she gave birth to Giovanni dalle Bande Nere, a Medici son of her third husband, an indomitable *condottiere* and progenitor of the grand dukes of Tuscany. There, on a morning in mid-October, 1911, five years after his release from the army, prisoner Benito Mussolini crouched in the courtyard in one of the small enclosures that for sixty minutes a day gave each prisoner a private space in the open air. He was washing his short cropped hair with water from a pail when a "Well, well, Mussolini!" startled him. He turned up his dripping head and saw a young man

1882 "*The village of Predappio lies in a wide basin blandished by sunshine in that region of east-central Italy called Romagna.*"

1883 *"Alessandro and Rosa Mussolini settled in a small house of rough stone where their first son was born."*

1888 *". . . a house which had seen better times, a gloomy old house called Palazzo Varano, its crumbling walls damp with moss."*

1891 "Rosa hoped that her children would receive a better education than she had received."

1892 "Within the walls of the Salesian Institute at Faenza there were eyes everywhere, the indifferent eyes of children and the watchful eyes of adults . . ."

1904 *"A Mussolini assiduously attending classes of the economist Vilfredo Pareto in Lausanne was not the only legend the agitator was to create out of his Swiss experiences."*

peering over a dividing wall and grinning pleasantly at him.

"Why, Nenni! You, too! They caught you, too!"

The youth grinned again, replied that yes, the police had thrown him and others into jail, and at once disappeared. To climb on a wall was a serious breach of discipline, and, if caught, young Nenni would have been punished for it.

"His wounds must have healed well, if he can do acrobatics of that sort," Mussolini must have thought as the other vanished. Whether Mussolini realized it or not, Nenni's presence in the Rocca was to prove a piece of luck. It was to change the heavy dulness of prison life into a moderately tolerable, moderately profitable, almost pleasurable experience. Although, according to the rules, during the first few days after their arrest prisoners were not allowed to go into the common room and talk to others, Mussolini and Nenni managed to meet again the next day. "The party is going to send me lawyers, good lawyers," Mussolini said with assumed casualness, "but I'm going to prepare my own defense." He was rewarded by an admiring "Really!" from the younger man.

Before their meeting in prison, Mussolini and Nenni had not known each other long, perhaps a month and a half, and most of this time they had been enemies. Pietro Nenni, who was to become the leader of the left wing of the Italian Socialist Party after World War II, was twenty years old in 1911, eight years younger than Mussolini. Like Mussolini, he was a son of Romagna, born of a poor family; he had been raised in an orphanage, and revolt against Catholicism and a strict school had made a rebel of him. He joined the Republican Party and in Forlì became the secretary of the local Republican chamber of labor. On the other hand, Professor Mussolini, as he called himself upon receiving a diploma as a high school French teacher, was the leader of the local Socialists; he was the executive secretary of the Forlì Federation of Socialist Organizations and editor of the Socialist weekly *Lotta di Classe (Class Struggle)*, which he had run single-handed since its foundation in 1910.

In Romagna Socialists and Republicans were traditional enemies. In farm questions the Socialists sided with the hired laborers and considered themselves the true proletarians, while the Republicans supported the sharecroppers against the landowners.

Mussolini, who in his *Lotta di Classe* had specialized in "anti-everything" articles — antipatriotism, antimilitarism, antiparliamentarianism, anti-Freemasonry, and against his own party — had written passionate tirades against the Republicans in a language hardly fitting the dignity that one associates with the title of professor. After one of these anti-Republican tirades, Nenni had gone to see Mussolini and requested him to withdraw publicly a false accusation printed in *Lotta di Classe*. So the two had met — and liked each other; but for the time being they continued their verbal battle as the political code required.

Yet, both Socialists and Republicans were extreme leftists and used to joining forces whenever a chance of action against established order presented itself. Soon Mussolini and Nenni found themselves fighting on the same side against vested authority during grave disorders in Forlì. The occasion was a general strike, a belated attempt to prevent the outbreak of the Italo-Turkish war. Two weeks after the strike — and the declaration of war — both men, each unaware of the other's fate, were arrested for leading roles in the disorders.

It was Nenni's first arrest and first jail term, but Mussolini was an old-timer and could have made a comparative study of European prisons: not only had he visited the jails of Italy and Switzerland, but also those of the Austro-Hungarian empire in Trent, a city then under Austrian rule, where he had spent several months. In the Rocca of Caterina Sforza he must have felt especially at home, for over the last decades it had become a sort of resting place for the male members of the Mussolini family. When Romagna was still ruled by the pope and the Rocca was a papal prison, Benito's grandfather had spent some time in it. Here Benito's father had served two terms of six months each as a consequence of his subversive activities. (The beginning of the second period had coincided with Benito's departure for Switzerland.) Twice in the past Benito himself had paid brief visits to the Rocca, and perhaps he now felt that it was up to him to maintain the family tradition by using the free services of the Forlì jail. (His brother Arnaldo was a law-abiding citizen and his father was dead. Ten months before Benito's arrest, Alessandro died in Forlì, where he had lived for the last two years of his life.)

Whatever feelings were aroused in him when he was once more within the gloomy walls of the old fortress, Professor Mussolini could do only one thing: prepare in mind and body for a stay that threatened to be long. This time the charges against him were serious, and neither his lawyers nor his own defense were likely to clear him entirely. The formal charges were numerous and detailed, but in substance he was accused of incitement to crime and class hatred, of complicity in causing acts of vandalism, and of resisting the police.

At that time Mussolini was a rabid antinationalist and for almost two years had filled his *Lotta di Classe* with antipatriotic propaganda. He had appropriated a sentence of the French antimilitarist Gustave Hervé and declared: "To us the national flag is a rag to be planted in manure," and, in his opinion, the *patria*, or fatherland, was an ideological cliché that served only to "pump the blood" of the proletariat. A frequent target of Mussolini's attacks had been the young Nationalist Party, founded in 1910 by a group of intellectuals. It had a strong patriotic slant and a program of expansion in the *terre irredente* (the territories still under Austrian rule) and into Africa. The program was not preposterous in its time. Imperialism, in the form of colonialism, was still very fashionable in Europe, and, apart from considerations of material advantage, countries with colonies were surrounded with an aura of dignity and respectability, as if they were members of an exclusive club. Italy had the two small colonies of Eritrea and Italian Somaliland but not the North African territories that had once been a part of the Roman Empire. Rome and its empire were still the measure of the aspirations of most patriotic Italians, and the Nationalists were not satisfied with Eritrea and Somaliland.

Early in 1911, when France occupied Morocco, the Nationalists realized that if Italy were to have a piece of the North African coast there was not much time to waste, and at once they had initiated an intense propaganda campaign to prepare public opinion for a military expedition to Tripoli. The Nationalist leaders, especially Enrico Corradini, used subtle arguments. They said that Tripolitania would provide an extension of the fatherland for the emigrants, who would no longer have to scatter over the world and do the humblest tasks for the benefit of foreign countries. The idea of more land appealed to the peasantry, usually unwilling to exchange the toils of the earth for those of war and generally aloof in political questions. For the Socialists Corradini had reserved a more subtle argument. Nationalism, he said, is nothing else but socialism at the level of nations: just as the proletariat must wage a class war against the capitalists to get a share of wealth, so Italy, a poor, overpopulated nation short of natural resources, must wage a war against richer countries and get her share of land and living space. Helped by the atmosphere created by the poets who sang the glories of ancient Rome and wept over the conditions of Italy, "the great proletarian," the Nationalists softened the hearts of the nation, including those of a few Socialists. But not Mussolini's heart. He had warned that before "conquering Trent, Trieste, and Tripolitania, there is Italy to be conquered, there is water to be brought to Puglie, reclamation work in the marshes of Rome, [and] justice to the south. . . ." Indeed, these words would have been a sign of wisdom had they not been later discarded, giving place to contrary ideas.

In matters of war, parties put pressures, governments decide. The prime minister at that time was Giovanni Giolitti, who is still remembered as the great old man of Italian politics before World War I, the man to whom Italy turned again and again in times of difficulty and crisis. A Piedmontese like Cavour, Giolitti was the antithesis of what is considered a typical Italian. Tall and of impressive carriage, cold, logical, and dispassionate, well-experienced in all phases of administration, he was a liberal by temperament but not given to unrealistic idealism. All his efforts tended toward the achievement of what seemed reasonable and possible; and within these limits he worked successfully for the improvement of social conditions through liberal reforms. In 1911 Italian expansion seemed to be a national interest and universal suffrage a possible liberal reform. The Nationalists were pressing for the first, the Socialists for the second. As if wanting to keep a balance between the two parties and please them both, Giolitti declared war on Turkey and granted suffrage.

When the newspapers announced that a war over Tripoli was imminent, Professor Mussolini decried the "mad adventure"; when the Socialist Party and the General Confederation of Labor called a nationwide general strike to protest, he approved the resolution of the Forlì Socialists to carry out the strike to its bitter end. The strike, which was a fiasco in most of Italy, in Forlì was a great success, a true revolt that lasted three days. When demonstrations began, the cavalry from Faenza came galloping into the main square of Forlì with unsheathed swords in hand. In the face of this charge, under the threat of the glittering blades and the no lesser threat of the resounding hoofs, the Socialists and Republicans decided to join forces. Mussolini and Nenni became the leaders of the resistance. The crowd disbanded but, undaunted and spurred by Mussolini's fiery eloquence, imposed total strike on the city, forced stores and factories to close, and turned off the lights in the streets. The next day and the following, in order to prevent the departure of the men called to the army, the rebels overturned a streetcar on a suburban line, pulled up railroad tracks, felled telephone poles, and cut telephone lines. Bravely, with sticks and stones, the strikers fought the armed police. On two occasions — once while Mussolini was haranguing them — at noises that on the taut strings of their sensitivity sounded like the pounding of ironshod hoofs on the pavement, they turned their backs and fled in panic.

At the end of the adventure there was clear evidence that the division of work between Mussolini and Nenni had been unequal, that the professor had spent his time talking and the young Republican fighting: Nenni suffered wounds on the head and chest; Mussolini did not receive a single scratch. At any rate, both words and wounds were in vain. Although the national strike was a failure, Professor Mussolini took great pride in the fact that the workers had practiced sabotage, a weapon with which he had familiarized them.

These are the events that brought about the charges against

Mussolini and for which he was sent to the Rocca for a forced vacation.

¶

On the day of the trial the *carabinieri* escorted the three prisoners into the courtroom. Mussolini, *Lotta di Classe* reported, was "closely shaved, with more vivid and sparkling eyes than usual, elegant, almost dandyish." The president of the court and two other judges heard the case, which was tried without a jury. Also in the courtroom were the prosecutor, three Socialist lawyers for Mussolini, four Republican lawyers for Nenni and Aurelio Lolli, another Republican defendant. It was certainly a *processone* (a big trial) as *Lotta di Classe* called it, an event in the small city of Forlì.

True to his word, Professor Mussolini spoke in his own defense "with his habitual, energetic precision, incisively." With greater oratorical skill than adherence to facts, he disclaimed any active part in the general strike and any other responsibility. In his opinion, too much importance had been given to his personal influence; the hour of agitators was over and the crowd was entirely on its own. All he had said and written against the Libyan war was evidence of his patriotism; his glorification of the general strike was theoretical, since a general strike is a myth whose "religiosity takes the place of past religions"; and his idea of sabotage was moral, civic, respecting the safety of the citizens. "I tell you, gentlemen of the court, that if you absolve me you will please me because you will return me to my work, to society. But if you condemn me you will do me honor, because you are not before a vulgar criminal . . . but an expounder of ideas who deserves your respect. . . . "

After this lofty closing, he was loudly applauded, and the prosecutor remarked that Mussolini had the gift of speaking very convincingly, which made him dangerous. He was found guilty of instigation to delinquency and sentenced to a year in prison. Nenni received a similar sentence (Lolli a lighter one). Later they appealed — and were transferred from the Rocca to Bologna, the seat of the appellate court. In the end, Mussolini served five months in jail and Nenni seven.

Mussolini's behavior in jail was exemplary; it calls to mind the good soldier he had been under army discipline. It was as if once in a while he felt relief in giving up the initiative, as if his callous assertiveness was a burden he was glad to shed — as if since childhood he had been a rebel not because he had wanted to be one, but because he had never happened to meet a will stronger than his own; because, in his early experiments with life, chance or fate had not led him into the deep groove of order and conformity in which flows the life of the law-abiding and the resigned, a groove in which, once forced by circumstance, he himself felt comfortable and secure. This readiness to relinquish his will, this easy adaptation to an existence dictated by others, was more than a passing mood; it was an ingrained trait, concealed most of the time by Mussolini's aggressive make-up. It was to be seen again in World War I, when he served as a good soldier, and, made more pronounced by his strange apathy and abulia, in the last years of his life when his will became entirely subject to Hitler's.

[margin annotation: good solder]

Being a good prisoner in the Rocca may not have been overly difficult for Mussolini. The old fortress was dark and dank, with no electric light or traces of modern sanitation. The best way of taking a shower was to carry a pitcher of water to the courtyard, as Mussolini had done on the day Nenni found him out, but the weather was not always co-operative. At night the somberly resounding paces of the wardens in their rounds and the sting of the bedbugs often kept the prisoners awake. Yet there were compensations. Mussolini and Nenni had each other's genial company and permission, which their lawyers had obtained for them, to have their dinner brought in. The good-natured companionship, the easy relations between prisoners and wardens, further toned down hardships and smoothed the sharpest edges of prison regulations.

Punctually, almost daily, a young girl came to see Mussolini. The professor, who had described himself as a bachelor to police and law authorities, introduced her as Rachele Guidi to Nenni and to other prisoners; but she was his common-law wife. Rachele, not quite twenty years old at the time, was short and plump, with regular features, a pleasant expression, and the red, roughened hands of a hard-working peasant woman. What made her strikingly noticeable among the dark-complexioned people of Romagna was the light-gold, almost platinum, color of her hair and the cold blue eyes that per-turbed those on whom they rested. Benito had first met her when, in pigtails, she was attending his mother's school, hav-ing moved with her family to Predappio from the neighboring countryside. Almost ten years older than Rachele, yet still in his teens, Benito occasionally substituted as teacher, and the picture of the lively little pupil with the long blond plaits be-came impressed in his memory.

Rachele belonged to a very poor family. Soon after her father's death, when she was seven and a half, she quit school to begin working for various families at farm and house chores. Her family, meanwhile, entered into relations with the Mussolini family — through the back door, so to say. Alessandro Mussolini was old and lonely. His health and spirits were weaker after his prison term in 1902, his boys were away from home; the death of his wife and the marriage of his daughter Edvige brought a sadness and an emptiness to his years that the widow Nina Guidi, Rachele's mother, did all she could to alleviate. In 1908 Alessandro sold his smithy in Predappio and with Nina went to Forlì, where, with her help until his death two years later, he was the keeper of an inn, the meeting place of the most militant local Socialists.

Benito and Rachele, who had not seen each other since her school days, met again in Forlì when she was sixteen and already desirable. A period of nomadism in his life separated them again, until in January, 1910, after a brief courtship spiced with passion and jealousy on his part, Benito took her to live with him, without formal marriage, in Socialist style. Rachele was of the same good stuff as Rosa Mussolini, vigorous, enduring, and loyal, but less intelligent, less am-bitious for her family, and of much sunnier temperament. She was at peace with life, contented with her lot, busy with the cares of the moment, though ready to fight for her rights as wife and mother.

In September, 1910, Edda, the first of their five children, was born. On the circumstances of Edda's birth many rumors were later to circulate both in Fascist and post-Fascist Italy. It was said that Rachele was not really Edda's mother, and although more than one woman was mentioned in this connection, according to the most persistent story Edda would have been the daughter of Angelica Balabanoff. Both Rachele and Angelica were strongly to disclaim these rumors, which they said were ridiculous and preposterous, but they never entirely killed them. Edda grew to look like her father rather than like either woman. These rumors are unimportant in themselves, but they show how in reconstructing the story of a man like Mussolini it is not always easy, and sometimes it is impossible, to separate fact from legend. Often, unknown interests are at play. In the instance of Edda's birth, it would seem that a birth certificate, or the testimony of persons who had seen the baby when newly born, would have dispelled any uncertainty, but so far as is known, no one has ever brought forth definitive proof.

Edda, at the time of Mussolini's imprisonment not much more than a year old, was with Rachele in Forlì, and in Rachele's arms she often visited her father in the Rocca. Visiting hours were short, and Benito often complained to Nenni that in prison he missed his woman, his baby, and his violin — he had learned to play the violin in one of his restless spells before leaving for Switzerland, but there is no evidence that he was a talented or skilled player.

Time in jail flows slowly. In winter the courtyard of the Rocca was icy cold, and the prisoners could not always take advantage of the daily hour of fresh air decreed by prison regulations. When they were together in the common cell, Mussolini and Nenni played cards, talked, and talked some more. Encouraged by the eagerness of his young companion, Mussolini indulged in an activity of which he did not believe himself capable: reminiscing — reminiscing encouraged by leisure, the very bareness of the cell, the medieval spirit of the fortress.

Time in jail flows exceedingly slowly. When Professor Mussolini was alone in his cell, nothing made the hours move fast, not reading, not working at a book on John Huss, the Czech reformer burned at the stake by papal order in 1415, not translating from the German a treatise on chemical dyeing for a small industry run by Socialists in Forlì. There was always more time to fill. Eventually, Benito Mussolini carried his reminiscing to its logical conclusion, autobiography, and in cell 39 of the Rocca of Caterina Sforza he wrote *"La mia vita"* ("My Life.")

This short booklet has often been considered the most genuine and spontaneous of Mussolini's autobiographical material, for as the years went by he looked upon himself, his past and present, through more and more highly colored spectacles. Yet it is doubtful whether "My Life" is genuine and spontaneous. Prisoner-author Professor Benito Mussolini says in the introduction: "My adventurous past is unknown. But I do not write for the curious, I write instead to relive my life. . . . I shall go back over what I was in my best years. I shall again pass along the road already traveled, I shall pause at the most memorable places, I shall quench my thirst at springs that I thought dried out, I shall rest in the shade of trees that I thought felled. I uncover myself. *Ecce homo.* I weave together again the cloth of my fate." And he began his narrative: "I was born on a Sunday, at two in the afternoon . . . The sun had been eight days in the constellation of 'Leo.' " This is hardly the sort of writing that a young man would do for himself. It is colorful reminiscence, which may have been attuned to the response that in daytime he read on young Nenni's face.

Childhood in Romagna: his experience at the Salesian school acquired the intensity of the tortures of the Inquisition (perhaps under the present influence of John Huss's tragic vicissitudes). An inhuman third-grade teacher, unbelievable punishments, a night of terror in the school courtyard when watchdogs chased him, a poor crazed boy, from corner to corner, and the feverish delirium that resulted next morning — these are Benito's most vivid recollections of his time in the boarding school.

Then, the two years in Switzerland, and on to more recent events: after his dismissal from the army he had been a schoolteacher in the old mountain town of Tolmezzo in the eastern Alps. There he found a strong, wilful population; second-grade pupils who did not let him rule them, but rebelled; sturdy women doing men's jobs while men were in foreign lands in search of work and bread; women who carried heavily loaded baskets on their backs, who toiled and farmed, who knew how to be aggressive in their love. He had not liked teaching in Tolmezzo, where his behavior, his cursing in the classroom, his sprees in town, and more than one romantic scandal had aroused much criticism. And in Tolmezzo the rain, which too often blotted out the nearby fields and pastures and the distant snowy peaks, was depressing, irritating. At the end of the school year he had not sought reappointment.

Further reminiscing took him to Oneglia, a bright city on the Italian Riviera betwen the deep blue Tyrrhenian Sea and the green hills on which citrus fruit grows, a sunny city whose administration was in the hands of Socialists and where lived his friend Serrati's family. There, with the encouragement and assistance of Serrati's brothers, he found a job teaching French in a private school and collaborated on a local paper of which he soon became the editor. In the *Lima* (the *File*) he wrote articles under the pen name "True Heretic," a name chosen to stress his antireligious fanaticism and to hide his identity, a necessary precaution, for school authorities would have found the virulence of his articles improper from a teacher. At the beginning of the school vacation he left Oneglia for good and, unlike Tolmezzo, with regret.

Then back to Predappio and, for a brief visit, in the very Rocca of Caterina Sforza where he was now. So, as past mixed with present, memories with reality, he relived twelve days he had spent in prison in 1908 for threatening with a weapon a man whom he had thought an organizer of scabs

— twelve days very similar to any twelve days now slowly going by — in the same seclusion, in the same company of common and political prisoners, burning bits of candle at night in order to read or fight bedbugs.

Further following his reminiscences, he was again in a region of the Alps, this time in Trent, an Austrian city, but traditionally Italian in culture and speech, where he had been called to be the secretary of the local chamber of labor and the editor of a local Socialist paper. In Trent he found himself among clerical conservatives and moderate Socialists, but also among "irredentists," Italian patriots although Austrian subjects, who felt that Trent, where stands one of the most impressive statues of Dante, was "unredeemed" and ought to be returned to Dante's country. In Trent he occasionally collaborated on the paper of one of these patriots, the Socialist Cesare Battisti, destined to die on the Austrian gallows for fighting on the Italian side in World War I. Association with these men may well have made a deeper impression on Mussolini's soul than he realized at the time, or realized later when agitating against the Libyan war. In Trent he knew, and fought verbally, a young Christian Socialist, Alcide De Gasperi, who, like Nenni, was to play an important role in Italy after World War II. In less than eight months in Trent, Benito led such a violent newspaper campaign against Catholics, conservatives, and government officials, and made himself so obnoxious by encouraging a plot against the Austrian police — and probably participating in it — that he was expelled from Austria. This expulsion added a thorn to his crown as martyr of the Socialist cause and earned him a congratulatory telegram from Angelica Balabanoff. His eight months in Trent produced another, more positive, result: a 104-page monograph on Trentino, a lucid and objective analysis and presentation of the linguistic, economic, and political conditions in Trent and the surrounding territories.

Once more he returned to Romagna, to his father in Forlì, to the common-law marriage with Rachele, to the founding of *Lotta di Classe*, and to events that did not need recalling because Nenni had shared them.

The closing sentences of "My Life" arouse the question

whether Mussolini was then a writer seeking literary effects or a man of little education using words at random, a skilful actor or an earnest repentant. "I have *wandered*," he writes (but the italics are not his), "*from one horizon to the other*: from Tolmezzo to Oneglia, from Oneglia to Trent and from Trent to Forlì. I have been three years in Forlì and already feel the ferment of wanderlust in my blood, pushing me on. I am a restless man, a wild temperament, *shy of popularity*.

"I have loved many women, but on these distant loves forgetfulness spreads its gray veil. Now I love my Rachele, and she also deeply loves me.

"What does the future hold in store for me?"

"My Life" is not especially well written, although Mussolini had begun to write early in his career and had written a great deal. Besides newspaper articles, and the pamphlets already mentioned, including the monograph on Trentino, he had written four short stories — he intended to write others and to collect them in a volume to be called "Perverted Stories," but he never did — and a serial novel published after he left Trent in the Socialist paper of Cesare Battisti. "The Cardinal's Mistress," was, in his own words, "a thriller for little dressmakers," and he considered that its success did not "speak in favor of the morality of readers of serial novels in daily papers." (But it had some success, and it was even translated into English.) Despite all this practice, "My Life" is hurried and dry, written in a succession of short, explosive sentences; the paragraph divisions are often disconcerting. Here and there a vivid passage stands out; for example, the moving description of his mother's death, quoted in Chapter 3.

The coolness and lack of feeling of this book are startling; the holy and the profane, family and friends, all are treated with detachment. On his First Communion at the Salesian Institute, he writes of receiving the holy wafer: "I swallowed it. It took an instant. God was by then prisoner in my insides." He describes the death of his grandmother in 1897: "My grandmother's room was cleared and we searched among her belongings for her will. Nothing was found. That room was then occupied by my parents." And of the death of a relative: "Before the end of the year another good piece of news reached me. [The first had been news that as a result of a love affair a fellow student whom he disliked had failed all his exams and seemed to be in a deranged state of mind.] Our relative from Mezzano had died and my mother had chanced upon several thousand lire . . . A nice catch."

He had shown some of this coolness for his family, though not so cynically, in an article he had written less than a year before on the occasion of his father's death. Despite the lofty opening: "I write these lines with trembling hand . . . to place a last homage of filial devotion on my father's grave . . . " and the even loftier conclusion: "Of earthly goods he has left us nothing; of moral goods he has left a treasure: the idea," the article was little more than a long, detached record of Alessandro Mussolini's political activities.

In "My Life," Professor Mussolini never gives thanks to the persons who had gone out of their way to help him. Of a school friend from whom he had borrowed books and money and who had assisted him in the study of the little Latin required for the diploma of French teacher, he writes: "Alberto Calderara, studious, a greasy grind." And he mentions only in passing the two Socialists who had helped him during the Swiss period and after, Giacinto Menotti Serrati and Angelica Balabanoff. It is almost certain that Mussolini owed several of the positions he held after his discharge from the army to Serrati's good offices and friendship. In addition, while teaching in Oneglia, Serrati's home town, the young professor had received a warm welcome and hospitality from Serrati's mother and his three brothers who, like him, were ardent Socialists.

Benito Mussolini and Angelica Balabanoff had never really lost touch and though each had gone his own way, their paths had often crossed. She had found time for several visits to Romagna (also, it is said, for one to Trent), and she had resumed her role of protector and encourager, the mentor eager to see a pupil test his ability and willing to share his political tasks. She had also shared the thrill and danger of a plot which, she believed, was intended to kill them both. It was April 30, 1911, and together in a village near Forlì they were celebrating May Day a day ahead of the calendar be-

cause Angelica had a busy schedule. At the inauguration of
the village's Socialist home, Benito spoke first, then Angelica,
and she was still speaking when loud shouts and the sound of
a few shots reached their ears. Outdoors, Socialist and Republican youths had come to grips, and a Republican had been
wounded. To avoid further disorders at the end of the program, the police rushed the speakers to a *carrozzella* (a horse-
drawn carriage), and there they sat between two *carabinieri*
while riding to Forlì under the escort of police in another
carrozzella. In the quiet of the countryside, at dusk, the only
sounds were the pounding of the horses' hoofs and the rattling
of the *carrozzelle* jolting over the stones of the unpaved road.
Suddenly a series of pistol shots snapped shriller than the
other sounds. The Republicans were taking their revenge.
They missed the speakers but wounded a *carabiniere* in the
second *carrozzella*. Benito, more realistic than Angelica,
called the episode a "miserable incident" which would not
have been reported even in the lowest class papers outside
Romagna. Like other similar episodes, the event contributed
to the belief that the Romagnoli were dangerous men, while
in truth in each Romagnolo there was, according to Mussolini,
a "bit of Tartarin's psychology" — in other words, all Romagnoli were boasters.

Nothing of this Mussolini chose to record in "My Life." Of
Serrati, he mentions only that in Switzerland the two of them
shared "a bohemian existence." Of Angelica, he writes that
with her he "brought to completion the translation of Kaut-
sky's book: *Am Tage der sozialen Revolution*," and that with
her he "began the translation of a Neo-Malthusian booklet by
a Zurich doctor, later translated into Italian under the title
"Fewer Children, Fewer Slaves." (In power, Mussolini was
to reverse his stand in favor of birth control and launch a
"demographic campaign," aimed at the rapid increase of the
Italian population.)

The coldness toward his benefactors evinced in "My Life"
is in perfect accord with the feelings that Mussolini expressed
in a letter from the Rocca to a friend: "It is such an effort for
me to be grateful. Gratitude: here is a sentiment *physiologi-
cally* very painful to me." (The italics are his.)

The most interesting, if shocking, side of "My Life" is not so much this lack of elementary affection and feeling of gratitude, a lack already evident in Mussolini's behavior and to become more conspicuous as time went on, but the revelation of his overdeveloped erotic instincts. In the fewer than ninety pages that make the book, in fact in the even fewer that cover the twelve-year period following the age of sixteen, Mussolini mentions some fifteen women by name and writes of others: "I do not mention names because [the affairs] are too recent."

His relations with women were brief and violent ("on a stairway . . . in a corner behind a door") and "alternated with altercations and brief spells of anger" — the anger that in Gualtieri had led him to wound his girl with a knife — while husbands were away or even asleep in another room. Women "loved him madly"; women with children committed "the most dangerous follies" for him. While he was still in Predappio or in its vicinity, his younger sister Edvige kept track of the victims of his love: he often asked to borrow money from her to take these girls out, and each time she obediently agreed. Each time she was naïvely surprised when he did not pay her back, and, instead, she had the unsought friendship of one girl after another.

This primitive, unrestrained sensuality, this proof of manliness — perhaps supermanliness in his mind — was not to subside with age. Over the years, numberless women, young and old, rich and poor, noble and plebeian, ignorant and highly educated, were his, often only for a few minutes. When he was still very young, before his long imprisonment in the Rocca and the writing of "My Life," he had occasionally gone out of his way to meet a woman, had even taken a long train trip to spend a couple of hours with a mistress. But at the height of his incredible career, when everything was to be regulated in Fascist style, women walked up a back stair of Palazzo Venezia to a private entrance, either at his invitation or under some pretext they had invented. He was not particular, but took them on sight and dismissed them when his passions were appeased; the relationship might last a quarter of an hour in all. Only a few women were his over long periods. Only Rachele, the proud peasant from Romagna, could keep her jealousy in check, bear the knowledge of his passing loves, and yet remain fiercely faithful to the end. (Information on Mussolini's affairs comes in the main from Mussolini himself and from gossip of the period. Some authors believe that the stories of his love life are evidence of his vanity and self-dramatization rather than strict truth. On the other hand, independent testimony, including that of his sister and of women who admit to having affairs with him, lends credibility to many of the stories.)

Professor Benito Mussolini completed his autobiography on March 11, 1912, and the next day he was released from prison.

His reminiscing had taken only a part of his time with Nenni. The two young men liked to discuss the books that their comrades and Rachele brought them. They read when alone, sometimes during sleepless nights, stretching the life of a candle by means that all prisoners know. During the day the medieval walls that had heard the war cries of Caterina's subjects and the echoes of the names of her husbands, her relatives, and her foes, Sforza, Riario, Medici, Borgia, resounded with shouts of admiration for discordant, outlandish names: Max Stirner, Georges Sorel, Friedrich Nietzsche, even Goethe and Schiller.

5

PHILOSOPHICAL BACKGROUND

> "The masses are a herd, and as a herd they
> are at the mercy of primordial instincts and
> impulses. The masses are without continuity.
> . . . They are, in short, matter, not spirit.
> We must pull down His Holiness the Mob
> from the altars erected by the *demos*."
>
> MUSSOLINI, September, 1922

THE five months of imprisonment in the Rocca were Mussolini's last period of intense, omnivorous reading — at least for a very long time, since only during the last two years of his life did imprisonment and confinement again bring him leisure for books. His release from jail in March, 1912, at the age of almost twenty-nine, marks the end of his formative years.

From the time of his early experiences in Switzerland until his death, he always asserted that he had no theories, no formulas; that in his opinion action comes first; that thinking has, at most, the role of explaining acts *after* they have taken place; that philosophical schemes are sterile, an impediment to freedom of action. It would be wrong, nevertheless, to believe that no philosophical or theoretical influences guided his conduct, and also wrong to explain both his advocacy of violent action and his egocentrism exclusively as results of his father's teachings and the spirit of rebelliousness prevailing in Romagna. Inherited Marxism, atheism, and the bent to rebellion were the foundations on which he built, foundations that became stronger and firmer as he found in his surroundings and in books confirmation and expression of his own impulses. As he gradually became acquainted with the numerous currents of international agitation, intricately interwoven, the colorful anarchism innate in him, a son of Romagna, lost some of its good-humor, and his leftism became slanted toward the trends that best suited his temperament, trends glorifying revolutions, heroes, and the ego.

Persons who knew him in his early political years said that he was not a true Socialist but a Blanquist: he knew little of Marx and of Socialist theories, nor did he show a genuine wish to learn them, but, at least from the time he first commemorated the Paris Commune in Lausanne, he was an enthusiastic admirer of Louis Auguste Blanqui (1805–81), a revolutionist who actively fought in several revolutions, first as a Republican and then as a Socialist. For his actions he was jailed so often and for such long periods that of the forty-eight years between 1831 and 1879 he spent thirty-six in jail. In view of his long imprisonment — his biographer Geffroy calls him *L'Enfermé*, the Prisoner — it is astounding how much he achieved. He founded several leftist papers and was the first to advocate dictatorship by the proletariat, the seizure of power by a revolutionary minority which would immediately institute a Socialist system. To defend the popular cause and to put his ideas into action, he organized the Parisian proletariat, preparing them for the great moment, and by 1870 he was heading a secret armed force of 4,000 men. Adolphe Thiers, acting president of the French Republic, had Blanqui arrested and jailed on the eve of the outbreak of that Commune of which Mussolini was to become such an enthusiast and which was the first test of Marxian doctrine, the first occasion on which the working class achieved political power. Following this arrest, his last, Blanqui spent seven years in prison, and thus he was unable to lead the Parisian movement which he had prepared and of which he was the soul. The *communards* offered three hostages — one of them the archbishop of Paris — in exchange for the release of Blanqui, but Thiers refused, afraid lest in freeing Blanqui he gave "a mind" to the Commune. The disorganization that resulted from his absence is one of many reasons for the early fall of the Commune. For half a century, whether he fought at the head of rebels or from a prison, Blanqui embodied the herald and the molder of new times.

In Blanqui, "the man of the barricades," "the martyr tribune," Mussolini found a natural object for hero worship, an
example and a guide for his actions. In Max Stirner, philosopher of the Ego, the "Only One," he discovered a reflection
of his inner self. The true name of Max Stirner was Johann
Kaspar Schmidt. He was a contemporary of Blanqui but died
much younger, at fifty. Stirner was an exponent of individualist anarchism; of him it was said that he "preached egoism in
the most absolute and logical way." In his book *Der Einzige
und sein Eigentum* (*The Ego and His Own*), Stirner rejected
all that in any way attempts to limit the individual and the
expression of the Ego, encouraging the Unique or Only One,
outside whom nothing exists, to place personal interests above
the interests of others. To all philosophers of egoism, as Mussolini himself once remarked, the state is oppression organized to the detriment of the individual, and, accordingly,
Stirner advocated total revolt against the state. In this revolt Stirner saw the liberation of the individual from all
social, moral, and even logical ties, the achievement of unconditional supremacy of the Ego which exploits everything
for its own enjoyment in complete amoralism. From Stirner's
writings Mussolini received permission and encouragement
to indulge his ambitions without considering their effects on
others, to follow his instincts without stopping to think which
were good and which bad. Mussolini's irreverence toward religious, social, and moral principles may well be the consequence of Stirner's teachings. Later, in the period of general
disillusion and disorientation after World War I, when old
ideals failed and old institutions were falling apart, Mussolini was consciously to return to Stirner and say: "Let the
way be opened for the elemental forces of the individuals, for
no other human reality exists except the individual. Why
cannot Stirner become fashionable again?" And: "Let us go
back to the individual. We shall support all that exalts, ampli-
fies the individual, that gives him greater freedom, greater
well-being, greater latitude of life: we shall fight all that
depresses, mortifies the individual." (Let, in Mussolini's later
interpretation, the Fascist squads have a free hand to do what
they want, kill Socialists, run about the country in search of

adventure, quench their thirst for blood and vengeance. Let them have a free life, in this sense, if this is what their instincts command.)

Although Stirner's memory stayed alive a long time in Mussolini, no hero or preacher of egoism had as much influence on him as the philosopher-poet Friedrich Nietzsche, if by influence is meant the conscious acceptance of views. Nietzsche himself would have been surprised had he known the sort of followers he was to have. He did not think much of agitators, "all too apt to be empty heads who flatten and inflate any good idea they get hold of and give it out with a hollow sound." Yet, it was precisely to these agitators, regardless of their political and philosophical tendencies, that he had the greatest appeal. Agitators, and unfortunately the future dictators of Europe, found justification of their wild goals and confirmation of their most destructive ideals in their own misinterpretation of Nietzsche's thought.

Nietzsche could equally fascinate Mussolini the Socialist agitator and Mussolini the duce of fascism; to the end of his life, Mussolini remained Nietzsche's admirer, used Nietzschean language and imagery, and tried to impersonate Nietzsche's creations. When old and no longer in power, Mussolini admitted that many times he had flung himself toward high and exalting goals in the wake of Nietzsche. Long before, in 1908, when he was an obscure teacher in Oneglia, he "devoured" a biography of Nietzsche by Daniel Halevy. He went to visit places nearby, in the peaceful gulf of Rapallo, the forest of umbrella pines and the glorious road climbing over steep rocks high above the placid sea, "where, at the time I was born, Nietzsche was conceiving *So Spake Zarathustra*." (Had Zarathustra entered Mussolini's horoscope together with the sign of the Lion?) Shortly afterward, in the autumn of the same year, Mussolini wrote three articles on Nietzsche for a Republican weekly of Forlì. Many years later, at the crest of his career, when asked by his biographer Yvon De Begnac what he thought of Nietzsche, he was to reply that he had expressed his definitive views on the German thinker in the articles of 1908. These articles, full of direct quotations, show that Mussolini had read several of Nietzsche's works and was able to illustrate some of the most striking aspects of his philosophical concepts.

What most impressed Mussolini was "this great Nietzschean conception," the superman, "the Nietzschean hero, the implacable and wise warrior," in contrast with the existing society that was the consequence of twenty centuries of Christianity. Nietzsche, Mussolini wrote, was violently anti-Christian. To Nietzsche, Christianity was the result of a spiritual revenge of the Jews over the Romans who had enslaved them and an inversion of values that the Jewish people achieved through Jesus. Jesus, Mussolini wrote in paraphrase of Nietzsche, was a visionary temperament endowed with "an extraordinary nervous energy" with which he could inspire the crowds. Thus the rabble, the slaves, had triumphed. This is the feat of the Jew, in whom Rome, which produced the last society of dominators, saw its very "counternature, its antithetic monster." (Thus, as early as 1908, the first seed of anti-Semitism was sown in Mussolini's receptive mind.)

Christianity and brotherly love, Mussolini said in essence, further paraphrasing Nietzsche, have produced wars, the terrors of the Inquisition, and the modern European, this small monster of restless and turbid conscience, proud of his incurable mediocrity. It was the preaching of equality, pity, and compassion that brought about weak and illuded men, sinners with worn-out nerves, men who asked of life only the preparation for death. But, wrote Mussolini, "a new species of 'free spirits' will come, fortified in war, in solitude, in great danger; spirits who will know the wind, the ice and snow of high mountains, and will be capable of measuring with a calm eye the full depth of the abyss — spirits endowed with sublime perversity — spirits that will free us from brotherly love, from the will to oblivion . . . that will triumph over God and nothingness . . . . 'Nothing is true, everything is permitted!' will be the motto of this new generation. . . . The apotheosis of egoism — here is the work to which the 'very free spirits' will devote their energies. . . . The superman spits in the face of any servile habit. He calls evil all that is compliant and low. . . . Christianity said: be mortified . . . renounce. The Nietzschean superman . . .

wants instead to conquer. . . . Nietzsche wants to teach men joy, the art of laughing, the art of dancing with a light foot."

The superman is endowed with the *will to power* that gives a purpose to life. "To create! This is the great redemption from sorrow and the comfort of life. . . . Nietzsche teaches: To that which is on the point of falling we must give a push. He whom you cannot teach to fly you must push, that he may fall faster." The superman will fight God and the common people, who with their little virtues do not know what is great and straight and genuine. But the superman will triumph over the common people and God and will impose his lion-like will on all. "The superman," Mussolini concluded, "is a symbol. . . . It is the realization of our weakness and at the same time the hope for our redemption. It is sunset and dawn. It is above all a hymn to life, a life lived with all the energies of a continued tension toward something higher, finer, alluring."

In the pattern of influences emerging the danger is evident. To a young man who searches for a hero to worship, Stirner and Nietzsche teach that he need not look outside himself for his hero; he himself can be the exceptional man who destroys and creates at his will. Even more dangerously, Nietzsche, the poet, imparts to this young man a fearfully vivid image of the superman, this extraordinary being who lives beyond good and evil and to whom everything is permitted. But Mussolini was a great actor, with a great ability to assimilate and make his own what he took from others, and during the whole of his life he kept the image of the superman before him. It was unavoidable that sooner or later he should try to act the superman.

At the time of his imprisonment in the Rocca, an incongruous and puzzling element complicated the pattern of individualistic influences. Mussolini was writing a book which was published the following year, *Giovanni Huss, il veridico* (*John Huss the Truthful*). The life of John Huss was part of the Protestant tradition and as such was almost unknown in Italy.

Mussolini had gone to considerable pains to gather his information. His aim was anticlerical propaganda, and in the preface he wrote: "In giving this book to the press, I formulate the hope that in the soul of its readers it will arouse hatred for any form of spiritual and profane tyranny: be it theocratic or Jacobinic." In its dry, choppy style, in the selection of episodes and quotations, the book is not without effectiveness. In the figure of John Huss, Mussolini saw the individualist who makes his own moral rules and decisions, who believes he discerns a universal significance in the answers he has found in himself, and who allows himself to be burned at the stake rather than submit to human authority, be it vested in inquisitors, popes, or emperors. Yet this short book is not in line with Stirner's amoralism, Nietzsche's anti-Christianity, and Mussolini's own atheism, and it seems an anticlimax after "Man and Divinity." It could be the work of a Lutheran pastor, for it is pervaded with a seemingly genuine faith in God and a purified and believing Christianity. While writing it Mussolini, the great manipulator of words, was impersonating his protagonist.

On the covers of Nietzsche's books Mussolini used to write a maxim by the nineteenth-century French philosopher Jean Marie Guyau: *Vivre ce n'est pas calculer, c'est agir* (To live is not to calculate, it is to act). For theoretical ideas on action he did not follow Guyau but a French social philosopher, Georges Sorel, whose fame was rapidly growing in France and in Italy. In Italy Sorel had become so fashionable that discussing him was a fad among Socialist intellectuals. Very early, Mussolini learned to call this engineer of bridges and roads, who had turned into a Marxian scholar in his middle age, *notre maître Sorel*, as his disciples called him, to use Sorel's language, and to appropriate Sorel's aphorisms. Like Sorel, Mussolini called *professionnels de la pensée* (professional thinkers) the intellectuals who claimed to speak for the people; he pushed the metaphor farther and labeled priests *professionali della menzogna* (professional liars).

Sorel's best-known book, *Réflexions sur la Violence,* was published as late as 1908 in France and 1909 in Italy, but for over ten years Sorel's essays, of which the book is a collection, were appearing in French and Italian journals as he elaborated his ideas on class warfare, strikes, and the use of violence. Directly and indirectly, reading his works or talking about him, Mussolini followed the evolution of Sorel's thought. He did not need the works of Sorel to learn about violence, which was innate in him, but in Sorel's essays he found what in himself was pure instinct framed into a theoretical scheme, scientifically formulated, and exalted as virtue. In commenting on one of Sorel's essays, he wrote in 1908, in the *Lima*: "So far as the concept of violence is concerned, my poor ideas have found rather authoritative confirmation in Georges Sorel." When Sorel's *Réflexions sur la Violence* was published in Italy with a preface by no less an authority than the philosopher Benedetto Croce, Mussolini was ready to review it and present its essential points to the readers of the newspaper *Il Popolo* of Trent.

From a pure Marxian, Sorel had become a syndicalist because he did not think that Marx had given sufficient attention to the means by which the proletariat was first to achieve and then to preserve its power. Syndicalists believed that labor unions and not the state should own and control the means of production. In reviewing an Italian syndicalist book for *Il Popolo* of Trent Mussolini wrote that "in traditional socialism it is the 'party' (a collection of incompetent, intellectual politicians) that assumes the delicate task of realizing socialism for the workers . . .; in syndicalism, intellectuals, *professionnels de la pensée*, ideologists, have no place. The labor union, embryo of the new society of producers, does not tolerate parasites. The party is possibilist; the labor union is revolutionary . . .; syndicalism tends to dissolve the forces of the state and to transfer as much as possible of the public administration into proletarian organizations."

To revolutionary syndicalism Sorel contributed the idea of social myths and the cult of violence. In his review of *Réflexions sur la Violence*, Mussolini commented: "According to Sorel, if great ideas have triumphed in the world, this is due to the fact that they have acted as myths upon the souls of the masses." It is immaterial whether a myth can be realized, provided it is sufficiently great, beautiful, and sublime to arouse heroism in the hearts of men, provided men are willing to achieve great deeds and sacrifices in its name. "A Christian myth was the Apocalypse, with the final defeat of Satan; a myth was that of the Reformation, of the French Revolution; and that of Mazzini's followers. The *Giovane Italia*, founded by the great Genoese exile [Mazzini], acted upon the Italians' souls as a myth, pushing them to conspiratorial deeds and battles."

The moving myth of the proletarian class is the general strike: the threat of letting the world starve will make the proletariat master of the situation. "The myth of the general strike," Mussolini wrote, "considered as the supreme battle — gives the worker the strength to achieve the revolution." On the occasion of his participation in the general strike for which he was sent to jail, he explained: "To the Sorelians the general strike must be the last, decisive battle to the finish that the proletariat wages against the *bourgeoisie*; it must be the beginning of a return to the producing class of the means of production and trade, held today by the capitalistic minority. Sorelians therefore put off the general strike to a distant future: and the general strike becomes a 'myth,' namely the ideological representation of a future possibility, used to keep awake in the proletariat the heroic sense of its mission in the world."

In his review of Sorel's book, Mussolini quoted this passage: "The purpose of force is to impose the organization of a social order in which a minority is governing; while violence aims at the destruction of that order." Then Mussolini added his explanation: "Force is the expression of authority, violence is the expression of revolt. The former belongs to the bourgeois world, the latter to the proletarian organization."

To remain wholesome and uncorrupt, Mussolini contended, socialism must not turn into a synonym for democracy; it must have the courage to be "barbarous." Strikes, proletarian violence, are pure acts of war, war in the open, without hypocritical attenuation, with the value of military demonstrations, and serve to stress class separation. Small concessions, "gentleness," tend to dampen the heroic spirit of the masses, to make the revolution impossible. "Proletarian violence," Mussolini quoted from Sorel, "actuated as a pure manifestation of the sentiment of class warfare, appears therefore very beautiful and very epic. It is at the service of fundamental interests of civilization . . . [and] it can save the world from barbarism." "[Socialism,]" Mussolini concluded, "becomes again terrible as it was in the beginning. This state of permanent war between *bourgeoisie* and proletariat will generate new energies, new moral values, new men who will be close to ancient heroes."

This concept of new men similar to ancient heroes evokes Nietzsche's free spirits. Both are violent and strong. Sorel, like Mussolini, is influenced by the German poet and his imagery. Sorel and Mussolini claim to work for the good of the masses, and Nietzsche despises the masses. This is a dilemma. Eventually, Mussolini was to incline toward Nietzsche's point of view, and to him the masses would become herds of sheep, instruments to be bent at his will and to his advantage. The cult of Nietzsche would persist for life: it was easier to erect altars to dead idols than to living ones. When Sorel modified his point of view in a rapprochement to antidemocratic monarchism, Mussolini, who was later to follow the same path, denounced him.

6

A JUMP AHEAD

> "I ask for ferocious men — I ask for one
> ferocious man with energy, with the energy
> to tear apart, with the inflexibility to punish
> and strike without hesitation — and so much
> the better if the culprit is in a high position."
> MUSSOLINI, February, 1918

Five months in jail added to Mussolini's halo of martyr-
dom and to his local fame. His comrades in Forlì hailed his
release from prison and celebrated it with a banquet in his
honor in the dining room of one of the hotels in town. The
banquet was well attended, either out of true solidarity for
the man being feted, or because the Socialists of Romagna,
hearty eaters by nature and thrifty by necessity, seldom had
a chance to savor a high-class meal. They came from as far
as twenty miles away.

In 1912, this was the measure of Mussolini's fame: it
spread over an area some twenty miles in radius, which included several small villages and towns in the proud hills of
Romagna. His influence was more restricted and did not ex-
ceed the boundaries of the Socialist federation in the electoral
college of Forlì, a federation which at that time reckoned
some two thousand members. Even within his small sphere of
influence he stood alone, in moral isolation. He had no
friends. He did make a favorable impression and exerted an
attraction, especially on young men like Nenni, but toward
them he felt no flow of warmth, no duties or responsibilities.
They, or the workers he addressed, were not his brethren, not
an object of love, but a tool at hand that perhaps someday he

would be able to bend to his own use. Perhaps . . . someday. Not at the moment, because the men under his influence were still too few.

If, in the hours in jail that he had not been able to fill otherwise, Mussolini had summed up the almost ten years he had spent as a Socialist agitator, he must have been dismayed by the smallness of his achievement. He had worked hard, studied — seriously at times, even Latin — written much and talked even more, but his painstaking efforts to elevate himself, to reach conspicuous positions and maintain them, had not led him far. Perhaps a few Italian immigrants in Switzerland and a few workers returned home from there, if inclined to think back — a pastime for which workers usually have no leisure — still recalled the half-romantic, half-truculent, youth who used to harangue them. A few Socialists in Trent thought well of him, and a few genuine revolutionists admired his fiery oratory, his vehemence, and his apparent moral intransigence. Otherwise he was little known. He was the editor of a weekly paper whose circulation did not reach a thousand copies, a Socialist whose greatest glory was five months in prison. He was a born gang leader, but his gang was minuscule, and there was no clear direction in which to lead it. According to an old Italian saying, it is better to be the head of an anchovy than the tail of a sturgeon, yet Mussolini was neither satisfied with his anchovy nor attracted by the status of tail. He wanted to become the head of a sturgeon. But what sturgeon?

Perhaps in jail he had planned to make his next ten years more fruitful and satisfy his ambitions in full. There are indications that he aspired to become director of the official Socialist daily paper *Avanti!* Perhaps, in order to get this position, he had resolved to use his elbows ruthlessly, with no regard for anyone, friends or enemies. Perhaps. . . . There is no end to speculations, but facts alone are the building stones of history. The fact is that there was barely time for his black hair to grow back on his closely cropped head before he was in a prominent position, a position he reached by pushing out more mature and respected, better-educated, members of the Socialist Party.

Mussolini made this jump at a national convention of the Socialist Party which opened on July 7, 1912, in Reggio Emilia, not far from the town of Gualtieri, his first teaching post. Reggio, a perfectly flat city in the plains of the Po River, was an industrial center, an agricultural market for the products of the fat land around it, and a small stronghold of socialism. Professor Mussolini arrived there in time for the opening session of the convention, the speeches of local and Socialist authorities. (A resolution was passed that morning in favor of two labor leaders in the United States — the Italian-American Joseph Ettor and the Italian Arturo Giovannitti — accused of conspiracy and murder during the recent textile strike in Lawrence, Massachusetts. Mussolini himself was soon to lead much of the Italian workers' agitation to rescue these men "from the legal snares of North American capitalism," from the "mercenary justice" which had "the task of repressing, of subduing and driving back, the working class" in those United States which he often called the dollar republic.)

In the afternoon Mussolini participated in the large outdoor rallies and read the posters that tapestried the city — protests against the Libyan war, which was not yet over, and the Nationalist propaganda in its favor. In the evening he was very nervous. He sensed political passion around him — hopes, rancors, and the expectation of some unusual happening. The Socialist in Reggio Emilia knew, as he did, that there was serious dissension in the party and that a crisis was imminent. Dissension had been frequent in the history of Italian socialism, which had begun as a vague, humanitarian movement against all forms of authority; it mixed class problems with the ideals of the *Risorgimento* and the well-being of the workers with Italian independence, and it aimed at all-pervasive goodness and universal brotherhood. This trend reached an apex of popularity in the time of Giuseppe Garibaldi, the hero of two worlds, idealist, "good man," and poet, who, after achieving Italian unity, adhered to the First International and called it "the sun of times to come." A more definitely political element was injected into Italian socialism at about this time by the presence in Italy of the anarchist Bakunin. It was

a socialism based on Bakunin's anarchism and the humani-
tarianism of the *Risorgimento* that Alessandro Mussolini embraced as a young man. Later, Marxism was introduced, not
by the working class but by the intellectuals, of whom the
best known, the most cultured and refined, was Filippo Turati.

The Italian Socialist Party, essentially Marxian, was
founded in 1892, when Benito was nine. Only with difficulty
did the many currents represented in the party manage to
hold together, and from the beginning there were factions
and occasional divisions into groups. Yet Mussolini had seen
socialism make great strides since he joined the party in his
student days: socialism was thriving in the moderate pros-
perity that at the turn of the century had replaced earlier
economic hardships. It provided the masses with an ideal,
a living faith; it improved their political education and
aroused their awareness of social rights and duties; in pointing to interests that extended beyond regional boundaries,
it helped to unite the Italian population, which had remained
regionally divided despite political unity. But certain recent
differences threatened to hamper further achievements. For
a long time Mussolini had been aware of a widening rift in
the ideologies of the party and the emergence of two strong,
antithetical tendencies, the reformist and the revolutionary.
The group that called itself reformist was led by Filippo
Turati and included some of the most highly intellectual Socialists. The reformists felt that a strictly interpreted Marxian
doctrine, teaching that a Socialist regime was to be established
only after the proletarian revolution, could well be "the sun
of times to come" but was much too pessimistic a view for
the present. They did not think the times were ripe for a proletarian revolution and felt that the working class could not
afford to wait for it but needed to improve its conditions at
once, that social advantages could be — and, in fact, were
being — obtained through patient collaboration with liberal
governments. They had obtained social reforms from the
liberal prime minister Giolitti, and their ascendency over the
party was great and still growing.

Mussolini belonged to the revolutionary wing, an intransigent group which would not give up the old ideals of Marxism, class warfare, and social change earned through direct action rather than obtained through compromise. Mussolini, the Blanquist, was instinctively against parliamentarianism, dialectic methods, political maneuvering, and the tactics of appeasement, avoiding open battle in order to win concessions that were only crumbs of the ideological whole. He was a soloist, incapable of collaboration, a man who could express himself in writing or in monologue but was poor at discussion and considered debate a waste of time.

From *Lotta di Classe*, he had opened a venomous campaign of words against the Italian Parliament, the "parliament of the underworld," the "most illiterate, most slothful, most corrupted in the world." He called the Chamber of Deputies "vain chimera, great circle of corrupters and corrupted, sovereign without scepter, Circe of honest navigators, quick and easy bargainer with the pirates of national happiness and honor, juggler of characters, hybrid, insincere and inglorious institution. . . ."

In his criticism of the reformists, "straw-stuffed figures that occupy the benches of the extreme left," Mussolini had gone further than most revolutionary Socialists, several times asking the party for the expulsion of the reformists. His agitation against them was usually restricted to his sphere of influence and did not reach far outside Forlì. On the only occasion that he presented his request for expulsion before a national convention — in 1910 in Milan — he met a personal fiasco. His speech was poor, disorganized, void of content; the reformists were victorious, and not even the revolutionary Socialists supported his point of view.

After the Milan Congress, and while Mussolini was jailed in the Rocca, other events had complicated the pattern of Socialist dissension. A small group of reformists moved further to the right and took positions that caused them to be suspected of patriotism and of favoring the Libyan war. Their leader was Leonida Bissolati, like his friend Turati a man of culture and a founding father of the Socialist Party, an honest, somewhat romantic, somewhat rhetorical man, like many learned Italians of that time. Since March, 1911, Bis-

1911 "*Benito Mussolini was a prisoner for five months in
the Rocca of Caterina Sforza, where that gallant
woman gave birth to Giovanni dalle Bande Nere.*"

1914 "In the almost two years of his impetuous and impulsive directorship of Avanti! the paper became more vigorous and aggressive, more uncompromising and rectilinear, better attuned to the tastes of the workers."

1916 "There is no doubt that Mussolini gradually came to like life in the trenches. A conscientious soldier, on occasion he went beyond the call of duty if this gave him opportunity to be noticed by his superiors and did not entail too much danger."

October 28, 1922 "The cabinet reacted to news of Fascist mobilization by proclaiming a state of siege. It appeared likely that the army would receive orders to resist the advancing columns."

1922 *"Mussolini, prime minister with dictatorial powers for one year, had been carried to his high position on the will of others, as a swimmer on the crest of a wave."*

solati had been the target of Socialist criticism: he had not refused to go to see the king who had summoned him for consultations, and he had become the first Socialist ever to set foot in the king's palace in the course of duty. Later Bissolati and two other reformist deputies — one of them Ivanoe Bonomi, who was to be prime minister of free Italy in the last year of World War II — committed an even darker crime. They joined the other members of Parliament in going to the royal palace to congratulate the king and queen on their escape, unharmed, from an attempted assassination. Bissolati also sent a personal telegram to the king.

In his provincial corner, Mussolini let his full contempt for Bissolati, the other two deputies, and the king flow freely from his pen. "We reject political assassination in our tactical conceptions, because today in Italy it is useless. Simply. This is the fundamental reason. The rest is empty talk," he wrote in his paper. "Between the accident which befalls the king and that which fells a worker, the former may leave us indifferent, the latter draws our tears. The king is by definition the 'useless' citizen. . . . We must have the courage to disqualify, publicly and solemnly, a handful of men who prostitute our party. Or shall we become a laughingstock? Alas, everything is possible in the land where the orange and the monarchic-socialist idyl bloom . . . ." Independently of Mussolini's colorful attacks, which fortunately did not travel far and probably did not reach those he attacked, the congratulations to the king aroused deep criticism among the Socialists. They revealed a promonarchic feeling often accompanied by a favorable stand toward the Libyan war, and this stand the Socialists could not let go unchallenged.

This was the background of the national convention in Reggio, with which all the participants were familiar, and the reason they expected a crisis. In addition, Mussolini knew that if things went well for him, his very words could precipitate the crisis on the morrow. And so he was nervous. He, the unknown peasant-journalist of Romagna, had been appointed chief accuser of men of principles and integrity, men whom he was sufficiently intelligent to judge his superiors both morally and intellectually. The revolutionary Socialists had assigned this task to him, both because they disliked the unpleasant role of the accuser and because they had faith in the effectiveness of his eloquence.

He had several friends in the revolutionary group. There was Angelica Balabanoff, who had followed his political development closely and encouraged him in his uncompromising stand; there was Giacinto Menotti Serrati, who, back in Italy at last, was pleased to advise his younger comrade for the sake of their earlier friendship; and there was also the spiritual leader of the revolutionary Socialists, Costantino Lazzari, an earnest, hard-working, persistent man whose every action was proof of his integrity. Lazzari had taken a liking to Mussolini, perhaps because in the young man from Forlì he thought he saw his younger self and his own devotion and adamant faith in Marxism; perhaps he mistook Mussolini's extremism for his own stern rectitude; perhaps he admired in his protégé the brilliance, the eloquence, and the imagination that he did not have. At any rate, Lazzari let Mussolini take the most important role at the national convention.

And so Professor Mussolini was very nervous: in the course of the first evening at the convention, he repeatedly touched the hunchback of a fellow newspaperman, for in the mystic substratum of his soul the ancient superstitions of his race were only slumbering and easily aroused. He slept little that night. On the morrow when he ascended the speaker's podium he looked pale and thin. His prematurely receding hairline, the waxy whiteness of his ample forehead, his trick of bringing his brows together in a somber and threatening expression, all made him look older than his age. The vast expanse of his black tie was not enough to divert attention from his ill-fitting suit. He saw in front of him the crowded theater, black with Socialists in their Sunday best. Everyone seemed to be there, both friends and adversaries: Turati with his long, flowing beard, which he was to shear off years later when fleeing Italy and Fascist persecution; Bissolati, spare and thin, with his chivalrous manners and kindly eyes; Serrati, short and heavy-set, despite the lean times he had been through; Angelica Balabanoff, small and plump under the load of her blonde braids; whitehaired Constantino Lazzari, serious and appreciative, who, years later, at seventy, was to be brutally beaten by the Fascists; and hundreds more. Behind him as he faced the audience was displayed a huge bust of Andrea Costa, who, upon his death two years before, had become the symbol of Italian socialism and for Benito was an encouraging link with his father's times.

Benito Mussolini's fears were not meant for public eyes. While the audience was still cheering his appearance on the podium, he straightened, swiftly dried his perspiring hands with his handkerchief, pushed his head up and his chin forward, silenced the crowd with his fiery eyes, and began to speak. As his short, dry sentences cut the thick air of the theater with the metallic sound of a guillotine, all eyes became fixed on him; at once he gained the assurance, the fervor, that talking to a large audience always gave him. His speech was long. First he reviewed his opinions of Parliament. "Italy is certainly the nation," he said, "in which parliamentary idiocy — that unmistakable disease so acutely diagnosed by Marx — has reached the most serious and mortifying forms. . . ." The Chamber of Deputies had voted universal suffrage simply to "vivify" Parliament. Suffrage, Mussolini said, "is the bag of oxygen that prolongs the life of the dying." "The usefulness of universal suffrage — from the Socialist point of view — is negative: on the one hand it accelerates the democratic evolution of bourgeois political systems, on the other it proves to the proletariat that it is necessary not to give up other, more efficient, methods of struggle."

Amid many more words, he came to the central theme of his talk, the attack against the reformist Socialist deputies and those of the right wing in particular. When Parliament ratified the annexation of Tripoli, he said in substance, when it voted new military expenses, when the police arrested many people at random after the attempt to assassinate the king, Socialist opposition had been practically inexistent. "Absenteeism, indifference, inaction: here are the words that summarize the deeds of the Socialist group. . . . Socialist deputies should have been . . . inflexible fighters, like Toledo blades, from life to death. The masses . . . cannot understand the moral effrontery of their political representatives:

their disgust for the inversions and exhibitionism of these men ends by increasing their skepticism toward ideas."

In the middle of his speech he introduced a motion, prepared with other revolutionary Socialists, for the expulsion of the three deputies who had gone to congratulate the king and of a fourth who had not but who was accused of being a *"tripolino,"* in favor of the Tripoli expedition. He ended his speech with a long tirade, partly historical and mostly polemical, and the audience responded with long and resounding applause, a true ovation. His motion was carried by a great majority.

Angelica Balabanoff, who had approved the motion as an influential member of the revolutionary section, also spoke, as if driven by a need to justify the action of the party. She was becoming a well-known figure at Socialist meetings, not only in Italy, but in many other European countries where she attended important international leftist gatherings, sometimes on her own, more often as a delegate of the Italian Socialist Party. She spoke Italian fluently with the added charm of a slight foreign accent. "If for reasons of principles," she said in Reggio, "we can afford to expel from the party men for whom other parties envy us because of the rectitude of their characters, it is a moral, not a personal, question. . . . In the attitude of our four comrades, [the proletariat] has seen an offense against the holy principles of class struggle and revolutionary faith."

Angelica Balabanoff was an inveterate, almost visionary, Marxist, and when she spoke of Marxism her homely face was transfigured. To the four deputies, she said: "We fulfil this duty of ours with far from light hearts. Knowing the historical vicissitudes that are removing you from the party, we can put ourselves in your boots and say that a day may come in which the proletariat may tell us, too, 'You do not follow our ideologies; you do not interpret our interests; you are not our voice; go away.' And we realize what a tragic day that day will be in our lives." Had this chubby little woman the power to read the future? She was to have an answer only two years later. For the present, all, even Bissolati, bowed to her.

For the present, Mussolini had reached the forefront of the

Italian political scene and had every intention of staying there. He enjoyed his triumph. The important newspapers spoke of him, described him as the fiery professor, as a violent, original, disdainful orator and thinker, as one of the most steadfast revolutionary chiefs who had drawn the warmth of his faith from assiduous contact with the working masses of the florid land of Romagna. In Paris, Amilcare Cipriani, the hero of early socialism and of the Commune, wrote in *L'Humanité*: "Today, among those who have triumphed at the convention of Reggio Emilia, there is a man, Mussolini, whose resolution was victorious. I like him very much. His revolutionary stand is mine, I should say ours — that is a revolutionary position which is called classic." (After reading this article, Mussolini, so very sensitive to praise, referred to Cipriani as HIM in *Lotta di Classe*.)

There were also critical voices, and one came from Paris, as the great praise did. Georges Sorel granted an interview to an Italian paper in which he said, according to the interviewer, "The battle engaged between the various sections of Italian socialism is harder to understand than the history of the Renaissance." He deplored the "elimination of intellectual worth" from the party. To this charge Mussolini replied that in the past Sorel had advocated an anti-intellectual, sublime, religious socialism, and that at Reggio "the religious soul of the Party (*ecclesia*) has clashed once more with realistic pragmatism. . . . Here are the terms of the eternal conflict between idealism and utilitarianism, between faith and necessity. . . . Humanity needs a *credo*."

Mussolini was right in this: the victory of the revolutionary section was in a sense a victory of idealism over utilitarianism, of faith over necessity. Yet he failed to see that the same old conflict existed inside himself, and if the mystic in him spoke feelingly about ideals and faith, the egocentric and cynic directed his actions, did not take idealism into consideration, and would always strive toward utilitarian aims.

Another paper commented that socialism had lost "the spirit of sacrifice which may make people renounce any competition for the triumph of the common cause." Socialist leaders with their partisan spirit did, in fact, lack the farsighted vision of what a united front might achieve for the good of Italy. It is conceivable that, had they been united and continued to fight together against militarism and war, they might have kept Italy out of World War I and prevented the rise of fascism. Instead, the four expelled deputies immediately founded an independent party and were joined by many former Socialists. Although Mussolini minimized the importance of this move, the old Socialist Party lost some of its vigor. It was further weakened by the leftist reformists' refusal to participate in the executive committee of the party on the grounds that after the national convention at Reggio there ought to be an entirely revolutionary experiment. Even Claudio Treves, the director of *Avanti!* and a brilliant lawyer and journalist, Turati's closest associate, resigned. All responsibilities fell into the hands of stubborn men who did not rise to the "intellectual worth" of their predecessors.

Mussolini, now a member of the executive committee, went back to Forlì, to his *Lotta di Classe*, his violin, and his too-often-neglected family. He should have been pleased with the turn of events, but he had not yet achieved what he wanted most, the directorship of *Avanti!* which the executive committee had entrusted to another man. For at least one day he gave himself up to one of his moods of discouragement, and on his thirtieth birthday he filed an application, his last, for a teaching position in an elementary school. It proved unnecessary. Three months went by, and at last the executive committee appointed him director of *Avanti!* He hesitated a moment before accepting, as if afraid that the load of responsibilities might, after all, be too heavy for his shoulders. It was typical of him to plunge into uncertainty and doubt, often even to draw back, when on the point of reaching a goal he had long striven to attain. In this case he accepted the position on one condition: that Angelica Balabanoff be co-editor. He had not consulted her, so certain was he that she would not refuse her help and support, that she would be willing to do whatever he and the party asked of her.

He left Rachele and Edda with Rachele's mother in Forlì and moved to Milan.

Milan, the big gray city from which on clear days one can see
the powerful arc of the snow-capped Alps across the plains of
Lombardy, for a long time had been Italy's economic heart,
the chief center of the nation's industrial, manufacturing, and
financial activities. It has a peculiar steadfastness and dignity
that come from its intellectual refinement; from both its
modern development and the tender attention it gives to its
antiquities; from the functional architecture of its factories,
banks, and office buildings; and from the exquisite Gothic
fastidiousness of its ethereal yet sturdy cathedral. In the tension
of economic evolution its population has lost some of the sun-
niest traits of Latin people and has become more eager, more
earnestly busy, more conscious of its duties and rights than
the rest of Italy. In the Milan of 1912, as in the Milan of our
day, there were the largest and best-organized working masses
in all of Italy, those in whom social education and conscience
had attained to the highest degree. There was also a wealthy
middle class, jealous of its cultural traditions, with high moral
principles and slightly complacent, at once liberal and trusting in the permanence of its social privileges.

In size and wealth, in the role it played in the national life
and the opportunities it offered, Milan differed from the small
provincial town of Forlì by an order of magnitude. A comparable difference existed between *Avanti!* and *Lotta di
Classe*. The weekly *Lotta* was one of some 250 local Socialist
papers in Italy, each of small circulation, each tuned to the
needs of a restricted group whose main views and tastes the
editor of each was likely to know. *Lotta di Classe* was founded
when Mussolini's presence in town made it possible. In the
two years of its existence Mussolini was completely free to
run it as he pleased, and it became a colorful, if culturally
unrefined, paper, the battlefield of his verbal battles and the
outlet for his aggressiveness.

The official organ of the Socialist Party, on the other hand,
was a daily paper with an established tradition. *Avanti!* was

founded in 1896, directed by Leonida Bissolati for several years, and was always in the hands of intellectuals. The best-known Socialists wrote for it, and workers from various parts of Italy and from abroad sent in regular reports. Though it had periods of slump and loss of circulation (due perhaps to overintellectualism), to many party members it was at the same time the symbol of the party and the tangible manifestation of socialism. Through these two functions it held together scattered groups and different ideological trends.

Mussolini must have realized that as director of *Avanti!* he was to have less freedom and greater responsibilities than as editor of *Lotta*. The directives he was to receive from the party executive might run against his inclinations and limit his initiative, although after the events at Reggio Emilia the executive committee was of one color only, revolutionary, as he was himself. In spite of these possible limitations, the role of director of *Avanti!* appeared of decisive importance: a strong and well-directed official paper, appealing to the workers and rallying them to the banner of extreme Marxism, could make all the difference between success and failure for the "entirely revolutionary experiment."

His moment of hesitation before accepting the position was justified but proved unnecessary. He rose to the new demands placed upon him. In the almost two years of his impetuous and impulsive leadership, the paper became more vigorous and combative, more uncompromising and rigid, and better attuned to the tastes of the workers; its circulation almost doubled. Realizing that neither a petulant nor a bellicose tone nor the foul language he had so often used in the past were fitting the director of a party paper, he gave up most of his too virulent "anti-isms" and began writing in a more sober and dignified tone. At the same time *Avanti!* became a tool in his hands, and he used it to increase his own influence, gain popularity, and assert himself as tribune and demagogue.

The recrudescence of economic crisis due to the Libyan war brought about another wave of dissatisfaction in the masses, of social agitation and strikes, and of repression that occasionally ended in blood. In all this, Mussolini, Sorelian and syndicalist at heart in spite of his growing aversion for

Maître Sorel, found the most natural subject matter for his articles. He encouraged and supported strikes, kept stirring the troubled waters, and gave to the paper an extreme insurrectional tone. Early in 1913, the army, which had been sent to keep in check the population of Rocca Gorga, a small village near Rome, killed seven people, including a five-year-old child. At once, Mussolini and his staff made this episode the occasion for extremely violent articles against the government and its "policy of carnage." *Avanti!* promoted a protest meeting in Milan and proposed a general strike. In its attempts to keep the agitation alive the paper was so pugnacious and outspoken that "the political authority — with the complicity of the judiciary power," (as *Avanti!* put it) brought suit against the director of the paper and its editorial board. When, over a year later, the suit came up for trial, the defendants had their hour of triumph and, strengthened by the documentation they had collected, turned into stern accusers of those who had been responsible for the deathly repression.

There is no doubt that through *Avanti!* Mussolini's influence over militant socialism — not over the evolution of its doctrine — was not negligible. It became evident at the next national convention, in the spring of 1914 in Ancona, when he obtained the expulsion of members of the party who were Freemasons. Freemasonry had acquired prestige and dignity in Italy in the middle of the nineteenth century when the society participated in the achievement of Italian unity. But Mussolini disliked its secrecy, the fact that he could not be certain who belonged to it, and the mutual support that members gave one another. In *Lotta di Classe*, he called Freemasonry "an association for furthering crime" and accused Freemasons of "elastic" morals, of "solemn documentable incoherences" and "criminal solidarity."

He was by no means the first Socialist to criticize Freemasonry, and the opinion that Socialist and Masonic ideals were incompatible had been vented for a long time in Socialist quarters, but the Masonic issue had been put aside when the issue of right-wing reformists had arisen. At the convention in Ancona, Mussolini introduced the most extreme of several anti-Freemasonry motions. It was carried, several

Socialist-Masons resigned, and the breadth of the party was
further reduced.

¶

Despite this success, Mussolini experienced more than one
failure during the period of his directorship of *Avanti!* One
of these failures is rather a piece of gossip than a historical
fact, but a piece of gossip on which all biographers insist and
at which Mussolini himself hinted repeatedly in later life.
Gossip is sometimes useful for probing a mind. According to
these stories, Mussolini's ego was deeply wounded because he
was not welcomed into the highly intellectual *salon* of Filippo
Turati and his companion, Anna Kuliscioff. She was Russian-
born, and in her youth she had had everything a woman may
wish, beauty, wealth, great intelligence, and as great a heart.
For many years she had been Andrea Costa's companion and
inspirer, and for this reason she was reckoned among the
pioneers of Italian socialism. Long prison terms for the Socialist cause had undermined her health, and with declining
health her beauty was fading, but she retained her charm and
her vivid intelligence. Anna Kuliscioff and Filippo Turati,
the sensitive, brilliant leader of the left-wing reformists,
gathered around them the intellectual *élite* of Milan and attracted foreign visitors. For almost thirty years their *salon*,
looking out on the innumerable pinnacles of the cathedral,
had been the meeting place of scholars and politicians from
many countries, literati, and friends and opponents. It was
open to almost anyone who was someone, but not to Mussolini.

In fact, Mussolini was in Turati's *salon* at least once, and
there he met Margherita Sarfatti, who was to become his
collaborator at *Avanti!* and, in Fascist times, write his official
biography, *Dux.* In a recent interview, Margherita Sarfatti
insisted that Mussolini was not excluded from Turati's *salon*,
and that he stayed away of his own choice because Turati held
political views different from his own. Most biographers,
however, do not share her point of view, and in her book she
herself relates Anna Kuliscioff's not-too-flattering comment
on Mussolini: "Actually, he is not a Marxist at all, nor a

Socialist either. He is not even a politically minded man. In fact, he is a little poet who has read Nietzsche."

From all that has been written about the Mussolini of this period and his relations with Turati, one picture stands out, that of a Mussolini extremely touchy in all questions of refinement, especially intellectual refinement. In the Italy of that time, culture and intellectual refinement went side by side with economic security and were the privilege of the same restricted class of people whose exclusive property they seemed to remain generation after generation. Most habitués of Turati's *salon* belonged to this class. Their common background and education united them even when their political views were opposed, and they had the same basic understanding of the issues over which they might be fighting.

Among men and women of this class, Mussolini was an outsider and an upstart. A psychologist might have recognized the symptoms of a strong inferiority complex in his aspiration to be welcomed and able to cut a good figure in a place where he did not belong and was decidedly ill at ease. Nowhere else did the ambivalence of his social origins become so hard to bear; nowhere else did the young man of peasant stock and traditions so intensely wish that he had reached the cultural level which his mother had dreamt for him and for which she had struggled. The realization of his shortcomings made him extremely self-conscious and therefore defiant; he stiffened to the point where his usual actor's skill and ability to adapt to circumstances failed him. He became noisy and tried to attract attention to himself by monologues in which his own ideas became dogma and anything he did not know was rejected. And thus he appeared less refined than he was and more out of place.

For all this, Turati disliked him with a dislike verging on contempt. Mussolini, to whom Turati must have represented the unattained cultural goal, was so deeply wounded that he nursed his rancor to the end of his life. Shortly before his death he was to admit, according to one witness, that the grudge he felt for Turati had exceeded all provocation and had affected the course of his political actions.

If this is in part gossip, other failures of this same period

are certainly factual. In the first elections held in 1913 under
the new electoral law, Professor Mussolini, the antiparliamen-
tarian, ran for deputy in his own electoral district of Forlì —
and failed. True, Forlì had long been a stronghold of republi-
canism, and his opponent was an older man, the Republican
incumbent. But then, had his three years of strenuous cam-
paigning for socialism left no trace? True, in the period that
preceded the elections he gave several speeches in various
towns and cities to promote the Socialist vote and only one,
in Forlì, to promote himself as a candidate. (He had stated,
with typical inconsistency, that "Parliament is the genuine
expression of the country.") But why had he not taken his
campaign more seriously? Was he indifferent to success?
When he learned that he was not among the fifty-three Socialist deputies elected in one of the greatest victories of
socialism, he appeared to be relieved (but of good actors it is
difficult to detect true feelings). It may well be that he had
announced his candidacy as deputy in one of his frequent
moods of uncertainty: it would have been flattering to be *the*
representative of revolutionary socialism in Parliament at
thirty years of age; but his antiparliamentary campaign could
have been a serious drawback. And out of Parliament he was
freer to follow his impulses, to turn his revolutionary propaganda to his own ends. Yet, when the chance came he failed
to take full advantage of it.

He missed an opportunity to show himself the man of
legend that he himself had created, the leader of a wide revolutionary movement. The opportunity was offered by a
public upheaval that flared up suddenly and spread like wild-
fire over most of Italy. Later known as "Red Week," it was
reminiscent of that Paris Commune that Mussolini had so
often and so enthusiastically celebrated. But while the Commune had had Blanqui as its soul and mind, Red Week was
without either. It started on June 7, 1914, which, being the
first Sunday in June, was also Constitution Day. Everywhere
there were celebrations, and Mussolini was in Forlì to speak
on "Marat, son of the people," unaware that anything was
amiss. Only upon his return to Milan did he learn that during
demonstrations in Ancona there had been yet another
"slaughter."

Ancona, a seaport on the Adriatic coast which at the time was second only to Venice in the volume of its maritime traffic, was becoming a "den of rebels" under the propaganda of two men, Mussolini's former prison companion, the enterprising Pietro Nenni, editor of the local Republican paper, and the internationally known anarchist Errico Malatesta. The two men had organized demonstrations on Constitution Day; in an attempt to prevent the demonstrators from going out into the streets, the police had killed three persons.

The next day in *Avanti!* Mussolini called the killing "premeditated murder, murder that has no extenuating circumstances," and prophesied that "tomorrow, when the news will be known in all Italian centers, both in the cities and countryside, the answer to the provocation will arise, spontaneously." And spontaneously it did arise, with only a bit of help from the Socialist Party and the General Confederation of Labor, which jointly called a general strike. Revolts and confusion followed, paralyzing activities from the top to the toe of the Italian peninsula. In Rome people expected at any moment the proclamation of an Italian republic.

Mussolini, the man of the barricades, stayed in Milan and did not see the barricades or the crowds of rebels that burned churches and city halls, attacked trains — scaring American tourists out of Italy — and seized property. It would be unfair to assert that he should have been in the thick of it, since strictly speaking his task was to spur all rebels through *Avanti!* He did a little more than his duty, and in Milan he left his office to harangue large crowds in the Arena, the huge stadium. He went so far as to make a timid attempt to lead a small group of demonstrators into the streets of Milan, but he did not go farther than the great cathedral, for in a narrow street behind it the police beat him on the head, though not so badly that the next day he could not go on talking at the stadium.

After three days the general strike was called off; *Avanti!* failed to provide effective leadership, and the revolt soon turned into a farce. Ancona and several towns proclaimed local republics, and there the rebels erected trees of liberty as symbols of the newly acquired freedom and confiscated goods belonging to the *bourgeoisie* — including the food found cooking on their stoves — for distribution to the people. Chicken went almost for nothing, and the new governments were nicknamed "chicken republics." In Ancona, where a state of siege was proclaimed, sailors landing from battleships dispatched to restore order were met by women and girls bringing them flowers and shouting "Don't fire on your brothers but on your superiors!"

Within a week the revolt subsided and order was reestablished.

In *Avanti!* Mussolini took credit for Red Week. "If a movement — like the present —" he wrote, "has been possible with the speed and simultaneity which have terrified bourgeois public opinion, this is due — it is not a sin of pride to affirm it — to our newspaper, which daily brings its word to the exploited of Italy. . . . We openly admit and claim our responsibility in these events and in the political situation that is forming [as a result]."

Despite this assertion, one gets a strong impression in reading the records of those days that Mussolini was taken by surprise and did not do much to steer and direct events once they had begun, that he had very little to do with the general strike, and did not even know the party's attitude toward it. The fact that his friend Nenni was arrested and sentenced to another long term in prison for his part in Red Week, while Mussolini was not even questioned or otherwise bothered by the police, may be a measure of their relative responsibility for the revolt. (The anarchist Malatesta, the most responsible of all, managed to escape from Italy while the police were hunting him.)

Failures can better be seen in the perspective of time. In June, 1914, Mussolini's failures were not as evident as his success, and Ivanoe Bonomi, the ousted reformist, could call him "dictator of Italian socialism in the present hour."

PART 2

PAUSE
AND
ASCENT

7

THE GREAT CHANGE OF MIND

> "Only war heightens all human energies to
> maximum tension and impresses a seal of
> nobility on the peoples who have the virtue
> to undertake it."
>
> MUSSOLINI, 1932

MUSSOLINI'S past successes and failures became totally
unimportant in the face of an event that many had dreaded
and few had expected, an event that occurred with precipitate
suddenness and stunned the entire world: the outbreak of
what is now called World War I.

There had been several ominous symptoms, but Mussolini
and most of his contemporaries had not given them the importance that history has since attributed to them. When, on
June 28 — two weeks after Red Week — a young Slav killed
the crown prince of Austria, Archduke Francis Ferdinand,
and his wife in the streets of Sarajevo in Bosnia, Mussolini
correctly analyzed the political aspects of the murder but did
not foresee its consequences: "The double killing," he pointed
out, ". . . has revealed the profound rift . . . between the
House of Hapsburg and the Slav world. . . . We must explain it as an explosion of national hatred. Austria is the
violent conqueror. . . . Austria is the obstacle in the path
of the Serbian design of expansion . . . [and] the brute force
which represses the labors and the aspirations of a people to
elevate itself. . . ."

Only on July 26 did the first headlines, fraught with alarm
and consternation, appear in Italian papers, and only then
did Mussolini envision a European conflagration. On July 28

Austria declared war on Serbia; by August 4 the war had spread to the major European powers, and Germany had invaded Belgium.

The outbreak of hostilities brought a widespread fear in Italy and abroad that the obligations of its treaties with Germany and Austria might drag Italy into a war that its people did not want. During the period of secret alliances that preceded and determined World War I, Italy was the junior member of a Triple Alliance, with Germany and Austria the senior partners; in the European balance of power it was a counterweight to the Triple Entente between Great Britain, France, and Russia. The causes of Italy's alliance were intricate and included the fact that she was not securing colonies, the consequent resentment against France who was acquiring new ones, and the desire to maintain and raise the prestige of the young country. Because the alliance was secret, the Italian people did not know its provisions beyond the fact that it guaranteed mutual defense.

The Triple Alliance, first signed in 1882, had been renewed several times, most recently in 1913. Then Mussolini denounced it as being contrary to Socialist ideals of internationalism and antimilitarism. Bitterness for his expulsion from Austria and aversion for the strong clericalism of the Austro-Hungarian monarchy may well have made him lean heavily on his pen, but there is little doubt that he reflected the opinion of most Italians when he criticized "the Italy . . . that becomes Prussianized with reckless arrogance; that becomes Austrophile with cynical indifference for its memories and its traditions." Mussolini, and the many people who felt as he did, failed to realize or admit that over the years the Triple Alliance had given the Italians the comfortable feeling that Austria, the "traditional enemy," would not try to regain the vast territories of northern Italy which had been part of the Austro-Hungarian Empire before Italian unity.

If the idea of an Austria turned into a friend for the sake of diplomatic opportunism could be comfortable and reassuring, an Austria allied with Italy in a war of which no one knew the causes or the aims was an appalling thought. The patriots who at the beginning of the *Risorgimento* had prepared and planned

Italian unity took care to instil in their aloof fellow Italians-to-be that hatred of Austria without which the movement for independence would have failed. Ever since the achievement of independence, elementary school teachers saw to it that glorification of the *Risorgimento*, with its heroes and ideals, would keep this hatred alive and make all good Italians believe that it had always been a most important element of the common tradition.

To the schoolboy Benito Mussolini, as to all Italian school children after the unification of Italy, modern Italian history was presented as a series of vignettes in strong colors: underground patriots, who called themselves *carbonari* (coal workers), covered with coal dust and soot, whispering in one another's ear, forming a long chain that extended from the top to the toe of the Italian boot; Silvio Pellico, wasting away in Austrian dungeons in Venice and at the Spielberg for having been one of the whisperers; Guglielmo Oberdan, hanged for his audacious attempt to kill Emperor Francis Joseph and rid the world of a tyrant; Garibaldi, in a red shirt, going to the conquest of Italy on a big white horse, with a handful of followers and a failing but indomitable wife riding by his side; the same Garibaldi, on horseback, shaking hands with Victor Emmanuel of Piedmont, modestly but unforgettably placing at the sovereign's feet a gift of conquered lands and then retiring to a small island; and, stranger than the rest and less comprehensible to the mind of a child, Mazzini shaping the fate of Italy — and consequently of Austria — from abroad, like a great puppeteer moving puppets through some mysterious, invisible power.

Mussolini could not escape the effects of this historical heritage, handed down to him at an age when the mind is most imaginative and malleable. He was exposed to it both in school and at home, where his mother, who taught her pupils history from approved textbooks, sang to her own children the battle hymns of the *Risorgimento*, to the sound of which intrepid soldiers had once marched against Austria.

All this must be borne in mind in order to understand Mussolini's aggressive demand for "absolute neutrality" on the eve of World War I and during the first months thereafter,

and his later change of mind. His Socialist ideas of internationalism and antimilitarism required neutrality as their
logical consequence, while the patriotic substratum made it
impossible for him even to think of a war on the side of
Austria, a war which, in view of the Triple Alliance, seemed
to be the only alternative to neutrality.

Many Italians, and especially the majority of those who
were in a position to exert political influence, gradually
shifted their stand from one of "absolute neutrality" to that
of "watchful neutrality," and then to one of intervention, as
circumstances evolved and the danger of a war on the side
of Austria and Germany faded away. Pro-French sentiment
was strong in responsible Italian circles — Italy often
quarreled with her Latin sister but could not cut family ties;
and the top intellectual stratum, including such leaders of
reformist socialism as Turati, admired British culture and
the British temperament. Only the clergy and their close followers felt greater sympathy for Catholic Austria than for the
powers of the Entente, atheist France, Protestant England, and
Orthodox Russia. The true Italian neutralists were the peasants, who in the Libyan war had seen an aim that they valued,
the acquisition of land, but did not see any reason, material
or sentimental, for the present conflict. By late fall, most of
those who had been in favor of absolute neutrality at the outbreak of the war were violently opposed to support of the
Triple Alliance but would not have raised obstacles to intervention on the side of the Triple Entente, should this prove
necessary for the defeat of the Central Powers.

Mussolini was only one of many Socialists, both in Italy
and elsewhere, who changed their mind about neutrality in
the war. In France, Belgium, and Germany, as soon as war
broke out, Socialists who had been convinced antipatriots
clamored to be allowed to enlist. Among them was that French
Socialist of extreme tendencies, Gustave Hervé, whom Mussolini admired and whose famous sentence "The national flag
is a rag to be planted in manure" Mussolini appropriated in
Lotta di Classe. The International proved ineffectual for
quenching the sudden fire of nationalism, and the sentiments
it had tried to instill in its adherents, pacifism, universalism,

and world-wide solidarity of the working class, were promptly dispelled by that strong loyalty to one's homeland which a war never fails to arouse. Thus in changing his mind Mussolini was only one of many, but the way in which the change came about was to single him out.

From July 26 through August and September, he hammered pro-neutrality propaganda in his articles and speeches and absolute Socialist neutrality in the large headlines of *Avanti!*

July 26: "Let a single cry arise from the vast multitudes of the proletariat, and let it be repeated in the squares and streets of Italy: 'Down with the war.' "

July 29: "Italian proletarians, stand up! This is the hour of firm resolutions and great responsibilities. Your blood, your bread, your future are in question."

August 5: "The neutrality of Belgium has been violated. . . . To be in direct or indirect solidarity with Germany means — at this moment — to serve the cause of militarism in its most insane and criminal expression."

August 13: "Neutrality until the end of the war, neutrality that will permit — at the right moment — the intervention of Italy in favor of peace: neutrality that should be maintained at all costs."

August 22: "The proletariat furnishes raw material, cannon fodder with which the states make their history. . . . War is the maximum exploitation of the proletarian class. After sweat, blood; after exploitation at work, death on the battlefield."

August 23: "The danger of Italy's help to the Austro-German bloc seems to us to have disappeared forever. Only the other hypothesis remains: Italy's intervention in favor of the Triple Entente. . . . But in order to declare war . . . against nations with whom Italy was allied for over thirty years and until yesterday, we should find a decent reason. . . . It would be repugnant to the Italian conscience to apply . . . the stab in the back."

August 26: "The show that the Nationalists offer us reaches

the apex of the grotesque . . . [and] these people, today, loudly proclaim that Italy must put aside her neutrality. . . . The thesis . . . is this: when Japan — very far away — enters the battlefield, is it possible for Italy to stay neutral? . . . For some, a 'neutral' Italy means an Italy degraded from Big Power to a secondary role. Are we or are we not a Big Power? *Ergo*: we must participate in the universal slaughter."

September 3: "Francophilism threatens to make common cause with the warmongers! No, a thousand times no! [We shall be] neutral as proletarians, neutral as Italians!"

September 22: "Workers! The Socialist Party, in this turbulent and frightening hour . . . reaffirms the existence of a deep and incurable antithesis between war and socialism, insofar as, apart from other formidable reasons, war, because compulsory, represents the extreme form of class collaboration, the annihilation of individual autonomy and of freedom of thought, which are sacrificed to state and militarism. . . .

" . . . The Socialist Party reaffirms its eternal faith in the future of the Workers' International, destined to bloom again, greater and stronger, from the blood and ruins of the present conflagration of peoples. It is in the name of the International and of Socialism that we invite you, O Proletarians of Italy, to maintain and accentuate your unshakable opposition to war."

September 30: "Italian Socialists have no reason to change their attitude of sympathy for the cause of the Triple Entente, but if [French revolutionists] demand that this sympathy induce the Italian Socialist Party to assume warmongering stands, they are mistaken."

Thus spoke Mussolini in his paper. These were the words that the Socialists read in the official organ of the party and that helped shape their opinion. But by early October insistent rumors were circulating in Milan and elsewhere: the director of *Avanti!* was wavering; his absolute stand for neutrality was not as absolute as he claimed; Mussolini hated Austria; Mussolini was very much in favor of France; he had even discussed plans for general mobilization in Italy; Mussolini was a man of two souls; there were two Mussolinis, the official spokesman of the party and the private individual, and the two did not see eye to eye.

Newspapers picked up facts and gossip. There had been, both in *Avanti!* and in a leading Roman newspaper, Mussolini's public denial that he had ever told "an influential person from the unredeemed lands" that war against Austria was not only unavoidable but also "the duty imposed by civilization on the Italian proletariat." The influential person, who published a denial of Mussolini's denial, turned out to be Cesare Battisti, on whose paper Mussolini had collaborated during his stay in Trent, and who was to be hanged by the Austrians for fighting on the Italian side.

There was a letter to a noted Socialist professor in Catania, Giuseppe Lombardo-Radice, who had resigned from the party on the neutrality issue. Mussolini wrote him that a war against Austria would not only encounter no obstacles on the part of the Socialists but would also find them "rather sympathetic."

There were long political discussions with a journalist whose penname was "Tancredi" at a table of the popular Café Campari in the *galleria* of Milan, in view of the Gothic cathedral. Mussolini allegedly revealed his true feelings to Tancredi and in justification of his official stand in *Avanti!* stated repeatedly that Socialist propaganda carried no weight and did not influence events, that the government was not so weak or the party so strong that the latter could affect Italy's future course of action. A bitter personal polemic followed Tancredi's revelation of his talks with Mussolini.

Altogether, it was a true political scandal. Newspapers of assorted political hues urged "Hamlet Mussolini" to abandon his equivocal position. He did, on October 18, in one of the longest articles he had ever written; but he made a fundamental mistake: instead of speaking for himself and telling the story of his own evolution, he spoke in the name of the party, although, in his usual dictatorial way, he had not consulted other members. The article, "From Absolute to Active and Working Neutrality," came as a surprise to everyone but Mussolini himself and his printer.

Absolute neutrality was a negative, comfortable formula which did away with the need of thinking, he said in substance. Socialists were divided on the neutrality issue, and their opinions ranged from opposition to any war except the proletarians' own to favoring intervention on the side of the Entente. From the beginning, Socialist neutrality had been "a markedly Austro-Germanophobe, and therefore Francophile, neutrality." (In this period Mussolini rarely mentioned Great Britain or Russia, for he knew very little about them and, as Turati had noticed, he refused to take into consideration anything that he did not know.) A war against the Austro-German Empire could free Italy once and for all from the possibility of any future reprisals; and should the Central Powers triumph and ask for the return of the Italian provinces which had once been under Austrian domination, not even the absolute neutralists would want Italy to stay out of the war. Mussolini concluded that absolute neutrality was a dangerous and immobilizing formula. Formulas could be adapted to events, but to attempt to adapt events to formulas was a mad and ridiculous undertaking. Italians enjoyed "the privilege of living in the most tragic hour in the history of the world"; did the Socialists want to be "inert spectators of this grandiose drama" or did they want to be protagonists?

In her book *My Life as a Rebel*, Angelica Balabanoff relates that on October 18, the day the article was published, she and Mussolini were on a train together, going to a meeting of the party executive in Bologna, when a Socialist carrying a copy of *Avanti!* came into their compartment and asked her to read what Mussolini had written. This was the first hint she had of Mussolini's change of mind. She was shocked, as were other members of the executive, who could not understand why Mussolini had not confided in them, confessed his doubts, and sought guidance. The meeting in Bologna was stormy and tumultuous. Accusations and recriminations rained on Mussolini's head. In the course of a re-examination of the party stand, he introduced a motion for conditional neutrality which received only one vote, his own.

"My succession at *Avanti!* is open," he told newspapermen as he came out of the meeting, and with these words he admitted his defeat, the fact that he had been forced to resign from the directorship of *Avanti!* Then, pale with frustration and repressed anger, he burst out: "So much is ridiculous in Italy, from pickled cucumbers to absolute neutrality! Ridiculous, ridiculous, everything is ridiculous!" To some people, Mussolini's predicament seemed sad rather than ridiculous: he had refused the financial settlement offered him and was left with no position, no work, and no income with which to support his wife and child. But whatever sympathy was given him was wasted.

Within a few days a rumor spread that Mussolini intended to found another paper and had already made the necessary financial arrangements. He denied the rumor, but on November 15, a little more than three weeks after the meeting in Bologna, the first issue of a new paper, entirely his own and avowedly in favor of intervention, was published in Milan. It was called *Il Popolo d'Italia* (*The People of Italy*) and bore two mottoes, Blanqui's "He who has iron has bread" and Napoleon's "A revolution is an idea that has found bayonets." Neither the name of the paper nor the use of the mottoes was original: there had been an *Il Popolo d'Italia* in Naples in the last century, and the two quotations were used as epigraphs on the title page of a book by Gustave Hervé. Mussolini, who had admired in Hervé the antimilitarist and antipatriot, now admired the Hervé who had changed his mind and promptly enlisted in the French army.

In an editorial in the first issue of *Il Popolo*, Mussolini cried loudly that "today, antiwar propaganda is cowardice" and flung an "auspicious cry" to the "young in years and young in spirit. . . . My cry is a word that I would have never pronounced in normal times, and that I instead raise loudly, with my full voice, with no attempt at simulation, with firm faith, today: a fearful and fascinating word: *war!*"

This article further incensed the Socialists and aroused their ire. On November 24 the Socialist section of Milan met in the People's Theater to examine Mussolini's case, in the mood of a revolutionary tribunal. On the walls of the meeting place someone had scribbled in huge letters: "Read *Avanti!* Boycott *Il Popolo d'Italia.*" When Mussolini arrived with a small group of "Mussolinians" — a term created for the occasion — he was hissed and greeted with shouts of "Traitor!

Judas! Rabagas!" * His face was gray and sweaty. He talked amid a storm of interruptions.

"I gather from the temper of this assembly that my fate is sealed," he said.

"Yes! Down with the renegade! Long live *Avanti!*"

"Today you hate me because you still love me! Twelve years of my life in the party should be a sufficient guarantee of my Socialist faith. Socialism is something that takes roots in one's blood."

The same men who, only two years before, in the concerted action with him in Reggio Emilia, had ousted four deputies from the party now expelled him. This is what Angelica Balabanoff had seemed to predict when she addressed her apologetic words to Bissolati and the other three deputies. No one apologized to Mussolini.

There is an intrinsic danger in the taking of extreme positions, for the more conspicuous one becomes, the more vulnerable. Mussolini had always called those who changed their minds "renegades," and of those who shifted to nationalism he had said: "For some time I have walked among wrecks of men. Italy is by now a tournament for perverters of all ideas, of all faiths, of all parties. I am ashamed to live in this Italy of tightrope walkers, of inert bystanders, of political jugglers, and of those who tolerate them with blissfully idiotic resignation. The reign of Rabagas is at hand!" But now he himself was the political juggler and had to bear the consequences both of his past rigidity and of his new flexibility.

He left the assembly pale and enraged and went straight to the editorial offices of his new paper to write a comment on his own expulsion. "I am ousted, but not tamed. If they consider me 'dead' they will have the terrible surprise of finding me alive, implacable, obstinately resolved to fight them with all my forces." A few Mussolinians left the party, whose ranks were further thinned; by this time the right-wing reformists, the Freemasons, and the Mussolinians were out.

* Rabagas was the protagonist of a famous French play by V. Sardou. In seemingly democratic speeches, Rabagas incited the people of Monaco to revolt against their prince; then, bribed by the prince himself, he took the opposite stand and was booed and hissed.

Mussolini found himself on the same side of the fence with interventionists like Leonida Bissolati, Cesare Battisti, Enrico Corradini, and the poet Gabriele D'Annunzio. A few weeks before, Gaetano Salvemini, later a voluntary exile from fascism and professor at Harvard University, had written to congratulate him on his "magnificent article on non-absolute neutrality." And there were others: after "the first roar of the cannons," Pietro Nenni, who was in prison for his part in Red Week, decided in favor of Italian intervention in the war.

Even before Mussolini's expulsion from the party, he and his collaborators on *Avanti!* had engaged in one of the bitterest, most venomous, most undignified wars ever waged in print. Mussolini accused honest, forthright Lazzari of having "a hidden past," of actions that had "diminished" his moral figure, and threatened to "dust off" documents that would furnish evidence against him. He accused of blackmail the caricaturist of *Avanti!* whose implacable pencil was daily making fun of him. He threw dirt at others, especially at his onetime friend Giacinto Menotti Serrati, to whom, with Lazzari and Angelica Balabanoff, he owed his amazingly rapid ascent in the Socialist Party. He asserted that Serrati, while living in the United States at the beginning of the century, had been an informer for the U.S. government, a "spy" denouncing Italian anarchists, and that he had the "moral responsibility" for the death of the Italian anarchist killed during political disorders in Barre, Vermont, in 1903.

Avanti! retaliated, called Mussolini "insane," "irresponsible," "alcoholic"; it accused him of loose morals, of having publicly denied that he was going to start a new paper while already planning it; of high sensitivity to flattery (he had been called "intrepid, the first and only hero"), of "spitting venom on everybody and everything," of "a shameful campaign of cowardice" and mudslinging, of establishing "that revolutionary and Socialist tenet: 'I am Benito the first and only one. You shall have no other God before me.'" More serious and damaging was the fact that ever since the appearance of the first issue of *Il Popolo*, the editors of *Avanti!* joined the chorus asking "Who pays?" and went on asking the same question day after day, with the insistence of the drop of water that wears out the stone on which it falls. "Who pays?" A six-page daily paper, with its own information service, its correspondents, and its serial novel, is not founded in three weeks and on pennies alone. Whose funds had Professor Mussolini received? Italian or foreign money? Were the persistent rumors of "gold from France" more than mere rumors? Professor Mussolini skilfully dodged these questions and answered only that his finances were "pure." When rumors failed to subside, he asked for an investigation, and the investigating committee, appointed by the city, returned a favorable verdict.

History, however, has neither decisively shown how *Il Popolo* was financed nor fully disproved that Mussolini received money from France. A later inquiry into this matter again cleared Mussolini, without halting the gossip. In *Mussolini Diplomatico*, published in 1952, Salvemini gives a documented analysis of known facts which seems to prove the existence of "French gold." A balanced evaluation of these contrasting opinions requires an answer to some questions: could the Mussolini of 1914 have been so important to the French cause that it was worth while to buy him? Was Mussolini likely to let himself be bought?

At no time could Mussolini be accused of being venal, neither as a poor young Socialist nor when he came to power. In his later life he was often to create the impression that he had no idea of the worth of money. He may have resented poverty, but he liked to display it ostentatiously, as the myth that spurred him on, as a condition with which he could identify himself. It is said that, in this period of his life, whenever he had to buy a new suit he would crumple it before wearing it, and though he owned good clothes, when he appeared in public he liked to look shabbier than the shabbiest workers. At home he lived a frugal life; in two autobiographies published after his death, his widow Rachele told of the simple tastes, few needs and ambitions, and peasant thriftiness that she shared with her husband. Although these autobiographies are ghostwritten and not particularly reliable in many ways, in these details they are trustworthy and confirmed by other evidence. Promises of personal financial advantage could not have bought Mussolini.

Nevertheless it was possible to buy him, if not for money, then for personal prestige, an outstanding position, or aid in the partial fulfilment of his will to power. He could not but be dissatisfied with the corner in which his extremism had pushed him. His talk of revolution in peacetime, his denouncing of colonial expeditions and all wars, his willingness to be jailed for his beliefs, had rapidly given him a glamorous reputation. But Mussolini was not one to be satisfied with a static position or with the ascendancy he had so far gained. He was moved by Nietzsche's will to power, and to him power was a constant ascent, an increasingly firm hold on more and more people, a dynamic state in which a pacifist Socialist had few chances to maintain himself if war broke out. In the fall of 1914, a serious and swiftly spreading war was being fought all around Italy; many former pacifists were giving in to their patriotic feelings, especially after it became evident that if Italy were to join the warring nations it would not be on the side of Austria and Germany; the expectations of success in a proletarian revolution were dim when compared with the sure glories of a war already begun.

Mussolini's question: "Do we want to be . . . inert spectators . . . or . . . protagonists?" in his article against absolute neutrality contained an implicit answer as far as he was concerned. He was not intended for the role of spectator. At the time he asked the question, he had already decided in favor of war, and soon afterward he unsheathed in public his newly acquired patriotic and interventionist sentiments. His motives were not strong inner convictions but contingent impulses adapted to opportunities and circumstances. His talks with Cesare Battisti, "the influential person from the unredeemed lands," and his wish to settle old scores with Austria, may have had considerable influence in awakening his dormant or repressed patriotism. In Trent, Battisti had been the exponent of the small, intensely patriotic group that wanted Trent and Trieste returned to Italy. At the outbreak of the war Battisti fled Austria and went to live in Milan, where he engaged in active propaganda for the intervention of Italy in the war; and news of his activities undoubtedly reached Mussolini. Yet other pressures may have been at work to bring about Mussolini's full conversion, and among these an offer of money to publish an interventionist paper does not appear either unlikely or improbable.

In view of the evidence, it seems almost certain that the, first funds for *Il Popolo d'Italia* were Italian, and that Mussolini received early suggestions, assistance, and help through a journalist in Bologna whose newspaper represented agrarian capital. This man is said to have been an emissary of the Italian Minister of Foreign Affairs, who wanted Italy's intervention in the war. It seems also certain that France, through the Socialist Marcel Cachin who later became a deputy, promised and soon delivered financial help. It would be difficult to ascertain how much was given, but remittances amounting to 100,000 francs ($20,000 of that time) were frequently mentioned.

But, one may ask, was Mussolini's weight in the cause of intervention so great that it justified buying him? History judges a posteriori that Italy would have gone to war in any case, and that Mussolini's shift from socialism to interventionism was of negligible importance. Yet a fair appraisal of the facts must take into consideration that the first suggestions of a new paper must have been made some time before Mussolini publicly indicated his readiness to change his mind, probably even before the first rumors of his wavering began to spread: very likely in September, 1914. At that time Italy's course of action was still uncertain. Intervention on the side of the Triple Alliance seemed unlikely, but the alliance itself had not yet been denounced, and the voice of the neutralists was still loud. The most important single element of organized resistance to intervention was the Socialist Party, and Benito Mussolini was the party's official spokesman and leader. He was acquiring a certain notoriety in Milan and its surrounding territory and had a certain number of enthusiastic admirers — one had gone so far as to write his biography, still in preparation in September, 1914, which was published three months later.

The "purchase" of Mussolini, if it did occur, achieved two aims. It weakened the Socialist front, sowing discord in its ranks and depriving it of a strong director for its official paper. It also gave the opposite field an able journalist who knew how to deal with the masses and how to arouse them for a cause, any cause. To this extent the "purchase" of Mussolini was a wise move, worthwhile to France and to the Triple Entente.

8

TWO DUELS AND FIVE WOMEN

"The spectacle of certain subversives, antimilitarist until yesterday, who today exalt
the institution that they wished to demolish,
is infinitely grotesque."
                    MUSSOLINI, October, 1914

IN his change of mind Mussolini does not seem to have
found peace of mind. The beginning of 1915 found him in a
state of turmoil, in a combative and exasperated mood that
exploded at the least provocation, as if he felt insecure in
his new position, on his own, and much concerned that he
might have lost that grasp on the working masses which was the
main factor in his past success; as if his insecurity had made
him so oversensitive and touchy that he could bear no criticism but had to try to drown it under cataracts of vituperation,
by outshouting his adversaries.

His paper became the forum for personal diatribes in
which he gave vent to his wrath. But expressing his rage in
writing was not enough to make it subside, and for once he
felt the need to pass from words to deeds, deeds that required
a certain physical, if totally misplaced, courage. Within the
span of little over a month he fought two of the five duels he
was to fight in the course of his life. (The other three took
place between October, 1921, and May, 1922.)

An anarchist lawyer, Libero Merlino, provoked the first
duel. After a meeting of neutralists in which Mussolini had
not participated and about which he had made some comments
in his paper, the lawyer sent a letter to *Avanti!* criticizing
Mussolini and saying: "the duce of the . . . interventionists
who *shouts in his paper* should have had the courage to appear

before the crowd gathered in assembly." It so happened that on the day this letter appeared in the paper Mussolini was in court where a suit against *Il Popolo* was heard. Seeing Merlino in the courtroom, he walked up to him: "Is the letter yours that *Avanti!* published today?" "It is mine." "And am I perhaps the 'duce' of whom you speak?" "You are." ". . . and you are a rogue and a rascal," Mussolini said and slapped the other hard in the face.

"Our director," said *Il Popolo d'Italia* on the following day, "administered to [the lawyer] such a series of slaps and blows of the fist that he pushed him against a radiator and kept him . . . glued to it under an uninterrupted barrage. . . . " The poor lawyer, who at first was as white as a washed rag and speechless, soon recovered his spirits and sent his seconds to Mussolini. They fought a duel that ended only when both were wounded slightly. Grudgingly, they shook hands. It was February 25, 1915.

On March 29 Mussolini fought a duel with Claudio Treves, Turati's close friend. He nurtured a deep resentment against this habitué of the Turati-Kuliscioff *salon*, this former director of *Avanti!* who had received a higher salary than he and whose collaboration he had refused. After Mussolini left *Avanti!* Treves resumed work for the paper and wrote articles against intervention. Mussolini, revealing his ability to turn political issues into personal slander, accused Treves in the pages of *Il Popolo* of being a neutralist in order to save his wife's money. Treves replied rather sharply. Having been called "he-wife," "Claudio Tremens," "Claudio the Rabbit," "vile," "revolting," "venal," and the like, he sent his seconds to Mussolini, although to do so was a breach of the Socialist code, which banned dueling as a militaristic and bourgeois practice.

The duel, which lasted longer than the first, was a mad succession of onslaughts undertaken before the signal to begin, of leaps forward and to the side, a furious agitation of sabers, a flashing of blades that crossed each other in the air, fell flat on shoulders, hit, and wounded. In the end, the anxious seconds and the doctors who were present ordered the fighters to stop.

The two opponents parted without reconciliation, as bitter as before.

Among the reasons for Mussolini's state of irritation after his change of mind may well have been the annoyances that several women caused him, for some of them did not accept easily or kindly his political behavior.

So far as it is known, Rachele was not among these last, and his conversion did not affect her seriously. After he had moved to Milan and left her in Forlì, Benito had gone to see her occasionally, but soon the frequency of his visits dropped considerably. Although he was quite satisfied with this arrangement and would have kept to it indefinitely, Rachele did not like it at all. He was surprised and embarrassed one day when she appeared at his office without warning with little Edda in her arms and said she wanted to live with him. He advised her to go back to Forlì until he found an apartment in Milan, but she was determined to stand on her rights — though not her legal rights, for they were not formally married — especially at a time when he was making a decent living. She had planned her move carefully with the help of a friend, and Benito had no other choice but to give in to her will. They settled in a small apartment where they moved a few belongings: their bed, Edda's crib, Benito's books, and the kitchen table.

Later, they slowly acquired what they needed. Benito would have bought everything at once, on terms, but the atavistic principles of peasant finance, well-rooted in Rachele, made her refuse to spend money before they had it. Rachele, the country girl to whom even Forlì had seemed too large, soon overcame her fears of the big city and learned to like the wide streets, the brisk pace of Milanese life, the few shows to which Benito took her on his press tickets, the shopping trips to Milan's open market, the *Verziere*, where food was cheap and she could realize the highest of housewifely aims, saving a few pennies. She was proud of her man, who could keep his family decently, if modestly, in Milan, and she drew some sort of aloof satisfaction from his rapid ascent in the Socialist Party.

Then one day Benito came home in a mood darker than any of his frequent dark moods. "We are back where we started from, and perhaps worse off. I quit the newspaper. I refused compensation. We have no money. Life will be hard . . . "

"We'll take it as it comes," the even-tempered Rachele replied and went about her chores, pretending that she did not mind, singing the cheerful songs that are heard in Italian homes when a woman is going about her housework. Benito, depressed and angry in turn, paced the floor, cursing under his breath, exploding in fits of rage against the people at *Avanti!* and against mankind and fate.

"Soon afterward," Rachele writes in her first book, "in order to give us the means to live, [Benito] went to Genoa, where his friend Captain [Giuseppe] Giulietti loaned him about two thousand lire." This amount was equal to four months' salary at *Avanti!* and much more than the family would spend during Benito's three weeks of unemployment. Why Mussolini should have borrowed such a large sum remains one of the minor puzzling elements in his behavior. (Because Giulietti, the leader of the maritime workers in Genoa, was known to favor intervention, gossip tried to link his loan with the founding of *Il Popolo d'Italia,* but he later denied that he had helped finance the paper.)

As soon as *Il Popolo* appeared, financial security returned to the family; but it did not give immediate self-assurance to Benito. He often sent Rachele to the newsstands to find out, without revealing her identity, how his paper was selling; and so they learned that *Il Popolo* was doing very well, especially when there were articles by "that fathead Mussolini," as the news vendor called him. Family life resumed its haphazard routine: Benito came home at irregular hours, often in the middle of the night, and some nights he did not come home at all, always claiming that he had been detained at the office of his paper. At home he shouted, scolded Edda, to whom he was more and more attached in his peculiar way, and bossed, even beat, Rachele. She did not mind the rough treatment and, though submissive in appearance, went on exerting her strong will. Benito often wrote articles at a furious speed at the kitchen table while Rachele looked on. Now and then he played the violin. Edda herself described her early years in a series of articles published in an Italian periodical in 1950: "As soon as I began to walk, my poor [mother] had hardly a quiet moment. In order to bring a nut to a little girl on the floor below ours, I once fell all the way down the stairs, while my father watched me bounce from step to step and instead of trying to stop me, stood swearing at the top of the stairs. . . . But the gravest danger I faced when I was only a few months' old. Father used to come home very late at night and . . . wake me up by playing his violin. Then he would close my eyes and I would go back to sleep. All this went well for some time, but then I took a liking to music and as soon as he would stop playing I started [crying]. One night . . . my father burst out in a violent rage and threw at me all the pillows, shoes, and [other] objects at hand; had not my grandmother arrived shouting "Benito, what are you doing?" and had she not promptly taken me away, I don't know what might have happened." As soon as Edda was five, he insisted that she too learn to play, perhaps in the hope that there would be at least one good performer in the family. Edda was receptive to the rhythm of music and, having been taken to the ballet, she imitated what she had seen and practiced dancing on her toes. Her parents did not encourage her, since even her father, for all his coarse boasting and revolutionary socialism, would have considered it absolutely improper if a woman of his family should appear on stage before an audience.

Angelica Balabanoff was the sternest critic of what she called Mussolini's betrayal. To her, the staunch, uncompromising Socialist, it brought the realization that she had been mistaken in her judgment, had misplaced her trust and had wasted the pains she had taken to improve his education and promote his ascent. Many years later Mussolini was to describe her as "an utterly boring militant, but of such a moral rectitude" that he wished all his opponents could be so endowed. It was against this moral rectitude that he clashed when he changed his mind, but even earlier their relations were strained.

Although he would not have undertaken to run *Avanti!* without her, he soon found out that it was uncomfortable to receive help and support, especially when these were apt to be sprinkled with lavish criticism and advice, as hers were. If he was a self-centered and dictatorial director, she was a demanding collaborator who too insistently acted as his conscience and was altogether too solicitous. On one occasion, when he was worried and fussed over his health, she arranged for medical advice, but then was indignant when she learned that he had fainted at the smell of ether — as he had once fainted at the smell of incense as a small boy in Predappio. She could not forgive him his fear of the sight of death — in *My Life as a Rebel* she tells that once, out of squeamishness, he refused to go to the morgue to identify the body of a youth from Predappio.

In Milan they lived in the same neighborhood, and one night on their way home from work Mussolini stopped by a clump of trees. It was during the early period of their collaboration on *Avanti!* and shortly after the convention at Reggio Emilia that had ousted from the party the right-wing reformists. "Here we shall hang Turati and the other reformists," Mussolini said. "And where shall we be hanged when the working class disapproves of us?" Angelica asked by way of reply. Piazzale Loreto was a mile — perhaps a mile and a half — away. Her eyes were again piercing the future, glimpsing the shameful hanging of 1945. (Her account cannot be regarded as hindsight, for she tells of this episode in *My Life as a Rebel*, published in 1938.)

By and by Mussolini came to consider Angelica Balabanoff a rival, and by July, 1913, she was no longer co-editor of *Avanti!* Yet on the surface their relations remained friendly. Her faith in his loyalty to socialism and his honesty were still intact when rumors began that his stand in favor of neutrality was not sincere. She still believed his repeated assertions that these rumors were the most slanderous calumnies, of the sort to which she herself had fallen victim more than once. She experienced her first shock of disappointment when she read his article on non-absolute neutrality on board the train to Bologna. It was then she exclaimed: "The man who wrote this has no place in the Socialist Party. He belongs either at the front or in a madhouse!" Yet at the meeting she was the one who suggested the financial settlement that he refused. Three weeks later, however, when *Il Popolo d'Italia* first appeared, all her illusions vanished. She considered him a traitor to the cause, guiltier and more despicable than Judas, for Judas betrayed one man, Mussolini the entire Socialist Party, all the workers of Italy. She was firmly convinced that he had changed his mind under the pressure of seductive offers and that he had written his famous article on non-absolute neutrality only after he had made all arrangements for his new paper and received assurance of financial help from France.

A few months later she left the country that she loved and resumed her wanderings: Switzerland, Russia, Austria, France, and finally the United States. There, in the thirties, she was to be an active propagandist against fascism and the "traitor" who led it. She was to return to Italy only after Mussolini's death.

Another woman was bitterly disappointed by Mussolini's shift to the cause of intervention and refused to see him again, the Mohammedan anarchist and neutralist, Leda Rafanelli. She had first set eyes on Mussolini on March 18, 1913, in Milan, when once more he celebrated the Paris Commune. Fascinated by the inspired, vehement words that he could always find for his favorite subject, she had written an article in his praise for an anarchist weekly. Flattered, he sent her a thank-you note, which opened the way to the romantic, curiously tantalizing relationship that followed. He asked to meet her; she invited him to her apartment. She was surprised when instead of the fiery worker-orator whom she expected she found at her door a shy gentleman in black attire, clumsily revolving a bowler hat in his very white hands, like a character in a farce. She warned him that her heart was not her own, but he insisted on coming to see her again: "We shall read Nietzsche and the Koran," he entreated, and assured her that he was "as free as air" and had no family ties.

Leda burned Egyptian perfumes and brewed Oriental coffee on a brazier in her living room, and she believed that she had "an intimate bond with the history of Cheop's pyramid," a link with a previous life many centuries back. In other ways she was extremely sophisticated, and she noticed his scanty knowledge in any field but politics, his blankness when she sought to lead him into the realm of spiritual and transcendental ideas. She soon discovered that he had no firm opinions but embraced those he had taken from the last book he had read; in discussions he gave in to her after only a few words.

Their relationship went on. Their romantic walks at night, their time together in her apartment or at the office of *Avanti!*, her coyness, and the Egyptian perfumes that disturbed him almost as much as did incense and ether, all these kept him in an exalted state. He would have liked her to become his mistress and inspirer, to assume the role in his life played by Anna Kuliscioff for Costa and Turati: the woman "who must incite and satisfy, and make senses, heart, and mind vibrate." Yet his spiritual surrender to her was not so total that he let her read his palm — she was skilled in this art, she said; but he was afraid of what his hand might reveal.

To her, as to Angelica Balabanoff, he admitted that he felt lonely, that he was refractory to affection, that he often felt as if he were going insane. This was his recurrent theme: "When I am in the madhouse. . . . " Sometimes she thought that he was right. His eyes were often crazed, and he wrote strange letters: "In order to keep my nerves exalted, I drank a large glass of absinthe . . . you know, the green liqueur that exerts its sweet and diabolic influence on the cerebral cortex and sends thirteen of every thousand Frenchmen to the madhouse. . . . How nice it is to be an idiot now and then." And in another letter: "You are perhaps the first woman who understands something of me. Criminals leave their skulls to students of anthropology; I should like to leave you my soul. So that you might complete your research."

This odd relation proceeded, interrupted from time to time, never very satisfactory, until political differences put an end to it. When he turned interventionist, she refused to see him again. In 1923 Mussolini's Fascists ransacked her home.

Unlike Angelica Balabanoff and Leda Rafanelli, Margherita Sarfatti, Mussolini's future biographer, raised no objections to his political conversion; in fact, she seconded it. When she first met him in Turati's and Anna Kuliscioff's *salon*, she was at once attracted by his positive qualities, his virile looks, his dynamism, his seeming nonconformism, and the assurance with which he put forward his views; and to him she expressed her wish to work for *Avanti!* Mussolini must have felt flattered: not only was she blonde and beautiful, intelligent, with a peculiarly feminine charm, but also, being the wife of an established lawyer, the daughter of a Socialist professor at the University in Venice, and from a wealthy family, she belonged to that class of intellectual Socialists that had often shunned him.

She became the paper's art critic and shared Mussolini's fiery socialism through the fall of 1914. Then she joined him in his venture with *Il Popolo d'Italia* and as its art and literary critic helped prepare its first issue. In 1914 her husband was one of the lawyers who defended the staff of *Avanti!* at the trial following the Rocca Gorga episode, and later, in early 1915, as a member of the commission investigating the funds on which *Il Popolo d'Italia* was started, her husband helped to clear Mussolini of the accusation of having received "French gold."

Even before this official sanction, Margherita had cleared Benito Mussolini in her mind. In her biography of Mussolini, she tells that she heard rumors of French gold before the appearance of the first issue of *Il Popolo d'Italia*. Feeling that Mussolini ought to be informed, she went to look for him at the offices of the newspaper. She found the staff occupying a few small rooms, hardly furnished at all except for a few tables and chairs, on the second floor of a modest building in

Via Paolo da Cannobio, a narrow, gray street in old Milan. The access from the street was through a dingy courtyard and up two narrow stairways. Mussolini was absent, but his closest associate, Sandro Giuliani, showed Margherita a contract for advertisements amounting to 4,000 lire (about $800 of that time). Her mind was set at ease, for Giuliani convinced her that, since several collaborators gave their services without remuneration, all the expenses for establishing *Il Popolo* were being met from this sum.

Il Popolo d'Italia was to remain in the small rooms in Via Paolo da Cannobio until 1921. When the lean years of fascism were over, the paper could have its own building; then the old rooms were transformed into a small museum, filled with Fascist trophies of battles and victories. Mussolini's own room in the old offices was a cubbyhole with a desk and chair and a single window which looked over a limited expanse of old roofs. Giacinto Menotti Serrati called Mussolini's room "the den," and Mussolini, who rather fancied himself in the role of lion, liked and retained the name.

Margherita Sarfatti was to have ample opportunity to become familiar with the den. Mussolini's association with her was to last almost twenty years, the longest association he had with a woman, Rachele excepted. Although she came to be considered, so to say, his official friend, it was not only love that drew him to her. It was again the fact, as it had been in his early acquaintance with Angelica Balabanoff, that in her he could confide in a way in which he could not have confided in a man, and from her he would accept suggestions and advice. It was to her credit that he lost some of his initial roughness, learned to be somewhat neater in his appearance, to care, or appear to care, about art and literature. With her vivid intelligence, her determined temperament, and her feminine intuition, she skilfully went about remolding the young man she had liked at first as he was and rendering him acceptable in higher spheres of society.

In a recent interview, Margherita Sarfatti asserted that her task had not been difficult. Mussolini, in her opinion, which is confirmed by others, had a prodigious gift for assimilation. All she had to do was to mention an idea casually, to make a suggestion or present an opinion in the course of conversation. The idea, opinion, or suggestion found an exceedingly fertile ground in Mussolini's mind and in a few days became a part of Mussolini's own thought. In Fascist times she was to be the editor of a Fascist monthly review, *Gerarchia*, to which the chief of government contributed articles which he considered the result of his deepest thought.

Mussolini was to put an end to their relation sometime about 1930. By then she was no longer a young woman, and Mussolini, at the height of power, must have felt that he no longer needed her advice.

While Mussolini was seeing Leda Rafanelli steadily and while he was becoming more and more sensitive to Margherita Sarfatti's charms, he was also having an unfortunate affair which caused him annoyance and irritation with a certain Ida Dalser, an intelligent, extremely high-strung woman from Trent. It is said that Mussolini had known her first in Trent and met her again in Milan in late 1913 or early 1914. She had tried several jobs and at that time she was running a beauty parlor, which she promptly closed when Mussolini promised to marry her — to her as to Leda he said that he had no ties of any sort. He got a small apartment for her, a fact that increased her illusions; but when he kept postponing their marriage, she began making violent scenes, sometimes in public, to his extreme vexation. One of Mussolini's biographers relates that one day she stood under the windows of his office and shouted invectives at him; whereupon he exploded in a sudden fit of rage, said it was time to put an end to this, grabbed a pistol, and would have rushed downstairs to shoot her had he not been held back by friends. In the midst of these quarrels Ida Dalser became pregnant and bore him a son, Benito Albino, in November, 1915. Early in 1916 Mussolini legally recognized Benito Albino as his son and renewed his promises of marriage to Ida, conveniently neglecting to mention that only a month before, on December 16, 1915, he and Rachele had celebrated a civil marriage.

Mussolini kept news of this marriage a secret, and as late as October, 1916, an official document published by Ida's relatives after the death of all those concerned, testified that "the family of service man Mussolini Benito consists of his wife Ida Dalser and of number 1 children."

The unfortunate woman was to live the rest of her life in perpetual agitation and shower her ex-lover with letters asking that he keep his promises. In 1917 she was interned, at Mussolini's instigation according to prevalent opinion, on the grounds that being from Trent she was Austrian and technically an enemy alien. Later she went back to Trent and resumed her letter-writing, requesting that Mussolini marry her. Mussolini always kept a cynical attitude toward her, and in 1920 he wrote a friend: "The person of whom you speak is dangerous, unbalanced, and criminal, a blackmailer and a forger. I had relations with her, I recognized her son, but she never was and never will become my wife. In the war she was interned and she made trouble for all the Italian authorities. You were not mistaken in judging her unbalanced. Tell me what she is doing and how she is living. At the same time have her watched and sent to jail, which is her natural place. . . . "

Mussolini's relation with Ida Dalser and the very existence of his son Benito Albino were not generally known while he was in power and were revealed after his death by Ida Dalser's relatives.

Ida Dalser spent the last ten years of her life — she died in 1935 — not in jail but in an institution for mental patients, where she was confined against the opinion of at least some of the doctors who examined her. Benito Albino grew under the supervision of two successive guardians, and Mussolini provided, at least in part, for his illegitimate son's sustenance, not directly but through his brother Arnaldo, who often took care of what was distasteful to Benito. Benito Albino died in World War II, under mysterious circumstances — some say in an institution like his mother, others, in naval action in which his ship was sunk.

9

MAN AND SUPERMAN
IN THE FIRST WORLD WAR

"It is the plow that shapes the furrow, but it
is the sword that defends it. And both the
plowshare and the blade are of tempered
steel, like the faith in our hearts."
                                    MUSSOLINI, December, 1934

Mussolini pursued his campaign for intervention to the
very end, with the single-mindedness and the intensity of one
following a fixed idea. He never realized, or he refused to see,
that Italy was still suffering from the effects of the Libyan
campaign, which had heavily taxed the national economy,
that she was not militarily prepared, and that she had more
to gain from staying out than joining the conflict. Thus he and
the other Socialists and syndicalists who rallied around him
and claimed the war would forever abolish the bondage of one
class to another worked in favor of the small minority that
committed the tragic mistake of leading Italy into the war.
The men forming this minority were moved by different
ideals: the king had been brought up as a soldier and was
anxious to increase his own prestige and that of his country;
Prime Minister Salandra made the same error of judgment
that Mussolini himself was to make in 1940 and thought that
the war would soon be over and Italy should enter at once or
miss a share of the loot; the Nationalists remembered that
Dante had sung of an Italy enclosed by mountains and sea
with the wide arc of the Alps marking her boundaries on land
— but in 1915 vast territories south and west of this arc were
still in Austrian hands; and other idealists saw in the war the

only possible way of completing the *Risorgimento* and Italian unity or were moved by indignation over Germany's aggression and her invasion of Belgium. All these groups of people, whose different ideologies converged in their wanting war, had one element in common, a misplaced patriotism. A sentence that Mussolini was to write on the third anniversary of the outbreak of war in Europe may be taken as representative of this common feeling: "Italy could not remain neutral, at the price of suicide, while her chivalrous intervention brought her at once among the most noble Nations of the world."

As late as April, 1915, both fighting sides were still courting Italy. Austria, realizing that Francophile sentiment was strong in Italy and that the scales were tipping in favor of intervention on the side of the Allies, was offering territorial concessions in return for an Italian pledge of neutrality. But the interventionists were against any deal. When old Giolitti, who as opposition leader was still a dominating figure in Italian politics, advocated a bargained neutrality, Mussolini assailed him in *Il Popolo*, maintaining that this course of action would be the hypocritical behavior of a beggar nation.

The Allies were willing to give Italy more than Austria was offering, provided Italy were to enter the war on their side, and Prime Minister Salandra, believing in a short war, was anxious to come to an agreement with them. On April 26 Italy and the Allies concluded the secret Treaty of London, whose provisions were not disclosed to the Italian Parliament. On May 3 the Italian government denounced the Triple Alliance. (It was justified in so doing, for the alliance had contemplated only defense and, in addition, Austria and Germany had not consulted Italy before going to war.) The government was compelled to move swiftly, because one of the secret provisions of the Treaty of London was that Italy should enter the war within a month. To make the war acceptable to the indifferent or hostile masses, a miracle was still needed, which neither Mussolini nor the other interventionists in Italy could perform. With a stroke of genius the government sent for the poet-novelist Gabriele d'Annunzio who at the turn of the century had been the pet of the literati and intellectuals and who for some years had been living in France.

D'Annunzio, a most prolific author, had been something of a child prodigy and had already made a name for himself by 1881 when at eighteen he left boarding school. His abundant prose and poetry had been a significant factor in the shaping of Italian thought. Although there is no evidence that Mussolini had read widely the writings of D'Annunzio, in his articles on Nietzsche in 1908 he remarked that the German thinker had influenced all modern creative writers including D'Annunzio. It was neither an original nor a profound remark, for it was common knowledge that Nietzsche had cast a spell on D'Annunzio. Despite the smallness of his body, of which he was painfully aware — "Am I a human substance or a pure will to art?" he asked himself — the poet had concealed from no one the belief that his was the role of the superman. The protagonists of his autobiographical novels were self-centered men, violent in their passions, who took the law in their hands and tasted all the joys, aesthetic to sexual, that life can offer, even the joy of killing; they were all variations of the Nietzschean superman. As for the real D'Annunzio, he had tasted almost everything, but the joy of killing he had experienced only vicariously, through his creations.

He was a great adventurer whose adventures were in the realm of the senses, a decadent voluptuary who enjoyed aesthetic and luxurious pleasures, a pagan who worshiped beauty. His villa on a hill near Florence, where he had a soundproof thinking room, was filled with red cushions and his garden with red roses. He wore lace underwear, fur-collared robes, or, if in an ascetic mood, the brown habit of a monk. He once announced to the papers that for a trip he had bought violet umbrellas and green parasols. He liked to assume childish attitudes, pretended not to know how a check is drawn, and for his savings preferred hiding places to banks.

Like Mussolini, D'Annunzio was oversensual and erotic. But while Mussolini, after the blunt hints in "My Life," kept his eroticism and love affairs to himself (many of these became known only after his death), D'Annunzio never refrained from analyzing his loves in great detail and openly. Thus *The Fire*, the novel that tells the story of his love for the actress Eleonora Duse who acted in the plays he wrote for her, gave to Rome abundant subject matter for scandal and gossip columns. Like Mussolini, D'Annunzio was a master manipulator of words; not always meaningful words. But unlike Mussolini's, D'Annunzio's words were poetic and reflected his unlimited imagination, his deep sensitivity to nature, which made him appreciate the color, touch, taste, smell, and sound of his environment, be this earth, sea, or air. His words flowed in swollen rivers, in precipitous and sparkling cascades. Carried away by the melody and impetus of his words, he went on pouring forth even when he had nothing more to say.

As a poet D'Annunzio had sung Italy's past and future glories. Like all his other passions, his patriotism was excessive. He was not only the son but also the lover of his country. He had begun writing patriotic poems when he was sixteen: "New days will come for our Italy: the standard on the Capitol will be resplendent in the sky-colored space, made beautiful by its glory. . . . And then to Rome will the battles and triumphs of antiquity return. . . . " Repeatedly he raised hymns to the sea, "glory and force of Italy," for he conceived his country as a great sea power, dominating the "free seas," her seas, proudly showing her beauty and her renewed Roman greatness to the world.

He had also been, and still was, the poet of irredentism: "Do not cry, soul of Trent. . . . Your mother will not abandon you. . . . " And: "O unvanquished Trieste, dream of our hearts, living wound rent in our flesh, you, not in vain, are waiting. . . . "

If any man could arouse patriotic feelings in the Italians and present World War I as a holy crusade, that man was D'Annunzio.

In 1915, at the age of fifty-two, he was a frail-looking man, five feet four in height, with a huge bald skull and a pointed chin ending in a tiny triangular beard, an almost ridiculous figure. But he was a great actor, an even greater actor than Mussolini. On May 5, 1915, he appeared on the cliff of Quarto, near Genoa, to unveil a monument to Garibaldi and his "thousand," who, fifty-five years before, from that same cliff, had sailed to liberate Sicily from the domination of the Bourbons. He was straight, agile, and as spry as a young man, and his eyes seemed to shine with divine inspiration. As he began to speak, his powerful personality seemed to be projected out of his body, to loom immense over the crowd and keep all spellbound. He was no longer the little man Gabriele D'Annunzio but the Archangel Gabriel descended on earth. Suddenly the sun pierced through the clouds and shone brightly and intensely in a sky that swiftly turned gloriously blue. The red cloth covering the monument dropped, and the bronze group sprang to view in the sunshine.

D'Annunzio began by extolling the creativity of the artist, a new Michelangelo, who had revived in hard bronze Garibaldi and his "thousand." His was an inflammatory speech, a call to war, filled with all the passionate elements a passionate poet can evoke. He addressed an Italy "which shall be greater by conquest, purchasing territory not in shame but by blood and glory. . . . Blessed are those who are twenty years' old," he said, "who disdained sterile loves in order to remain virgin for the love of the *patria*."

D'Annunzio's call to war resounded along the entire Italian peninsula, stirred wary patriots, aroused those slumbering, and marked the end of Italian neutrality. But some of the men who for months had done active propaganda for intervention felt that they had been cheated and outwitted, and that in a single hour the poet had stolen from them the glory of leading Italy into the war, a glory that was their due.

Mussolini must have been among those who felt unhappy at D'Annunzio's performance, for he wrote an article on the ceremony at the Quarto cliff without mentioning the speaker: "Yesterday, Genoa said its great word of faith. She said it in front of the sea, on the faithful cliff, before an innumerable crowd. . . . All Italy was there to celebrate the inaugural rite. . . . War! the people shouted yesterday with unanimous voice. War!" A few days later D'Annunzio spoke again in Rome and again aroused an enormous enthusiasm; again Mussolini wrote no comment on D'Annunzio's speech and did not mention D'Annunzio's name.

Never in later years was D'Annunzio to doubt that he, the Archangel Gabriel, had led Italy into the war, that the decision in favor of intervention was due to his words; but Mussolini, as late as 1917, was still to claim that he alone had been chiefly responsible, and to write: " . . . that work against neutrality which I undertook in the first issue of *Il Popolo d'Italia* — without stupid modesty — was the moving energy of the unforgettable revolutionary days of [May] 1915. . . . "

In Mussolini's behavior toward D'Annunzio, in the way in which he almost entirely ignored the poet at a time when all Italians and especially the interventionists were acutely aware of him, it is easy to recognize the same inferiority complex he had exhibited among men of higher intellectual refinement whose presence made him uncomfortable in Turati's *salon*. This reaction toward D'Annunzio was to persist for a long time, yet Mussolini was able to absorb much more from D'Annunzio than from any other intellectual. In fact, directly or indirectly, consciously or unconsciously, Mussolini was to imitate, sometimes copy, the poet's style, his imaginative political creations, and even his handwriting; and most of the Fascist choreography was to be D'Annunzian.

The first instance in which Mussolini imitated D'Annunzio came at a time when he was ignoring the poet's propaganda for intervention. In "Notte di Caprera," the only poem by D'Annunzio which we are certain Mussolini read, the poet addressed Italy: "O mother, and may what we will give thee win in sanctity what we [already] offered thee. Yet we offered thee what in us was divine." On May 24, 1915, when Italy declared war on Austria, Mussolini wrote: "O mother Italy, we offer thee, without fear and without regrets, our life and our death."

On the night of May twenty-third Italian troops crossed the border into Austrian territory. Thus began that tremendous static war, that war of positions in the high mountains and along the snowy crest of the Alps, where in their hastily dug trenches Italian soldiers, poorly equipped and supplied, faced an enemy entrenched in better and higher positions and equipped with more powerful artillery. Only the endurance and patience that were the millennial heritage of the Italian race could make the soldiers hold their vulnerable positions as long as they did, even after the enemy concentrated much larger forces as a result of the collapse of Russian resistance. Only Italian resilience could turn as serious a setback as the rout at Caporetto in the fall of 1917 into a full victory within a year.

Italy was totally unprepared for a long and tough war. As Mussolini was to point out in November, 1917, all during 1915 "the Italian soldier was in the war under conditions of absolute inferiority. Battalions upon battalions moved to the assault, opening the way through barbed wire with . . . hoes, rifles, and [their] hands. Regiments upon regiments clung for months to mountainsides where a boulder rolled down from their higher position was all the Austrians needed for their defense."

Mussolini did not volunteer for the army. Many years later, when dictator of Italy, in entries about himself in the *Enciclopedia Italiana* and in an Italian Who's Who, he claimed to have "enlisted," and he let his biographers repeat the statement, thus helping to create the legend of Mussolini the volunteer and war hero. The truth is that in the first months of the war *Avanti!* and other papers accused him of not wanting to join the army, of being afraid not only of Austrian lead but also of Italian (Socialist) bullets "fired from behind" in revenge for his treason. To these accusations he replied that he had tried to enlist but was rejected because his class was due to be recalled soon. These were the army's rules, he said. "In wartime," he wrote, "one does not discuss military orders and ordinances, one accepts them." But his justification sounds like the flimsy pretext of one who would rather fight a war from an office desk with pen and ink than at the front lines with gun and grenade. And it is quite in character for

Mussolini to ask for action with great insistence and determination, only to waver or even withdraw when the chance to act was at hand.

Not all men react in the same way, and many of those "young in years and young in spirit," to whom Mussolini had flung his war cry in the first issue of *Il Popolo d'Italia*, enlisted as soon as Italy entered the war, although it might have been against army rules. Among the volunteers was Leonida Bissolati, who left at once, although he was fifty-eight, and in July was seriously wounded in action. From that moment Mussolini acknowledged Bissolati's chivalry and valor, though continuing to oppose him in the political field. D'Annunzio also volunteered, and in the war he found an opportunity to be all he had ever wanted to be, the adventurer and the superman.

With unusual perception the Italian military command realized that the poet would best serve the cause of his country if allowed to follow his whims and build his own myth. And this he did, thoroughly and successfully. He was a lieutenant in the cavalry when he volunteered, and was successively a pilot, infantryman, and sailor. But he was at his best when he had wings — he the Archangel Gabriel. Aviation was in its infancy, and flying in any plane was very hazardous, but D'Annunzio had already flown with the pioneers of flight and sung the "aerial fever" of speed, the advent of aviation. He did not mind danger. He once said: "Danger is the axis of the sublime life," a paraphrase of Nietzsche's "to live dangerously" that was to become a Fascist slogan. He was past the prime of life, and for Mother Italy he would not have minded dying. The first two of his many exploits, all of which had the flavor of comedy and were looked upon as gay Sunday outings by serious strategists, were flights over the two "unredeemed" cities of Trieste and Trent, on which he dropped not bombs but messages of love and encouragement. After the flight over Trieste, the first in time, the Austrian command placed a price of 20,000 crowns upon his head. Undeterred, the soldier-poet wrapped in Italian flags the leaflets with his message to the inhabitants of Trent, the "Trentini, people of ours for love and sorrow, brothers in eternal Dante."

Mussolini ignored D'Annunzio's feats. While he had no excuse for not taking note of the first flight, he had justification in the case of the second: he was no longer in Milan and was now serving as a soldier in the trenches. At the very end of August, 1915, the army had called him to active service. He then wrote the parting sentences worthy of an impatient warrior: "The hour long yearned for has arrived. . . . It is with truly glad spirit that I put down the pen to grasp the gun." Having donned the uniform and plumed hat of the *bersaglieri*, as he had over ten years before, he left Milan on September 2; on the eighteenth he spent his first night in a trench. He was on active duty for seventeen months, until wounded, and he spent about a third of this time in the front lines. He was a conscientious soldier but never accomplished a remarkable, let alone a heroic, deed.

In the periods in the front lines he kept a war diary which appeared in installments in *Il Popolo d'Italia* and was later published in a slim volume. It is a dry and repetitious record of what was going on in the small section of the front that Mussolini could observe without straining his eyes. Although there is no doubt that he was striving for literary effect — the sky is often cloud-laden, the sun stays radiant even when covered by "a veil of fog," rivers are "sky-blue" — he never gives a full and satisfying description. The hamlets and villages he passes on the way to his post, many of which have always attracted tourists for the charm of their characteristic lanes and cottages, for their position, and the grandiose landscape surrounding them, have no shape, no substance, no individuality in Mussolini's diary. He does not notice the valley he crosses, he never takes in the sight of those mountains that he and his companions strive to conquer — steep, inaccessible mountains, so terrible to fight for and yet so beautiful when their golden pinnacles and jagged rocks turn gray in the summer dusk or, in winter, when snow and ice make them so dazzling that they seem to multiply the power of sunlight. He never tries to interpret the action of his battalion as a part of the wider action of the army (perhaps because of security regulations), never makes reference to other theaters of war. But the very repetition of incidents, each exclusively of local scope, the very lack of a wider frame of reference, leaves in the reader's mind a vivid and detailed image of the incredibly hard existence of the soldiers in mountain trenches. Trenches that offered little protection against shells and grenades, against rain, snow, and ice; trenches to be reached only under the cover of night, over steep paths often slippery or altogether impassable, exposed to enemy fire; where the soldiers sometimes remained for days without the expected distribution of food and ammunition. Trenches where life went on as it could, in slime, afflicted by lice, where disease spread fast and death was the habitual visitor . . .

Mussolini, like other soldiers, adjusted to life in the trenches. He got used to the roar of cannons, the blast of exploding shells, the whistling of the wind in mountain gorges and around mountain tops, the thunder of avalanches, and the precipitous fall of stones along steep, rocky slopes. He, like other soldiers, became accustomed to days and nights in the rain, to the "cold water" from the sky that "washed" his skin, entered his shoes, and left him "soaking wet, drenched to the bone," at a time when he may have had only "a cold sip of coffee" in his stomach. He stood watch in the snow, "drunk with white"; he piled up sandbags behind which to hide and dug and built to strengthen his shelter. He became accustomed to never having enough to do, to the boredom of that constrained existence.

More important, more dangerous for the future of Italy, the once squeamish Mussolini, like millions of other soldiers, got used to the sight of death. His diary becomes a systematic account of death. As his previous squeamishness diminished and then vanished altogether, he not only recorded the number of dead but described them with increasing realism. "The dead are covered. One sees only the rigid hands, black with trench mud . . . . The *zappatori* lay the dead on stretchers made of tree branches and sacks . . . . Now we resume chatting. We whistle. We sing. When the spectacle of death becomes habitual, it makes no impression any more . . . ." He can now indulge in gruesome details: a body becomes "a shapeless mass." He reports that "In the mule track there is a trail of blood and brain matter." "On the [hill] top there are still some ten bodies . . . . One has no head . . . ." It seems to make little difference to him whether that blood and brain matter, that headless body, belonged to a friend and companion or to an unknown soldier.

There is no doubt that Mussolini gradually came to like life in the trenches, which gave him a sense of physical well-being; that he was a conscientious soldier who on occasions went even a bit beyond the call of duty, if this gave him an opportunity to be noticed by his superiors and did not entail too much danger. There are proofs of these facts other than in his war diary. There is his promotion to corporal on February 29, 1916: "For his exemplary activity, his high spirit as a *bersagliere*, and his serenity of mind. Always first in any undertaking of work and daring. Indifferent to hardship, zealous and scrupulous in the accomplishment of duty." In between these lines the reader senses an unsuccessful effort on the part of the writer to find one single reason for Mussolini's promotion, one truly outstanding action or soldierly deed.

There is also a letter that his captain wrote years later, in 1919. The last round of abuse between Serrati and Mussolini was then being fought in *Avanti!* and *Il Popolo d'Italia*. It was the bitterest of all rounds, the one in which the two protagonists threw the greatest amount of mud and dirt at each other. When *Avanti!* repeatedly accused Mussolini of being a coward who had done all in his power to avoid the front lines during the war, Mussolini published the letter he had received from his captain: "I perfectly remember the episode at the Ursic . . . in which you [and two others] went out the morning after you had arrived in the trenches, in a voluntary patrol, to exchange a few hand grenades with the Austrians. . . . I remember that when called to the headquarters of our army to write a historical diary you refused to be a shirker working as a scribe and came back . . . to the trench. I also remember that . . . like any *bersagliere*, you accomplished at night the dangerous task of transporting food and bread . . . under the usual rain of bombs. . . ." Another officer, a lieutenant, also came to Mussolini's rescue on the occasion of Serrati's attack in *Avanti!* But except for

some vague praise this officer's letter contained only a reference to an insignificant instance: "When I came to call you
. . . I found you busy using your shoes to empty the shelter
in which you had spent the night, of the muddy water that had
penetrated into it."

If there is no doubt that Mussolini was not a bad soldier
when on active duty, there is also no doubt that he embel-
lished and distorted facts to his advantage. The vanity that he
displays in his diary is so naïve that it does not irritate.
He believed that all officers sought him out, that everybody
wanted to meet him, the great journalist Mussolini. He
missed no occasion to put himself in the most advantageous light, to relate a word of praise, a favorable comment
upon his behavior. Later, when no longer in active service,
he boasted of his seventeen months in the trenches, but he
spent two-thirds of this time either in the rear lines with his
company, or on leaves — rather more numerous than one
would expect — or in hospital, although he had no fever to
speak of and others in his condition stayed in the trenches.
He also applied and was accepted for an accelerated course
for officers. Certainly not of his own will did he go back to
the trenches after only six days at a training school; his
superiors did not want to make an officer of a man who
had been a subversive. (Pietro Nenni also was dismissed from
a similar school, for similar reasons.)

One day in February, 1917, during one of those lulls in the
fighting that seemed established by tacit agreement between
enemies, Mussolini saw the light of a cigarette in the enemy
lines and threw a hand grenade. His captain deplored the
action: "Now *they* will do the same to us." But Mussolini was
pleased with himself and noted in his diary that the cigarette
had gone out ". . . and probably also its smoker." It is said
that he was pleased when he learned that he had killed at least
two men.

Two days later Fate took her revenge. Mussolini was prac-
tice-firing a howitzer when a shell exploded inside it. Five
soldiers died. Mussolini had always believed that luck was
on his side, and so it seemed this time. He survived. He was
"struck by a hail of splinters and thrown several meters

away." He suffered a large number of wounds, and at least
forty splinters remained embedded in his body. It was his
turn to be carried on one of those stretchers that he had so often
and with so little emotion seen loaded with the wounded and
dead. He was taken to a first-aid station, then to the nearest
field hospital. High fever and infection of a large wound
in his leg hampered recovery.

Two weeks after the accident the king visited Mussolini's
hospital. A newspaperman wrote the story of this visit for a
Milan paper, and later Mussolini published it as an appendix to his war diary. The whole thing, the sentences exchanged between the king and the former antimonarchist who
in the past had piled violent abuse on the House of Savoy,
the wide publicity given the story, would be comic indeed if
anything that touches on Mussolini did not have a tragic con-
notation for the destiny of Italy.

"The sovereign," the reporter wrote, "entered the ward
where Mussolini had just been brought, returning from what
is for him the most heart-rending operation: the daily treatment
[of his wounds]. Mussolini was slightly depressed . . . .

"Having come near his bed, the king asked Benito Mussolini:

" 'How are you, Mussolini? '

" 'Not so good, your Majesty.'

"The [doctor], Captain Piccagnoni, questioned by the
sovereign, added precise details:

" 'The fever began eight days ago, when an infective com-
plication set in the leg wounds: the temperature exceeded
104°. . . .' The king was listening, looking to the wounded
man's face:

" 'You must be suffering a good deal, even if you are
strong, with the pain of being held immobile.'

" 'It is a torture, your majesty, but one must be patient.' "

They went on talking about the cause of the accident, and
then the king said that from a general he had heard words
praising Mussolini.

" 'I have always tried to do my duty with discipline, as do
all other soldiers . . . .'

" 'Very good, Mussolini,' the king interrupted, 'you must
bear immobility and pain with resignation.' "

And after this profound exchange the king moved on to other patients in the hospital.

While Mussolini was in the army, first on active service, then recovering from his wounds in a hospital, D'Annunzio, the soldier-poet, suffered a setback in his exalted role of wartime superman. In January, 1916, he was on a reconnaissance flight over Trieste and the Istrian coast when the motor of his hydroplane stalled. From a considerable height, in bad weather and fog, he brought down the plane on the sea but did not avoid hitting a sand bar. Thrown out of his seat, he struck his right temple against a machine gun. He was dizzy for only a few minutes and then dried the few drops of blood from his temple and pretended he was not seriously hurt. Next day he again flew over Trieste. A month later, when he looked at himself in a mirror, he found that his visual field was impaired; he could see only the top part of his head; concerned at last, he summoned an army doctor. His right eye was lost and his left in danger. For several weeks he was confined to his bed in a darkened room. In this period of forced inactivity he wrote a book about the event, *Notturno*, on more than ten thousand long strips of paper, one line at a time, in a handwriting that he could not control by following it with his eyes. To those who expressed their sympathy he answered serenely and with detachment. "Do not worry about my eyes, O brother," he wrote to the French novelist Auguste Maurice Barrès, "but save the beauty of the world for newer eyes."

The following September he tried again to fly, but the bandage over the lost eye bothered him. He gave up his wings for a few months and resigned himself to being an infantryman. He participated in military actions of a certain importance and with his passionate words spurred his battalions into action. But the Archangel Gabriel could not live long without wings. In 1917, against his doctor's advice, he resumed his flights.

In his next epic deed, D'Annunzio planned, organized, and led a series of three raids in a formation of more than twenty planes over the enemy port of Pola, on the southern coast of

Istria, where the Austrian fleet was at anchor. Each time he dared the enemy's powerful searchlights and guns, and his own plane was hit, though not badly damaged; each time tons of explosive were dropped and caused serious damage to port installations. It was in the third of these raids that the poet, in a sudden flash of inspiraton, for the first time launched the war cry, inspired by an old Greek cry, that was to become identified with fascism and Mussolini: *Eja, Eja Alalà.* He and the other flyers were preparing to leave. "The mechanics had already put the propellers in motion," D'Annunzio himself related. "The green red blue yellow flames, multicolor like the veil of Iris, erupted from the tail pipes . . . . My impatient companions . . . threw their 'Hurrahs' at me, flung the barbaric cry . . . . Suddenly, not from my school memories but from my deepest darkness, the other cry sprang up and went through my chest, like the flick of an arrow . . . . After I spoke to them, they all wiped the 'Hurrahs' from their mouths with the back of their hands . . . . I ordered: Silence. Not here but over there, over Roman Pola, we shall consecrate the cry of the new strength of Italy. When all bombs have been dropped on their targets, each crew member . . . will stand up and launch the cry through the barrage fires." And thus, the Fascist cry was born long before fascism.

Mussolini, well on the way to recovery from his wounds, ignored the cry that almost daily he would shout or hear shouted at him by the crowds once he realized its effect and made it his own.

His recovery had been very slow and was not yet complete. The hospital in the war zone where he had been taken after the accident was bombarded by enemy planes, and slowly, as it was feasible, all patients were evacuated. As soon as his condition permitted, Mussolini was transported to a hospital in Milan. The infection of his right leg had reached the bone, pieces of which had to be chipped off, and all treatment was extremely painful. In the middle of June, still in the hospital, he resumed writing articles for his paper. In early August he was allowed to go home, although the wound in his leg had not healed and required treatment. By October he was limping only a little, and soon afterward he appeared in excellent shape. He did not try to return to the army, although, unlike D'Annunzio's loss of an eye, none of his injuries was permanent. Again, as at the beginning of the war, his office and his newspaper seemed fully to satisfy his need for action.

The war on the Italian front was then in its third year. In the first year, between May, 1915, and May, 1916, the front had not changed appreciably. As the soldiers became better prepared and strategy more skilful under General Luigi Cadorna, the Italians consolidated their positions and undertook several offensives. They advanced at various points and obtained some advantages but, forestalled as much by Austrian resistance as by bad weather, flooded rivers, and the enormous difficulty of the terrain, they were not able to fuse their gains into a strategic victory. In May, 1916, the Austrians took the offensive and the Italians suffered a limited reverse in the course of which many irredentists were captured and executed for fighting on Italy's side. Among them was Mussolini's old friend Cesare Battisti, who henceforth became a martyr and a symbol. Italian soldiers fight well if they know why they must fight. At the beginning of the war they were confused and did not see the reasons for suffering tremendous hardship; their feelings toward the war were at most lukewarm. As soon as the enemy entered Italian territory, the soldiers rallied, struggled vigorously to contain the offensive, and only a few months later turned the rout into one of the Allies' major victories in that year, the capture of the city of Gorizia and of the supposedly impregnable Monte Sabotino which guards its approach from the north.

Early in the summer of 1917, when Mussolini resumed his journalistic activities while still in the hospital in Milan, a slow process of deterioration of civilian and military morale was beginning to spread over the entire country, which had not expected the war to last so long or to demand so great a sacrifice. Mussolini, hypersensitive to moods, noticed the onset of "defeatism" and in June warned his readers of its danger. "For the past few weeks," he wrote, "our nation has been going through a profound crisis. We no longer walk on solid ground; uncertainty troubles our souls; many think about tomorrow with an anxiety rendered more acute by love of the *patria* . . . ." Defeatism concerned him more than anything else. Like most Italians, he considered it a national problem, exclusively Italian, while in fact it was as strong in other allied countries, which were also exhausted by the long and costly war.

In Italy defeatism was in great part due to a resurgence of animosity between the former interventionists, who now called themselves nationalists or patriots, and former neutralists, now called pacifists. Among the symptoms of defeatism were the bread riots, due to the improvidence of the government, that occurred in Turin and other cities, in which some forty persons were killed and for which Lazzari and Serrati were sent to jail. More and more insistent were the loud accusations against the *imboscati*, or shirkers, who in increasing numbers, according to the patriots, were finding niches in some "essential" job and dodging active duty in the front lines. Equally disheartening was the spectacle of the *pescecani*, or sharks, the war profiteers, who were said to be amassing huge amounts of money in war contracts. And always a factor was the propaganda of the pacifists.

In the summer of 1917 Pope Benedict XV, in a note to all belligerents, called for a "white peace," a peace of compromise without territorial losses or gains, and referred to the war as "useless carnage." The papal note greatly irritated Mussolini, who called it a "safety belt thrown by Benedict XV to the Central Powers," and "the greatest act of sabotage of our war of defense and national revenge that has been perpetrated since May, 1915." With the clericals, whose thinking was influenced by ecclesiastical authority, the Socialists pursued their propaganda for peace, although it was becoming more and more evident that the moderates among them would rather help than sabotage the war and believed that the proletariat had more to gain from an Italian victory than from a defeat. Yet the Socialist Claudio Treves, Mussolini's rival in the duel of 1915, invented a slogan that was to pass from mouth to mouth and be scribbled on wall after wall, until it reached the fighting men: "Next winter no longer in the trenches." This motto, which was only the echo of the hopes of all, had such effect upon the wavering and uncertain, the tired and desperate, that it can be regarded as a most successful piece of defeatism.

In the last days of October, 1917, in this atmosphere of depression and disunity, to a nation whose resistance was undermined, the military defeat of Caporetto came as a severe blow. Italy, at first only at war with Austria, had declared war on Germany also, and Bulgaria had joined forces with the Central Powers. German, Austrian, and Bulgarian armies now broke the Italian lines and rushed down the mountains, along the roads that led to Caporetto, and eventually to the Piave River. These roads Mussolini had traveled to reach the trenches and military positions to which he had been assigned during his military service, and the lands that were now tramped by the enemy were well known to him. Like all Italians, he was stunned. The impossible was happening: the brave soldiers in whom the nation had placed its full confidence and faith were retreating in a true rout. The Italian inferiority complex made the disaster appear worse than it was, and the expectation of a large-scale enemy invasion loomed, ominous, over the population. In reality, despite heavy losses, the setback on the Italian front was not as bad as had occurred on other fronts, not as dangerous as the French reverses that had allowed the Germans within a few miles of Paris.

Mussolini at first correctly analyzed the military reasons for the defeat: the collapse of Russia had allowed the enemy to withdraw most of its forces from the eastern front and to concentrate them on the Italian. He also surmised mistakes on the part of the Italian high command which later were confirmed. (The largest contingent of troops was stretched out in the front lines, and too few were in a position for defense in depth. The reserves were too far back and did not arrive in time. The Italian armies had no experience in meeting a large-scale attack, and after the long war of position they did not know how to move swiftly and reform their lines.) As time went by, however, and especially after the war, he was to blame Caporetto and other ills upon defeatism, which had been only a contributory factor. Thus he was to reopen and keep open a most unfortunate rift between the "patriots" and the "defeatists."

For the moment the Italians achieved the near-impossible. As Sir William K. McClure, the *London Times* war correspondent for the Italian front, was to write, "The retreat, with all its confusion, its mistakes and its tragedies, remains an astonishing achievement. The resistance which followed it, when the retiring armies turned and stood at bay on the mountains and on the Piave [River], was the greatest of Italian victories." In the nation, as Mussolini himself recognized, the people rallied and stood together, afraid at first, then determined to have their revenge. "In all the manifestations of these days," Mussolini wrote, "from the mass gatherings to the fund-raising for the refugees [from invaded lands], there is such a vibrant ardor that it appears exacerbated. The cities respond. The cities stand firm. Even in the countryside the danger of the invasion shakes the masses." This tremendous effort of the entire nation bore its fruit, and a year to the day from Caporetto Mussolini could announce that the Italian armies had begun an offensive and that victory was in sight.

D'Annunzio's last exploits were the famous *Beffa di Buccari* (the practical joke at Buccari) and a flight over Vienna. Neither was of military importance, but their propaganda value was great. In the first, planned by the poet and led by Costanzo Ciano, the father of Mussolini's future son-in-law, three motorboats carrying thirty men entered the well-guarded bay of Buccari near Fiume, sent off a few torpedoes against enemy merchant ships, and dropped three bottles into the water, each containing a copy of a scoffing message signed by D'Annunzio, who declared that he, "the principal enemy," had come to make fun of the price on his head. In the flight over Vienna, achieved in full daylight, he dropped leaflets with one of his usual messages, which ended *"Viva l'Italia!"* In all, seven Italian planes reached the Austrian capital, were chased by Austrian fire, and flew off without giving battle, since this was not a military but a propaganda feat.

By the end of the war the soldier-poet had received three promotions for merit and, both from the Italians and the Allies, a vast array of decorations, including one gold and five silver medals.

Mussolini had his promotion to corporal.

The war on the Italian front ended on November 4, 1918. In the offensive begun on October 24, the Italian armies, with some help from the Allies, had been pushing back the enemy, up those valleys that it had ruthlessly and defiantly invaded the year before, and reconquering the land where the enemy had brought havoc, burned, and killed. They relentlessly pursued the retreating German and Austrian armies out of Italian territory, deep into Austria.

"The greatest joy is accorded to us: that of seeing an Empire annihilated, the violator of ours and others' freedom," Mussolini had written on November 2, and two days later, in a style that begins to be D'Annunzian, he could exclaim: "This is the great hour! . . . The hour of divine merriment, when the tumult of emotions suspends heartbeats and tightens the throat. The long passion, at last crowned by triumph, draws tears of joy even from eyes that saw much and wept much . . . ."

Italy had won the great victory of Vittorio Veneto and signed an armistice with Austria.

"Peal of bells, clangor of military bands, flying of flags, choruses of people: This is what is adequate to the indescribable events of these days," wrote Mussolini on November 5.

Peal of bells . . . . The innumerable churches of Italy, in cities and villages, on hilltops and along the seashore, in valleys and on the flanks of steep mountains, rang their bells loudly for hours at a time, calling all the people to rejoice because the war was won. And the people rejoiced. Choruses of people offered thanks to God and sang hymns to the victorious *patria*. The national flag, the *tricolore*, was displayed everywhere with pride and reverence. From mouth to mouth, from the Alps to the sea of Sicily, the words "victory" and "peace" were repeated. But many mourned because peace and victory could not bring back the 600,000 dead or restore to health the numberless wounded who had lost limbs and eyes on the battlefields.

Each city held celebrations for the victory. And in a celebration in Milan, on November 10, Mussolini had a small part. As one of several speakers, from the height of the granite base of a monument to Milanese heroes of the *Risorgimento*, flattened against an obelisk, he said a few conventional words to a large crowd, which loudly cheered him. When the last cheers died away, Mussolini climbed down from the monument and walked to a truck filled with young men in a new military uniform: black fezzes, black pullovers under the coats, black flames on the coat lapels, black stripes on the hunters' pants. Even their flags were black. They were *arditi* (literally, daring men), known also as "Black Flames," soldiers and officers picked for their courage and recklessness in action, daredevils who were trained to rush to the assault with a grenade in each hand and a knife between the teeth, known for gallantry in battle (and as a menace to the civilian population).

The *arditi* in the truck made room for Mussolini and drove away through the streets of Milan. They stopped at one of the fashionable cafés, where they ordered champagne. There Mussolini spoke to them. The military command was at that time considering the advisability of dissolving the *arditi*, which with their ruthlessness were causing serious trouble. But Mussolini made it clear that he stood by them:

"*Arditi*! Fellow Soldiers!

"I defended you when the Philistine was defaming you. I feel some of myself in you, and perhaps you recognize yourselves in me. You represent the admirable, warlike youth of Italy. The flash of your knives and the roar of your grenades will wreak justice on all the wretches who want to hinder the advance of the greater Italy! You shall defend her! We shall defend her together!

"Black flames, . . . to whom the honor?

"To you."

Perhaps it was the fumes of champagne that made Mussolini predict the future in his toast. This moment can well be considered the conception of the Fascist Blackshirts.

The next day a group of *arditi* came to his office bearing a black flag with a white skull upon it (the *arditi* used skulls and crossbones for their symbols and insignia). It was a gift for Mussolini. Were they moved by gratitude or the hope of support against those who opposed them? Mussolini hung the flag on the wall behind his desk, and a tacit pact was thus sealed between the newspaperman and the daredevils. Mussolini now had a devoted bodyguard.

Undoubtedly, this group of *arditi* had fallen under that "charm" which at about this time many who had occasion to approach him had begun to notice in Mussolini. Perhaps his physical condition had something to do with his charm: in his war diary and in letters to his sister Edvige he had repeatedly stated that the air of the high mountains and the hard life of the front lines were good for his health, and indeed he was in exceptionally good health. The persons who had known him when he was still at *Avanti!* and had not seen him until after the war were struck by the change. The thin, pale, feverish-looking young man had turned into a sturdy figure with thick neck and wide chest, with a good set of muscles that, once in power, he was always willing to exhibit with great pride. Evidence of his strength and virility is the fact that in the war period he fathered three sons: his "secret son," Benito Albino, by Ida Dalser; and Vittorio and Bruno by Rachele, in September, 1916, and April, 1918, respectively.

Benito Mussolini's vitality was in itself an element of attraction, a cause for admiration; but it was not the main factor. Most of those who came under his spell said that his charm was something that defied definition. One of his collaborators of Fascist times, Giuseppe Bottai, writing in 1949 about the period immediately after World War I, found no better words to describe it than "There was already in him, so to say, something 'Mussolinian.'" The pro-Fascist G. Pini and D. Susmel, co-authors of a four-volume biography of Mussolini, wrote: ". . . a charm the like of which nobody had; an undefinable *quid* of psychic and spiritual nature that many have striven to represent without ever perfectly succeeding." Some writers tried to be more specific, and among them was the founder of Italian futurism, F. T. Marinetti, who noted early in 1919: "Square and grinding jaws . . . . The eyes move swiftly, ultradynamic. The extremely white cornea of a wolf flashes right and left . . . ." Others described "the square head like a boulder," his "magnetic eyes," "his magnificent Napoleonic jaw" (later, as the cult for everything Roman developed, Mussolini's was to become a "Roman jaw"), "his body and soul cut in travertine marble," "the immense, impossible-to-be-contained glance," and his voice, which "vibrated with infinite echoes," that "male, metallic voice." The two Fascist biographers concluded: "Evidently there was something in him which no one else had," if such exalting descriptions could be written long before his political triumph.

Along with the awareness of his charm came the first mention of the word "good," which was later to be found in memoirs of people who saw him daily over many years. These people called him good because he would rather give a few lire to supplicants than discuss their cases with them; because he had friendly ways with a few "inferiors" and knew how to give "a very large tip and a potent handshake" to a driver; because he did not denounce or punish subordinates whom he caught in petty theft or some other trivial offense; and had occasionally found work for a needy person; because, as many fathers do, he would rather let Rachele scold their children than take the initiative himself.

Of interest in relation to this "goodness" are the sentences written by Torquato Nanni, an honest lawyer and journalist of Forlì, one of the few Socialists with whom Mussolini had maintained friendly relations since his youth. (In 1934 Mussolini was to let this old friend be sent to the *confino*, compulsory domicile, for not bending to Fascist orthodoxy; in commenting on this fact, Mussolini was to say: "[Nanni], almost a dwarf, with a most generous heart, preferred to sink rather than ask for mercy." And Mussolini preferred to let his upright friend sink than be just.) Nanni had written the first biographical sketch of Mussolini — twenty-three pages long — at the very end of 1914, when the uproar about Mussolini's conversion to interventionism was at its peak. It was published early in 1915 over Mussolini's objection: "Biographies, so long as I live, *never!*" The booklet was in circulation only a short time; in 1924, however, when Mussolini was prime minister, Nanni included the earlier material in a book on socialism in which he examined his old friend "in the light of Marxian criticism." He then wrote: "This good [man] who has an excellent heart, and sometimes an even feminine sensitivity, when in the field of combat does not know any limit to his violence, is not moved by affection, friendship, sentiment; any other touching appeal has no echoes in that heart, in which there is room only for his passion. What counts is his intention and not those of others; his will and not the wishes of others."

Detachment; a compulsion to choose always the easiest course in dealing with the importunities of beggars and petty offenders; egoism; an extremely well-developed actor's ability to enhance his usual appearance; his incredible skill in appearing wholly dedicated to a cause; an intuitive knowledge of mass psychology; these must have been the elements of Mussolini's "charm," of the magnetic attraction that he was beginning to exert over the youth of Italy.

Mussolini's former friend, Giacinto Menotti Serrati, the director of *Avanti!*, gave another explanation. In 1919, in one of his bitter polemics against Mussolini, Serrati wrote: "He is a rabbit; a phenomenal rabbit: he roars. People who see him and do not know him mistake him for a lion."

10

1919 AND AFTER

"If I were not a cynic, insensitive by now to anything that is not adventure, today the cold block that is my soul would break apart in a warm, vindictive fit of laughter!"
MUSSOLINI, January, 1919

THE year 1919 was a year of disillusion and disappointment.

Several times during the war Mussolini had predicted that Italy's return to peacetime conditions would be easy. He once wrote that the transition from war to peace would be smoother for Italy than for any other of the warring nations. A victorious army, he explained, is never a source of disorders for its country. Italy's high birth rate would rapidly make up for the loss of human lives in the war. There would be little damage, since the enemy would not advance far on Italian soil. (Mussolini wrote this before Caporetto.) The population, war veterans included, would be tired of violence, and so peace would bring a decrease in tension, certainly not civil war. The mention of civil war reflected the awareness, in all European countries, that armed nations may well turn against their governments: by the time Mussolini made this prediction the first Russian Revolution, the so-called March Revolution, had already taken place, Czar Nicholas had been dethroned, and Aleksandr Kerenski was trying vainly to restore army discipline and order in the country.

Unfortunately, Mussolini proved to be a very poor prophet, and of all the victorious countries Italy experienced the greatest difficulty in adapting to peace. In the war she had acquired the right to call herself a great power, but the price she had paid was extremely high, and in the years immediately after the war she suffered a psychosis such as only defeated countries usually suffer. Part of her ills were real and part imaginary, or at least greatly aggravated by self-pity and a misleading interpretation of the symptoms. The gravest of the real ills was the country's economic condition, for the war had been a huge financial drain. When all expenses were totaled, the cost of the war was put at 148 billion lire, or twice the entire expenditure of the nation from unity in 1861 to 1913 (a period which included a war of independence and the Libyan war). War damages alone amounted to 12 billion lire; the public debt was increasing with each passing month; the once strong commercial fleet was in large part destroyed. During the war Italy had received credit and supplies from the Allies, but the improvident and weak governments that succeeded one another did not seek provisions for continuing assistance. The first year of peace brought greater economic hardships to the population than any war year.

Under these conditions the problem was not so much how to replace the dead, as Mussolini had indicated, but how to provide for the three million returning veterans, many of them young men who had never learned any trade but war. During the war the morale of the soldiers had been kept up with promises — land for the peasants and work for everyone under fair conditions — but on their return home the veterans found the old owners on the land and no jobs open. For lack of raw materials Italy had to slacken the remarkable industrial effort she had made in wartime. Most of the veterans, and especially the young officers, did not have the preparation or the moral strength to face this abnormal return to normality. Their spiritual baggage consisted of suffering, rancor, illusions, and the habits of idleness in the trenches. They all had vague hopes and aspirations toward something new, something better and brighter than what the past had been, and at first events seemed to justify these hopes: the Austro-Hungarian Empire had gone to pieces; the Ottoman Empire was in the last phase of disintegration; Russia had replaced a tyrant with a republic of the people. The old world was collapsing, and it was reasonable to expect that in Italy as well the old social structure would give way to a new and more promising order.

A strong and enlightened government might have been able to cure the worst ills, to take advantage of the highest ambitions; instead, a succession of weak and inefficient governments allowed the situation to deteriorate into chaos. Two political groups, the heirs of the old neutralists and those of the interventionists, were the source of Italy's more imaginary ills. On one side, the Socialists reaffirmed their aim of a proletarian dictatorship, gave their adherence to revolutionary Russia, declared their open hostility toward all "responsible for the war," and encouraged strikes and violence, thus creating an enormous fear of bolshevism out of all proportion to the real danger. On the other side, excessive patriotism and nationalism gave Italy an enduring impression that she was badly cheated in the peace treaties and that sooner or later she would have to do something about it.

With the secret Treaty of London, France and Great Britain had promised Italy the ethnically Italian Trentino, the Austrian South Tyrol, and the predominantly Slavic Dalmatia; also pledged to Italy was a part of the possible territorial acquisitions from Turkey and an equitable compensation if England and France acquired German colonies. (No provision was made to give Italy the Italian city of Fiume, a free port when under the Austro-Hungarian monarchy.) But President Woodrow Wilson, who had led the United States in the war, advocated a peace settlement based on the new principle of self-determination of peoples and made it clear that he was not bound by secret treaties. In answer to his Fourteen Points, D'Annunzio, still cherished by intellectuals and war heroes, wrote an article entitled "Victory of Ours, You Shall Not be Mutilated!" and thus launched the myth of the mutilated victory, from which the Allies wanted to cut off limbs, that is, territories due to Italy. This myth became the symbol in which the lofty patriotism of the war could find a new aim and continued reason for existence.

The Italian government encouraged the outburst of patriotism as a justification of its territorial claims at the peace conference. Yet, while the Italian representatives at the peace conference were taking an uncompromising and unreasonable stand over Fiume and Dalmatia, which irritated Wilson and hardened him in his position, they lost their chance of getting any appreciable compensation in Africa and anything at all in Turkey. Eventually, Dalmatia was assigned to the newborn nation Yugoslavia.

These then were Italy's ills in the early postwar period: the broken-down economy that provided the background against which all other symptoms must be viewed; the enormous difficulty that the returning men found in adjusting to peace conditions; the lack of statesmen of sufficient stature to meet the problems of the hour; the attitude of the Socialists that protracted defeatism and created an inordinate fear of bolshevism in the middle classes and among property owners; and a much-thwarted patriotism that embittered a good section of the population and drove it to react violently against the new defeatism.

In the social and political unrest that followed closely the last celebration of victory, fascism found the most favorable conditions for its birth and growth.

The beginnings of fascism were modest. In the old part of Milan there is a little square, Piazza San Sepolcro, almost filled by a church which bulges between two Romanesque bell towers. In 1919, opposite the church, there was a low gray building in neoclassic style, the Palazzo Castani (which later was rebuilt by the Fascists), and in a "Club for Industrial and Commercial Interests" in this palace, on a Sunday morning, March 23, Mussolini founded the *Fasci di Combattimento*. (The word *fascio*, from the Latin *fascis*, a bundle, was not new in politics. Sicilian peasants in 1893 had formed revolutionary *fasci*. In 1915 Filippo Corridoni first, and then Mussolini himself, founded interventionist *fasci*, which later merged. After Caporetto there had been a parliamentary *fascio* for national defense, and Marinetti's futurist *fasci*. The word fascist was in current use and in recent years had acquired a rightist slant.)

For three weeks, through *Il Popolo d'Italia*, Mussolini had called for a "national rally of Italian interventionists," but on that Sunday morning of 1919 perhaps at most a hundred persons were present, half of them from Milan. Fifty-four delegates unanimously indorsed three declarations, presented to them by Mussolini, which for a time were to be the only Fascist program.

In the first declaration, after turning their thoughts to the dead, the disabled, and the prisoners of the war, the Fascists pledged their support to all claims of veterans' associations. In the second, they declared themselves opposed to "the imperialism of other peoples to the detriment of Italy and a possible Italian imperialism to the detriment of other peoples." They accepted the principle of a League of Nations and asked for the integration of Italy "on the Alps and on the Adriatic Sea with the reclamation and annexation of Fiume and Dalmatia." In the third declaration the Fascists proposed to "sabotage with all means the [electoral] candidacies of all neutralists." While Mussolini presented and analyzed his three declarations, groups of *arditi* in the square below were keeping watch in the fine spring rain.

Of this performance, which marks the birth of fascism, two facts are of significance: first, the meeting was chaired by a captain of *arditi*, other *arditi* were present, and groups of *arditi* provided protection against possible interference; second, the meeting took place in a club of men of property. The first fact is self-explanatory: the tacit pact between Mussolini and the ruthless *arditi* still held, and Mussolini had come to rely on their armed support. In its very inception fascism was a movement of militaristic tendency and organization.

The second fact needs some explanation: Mussolini had traveled far from his Socialist days. For some time after his expulsion from the party he had called himself a Socialist, a revolutionist who in the war had seen a means of a social change that would take the place of revolution. He had called his paper a Socialist daily, although it is almost certain that he received financial help from Italian landowners (in addition to the less-certain "French gold"). In August, 1918, however, in order not to be confused with "other Socialists," Mussolini replaced the subtitle "Socialist Daily" with "The Daily of Fighters and Producers" (some time before he had dropped the mottoes of Blanqui and Napoleon). His paper, he explained, would remain his own personal mouthpiece but would increasingly express and support the interests of fighters and producers. By "fighters" Mussolini meant to indicate all soldiers, from Generalissimo Diaz to the youngest infantryman. Producers were not solely laborers, because "there is work which does not cause sweat . . . or the famous calluses on the hands."

Thus he had seemingly repudiated his previous stand against capital; he began courting groups especially strong because of either arms or money; and he abolished all boundaries to his sphere of action. His move was shrewder than he could have guessed at the time. In the summer of 1918 he could not have foreseen the enormous difficulties that the veterans were to encounter in their return to peacetime life, the too-rapid demobilization, the lack of provisions for their absorption into the machinery of the national economy, their feeling of being let down, and their consequent search for new ideals. He could not have foreseen that he would exploit the veterans' unrest, become their leader, and provide armed defense for "non-sweating producers."

The fact that fascism was born in the "Club for Industrial and Commercial Interests" proves that as early as 1919 capitalists were welcoming Mussolini and the prospect of his armed protection. In its active form, the Fascist defense of capital was to come only in the following years. At the time he founded the Fascist movement Mussolini was still groping for a line of conduct, and he left all doors open. As a result of the war, which had extolled individual feats of valor, he experienced a return to Stirnerism ("Why cannot Stirner become fashionable again?" he asked) and encouraged an individualism that bordered on anarchy. At the same time he tried to regain the contact with the masses that his defection from orthodox socialism had interrupted. In his paper he approved the first of the postwar strikes and the first occupation of a factory. To the workers of this factory who, faced with a refusal of their requests, closed themselves in their plant, excluded management, and went on with their work, Mussolini praised "this creative strike that does not disrupt production." He did not limit his praise to articles in his paper but went to the factory itself and delivered an exalted speech. He placed himself, as an individual, in competition with the entire Socialist movement.

Of this lack of a sure line of conduct he must have been acutely aware, if, in commenting on the birth of fascism, he could say: "We allow ourselves the luxury of being aristocratic and democratic, reactionary and revolutionary, legalistic and illegalistic, according to the circumstances of place, time, and environment in which we are compelled to live and act."

Despite the vagueness in political orientation of early fascism, one trait was prominent: an exacerbated nationalism that called for full recognition of the "values of victory." In this respect, Mussolini's nationalistic evolution after the war may be regarded as typical of the group that adhered to the foundation of the *fasci*.

At the end of the war Mussolini was an enthusiastic admirer of President Woodrow Wilson, whom he was soon to look upon as the bitterest foe of Italy. Early in 1918, Mussolini applauded when Wilson, the first great propagandist of American ideals abroad, announced his Fourteen Points, which expressed his ideals of a just peace based on national self-determination. The principle of self-determination was new, and though by now it has become an intrinsic part of Western culture, in 1918 its meaning was not entirely clear. From a practical point of view, as Wilson himself was soon to discover, it was not fully applicable along the old national boundaries of European countries, where populations had mixed and ethnical groups were inextricable. Some degree of misunderstanding between Wilson, the idealistic reformer, an almost naïve Anglo-Saxon crusader, and the passionate Italian people was perhaps unavoidable. Mussolini himself remarked that the Italian *forma mentis* was not bent toward the "social mysticism" of the Anglo-Saxons. "Certain movements in the Anglo-Saxon world are hardly understandable to us, descendants of Latin Rome that was intensely practical and political even in religious matters."

For Mussolini, and among those interventionists who felt as he did, the misunderstanding was much greater than it was for other Italians. Mussolini interpreted self-determination as the right of Italy to her territorial claims. "These rights," he was to write in early 1919, "are so glaring in the reality of history and life, that the President will have no choice but to consecrate them with his solemn word. *They are rights of a people who has been prodigal in shedding its best blood.*"

Understanding, at any rate, is not essential in igniting the spirit with a new credo: acutely in need of something new to believe in, many Italians turned to Wilson, the American messiah, for the new faith he had to offer. The other messiah of those days was Lenin, but in Italy he was not yet popular, and only one group of Italian Socialists placed its hopes in him. Mussolini, usually wavering and uncertain, always changing opinions, for once did not hesitate long when faced with a choice between Lenin and Wilson. The Russian experiment had fascinated him at its very beginning. Kerenski had briefly been his hero, the "man who was Russia" as Napoleon had been France. But Kerenski had disappointed him, for he had not rallied the army against the Central Powers and was therefore responsible for the Italian defeat at Caporetto. Lenin had been instrumental in arranging a separate peace between Russia and Germany, and he could arouse no sympathy in Mussolini's heart. Wilson had not only led his country into the war on the side of the Allies and given the war its previously lacking ideological purpose, declaring it a war to end all wars, but in May, 1918, he had signed a law that gave him extraordinary powers. "From now on," Mussolini had commented, "he will be above all a *dictator*." If the ultrademocratic United States could have a dictator, then "dictatorship is not necessarily 'reactionary' . . . "

It is of interest that Mussolini had begun to think and talk much about dictatorship at about this time. It does not matter that he announced himself "decidedly against any form of dictatorship" or that he advocated such a system as "a necessary, exceptional regime for the exceptional period of war." The important point is that dictatorship came to occupy a prominent position in his thoughts and that in his mind it was associated with a democratic republic and its president.

In the last days of the war and the first months after its end Mussolini rarely wrote an article for his paper without mentioning Wilson, and almost always he praised him. "All Europe is at the feet of this man, who came from the other side of the ocean and is neither emperor, captain, nor prophet, but is all this, in a harmonious synthesis that transports the populations. . . . He is the greatest of emperors. . . . Wilson's empire has no boundaries because He does not rule over territories 'but interprets the needs, hopes, and faith of the soul. . . . "

The article containing these exalted words appeared in *Il Popolo d'Italia* on January 5, 1919; and in the evening of that day Mussolini had an occasion to meet the President of the United States. Wilson, on a good-will visit to Italy, stopped for a few hours in Milan, where he was the guest of honor at a gala dinner in the foyer of La Scala, Milan's opera house.

Since its opening in 1778, La Scala had been not only one of the greatest centers of lyric art in Europe but also a scene of importance in the expression of European social and political life. In that theater the emperors of Austria had given formal balls for their Milanese subjects; Italians had celebrated the end of the Austrian domination and, a few years later, the crowning of Napoleon III; during the *Risorgimento* the richly decorated boxes had provided safe meeting places for conspiring patriots; at all times, special performances of music into which the audience read political innuendo gave occasion for outbursts of cheering or hissing. It was appropriate that Milan should honor Wilson at La Scala.

Wilson's popularity in Italy was at its peak — only a few days later it was to begin to wane, and soon Mussolini was to pour abuse upon him. For the moment Italy was in a frenzy over Wilson, and in his paper Mussolini joined the

chorus who shouted *"Viva* Wilson," and indeed were shouting *"Viva* Wilson" in the square before La Scala while the
guests were eating dinner. At the gala affair he had no chance
to talk to Wilson: he was still a rather obscure newspaperman
and had not yet learned English. He sat at a distance from the
guest of honor, among other newspapermen, ill at ease in a
rented full-dress suit. The evening brought no enlightenment
to him. G. A. Borgese, then a correspondent for the *Corriere della Sera* of Milan, related in his book *Goliath* that
he was sitting next to Mussolini; while Borgese and another
newspaperman were discussing the League of Nations proposed by Wilson, Mussolini added only grunts of disapproval
and shrugged his shoulders. Six days later he wrote in his
paper: "Why the League of Nations? To avoid wars, it is
said. . . . Is it really necessary, in order to avoid wars, that
the 1,500,000,000 inhabitants of our planet, none excluded,
be part of this league from the very first moment? Would not
an alliance . . . between the United States, England, France,
Italy, and Japan be, as a first step, a formidable guarantee of
peace?" And he was still convinced that Italy had a right to
the territories promised in the Treaty of London, as well as to
Fiume, whose National Council had requested annexation
to Italy the previous October. He felt very strongly that Italy's
aspirations should be given priority over those of the newborn Yugoslavia, whose very existence was due to the Italian
victory, to the fact that *Italy* had defeated Austria and set
free the national groups that Austria had held under her rule.

The lack of comprehension shown Wilson's proposals by the
numerous Italians who shared Mussolini's patriotic views
was soon to become one of the major causes of political unrest in Italy, one of those conditions that were to prove
favorable to the rise of fascism.

Mussolini's patriotic intransigence burst out in the same theater, La Scala, six days after the gala dinner in honor of Wilson.
The occasion was a speech that Leonida Bissolati proposed to
give to explain his views. During the war Bissolati, twice

wounded, had twice returned to the front lines, despite his age and against medical advice. He left the front only when called to participate in the government and organize Italian resistance. He had recently resigned his post in government because of differences with the foreign minister, Sidney Sonnino, who wanted to advance extensive territorial claims at the peace conference. Bissolati, instead, had taken a stand for which Mussolini had labeled him "a fanatic *rinunciatario*" (renouncer), a word newly coined that in Mussolini's mouth acquired implications of baseness and treachery. In an interview with a correspondent for the *London Morning Post*, Bissolati had expressed the opinion that Italy should renounce the South Tyrol, which the Italians called *Alto Adige*, and Dalmatia in exchange for Italian Fiume.

In his stand Bissolati was more Wilsonian than Wilson himself. Wilson had realized the need for compromise between the principle of self-determination and other impelling political interests in Europe. Thus France was to annex Alsace-Lorraine, although the annexation would go against the will of over a million Germans residing in those regions; and Czechoslovakia was demanding boundaries that would include large German groups. In the case of Italy, the Alps provided such a clear-cut natural boundary, such a unique line of defense, that Wilson was willing to sacrifice self-determination in the German-speaking Alto Adige and let it become part of Italy, as indeed long before him Dante and Mazzini had urged.

Thus Alto Adige was not an issue for long, but Fiume and Dalmatia remained a reason for disagreement throughout the peace conference and were the cause of lasting Italian unrest. Fiume was a seaport with a predominantly Italian population, but the surrounding territory was Slavic. At the time the Treaty of London was signed, it was decided that if Italy was to have Trieste, on the west coast of Istria, the Austro-Hungarian monarchy should keep Fiume on the east coast. After the collapse of Austria, the Croats and Slovenes asked that Fiume be included in their new country, Yugoslavia, and it was to this that the Italians objected.

Dalmatia was a greater issue. It had been part of the

Roman Empire and, in more recent times, of the republic of Venice; its culture was Italian, and the patriots were horrified at the prospect that its numerous Roman monuments, its jewels of Venetian architecture, and the thousands of Italians who lived in Dalmatian towns should fall into the hands of the Yugoslavs. Since Roman times the Adriatic Sea had been *Mare Nostrum,* our sea, and according to many Italians — but by no means all — Italy needed both shores of the Adriatic for her defense. In fact, some responsible military men maintained that Dalmatia would be useful only for purposes of offense, but that for the defense of Italy it would prove a burden rather than an asset.

In proposing that the Italians renounce both Alto Adige and Dalmatia, Bissolati aroused the anger of the "patriots." For this reason, on the day Bissolati was to speak Mussolini went to La Scala determined to make trouble. He sat in a box and swept the theater with his darkly glowing glance. In another box he saw a brother in nationalistic faith, Filippo Marinetti, founder of futurism and lover of anything new: cubist painting, futurist poetry, the "renovating" war, new lands for Italy — and new recipes for Italian cuisine. Mussolini's glance moved from Marinetti to the audience below and the many men in uniform scattered here and there. He was pleased. He knew that he could count on them, since the great majority of those who had gone through the war felt that abstract idealism was not a sufficient reward for three and a half years of suffering and sacrifice. These and many other Italian patriots wanted Alto Adige and Dalmatia because they had been promised to Italy in the Treaty of London — and wanted Fiume as well on the basis of self-determination.

When Bissolati appeared on the stage of La Scala, tall and thin, looking pale and tired, a loud tumult of voices broke out. Some in the audience cheered, most booed him, and first among these was Mussolini, who was pleased that with his help and that of Marinetti and many officers in the audience the tumult lasted almost an hour. When it seemed to subside, Bissolati began to read his speech, raising his voice above the constant murmur in the theater. He managed to read about half of his address, then a great noise broke out again, as if at the expected signal of an invisible maestro: "Croa-tian, Croa-tian," the audience shouted in cadence.

Bissolati tried to proceed, but then, according to Borgese, who tells this episode in *Goliath*, "Bissolati recognized Mussolini in the chorus. That unmistakable voice, dishearteningly wooden, peremptorily insistent, like the clacking of castanets. He turned his head to the friends who were nearest to him and said in a low voice: '*Quell 'uomo no*' ('I will not fight that man'). From that moment on he read his pages only as a formality, to himself. No applause was audible at the end. The crowd, part triumphant, part impotently disgusted, cleared the theater." Commenting on these events, Borgese remarks: "It seemed as if a deadly blow had been struck at freedom of speech and thought. . . . "

Almost as if they wished to confirm Borgese's opinion, the two Fascist biographers, Pini and Susmel, relate that while Mussolini was engaged in booing and hissing, one of Mussolini's staff writers enthusiastically applauded Bissolati, and they conclude: "Of course he had to leave the paper."

Bissolati's hardly delivered speech was his political testament. He was to die a little more than a year later, and then Mussolini was to write a eulogy of his dead enemy. Meanwhile, Mussolini and Marinetti could be proud of themselves: with their action at La Scala they fostered that one-sided, blind resistance to any compromise which was to be the undoing of the Italian cause at the peace conference and leave the nation with the bitter taste of disillusionment.

It was this sort of nationalism that bound together the group convened in Piazza San Sepolcro for the founding of the *Fasci di Combattimento* and the few other persons who, though not present, notified Mussolini of their adherence. These Fascists "of the first hour" — *sansepolcristi*, as they were later called — were otherwise an heterogeneous bunch. Among them were Marinetti and other futurists, several *arditi* and officers of the regular army, anarchosyndicalists, Republicans, former Socialists, and ultraconservatives. Although several cities and towns had sent their representatives to the rally, for many months fascism was to remain almost exclusively a Milanese movement. The few *fasci* that soon were established outside Milan, mostly in northern Italy, at first added little to the movement.

It is indicative of the general postwar disorientation that in the spring of 1919 Pietro Nenni, who continued to cling to his Republican ideals, became one of the founders of a *fascio* in Bologna and brought to it his usual enthusiasm, only to break away from his briefly Fascist past the next year and become the Socialist that he is today.

For a while fascism remained identified with Mussolini and was as uncertain of its trends and aims, as inconsistent, as proud of its lack of programs and of its opportunism as was its founder himself. In June, in preparation for the elections, although the date had not been set, the Fascists published their program. It was a leftist, rather revolutionary program that included universal suffrage, with specific provisions for the vote for women (who, however, were excluded from the polls throughout the Fascist period); support of workers' demands and a share in the management of industry; disability and old-age insurance; the institution of a national militia; a progressive tax on capital, "a real partial expropriation of all wealth"; an 85 per cent tax on war profits; and the confiscation of all ecclesiastical property. It also contained a declaration to the effect that "revaluation of the war" was the chief objective. It has been said that this program was more leftist than Mussolini would have wished. But it may not be so, for, throughout 1919, Mussolini, while undoubtedly receiving help for his paper from capitalists, was still striving with all his power to lure the masses away from the Socialist Party and, through promises or threats, into his own sphere.

Fascism owed its very existence to Mussolini's hatred and spite against the party which in 1914 had ousted him. He could nurse his rancors a long time, and his rancor against *Avanti!* and its director Serrati and other members of the Socialist Party had not subsided. It had increased with the end of the war and the return of soldiers to civilian life, which gave new importance to the masses. Mussolini attempted to win their love, and at the same time fought the Socialist Party.

It is not without significance that he launched his first appeal for the national rally to found fascism only two weeks after he had seen the first Red demonstration of the postwar period. A parade of workers, whose number he gave as "twenty to thirty thousand" from Milan and adjoining towns, flooded the streets, carrying red flags and antiwar posters, shouting "Long live Lenin!" and reviling the middle classes and the military. This demonstration made such a deep impression on him that he was to recall and describe it in an "autobiography" (written by his brother Arnaldo) published in 1928.

Even more significantly, three weeks after its foundation, on April 15, fascism moved to its first attack. While Mussolini sat in his den with a large pistol and a glass of milk on his desk, Marinetti with other futurists and *arditi* staged a "spontaneous, patriotic demonstration." That day there was a Red rally at the Arena in Milan. When Marinetti, who had climbed on a stone lion on a nearby monument, heard the first notes of "*Bandiera rossa*" ("Red Flag"), the hymn of the workers, he gave the signal for battle. After some pistol shots and the disbanding of the Reds, the Fascists moved on to assault the offices of *Avanti!* Because a soldier was killed, the Fascists entered the offices, wrecked the press shop, machinery, and furniture, and set the place on fire.

The absence of Mussolini from the streets, after the legend he had created of his heroic self and his repeated assertions of the need for action, puzzled many people and started wild rumors. Some thought that he had been killed; others said that he had been wounded or arrested; and there were those who insisted that, disguised as an *ardito*, he had led the assault on *Avanti!* But Mussolini, the armchair general, had barricaded himself in his office. Barbed wire entanglements in the courtyard protected the entrance to his den; daggers, pistols, and grenades were ready on a table; on the roof several youths kept watch; and other men were at pistol practice in the cellar. He gave orders and was kept informed over the telephone, and now and then he stirred his milk with a

spoon — the never-missing glass of milk, symbol of tem-
perance and thrift, one of the props for Mussolini's stage.

That day the "forces of bolshevism" ignored him, and his
fortress remained unchallenged. The men who had won the
day for him arrived from their battles, gathered in the courtyard below his office, and called to him to come out. From the
balcony he said only a few words, to the effect that the
Leninist hordes, descendants of wartime defeatists, who still
believed they could sabotage and "mutilate" victory, had
met with men determined to do anything rather than let the
fruits of victory go to waste. He hailed a new Italy, as strong
in peacetime as in war, and was answered by repeated cries
of *"Viva* Italy!" and loud applause. A delegation brought to
his office a new sort of sacred relic, a piece of charred wood
from the burning offices of *Avanti!*

This was the first victory of fascism over "bolshevism," the
first "punitive expedition" against the Socialists. The fact that
the police did not intervene and that no newspaper took a
strong lead in condemning the act of vandalism against
Avanti! encouraged the Fascists and drove them to more and
more wanton punitive expeditions. Although the number of
men involved was to remain small, the episodes of violence
and destruction were to multiply, to become more acute and
spread from Milan to all of Italy. The majority of the population was to become so weary of these disorders, this rioting
and bloodshed, this state of civil war, that it began to hope for
a strong government, for a strong leader, for anything that
might put a stop to the chaos that was Italy.

In June and July the unrest due to the *carovita* (high cost of
living) reached a peak. Although the government was spending 200 million lire a month to keep down the price of bread,
other prices were soaring with the inflation and only salaries
lagged behind. The exasperated masses, under strain since the
beginning of the war, unwilling to put up with near-famine
conditions, took matters in their hands, invaded and pillaged
shops and storehouses, demanded lower prices, damaged

property and let food go to waste in their illusory hope of improving matters. Their action spread rapidly and became national. Here and there groups of workers formed so-called Soviets, committees to requisition food and keep prices down; here and there these committees enforced a 50 per cent reduction in all prices.

The crisis was acute. Had the Socialist Party been strong, it could have organized that dictatorship of the proletariat that it was advocating. But the Socialists were divided, as they had been so many times in the past, and ineffectual. They took the attitude that the revolution was nearing and would come by itself as the logical conclusion of the current conditions. Costantino Lazzari asked the Socialists to be vigilant, since events would precipitate their "fated" conclusion. The independent Socialist group headed by Bissolati hoped that the ruling classes might peacefully surrender their power to the working classes, and Turati's reformists were altogether against a seizure of power on the part of the proletarians.

The masses were left without directives, growing mobs felt that revolution meant a pillaging on a larger and larger scale, and the resulting acts of vandalism instilled an ominous fear of bolshevism in the middle classes. It was increased the more in some parts of Italy as the peasants, who during the war had heard the slogan "the land to the peasants," invaded large holdings as squatters, to the applause of many members of the army.

Yet, precisely because it was left without directives, the near-revolution subsided before either the Socialist Party or Mussolini realized that this was the very hour of "bolshevism" in Italy. All that Mussolini did in this time of crisis was to write two articles mirroring the prevailing confusion of ideas. In a single breath he said that the government cannot multiply goods that do not exist and that greatly increased production was the only way out (but he did not explain where raw materials for this production were to come from); that "the less the government interferes in national economical matters, the better" and that the government had not used sufficiently strong preventive and repressive measures to meet the crisis.

One possible and plausible explanation comes to mind for Mussolini's hurried and superficial treatment of events so grave: he was among the few who did not suffer economic hardship. Unlike most veterans, he had faced no unemployment upon return from the front lines; on the contrary, his return had coincided with his rise from dubious social status to that of a well-to-do bourgeois with a moderate financial security, which very few then enjoyed in Italy. The postwar period coincides with a phase in his evolution which may be called "the period of spats." He was striving at this time for a certain refinement which was not natural to him, encouraged by his friend Margherita Sarfatti: his black suits, the rented evening clothes, the bowler hats, and the celebrated spats are signs of his newly sought elegance (in this attire, black suit, bowler hat, and gray spats, he took flying lessons in 1920).

He had not given up all pretensions to poverty, or at least to thrift, of which the glass of milk on his desk was the symbol. He did not live in luxury and could ask with clean-enough conscience: "Who should fill [the empty coffers of Italy]? Perhaps ourselves? We who own no houses [he rented a comfortable, middle-class apartment], no cars [he rode *carrozzelle*], no banks, no mines, lands, factories, bank certificates?"

The first elections after the war took place on November 16, 1919. After a vain attempt to form a bloc of leftist groups, Mussolini was one of twenty candidates on an exclusively Fascist ticket, including Filippo Marinetti and Maestro Arturo Toscanini, later an anti-Fascist and an exile in the United States. Mussolini's fiasco was worse than the most pessimistic predictions: The Fascist ticket received 4,657 votes out of the 270,000 in Milan. The Socialists, on the other hand, in their biggest national victory, won 156 of the 535 seats in Parliament. Despite the errors and the weakness of its leaders, socialism, with its promises and its propaganda against those who had led Italy into a costly and useless war, had still a tremendous appeal for the masses. The other victor in the November election were the *popolari*, the Catholic party, founded a year earlier when the pope had withdrawn the *non expedit*, which had hampered Catholic voting.

Next day *Avanti!* published a mocking announcement:

"This morning a dead body in a state of decomposition was fished out of the *Naviglio* [the large canal of Milan]. It would seem to be the body of Benito Mussolini." A procession of Socialist workers with torches carried a coffin past Mussolini's home to celebrate his political death.

Mussolini's frustration found expression in an act of violence: that same evening, while a large group of Socialists were celebrating their electoral victory in front of *Avanti!* a hand grenade exploded in the air and wounded many. The grenade was of the type that the *arditi* carried, and there was no doubt that the Fascists were responsible. A delegation of Socialist leaders, including Turati, Treves, and Serrati, formally requested the dissolution of the *fasci* and *arditi* and the arrest of Mussolini. The second part of the demand was easier to satisfy than the first, and Mussolini was sent to jail. His arrest immediately after his political defeat aroused criticism, especially among fellow journalists, and Senator Luigi Albertini, director of the liberal *Corriere della Sera*, personally intervened on the ground that Mussolini was a political wreck and it would be foolish to make a martyr of him. He was released twenty-four hours after his arrest, but his case was not dismissed. With others, he was accused of organizing armed bands "in order to commit crimes against persons" and of ordering the throwing of the grenade. The investigation dragged on; by the time his case was ready for trial, Mussolini was a deputy in Parliament. The case against him was dropped.

His electoral defeat and arrest marked a low point in his career and his faith in himself. In November, 1914, when he was ousted from the Socialist Party, he had been able to look ahead toward new aims, a new orientation, and his own newspaper. Five years later there was little he could place on the scales to balance his failure: his collaborators began leaving him, the circulation of his paper dropped, and the paper was running in the red.

His friend and confidante, Margherita Sarfatti, noticed that the offices of *Il Popolo d'Italia*, deserted by all, were so empty that they seemed too large. In her biography of Mussolini, she wrote that in this period he was given to "occasional expressions of profound bitterness," especially when his

closest associates left him, and to "crises of dissatisfaction"
with his paper; that now and then he declared he wanted to
sell the paper, which was not run the way he wanted — and,
anyhow, he had been a journalist too long; that he would say
he had many other abilities: he was a very good bricklayer,
he was learning to fly a plane, he could always wander about
the world with his violin; that he wanted to write plays and
be an actor in them.

He talked much of changing occupation, but did nothing
about it. He remained in his den, barricaded against possible
reprisals, and went on writing fiery articles against this and
that. Luck was usually on his side, and at first slowly, then
rapidly, the wheel of fortune turned in his favor. Almost independently of his will and his action, throughout the second
half of 1920 and all of 1921, numerous *fasci* were founded
and Fascist gangs sprang up, often in retaliation against local
groups of Reds.

One of the main causes of the rapid spread of fascism was
the exaggerated fear of bolshevism that gripped the bourgeoisie. In fact, the danger of bolshevism did not last long in Italy.
Mussolini himself had realized this as early as August, 1920,
writing "the acute period of the Bolshevist infection is over"
and "Italian bolshevism is lying on the ground, breathing its
last breath, under a mortal blow." Soon, however, he recognized
that he could use this fear of bolshevism as a weapon in his
favor, and he did all he could to keep it alive, never neglecting
a chance to exaggerate Bolshevist activities and to incite reprisals against them, thus making the danger appear much
greater than it actually was.

As for himself, sometimes he was alarmed even by fascism,
this creature of his which did not submit easily to the will of
others. Now and then Mussolini considered the possibility of
disengaging himself from fascism and repudiating it completely; instead, he channeled its forces and used them to his
own ends. Meanwhile, he received a valuable lesson from
Gabriele D'Annunzio, the superman of World War I. He was
to draw much profit from this lesson, learning how an individualist and an adventurer could use national forces and the
national scene to stage a dramatic personal adventure and
fulfil his ambitious needs.

11

THE EXAMPLE

"We, who detest from the depths of our soul
all Christianity, from Jesus' to Marx's, look
with extraordinary sympathy upon this 'resurgence' of modern life in the pagan cult of
force and daring."

MUSSOLINI, December, 1919

BENITO Mussolini and Gabriele D'Annunzio met for the
first time in June, 1919, in Rome, and before this meeting
they had been corresponding for several months. Toward the
end of 1918 the poet had sent a letter to the director of *Il
Popolo d'Italia*, to which Mussolini had answered: "Our ideas
coincide on these fundamental points: 1. The Italian victory
must not be mutilated, not even under the pretext of democracy
or of a Wilsonianism interpreted the Croatian way. 2. It is
necessary to undertake a profound renovation of our national
life from and on the terrain of our victory. 3. We must block
the way to the saboteurs of the war. . . . Is this all right?"
The poet, the prodigious producer of ideas, had no use for
generalizations of this sort and dropped his correspondence
with Mussolini at its very start. Yet the exchange of letters
gave Mussolini a pretext to ask D'Annunzio to write "a word"
for *Il Popolo*. The poet granted the "word" in a telegram in
which he asked Mussolini to reserve three columns for an
article to be published at once.

The article was in the form of a "Letter to the Dalmatians"
and was published in January, 1919, on the first page of *Il
Popolo*, over six columns, under the heading: "Italians, Listen
to the Message of the Intrepid One." Full of patriotic pathos
evocative of Italian sacrifice in the war, enlivened with images
of Italian masterpieces in Dalmatia, the "Letter to the Dal-

matians" did its share to build up Italian inflexibility in her
territorial claims for the eastern shore of the Adriatic.

Il Popolo d'Italia went on publishing all that D'Annunzio
had to say, and the poet, no longer a soldier, no longer busy
planning and performing heroic deeds, was doing a great deal
of talking. He talked in Rome, from the balcony of his hotel,
or in a Roman concert hall, mentioning Dalmatian towns that
in his opinion were Italian and ought to be returned to Mother
Italy, and requesting the annexation of Fiume. Fiume was
then occupied by Italian and French forces on behalf of the
allied command, and many patriots could not understand
the government's delay in declaring the annexation which the
Fiumani themselves had asked. With his inflammatory
speeches, D'Annunzio added fuel to the fire.

On May 24, in celebration of Italy's entry in the war, the
poet had been scheduled to speak in Rome but for fear of
disturbances the government vetoed it. *Il Popolo d'Italia* sent
the poet a telegram of solidarity, to which D'Annunzio replied: "I am ready. We are ready. The great battle starts.
. . . " He did not specify what battle was starting, but announced all the same that there would be a victory.

Soon the rumor spread in Rome of a conspiracy in which
Mussolini and D'Annunzio, together with a general and a Nationalist leader, would take part and which would be directed
at overthrowing the parliamentary system and replacing it
with a military government. The general in question denied
these rumors, and nothing happened.

Neither Mussolini nor D'Annunzio had sought a meeting.
The machinations of a newspaperman, who told Mussolini
that D'Annunzio wished to see him and D'Annunzio that Mussolini had asked to meet him, are held responsible for the
interview between the highly sophisticated poet and the clumsily bourgeois journalist. It took place at the Grand Hotel,
near the old stone fountain of Piazza San Bernardo and the
sun-baked ruins of Diocletian's baths, and it lasted a full hour.
Although neither man revealed the subject of their conversation, subsequent events gave a clue to it. They must have
discussed certain plans that would be put into action in the
following months. Shortly after this encounter Mussolini went
back to Milan.

On September 12, 1919, Mussolini received from D'Annunzio a message which bore the date of the previous day: "My dear companion: the die is cast. I am leaving now. I am getting up from bed, with a fever. But delay is not possible. Once more the spirit will predominate over the flesh. Summarize the article that *Gazzetta del Popolo* will publish and report the last part in full. And support our cause vigorously during the conflict."

Thus the poet announced to the journalist that he was marching on Fiume to occupy that city. He had seized a propitious occasion: following riots, the allied command had decided that the Italian garrison in Fiume should be replaced with other contingents. One of the top officers of the garrison, a Major Reina, made his troops swear they would come back to take the city and asked D'Annunzio to lead the expedition. The poet was typical of those officers who had grown accustomed to the war with its excitements and rewards, its exaltation of the personal feat, its freedom from daily cares and uncertainties. When peace "broke out," as suddenly and unexpectedly as had the war itself, these men experienced a letdown. They unconsciously looked for ways to continue the wartime existence which had lasted so long that it seemed there had been no previous life. D'Annunzio in particular had found in the war self-glorification, fulfilment of his dreams as superman, and an escape from creditors and financial harassment. To him peacetime meant a return to debts and old mistresses, and the sad admission that he was getting on in years. To be free from worries and stay young he had to remain a warrior, and so he accepted Major Reina's request that he lead the expedition to Fiume.

A few army and navy units deserted to follow him, bringing trucks, tanks, and supplies, in what was the first mutiny in the history of the Italian army. (It is said that soon afterward the king had to write personal letters to high officers to prevent them from deserting.) Demobilized *arditi*, who did not know what to do with themselves, and other adventurers increased the ranks, and when D'Annunzio, self-appointed hero, marched into the city he had about a thousand men behind him (and more were later to join him). He occupied Fiume in the name of an Italy which had given him no mandate for such a move.

By the time Mussolini received D'Annunzio's message, the poet, who had assumed the title of *comandante*, was already the ruler of Fiume. It is unfortunate that there was no camera to snap a picture of Mussolini as he read D'Annunzio's message, that no one was there to describe that moment. The expression on his face must have been revealing. Did the message take him by surprise? Or was he expecting D'Annunzio's move? Was he pleased or perturbed? D'Annunzio was now fulfilling promises that Mussolini himself had made to the people of Fiume. In that city, shortly after the end of the war, he had given a talk: "People of Fiume! I tell you that Fiume will be Italian at any cost! . . . You may count on me, always. I shall keep agitating in your behalf until . . . the question of Fiume is resolved. . . . On the other shore [of the Adriatic Sea] there are thousands and thousands of your brothers determined to dare all for you . . . " He had then been the first politician to go to Fiume after the war with encouragement and reassurance. The response was a roar of applause. Now he, the man of action, was in Milan, while D'Annunzio was in Fiume in defiance of the government and the Allies.

From his armchair in the den Mussolini poured out praise for D'Annunzio and his feat.

Then he received another letter from the *comandante*: "My dear Mussolini: I am surprised at you and the Italian people. I risked everything, gave everything, got everything. I am master of Fiume, its territory. . . . And you are trembling with fear! . . . Any other country would have . . . overthrown [the government]. And you go on babbling, while we fight. . . . You do not even help us with a fund drive and a collection. . . . Wake up! And be ashamed of yourselves. . . . Isn't there anything we can hope for? And your promises? Shake yourselves up, lazy ones, from your eternal siesta. . . . "

To this scorching reprimand Mussolini replied with an inconclusive letter: "I want to prove to you that I have worked strenuously. That I am resolved to everything. But we must understand each other. We must define the political objectives at home. I remind you of our conversation at the Grand Hotel in Rome. . . . Tomorrow I shall launch an appeal for a national fund drive for Fiume. . . . We must also watch bolshevism. There are 450,000 strikers. . . ."

The tenor of D'Annunzio's letter indicates that at the time of their encounter in Rome Mussolini had made certain promises which he was not keeping. Mussolini, however, could not afford to be on bad terms with the man whom all patriots applauded, whom even the baffled Allies did not condemn or try to chase from Fiume, the man he himself was taking as a symbol in his campaign for the November elections. "Whoever votes for the Fascist bloc votes for D'Annunzio, Fiume, and the greatness of Italy," the posters read. To placate the poet, Mussolini made an appeal for funds for Fiume; he sent messengers of good will, and on the first day of good flying weather he flew to Fiume. It was October 7, and the *comandante* had been in power for less than a month.

Mussolini's visit to Fiume lasted less than twenty-four hours, just long enough to give him a first impression of the city under D'Annunzio's rule. To this visual image he was to add details that others related to him but he did not see, for this was his only trip to Fiume in the fifteen months it was held by D'Annunzio. Though the final picture that formed in his mind was in part vicarious, it was to remain vivid and challenging and be an example to emulate, an example that heightened his indubitable sense of inferiority to D'Annunzio, sharpened his rivalry, and showed him what a man imbued with Nietzschean philosophy and endowed with a will to power can achieve, even with small means.

In Fiume Mussolini saw a picturesque scene staged by a great actor for his own performance. It was the product of a poetic inspiration and a sense of aesthetics that Mussolini lacked altogether; of a dramatic skill of which Mussolini had a full measure; and of an immensely more fertile imagination than his. On this scene Mussolini saw a choreography designed for large masses; he observed the minutest elements and stored them in his exceptional memory. The lesson he learned had many aspects.

The *comandante* had seized Fiume by what is more realistically described as a gay parade than a military expedition. Yet, on the military side, the march on Fiume had shown that some units were willing to desert the regular army and navy to follow an adventurer with personal appeal, and that in an undertaking of this sort the regular forces could be counted upon not to put up a stiff resistance but rather to sympathize and help, at least passively. In Fiume the *comandante* was an absolute ruler, though he had had no training for this role and governed not according to traditional patterns but following his own whims. He lived his adventure day by day, in a sort of frenzy, on a full diet of acclaim, of professions of affection from his subjects and from the illegal army he had gathered around him. He had organized his army on the pattern of the ancient Roman legions, with Roman titles and insignia, following that excessive cult of Rome to which he had given expression in his early poetry and oratory. Whether his legionnaires were deserters, former *arditi*, adventurers, or men running away from the Italian police, they were ruthless and restless, seeking novelty and action, and loyal to D'Annunzio and the "liberation" of Fiume — their motto was "Either Fiume or Death."

Fiume, a not especially attractive or distinctive seaport at the foot of low hills, had turned into a vibrating city, alive with nine thousand legionnaires who sang and shouted, a city adorned with waving banners and flags that added touches of bright red and green to the old gray buildings. On the largest balcony in the city, on the building decorated with the greatest number of flags, the government palace, the *comandante* came out day after day and spoke to a crowd in which black shirts, black insignia, and black flags prevailed. His grandiloquent speeches, inspired by Greek and Latin oratory, often ended in a dialogue with the crowd in the square below, a back and forth swinging of enthusiasm and passion between speaker and audience (which later came to be regarded as typical of Mussolini and the Fascist crowds). "To whom Fiume?" the poet asked. "To us!" the crowd answered in one roar. "Do any of you doubt my faith?" "No, never!" "Am I still worthy of leading you?" "Yes! Yes! Yes!" And the final chorus: "For Fiume, for Italy, for D'Annunzio: *Eja, Eja, Alalà.*"

On his visit to Fiume, or from other visitors there, Mussolini learned of certain innovations that were later identified with fascism: the introduction of the death penalty, which did not exist in Italy except under martial law; a new form of punishment, the forced administration of castor oil to purge adversaries of their wrong ideas; the invalidation of the results of a plebiscite if they went against the ruler's wish; the proclamation of a charter with a provision by which in time of emergency the city council could appoint a *comandante* with full dictatorial power — D'Annunzio considered the current time one of emergency.

D'Annunzio called his government in Fiume the Regency of the Carnaro, after the gulf on which the city lies, and its charter, *Carta del Carnaro.* This was a piece of delightful and imaginative literature that Mussolini could not fail to appreciate — for its stress which is on production, if not for its aesthetic value. Mingling elements of Latin culture, Italian nationalism, medieval communal institutions, and vaguely Marxian theories, the *Carta del Carnaro* gave to Fiume "a genuine government of the people — *res populi* — founded on productive labor and . . . ordered according to the widest and most varied forms of autonomy, as it was interpreted and applied in the four glorious centuries of our communal period. . . . Only assiduous producers of the commonwealth and assiduous creators of the common power are the real citizens of the Regency." These producing citizens were to belong to one of ten corporations; the first nine were for citizens furnishing all kinds of work, manual and intellectual, and the tenth was reserved for "the mysterious forces of the toiling and ascending people . . . consecrated to the unknown genius, to the apparition of the very new man. . . . " Each corporation was autonomous, levied its own taxes, provided for mutual assistance, invented "its insignia, emblems, music, its songs and prayers . . . its ceremonies and rites. . . . "

Thus in Fiume was sown a seed of the Fascist corporative state.

While in Fiume, Mussolini talked with D'Annunzio for an hour and a half, but what they said to each other is not known with certainty. According to rumors and to allusions in their correspondence, the "Intrepid One," drunk with success, was impatient to make some other move, any move, even to attempt to lead an insurrection in Italy, with the promised support of the Fascists. Mussolini, it is said, dampened the poet's enthusiasm, temporized, expressed hopes for the coming elections, and advised waiting for the results of the elections before taking further action. It also is said that on this visit Mussolini brought to D'Annunzio the first receipts of the fund drive for Fiume.

The fund drive launched through *Il Popolo d'Italia* was exceptionally successful, and within a few weeks three million lire were collected, but though Mussolini may have taken some of this money to Fiume, not much more reached the city. A good part of the fund went into his electoral campaign, with either the poet's consent — and this may have been a subject of conversation in Fiume — or at least his failure to protest effectively. On October 30 Mussolini wrote D'Annunzio: "We are organizing bands of twenty men each with some sort of uniform and weapons, both in order to insure our freedom of speech and for the other events for which we are awaiting your orders"; and ten days later he wrote again: "Following the authorization that you gave to Michele Bianchi [Mussolini's collaborator both at the paper and in the organization of the *fasci*], I am meeting the expenses of this exceptional period with the funds of the drive. . . . "

Thus the money that patriotic Italians thought they were giving to feed and clothe the legionnaires holding Fiume was instead being used to organize and arm the first Fascist squads. The specious motive was that these squads would stand ready to help the *comandante* in Fiume when the moment came, but events were to show that Mussolini had never meant it to be so. The defection of Mussolini's closest associates after his electoral fiasco, which Margherita Sarfatti so sympathetically describes, was not due so much to his lack of political success as to his unscrupulous use of the funds meant for Fiume. Whether D'Annunzio really intended to use the Fascist squads for a vast action in Italy, or whether he could not be bothered with administrative details, in the misuse of the funds he shared the guilt with Mussolini. The importance of the squads was to appear evident when they multiplied, terrorized the country, and brought it to the verge of civil war.

Meanwhile, Mussolini was going through that period of discouragement which his failure in the elections had brought about. His correspondence with D'Annunzio reflected his low spirits and made it clear that to him the poet's friendship was at that time even more important than before; and that he felt keenly the increased distance between the poet's position and his own. Jealousy, or envy, placed a dash of servility in his letters to D'Annunzio: "Count on me again, now and always. I consider myself the most devoted and disciplined of your legionnaires. And I set no limits to my discipline," he wrote immediately after his electoral defeat. In his subsequent letters he reasserted his absolute and "unchanged devotion" and made a few timid suggestions, stating that the last word was to the poet.

The months went by. D'Annunzio held Fiume, receiving unofficial support and supplies from the government and the army, organizing his own pirates, who went as far as to capture a ship with a valuable cargo which had stopped at Sicily on its way to South America. Mussolini worked at his paper and slowly recovered his usual confidence in himself.

In September, 1920, D'Annunzio began thinking again about a large-scale operation in Italy, aiming at a coup d'état. Through messengers, letters, and memorandums, there was again an exchange of views between poet and journalist. But Mussolini was not at all enthusiastic. Among the possible reasons for his pulling back, two were insistently repeated.

According to one, Mussolini did not relish the idea of a movement in which he was to play second — if not third — fiddle,
especially when he was already entertaining ambitious
schemes of his own. According to the second, D'Annunzio was
showing himself to be too much the leftist, both in the way he
talked and in some of the provisions of the *Carta del Carnaro*,
which he had promulgated early in September. For his coup
d'état D'Annunzio counted on the Fascist squads, which were
growing stronger and multiplying, but he also wanted to make
an appeal to the workers of Italy, it was rumored, and this
would have alienated the industrialists and landowners who
in the last few months had begun to give financial support to
the Fascist gangs.

In order to gain time, Mussolini sent memorandums to
D'Annunzio, in which for the first time in writing he mentioned a March on Rome. (This march was to be the third
phase of a program whose first two phases were the occupation
of the territories that Italy had claimed but had not obtained
and a pause in the action in order to see how Rome, Belgrade,
and London would react.) It is of interest to note that for
D'Annunzio's coup d'état Mussolini advised the deposition of
the monarchy and the installation of a republic, for at this
time he was strongly republican. He indicated the spring of
1921 as the best time for the coup d'état.

Before the spring of 1921, however, D'Annunzio's fortunes
were to change. In November, 1920, Italy and Yugoslavia
signed the Treaty of Rapallo, which settled their territorial
differences and made Fiume an independent state. (Italy had
already gotten Trentino and Alto Adige; now Dalmatia was
assigned to Yugoslavia, with the city of Zara going to Italy.)
The poet ignored the Treaty of Rapallo. To the order that he
surrender Fiume, he answered: "I disobey"; and when the government resorted to a blockade of the city with troops and
battleships, he declared war on Italy. The "war" started on
Christmas Day, the "Christmas of Blood," as D'Annunzio was
to call it. A few men were killed and several were wounded. A
shell from a battleship slightly wounded the *comandante*. Determined to let his blood run to its last drop for the cause of

Fiume and Italy, he repeated the call of dying gladiators, *Morituri te salutant.* But two days later, convinced that Italy had not proved worthy of his dying for her, he quietly left the city.

Mussolini, unexpectedly reasonable, did not object to the Treaty of Rapallo, although it gave Italy about as little as the *rinunciatari* had asked. Commenting on the Treaty of Rapallo, Mussolini wrote: "We frankly declare that we are pleased with what has happened [in regard] to the eastern boundary line, and we believe that this satisfaction will be shared unanimously by Italian public opinion. For Fiume, also, the solution of Rapallo is not the ideal one, which would be annexation, but it is the best of those proposed so far." And in another article: "Italy needs peace . . . to start on the road of her unfailing greatness. *Only a maniac or a criminal would think of unleashing new wars not imposed by sudden aggression.* For this reason we consider that the agreements for the eastern boundary and for Fiume are good." Later he vacillated, stressing the good provisions of the treaty and condemning its deficiencies, especially those that concerned Dalmatia. Criticized by many of his own followers who had expected a more aggressive stand from him, he ended by saying that he approved of the treaty only because, like all other treaties, it was not eternal, and sooner or later it would be revised.

When the Italian government undertook the siege of Fiume, from his desk in the den Mussolini wrote articles to deplore this act of civil war, which he called a crime and an infamy; but as soon as D'Annunzio left Fiume and the city accepted the conditions imposed by the Treaty of Rapallo, he became sensible again, regained his "optimism," and took a philosophical view of events: "We must find comfort," he wrote, "in the thought that the tragedy has not turned into a catastrophe, with the planned destruction of the city and port, with additional slaughter of men, and the death of D'Annunzio." As always, whatever emotions he had experienced for the fate of Fiume and its defender, they had spent themselves through his words, and the end of the Fiume episode found him ready to forget his past feelings and turn his mind to new problems.

But D'Annunzio and his legionnaires had expected material help from the Fascists, who were to order their squads to initiate a vast upheaval in Italy. Mussolini's past "moral support," through articles in a paper of limited circulation, did not satisfy them. They accused him of treason, of having abandoned the cause of Fiume in the decisive hour. D'Annunzio warned his legionnaires against leaving him and joining the Fascist movement, in which there was no "sincere political faith inspired by a clear philosophy."

Mussolini's desertion of the cause of Fiume appeared so inexplicable to so many people that soon an explanation was advanced: Mussolini, it was said, had made a deal with Prime Minister Giolitti, who had promised immunity for him and his Fascist squads, provided he kept his hands off Fiume and the enactment of the Treaty of Rapallo. The rumor did not appear without foundation. The squads were keeping busy. In September, 1920, the workers' agitation had reached its climax with an extensive and widespread occupation of factories, where the workers had established administrative councils. At about the same time peasants, organized in "Red leagues" and co-operatives, had occupied stretches of land and pressed their demands upon landowners. Although Giolitti had worked out a compromise which returned the factories to their owners, the compromise had left both workers and owners dissatisfied. The Socialist leaders, still encouraging local outbursts of passion, designed to keep the idea of the revolution alive, were unable to channel sporadic and individual actions into an organized movement with well-defined aims. Under these conditions, the middle classes, which had at first been willing to make concessions toward the most urgent social reforms, were vexed by the repeated provocations and frightened by the specter of bolshevism.

Industrialists and landowners joined in a counteroffensive by supporting the Fascist squads, which from their very beginning had relentlessly fought the Socialists. The Fascist squads had so far been limited in number and importance, but in the fall of 1920 they began to spread from Milan to other parts of Italy, especially in the Po Valley and in Tuscany. There they seemed to set themselves to the systematic destruction of all that represented socialism. By November, 1920, the clashes between Fascists and Reds were so alarming that the moderate paper *La Stampa* of Turin commented: "The facts show, with dreadful eloquence, that the contrast between Fascists and Communists is becoming more and more savagely acute and by now has taken the form of real warfare. Educated at the same school, moved by the same adoration of the principle of violence, Fascists and Communists no longer have power to keep themselves in check, and in the mad transport of their passion, excited by blood, hatred, and the spirit of revenge, they throw themselves at each other with guns, pistols, grenades, and daggers."

The greater share of the "guns, pistols, grenades, and daggers" were on the Fascist side, and the Reds were more often unarmed. The Fascists did not even have to buy all the arms they needed; sometimes they obtained them with the sympathetic connivance of the army. The army was in favor of fascism and very much against socialism, which in its campaign against those responsible for the war often attacked veterans and military men. In isolated episodes in the streets of several cities, the Reds had insulted, reviled, and beaten officers, even spat upon them, and fellow officers keenly resented this offense. The Fascists, who presented themselves as avengers, often obtained ammunition and weapons directly from army depots.

Not only the army but also the police connived at Fascist terrorism and very seldom intervened to prevent aggression against the Reds. These are the incidents from which may have sprung the rumor that Mussolini had made a deal with Giolitti. The rumor is hard to prove or disprove, but if in late 1920 Mussolini had not made a deal, he did so in the spring of 1921: in April Giolitti dissolved Parliament, called elections for the following May, and invited the Fascists to enter his own national bloc. He hoped he could thus counterbalance the strength of the Socialists and *popolari* in Parliament, and he believed that by giving the Fascists recognition and official status he could absorb them and make them turn from lawlessness to a well-considered respectability.

Mussolini accepted Giolitti's invitation but gave no signs

of checking his combativeness. "Into Parliament will go a platoon of Fascists loaded with aggressiveness," he said in one of his electoral speeches. "They will go there to work for the people and the nation beyond any [personal] ambition."

As was to be expected, now that he had joined Giolitti's bloc, Mussolini was successful: he and thirty-four other Fascist candidates were elected to Parliament.

The following November, at Mussolini's own suggestion, the Fascist Party was founded, despite the fact that for a long time he had boasted that fascism was not a party but a movement, not bound by programs and formulas, a true "anti-party."

On the eve of the foundation of the Fascist Party, Mussolini was still asking himself what its aims could be, and answered: "It could have one function, though a transitory one: to channel and hold together a bundle of young energies, which otherwise would become disoriented and disperse, around a notable single energy who might use them . . . for his own ends, which, it is fair to hope, will continue to be conceived in harmony with the true interests of Italy." According to a report prepared on the occasion of the foundation of the party, there were at that time some 2,200 *fasci* with 320,000 members.

The civil war did not abate, despite attempts at "pacification" and the signing of "pacification treaties" by both Socialists and Fascists. Tired of violence and disorders which continually upset the rhythm of life, the nation began talking of a return to normality that could be brought about only by a strong government. Astute Fascist propaganda presented fascism as the only force that could suppress and keep in check the wave of subversive agitation and thus dispel forever the danger and the fear of bolshevism. As the head of the Fascist movement, Mussolini appeared to be the man who could embody the strong government.

In the growth of fascism and in the civil war, Mussolini was little more than a spectator, always hailing the same group, like a fan encouraging his favorite team at a baseball game. Fascist squads sprouted wherever there was a Socialist group to give battle to and a former army officer, still imbued with the spirit of adventure that the war had created, to lead them. Former officers of this type took the initiative and gathered around themselves boys too young to have been in the war and sorry to have missed it, veterans unable to disarm in spirit, men who could find no employment and welcomed whatever food and pay was given a *squadrista*, and the usual malcontents who always like to move in troubled waters. Mussolini had been and remained the symbol that held together the loosely organized proselytes. In *Il Popolo d'Italia* he spoke for them and extolled their magnificent deeds, violently decrying the outrageous treachery of their enemies, interpreting their lofty patriotic sentiments and their immense cult of "a great Italy," to which they had resolved to dedicate their lives. His speeches to local groups, his occasional attempts to avoid excessive violence or to encourage an act of revenge against the Bolshevists, the personal words of praise that now and then he dropped, as from a great height, on some of the most active gang leaders or local Fascist authorities, were sufficient to maintain admiration and their loyalty to him. Whether the bonds that tied his adepts to him were made of faith, misunderstanding, or unconcern, all Fascists regarded him as their duce.

12

THE MARCH ON ROME

"Fascism is a movement of reality, truth, life,
adhering to life. It is pragmatist. It has no *a
priori* isms. No remote ends. It does not
promise the usual heavens of idealism. It
does not presume to live forever or for long.
MUSSOLINI, July, 1919

On October 3, 1922, a high official at the Ministry of
Interior remarked: "If after this challenge the government
remains at the window as it has done so far, it will cover itself
with ridicule." That day *Il Popolo d'Italia* had published the
military regulations for the Fascist militia, which created a
Fascist army outside the regular Italian army, an act clearly
illegal and unconstitutional. The government did stay at the
window, assuming an attitude of "wait and see."

The prime minister was Luigi Facta. In February of that
year he had succeeded Ivanoe Bonomi, the former reformist
ousted from the Socialist Party by Mussolini in 1912. Bonomi
had succeeded Giolitti, who had resigned the previous summer
after the Parliament whose elections he had called proved
unwilling to support him; his own national bloc had split
into unco-operative groups. His fatal mistake had been to
seek an alliance with the Fascists.

Luigi Facta was an honest but weak man, good-natured,
devoted to his king and his country, hopeful in the most hopeless situations, always trusting that in the end everything
would turn out for the best. He was the man least suited to
meet an emergency. Faced with this new act of shameless arrogance, he did nothing at all, and the birth of the Fascist

militia was not challenged. His sole justification was that in the militia's oath of allegiance there was nothing to which a constitutional government could object: "I swear in the name of God and Italy, in the name of all those who fell for the greatness of Italy, to consecrate myself wholly to the service of Italy."

Three weeks later, on October 24, a gigantic rally took place in Naples. It was, as it was meant to be, a display of Fascist force, the first after the organization of the militia. On that occasion the Honorable Benito Mussolini, deputy in Parliament, restated the demands he had made on previous occasions. He said that fascism wanted "to become the State." The Fascist Party was ready to enter the government; but the government had not granted the prompt elections that he had urgently and repeatedly requested. It seemed uncertain that a legal solution would be possible: "The problem, not understood in its historical terms . . . becomes a problem of force."

In the past few months fascism had grown more arrogant and belligerent, better organized for its campaigns of terrorism, while the position of the government, under the weak premiership of Luigi Facta, was growing more and more precarious, and the nation was coming closer to a state of chaos. The drama reached its climax when, at the end of a governmental crisis that had proved the utter inability of the leading statesmen to cope with the situation, a group of Socialists called a general strike. In the mind of its organizers the purpose of the strike was to defend political and syndicalist liberties against "reactionary factions," thus helping the government re-establish law and order. It was a naïve move, inspired by the old myth of the general strike in which Socialists still had faith despite its invariable failure; it was also a move which exasperated the population and played into the hands of the Fascists. The strike took place during the first days of August, and it involved some public services. The Fascists presented the government with an ultimatum in which they stated that

unless the strike was halted within forty-eight hours they
would break it up; and at the same time they took over some
of the services on strike and ran them at a reduced pace. In
some cities the Fascists — and sympathizing students — distributed mail, operated streetcars and trains, and earned for
themselves the gratitude of the local population.

This was the turning point in Mussolini's career. His great
sensitivity to public opinion told him that his time had come
and he should no longer put a check on his ambition. He declared that fascism was "inevitably" on the point of becoming the state; in its ranks would be found "the necessary
forces to administer the nation." From that moment he kept
ready for the most opportune occasion and wrote and spoke
as one on the eve of seizing power. Yet he was always more
aggressive when addressing a crowd than when he spoke to a
small group, and in spite of his drastic, revolutionary
speeches he did not cease to explore more constitutional ways
of reaching power. He tried to find a "legal solution," a coalition government with other parties.

Mussolini had been in contact with all the exponents of
Italian politics, the men who had been prime ministers in the
past and seemed acceptable for this role in the future: the
present premier, Luigi Facta; the eighty-year-old statesman
Giovanni Giolitti, to whom the country always gave its confidence in hours of crisis; Antonio Salandra, who as head of
government had led Italy into World War I; and Francesco
Saverio Nitti, who had been prime minister at the time of the
occupation of Fiume and at whom Mussolini and D'Annunzio
had hurled the most vitriolic abuse. To these men Mussolini
had laid down his conditions for collaboration. He did not
insist on the post of premier for himself but asked several
ministries for the Fascists. Nothing had come of these consultations, and for this reason he spoke in Naples of "a
problem of force."

After the general strike and the Fascist reaction, he continued to keep in touch with D'Annunzio. Their relationship
involved a mutual profession of friendship—and a constant
watch on each other's movements. The poet, who had retired
to a villa on Lake Garda, remained in the background, but

now and then his youthful spirits burst forth in one of his colorful, grandiloquent speeches, in dazzling if vague promises of great feats, that made his popularity flare anew. Popularity revived the rumors, which never died out entirely, of *his* intended march on Rome. But then an accident stopped them for a while.

On August 13, D'Annunzio, novel Humpty Dumpty, had a great fall from a window of his villa and cracked his skull on the gravel in the garden below. He recovered, miraculously, but remained weak and frail. No investigations were made or questions asked on the causes of the accident. The poet called it "my mysterious fall" and once said that "Italy" had given him a push; but he did not specify whether the push had been figurative or literal. In later years someone remarked that Fascist toughs had often prowled in D'Annunzio's garden. By October D'Annunzio had resumed sending messages and promising great feats when the proper time came.

Apart from his old jealousy of the poet, Mussolini had other reasons for avoiding joint action with D'Annunzio. The poet was in favor of deposing the king and raising to the throne the king's more attractive cousin, the Duke d'Aosta, who had won praise in World War I for leading an "invincible" army. According to Margherita Sarfatti, who was very close to Mussolini after the war, the future duce did not want a king with a strong will and public favor. Besides, as a result of his upbringing and past political associations, Mussolini was at heart a republican and would gladly have done away with both Savoy and Aosta. Ever since the founding of the *fasci* in Piazza San Sepolcro, Mussolini had repeatedly asserted that fascism was of republican leanings; however, monarchic sentiment in the Fascist ranks was very strong, so strong that dissension and squabbles over "republican tendencies" caused a serious crisis which had threatened to split the Fascist forces.

Mussolini, who had deftly wiggled out of the impasse, more recently had come to realize that Italian life was "depending heavily on the Savoy monarchy," as he said in his speech at Naples. Accordingly, he reassured the monarchy of his good intentions, making it clear that he wanted no change in the direction of a republic, and hinting he was not in favor of the Aosta branch of the royal family. At the same time, as if he wanted to specify that he expected something in return for his monarchic stand, he warned that from the monarchy he expected no opposition. And he repeated this in his speech at Naples.

He gave his speech in the morning; in the afternoon he inspected the six thousand Fascists who had gathered in Naples and stood in perfect military formation. To them he swore: "I tell you with the solemnity that the moment calls for: either the government will be given to us or we shall take it, descending upon Rome. It is now a question of days, perhaps of hours." The Fascists answered in a roar: "To Rome! To Rome!"

Late that same evening Mussolini sat in a secret meeting with top Fascist officers. Great decisions were made. The date of the March on Rome was set for October 28, only four days ahead. For several weeks Mussolini had been talking of a March on Rome, but only eight days before, on October 16, had he formally proposed it. Two Fascist leaders, experienced in military techniques, said that it would take six months' preparation. Mussolini wanted it in a matter of days, for in his opinion the element of surprise was paramount. He may also have felt that to start a March on Rome would give him a great advantage in bargaining, even though the March might not be sufficiently well-organized for a successful conclusion. Under the threat of columns closing in on the capital, the government might make important concessions. Supported by other impatient members of the party, his rashness and ambition prevailed over the voice of caution and technical competence. That day a quadrumvirate was designated to take over all power once the preparations for the March were made.

In Naples the moment had come. It was decided that a secret mobilization of the militia would begin as soon as the Fascists gathered in Naples returned to their homes; total mobilization would be proclaimed on the night of the

PROCLAMATION

OF THE FASCIST QUADRUMVIRATE

27 October 1922

Fascists! Italians!

The hour of the decisive battle has come. Four years ago at this time the national army unleashed the supreme offensive that led to victory: today, the army of Blackshirts seizes again the mutilated victory and, pointing desperately toward Rome, restores it to the glory of the Capitol. From today princes and *triari* are mobilized. The martial law of Fascism goes into full effect. On direct order of the duce, military, political, and administrative powers of the Executive of the Party are assumed by a secret Quadrumvirate with dictatorial mandate.

The Army, supreme reserve and safeguard of the nation, must not participate in this struggle. Fascism states again its highest admiration for the Army of Vittorio Veneto. Neither does Fascism march against the police but against a political class of half-wits and idiots that in four long years has not been able to give a true government to our nation. Be it known to the classes forming the producing *bourgeoisie* that Fascism wants only to impose discipline on the nation and help all forces which may increase its economic expansion and well-being. The people who work, those in the fields and factories, those in transportation, all the employed, have nothing to fear from Fascist might. Their rights will be loyally protected. We shall be generous toward unarmed adversaries. Inexorable with others.

Fascism bares its sword in order to cut the too-numerous Gordian knots that enmesh and sadden Italian life. We call upon the Supreme Lord and the spirit of our five hundred thousand Dead to witness that only one impulse drives us, only one will bring us together, only one passion enflames us: to contribute to the safety and greatness of our Homeland.

twenty-seventh (Mussolini had already written the text of the proclamation). Once these decisions were made, Mussolini conferred supreme powers upon the quadrumvirate; he then disappeared from the scene until the morning of October 30.

A few words on the members of the quadrumvirate may give some indication of the forces behind fascism. Of the four men, Michele Bianchi, secretary-general of the Fascist Party, was the closest to Mussolini in his political views and career and had been his associate for the longest time. Bianchi, born in Calabria in 1883, only a week before Mussolini's birth, was a newspaperman who had been in turn a syndicalist, an interventionist, and an army volunteer. As one of Mussolini's collaborators on *Il Popolo d'Italia* he had been a Fascist "from the first hour," for he had been present at the first meeting in Piazza San Sepolcro. Stubborn and indefatigable, he was willing to stay behind the scenes provided he could exert his driving force upon men and events, and this he did with a perseverance that bordered on fanaticism. He had been one of the men who on October 16 supported Mussolini's decision to undertake the March on Rome, against the advice of military experts. Mussolini was to say later that Bianchi had been the political brain of the quadrumvirate.

General Emilio de Bono, oldest of the four members, was fifty-eight in 1922. He was a bald, frail-looking little man with a full white beard, and he had risen to leadership in the African campaigns. In World War I he had held positions of high command. His participation in the command of the Fascist militia before he retired from the regular army was a breach of discipline for which he was called to answer —but no action was taken against him; and this is one of many signs of the army's sympathy for fascism. To fascism De Bono contributed his experience in organization and army tactics and his personal contacts with army men. He would have liked to have had six months to prepare for the March on Rome.

Captain Cesare Maria de Vecchi, a year younger than Mussolini and Bianchi, was a landowner from Piedmont, a monarchist, and a lawyer in good standing with the royal court. In his youth he had done some painting and had written poems; in the war he had distinguished himself, earning six decorations and several promotions. After the war he organized the Fascist movement in Piedmont. De Vecchi represented a conservative, almost feudal, element in fascism, and his faith in and devotion to the House of Savoy had done much to overcome the initial republican tendencies of the party.

The last of the four men was twenty-six years old and a typical specimen of the veterans of the younger generation, physically and spiritually molded by experiences in the war. His name was to become the best known of the four: Italo Balbo. He was brilliant and attractive, with long and usually unkempt hair. Later, Balbo was to write a book, *Diario 1922*, a good source of information about the events of that year and his own attitude toward them. He was eighteen when he went to war and learned to command and to obey, with a strong preference for command. The years immediately after the war had destroyed his leftist ideals. Socialists had insulted him in the streets, as they had often insulted army officers whom they considered responsible for Italy's part in the war, and in his disillusion he had then turned to fascism. Mussolini promised that fascism would bring about a complete renovation of values; meanwhile, it created the mirage of a new Italy in which the young people who had fought in the war would be at the helm of government.

Balbo became a self-appointed general in his native Ferrara, and from that city he led a march on Ravenna and one on Bologna — 63,000 men participated in the second, according to his figures. The spirit of adventure dominated him. The sight of blood, of buildings set on fire by his Fascist squads, the perpetration of violence, elated him as no drug could have done. His feats were the test of his efficiency and a rehearsal for later exploits.

Mussolini had come to rely on Balbo for information and advice in questions of strategy. He called Balbo "a magnificent *condottiere*" and on him shed occasional words of praise, sometimes accompanied by a kiss or a hug, which filled Balbo with immense pride; and this pride generated admiration for the giver. Yet young Balbo perceived some of the older man's limitations. It was Balbo who suggested the men for the quadrumvirate, and in later years, it is reported, he was to boast to friends that he had engineered the quadrumvirate, excluding Mussolini from it.

It is true, as Balbo knew, that Mussolini was too irresolute and too inexperienced to be the commander of military forces, but in order to function properly the quadrumvirate, like fascism itself, had great need of Mussolini. Like fascism, the quadrumvirate was made up of heterogeneous elements that would have come apart without some cohesive force to hold them together. That force was Mussolini; not Mussolini the man, but Mussolini the myth, in which his followers wanted to believe: in short, Mussolini the superman.

He had acted his part so long for the benefit of the crowd that his impersonation had become second nature to him. Often in the history of mankind the masses have felt the need to create a hero and attribute to him superhuman qualities. In Mussolini's case, the creation of the hero had been a joint achievement of the hero himself and of the Fascist masses in search of someone who would fulfil their mystic need to lavish loyalty and devotion on a leader. The reason Mussolini's words had a magic effect on the crowds was that both he and the crowds expected them to have just such a magic effect. It was as if the crowds impressed their will on Mussolini, took hold of him, molded his thoughts and words, and drove him on with their fanatic devotion. To him, making large masses respond had become a necessity; and he did so with the tone of his voice, with his gestures, with the expression of his eyes. It is bewildering to read the words that aroused such boundless enthusiasm and to find that without Mussolini's presence, deprived of his voice, they are banal and hollow.

Without an audience, Mussolini was a shell, as hollow as his words seem without his voice. Without Bianchi's and Balbo's continuous rewinding of his enthusiasm, he became again the lonely man, irresolute, giving in to the last opinion he had heard, shrinking from action when the moment for action arrived. A chief who needed periodic rewinding would have been a hindrance during the March on Rome, and it may have been at the suggestion of the quadrumvirate that Mussolini quietly left Naples for Milan on October 25. On the other hand, he may have welcomed the idea of spending the turbulent days ahead in a city close to the Swiss border and to sanctuary in the case of a Fascist failure.

Mussolini arrived in Milan on the morning of October 26 and at once resumed negotiations for a coalition government. His speech at Naples had caused considerable alarm in official quarters, but the government was still at the window, uncertain whether to resign. Mussolini's behavior in the days following his speech show that he had by no means closed his mind on the decision to march on Rome. He was still pondering whether to postpone it or to call it off altogether; and in either event he kept ready a car in which to flee to Switzerland.

He could not but feel the uncertainty of the situation. What would happen if the Fascists were to push the expedition to its ultimate conclusion and try to seize the capital? The difficulties of transporting a large number of men within marching distance of Rome were enormous. A considerable number would necessarily be engaged in occupying and holding key cities, seizing weapon and ammunition depots, and in disarming *carabinieri*. Not all the Fascists would be available to march on Rome. If the government were to decide to defend the city, if the army were to obey orders and turn on the Fascist columns, fascism might lose the battle for Rome. But these were big "ifs." The government was weak, the army had always been friendly toward the Fascists and had tolerated their excesses. On the other hand, the end of the Fiume episode, with its Christmas of Blood, had taught Mussolini that the sense of discipline could be strong in the army.

The very fact that on October 26 Mussolini resumed negotiations for a peaceful solution proves his state of mind. He pushed negotiations at an accelerated pace until the afternoon of October 29. In those four days wires and letters were exchanged and long-distance calls were made, intercepted, and recorded. Much of this documentary evidence was published after the fall of Mussolini and helps to reconstruct the story of the March on Rome.

By October 26, not even in Fascist circles was the date of the March clearly known. A few excerpts from telephone conversations may give an idea of the confusing state of affairs. On that day the office of *Il Popolo d'Italia* in Naples called the editorial offices in Milan:

Naples: "There are rumors here [it is] for tonight."

Milan answered: "Well, here we don't know anything. Do you want to talk with Mussolini?"

"Yes, ask him to come to the phone for a moment."

"Wait. . . . The director says that at this moment he can't get away; he says to tell me if you have something to say."

"Since everybody here is alarmed and says at midnight, at midnight — is there some truth in it or isn't there any truth?"

"Wait a moment. . . . Mussolini says that this evening he goes to the theater . . . so you well understand . . ."

"But here there is a great alarm because everybody says at midnight, at midnight . . ."

"But no, no; *he* says no."

Mussolini did go to the theater that night. He went to more than one theater. Some reports say he was accompanied by his wife and daughter, others by his close associate Margherita Sarfatti and her daughter. On his reasons for appearing in a public place opinion is divided. Those who wish to represent Mussolini as a consummate politician say that with his relaxed appearance he wanted to make people believe that there could be no truth in rumors of a March on Rome; those who want to stress his wavering nature say that only by evading contact with his office could he avoid being pestered by subordinates and forced to make decisions.

Meanwhile, the worried cabinet in Rome handed its port-folios to Facta, the prime minister. It was now up to him to decide whether the entire cabinet should resign.

On the evening of the twenty-sixth, while Mussolini was at the theater, Michele Bianchi in Rome declared to the news-papers: "The only possible solution of the crisis consists in entrusting the succession of Facta's cabinet to the Honorable Mussolini. The party which has determined the crisis is the Fascist Party; it is therefore the head of this party who must be called to form the new cabinet. . . . Who represents the country at this moment? We do. The day before yesterday there could be talks of a coalition directed by other top men with our collaboration. But today the situation is radically changed. . . ."

Mussolini in the post of prime minister, fascism the master of the government: this is what Bianchi had been working for all along. Knowing that Mussolini might be willing to settle for less and was pushing negotiations, Bianchi kept a wary eye on what was happening in Milan. He called *Il Popolo* that same night, or, more precisely, at 2:45 A.M. on October 27. Bianchi talked with an editor of the paper, bringing him up to date on the events in Rome. Then he said:

"So, are we still agreed on what we said in Naples?"

"Yes . . . but . . . there is something new."

"What is it?"

"How can I tell you on the phone? There is some softening in sight."

"Oh, oh."

"But, see here. . . . I tell you that I foresee that this soften-ing, which in any event will be only for a few days, will be rejected by both sides."

At this point another man snatched the receiver in Milan and asked about things in Rome. Then Bianchi said:

"As far as we are concerned, we must not retreat a single step."

"Absolutely."

"It seems to me that our path is clearly marked out."

"Firmly."

"What you are telling me is of great comfort; have courage!"

"Goodbye, Michelino."

This conversation did not entirely reassure Bianchi. He pondered it for a quarter of an hour and then called Mussolini personally:

"Benito. . . ."

"What is it, Michelino?"

"I and the others want to know what instructions you are giving."

"My instructions?"

"Yes, and what is new."

"The news is this: Lusignoli [a senator, prefect of Milan, and intermediary between Mussolini and Giolitti] went to Cavour [Giolitti's residence in Piedmont] and says that he can snatch four important portfolios and four underportfolios from Giolitti."

"What portfolios would they be?"

"Navy, Treasury, Agriculture, Colonies; then there would be War, which would be given to a friend of ours; then there would be the four undersecretaryships."

"What then?"

"Then he [Lusignoli] has sent me word that he will be back at nine in the morning."

"Benito. . . ."

"What is it?"

"Benito, are you willing to listen to me? Do you want to hear my firm, irrevocable resolve?"

"Yes . . . yes. . . ."

"Answer 'No.'"

". . . Of course, the machine is wound up now; nothing can stop it."

"What is going to happen is as fated as Destiny itself. . . . It is no longer the moment for discussing portfolios."

"Of course."

"So we are still agreed; may I pass this on in your name?"

"Wait before you do. . . . Let's hear what Lusignoli has to say. . . . Let's try to talk again tomorrow. . . ."

A few hours later Salandra called Mussolini from Rome. In view of the cabinet crisis, he wanted Mussolini to come to Rome and be at hand. But Mussolini was not going to do so under any circumstances; he felt much safer and much more comfortable in his office in Milan.

Fascist mobilization had begun. Many provinces reported to Rome that Fascists were requisitioning cars and weapons, taking prisoners, cutting telephone lines, and occupying public buildings, railroad stations, and army depots. They were arriving at assembly points by train and truck. According to plan, the quadrumvirate had set up headquarters in Perugia, and there it was to exert the full political and military power conferred by Mussolini; instead, it lost control of events. Throughout the critical days, Perugia remained cut off from the bulk of Fascist forces, isolated on its hilltop, hardly informed of the progress of operations. Of the members of the quadrumvirate, Bianchi spent much time in Rome; as secretary of the Fascist Party, he issued statements and granted interviews in which he increased demands on behalf of fascism and Mussolini. De Vecchi kept busy trying to influence the royal court and the Nationalist Party, and Balbo traveled between Perugia, Florence, and Rome in an attempt to obtain information and to act as liaison with certain groups of mobilized Fascists.

One report of these days comes from Enrico Corradini, the Nationalist leader, in a letter to Giolitti, who on October 27 was celebrating his eightieth birthday in the quiet of his native Piedmont: ". . . there is a beginning of action on the part of the *fasci*, who according to fragmentary information intend to exert strong pressure to obtain the formation of a Fascist government. The truth, it seems, is that Mussolini shows signs of giving in to his extremists. Meanwhile, the king has arrived in Rome. . . ."

The king arrived in Rome on the evening of October 27, called back from his summer place by Prime Minister Facta, who had recognized at last the gravity of the situation. About 11:00 P.M. Facta handed the king the cabinet's resignation and had a long talk with him.

On the evening of October 27 Mussolini was again at the theater. He then went to his office, heard the latest news, worked late, and returned at 6:00 in the morning. It was the fateful morning of October 28, the day of the March on Rome. The entry at *Il Popolo d'Italia* was barricaded, and seventy Fascists were ready to defend the building (*Il Popolo* was no longer in Via Paolo da Canobbio; from the time the fortunes of fascism had changed, it occupied an entire new building). That morning Mussolini went more than once to the *prefettura* for consultations with Prefect Lusignoli, who spoke for Giolitti; he also participated in skirmishes in the street in front of the newspaper office and spent a great deal of time on the telephone.

The news that reached Mussolini was not good. The cabinet ministers had reacted to Fascist mobilization by declaring a state of siege, and by 8:30 A.M. the proclamation was being posted on the walls of Rome and telephoned to the provinces. Military authorities everywhere had begun to take over the civilian administration, and it appeared very likely that under these circumstances the army would receive orders to resist the advancing Fascist columns. In fact, the army had already begun to blow up stretches of railroad track and otherwise hamper the progress and supply operations of the marchers. The quadrumvirate, isolated in Perugia, was not exerting its military functions, and the many groups and columns of Blackshirts proceeded under their own commanders, according to a vaguely pre-established plan, without having any certain knowledge of what the rest of the Fascists were doing. They were poorly armed, short of food and drinking water; no provisions had been made for quarters or camps on the March.

At 10:00 A.M. Mussolini received a call from the Nationalist deputy Luigi Federzoni in Rome. Since all long-distance calls not on government business were forbidden, Federzoni was phoning from the Ministry of Interior. He reported: ". . . if a *de facto* situation like the one now in progress continues, [this] will happen: the king will leave the throne. Here there is absolutely nobody who can represent the *fasci* and with whom we can consult about the situation. De Vecchi has not yet arrived in Perugia. De Bono has insistently told me to be sure to let you know all this, and he begs you to come immediately to Rome."

Mussolini answered: "I cannot come because in Milan action is under way. We must inquire in that place known to you, the supreme command. I'll accept any solutions that the supreme command wants to adopt."

"But how can the command . . . let you know, if it cannot communicate with Milan?"

"You take care of informing me. Keep in mind that the movement is very serious all over Italy."

"Now the question is not to destroy the support, otherwise everything is lost."

"Get in touch at once and say that Mussolini will consent to whatever the commanders decide. . . ."

It is hard to say whether Mussolini was temporizing, whether he realized that the quadrumvirate would see that they got for him as much as it was possible to get, or whether he was so confused, so uncertain, that he actually meant to surrender his will to the quadrumvirate.

At about the time Mussolini and Federzoni were talking by phone, Prime Minister Facta went to the Quirinal to present to the king for his signature the decree of the state of siege. But His Majesty took the initiative he had never taken in the past and refused to sign. During the night, it is reported, he had consulted with his top generals, asking them whether the army could be counted upon to fight the Fascists if so ordered; he received the reply that the army would do its duty — but perhaps it would be better not to put it to the test. It is also possible, as many Italians were to maintain, that the king refused to sign because he feared civil war and did not want Italian blood to flow. Facta was thunderstruck: according to the prime minister's version of the story, the king had given consent to the state of siege the night before. Now Facta was compelled to revoke the decree and face the nation's criticism.

Wires were sent to countermand the decree, and chaos increased. In some places the revocation arrived before the original order, and local authorities could not make out what was meant; in others orders and counterorders were received with skepticism and disregarded. The military authorities hesitated before relinquishing the administration of cities and towns to civilians from whom they had taken it only hours before. The general public could not understand what was going on, whether there was or was not a state of siege, and for some time not even the Fascist command at Perugia had the answer. Then, as if Nature in a fit of perversity wanted to add to the general confusion, it began to rain steadily all over Italy. The unsheltered Fascist columns waited outside Rome for the order to march. It was one of those heavy rains that suddenly wipe out the last mildness and balminess of an Italian October and usher in the leaden days of autumn.

If the lack of prompt news from the marching columns caused disorganization in the command of the insurrectionary movement, it also aroused a disproportionate fear in Rome, and in the end it worked in favor of Mussolini. The king and the government, poorly informed, overestimated the number, strength, and determination of the Blackshirts, some of whom had already been driven back to their homes by the rain and the scarcity of food. With very little bloodshed, with a few tanks and planes, the army could have easily pushed back the Fascists. But this is hindsight, and at the time the men in power in Rome did not have all the elements with which to judge the evolving situation.

In Milan the men around Mussolini acted as watchdogs, followed all his moves, listened to his words, and made certain that he would not give in to pressures but would increase his demands each time he obtained a concession. When news reached him that the state of siege had been revoked, Mussolini knew that Rome was in panic. This increased his confidence, and he took a firmer stand. He began to see himself the master of the situation, at the head of the government, as Bianchi and

Balbo had declared he should be. When Federzoni and De Vecchi telephoned to say that he ought to come to Rome, he replied that he would only if the king called him for consultation; then, and then only, would he leave Milan. When the king's own adjutant informed him that His Majesty wished to see him, he replied that he would not leave Milan unless asked to form a cabinet. Thus before the end of the twenty-eighth Mussolini was dictating his conditions to the king.

At 1:30 A.M. on the following day, De Vecchi telephoned Mussolini again. A few hours earlier the king had asked Antonio Salandra, the former prime minister, to choose a cabinet. Salandra was a man of the right. De Vecchi, the conservative Piedmontese with a feudal loyalty to his king, advised Mussolini to comply with His Majesty's (and Salandra's) wish that he collaborate in a Salandra government. Mussolini refused, "more than absolutely," to accede to this request. He also refused to go to Rome to be available in case of further developments.

He wrote instead an article for the morning issue of his paper, and a condensed version was wired to the Naples office. The wire, intercepted, left no doubts in Rome. "Victory already appears to be widespread, with the nation's near-unanimous consent, but victory should not be mutilated by last-minute concessions. It is not worth mobilizing only to arrive at a Salandra compromise. The government must be decidedly Fascist. . . . At this time the solution of the crisis may be possible within the compass of the most orthodox constitutionality; but tomorrow it will be too late. The irresponsibility of certain Roman politicians oscillates between the grotesque and the fatal. They must decide. Fascism wants power and will have it."

Later that morning Mussolini received one more telephone call from De Vecchi. Salandra had given up his attempt to form a cabinet; De Bono and De Vecchi had stressed the urgency of a solution, saying that they would not be responsible for the discipline of the Fascist troops camped outside Rome under the steady rain; through De Vecchi, the king asked Mussolini to form a cabinet. Mussolini, not satisfied with this message, requested a telegram in confirmation. "As soon as

I get the wire, I'll leave by plane," he said, but when the wire was delivered, he decided to take the night train.

This gave Mussolini time to take certain precautions. He had already sent messages to D'Annunzio to keep him informed and to obtain his approval of the March on Rome, thus forestalling any possible outburst of criticism. From the soldier-poet, still weak after his fall, nothing more concrete than words was expected, but coming from D'Annunzio even words could be a peril. The messengers brought back a message that contained no threat: ". . . Victory has the clear eyes of Pallas. Do not blindfold her. . . ." Reassured from this quarter, Mussolini had still a serious worry. He did not want his first days in power to be troubled by a general strike, and he was well-acquainted with Socialist policies; he remembered the last strike too vividly not to expect some attempts at retaliation. He could not prevent the Socialists from calling a strike, but he could deprive them of the means of giving publicity to it and passing directives to large numbers of potential strikers. At his orders, the Fascists burned to the ground the new offices of *Avanti!* — the fourth time the Fascists had set the offices on fire since early 1919. For two weeks the paper's voice was silenced, and then it began to publish in Turin.

Mussolini arrived in Rome on the morning of October 30. Many years before, when still the obscure editor of *Lotta di Classe*, he had written one of his most violent articles on Rome, calling it "parasitical city of furnished-room keepers, bootblacks, prostitutes, priests, and bureaucrats . . . city without a proletariat worthy of the name . . . focus of infection of the national political life . . . huge vampire . . . city that sucks the best blood of the country . . ." But in 1919 his opinion had changed, and on the occasion of President Wilson's visit to the capital, he had written: "President Wilson, approaching Rome, will feel the subtle and undefinable emotion that all civilized men feel when, once the burned and proud solitude of the *Agro* [the Roman *campagna*] and the pines that surround the seven hills with ever-living green are behind them, there appears amidst all its cupolas, its towers, columns, and palaces, in its light and its shadow, Rome unique and immortal."

Benito Mussolini did not look at his best when he arrived in immortal Rome. He had scarcely slept for several nights, and he had been under tremendous tension. His face was haggard; he was wearing black shirt, black trousers, and white spats. In the Quirinal, to which he went directly from the station, he shook hands with the king and said: "Your Majesty, will you forgive my attire? I come from the battlefields."

The Fascist regime had begun.

PART 3

IN
POWER

13

THE PRESIDENT

"Our action will be directed against any form
of dictatorship which could not but end in a
new barbaric manifestation: and our revolution, if it is inevitable, must have a Roman
and Latin imprint. . . . "

MUSSOLINI, March, 1919

Mussolini, prime minister with dictatorial powers for one
year — "The President" (of the cabinet), as he was called —
had been carried to his high position on the will of others,
as a swimmer on the crest of a wave. Judged by the events
of the few days or weeks that had preceded it, his victory
seems due as much to the weakness of the existing government, the army's connivance, the alertness of his watchdogs
in Milan, Bianchi's political stubbornness, and other circum-
stantial causes as to his ability as a politician and leader or to
his popularity. (In his first years in power his popularity was
to grow immensely and fast, but for the moment it was not
overwhelming.) But in the confusion of the moment, when not
all the facts were known and some were purposely concealed,
he appeared as the hero of the March on Rome, a physically
strong, dynamic, mentally alert, outwardly self-reliant man.
And at thirty-nine he was the youngest prime minister in
Italian history.

With a moderation that was the more remarkable coming
after the seemingly violent conquest of power, he formed a
true coalition cabinet in which he kept for himself the Ministry of Foreign Affairs and the Ministry of the Interior. Only

four ministers out of fourteen were Fascists; the others included Social Democrats, *popolari*, liberals, General Armando Diaz, the victor of Vittorio Veneto, the very popular admiral Paolo Thaon di Revel, and the liberal philosopher Giovanni Gentile (who immediately began to introduce liberalizing reforms in the schools). Thus he pleased many groups, from the armed forces and the academic world to the Vatican, softened the opposition by surprising it, and presented himself in the best light he could to the eyes of the world.

The world, somewhat puzzled and baffled, suspended judgment but turned on him its benevolent attention. After the proofs of decadence, often of decay, that older institutions had given in many European countries, the Fascist experiment with youth and energy was a factor of hope rather than concern. It was to show whether patriotism, enthusiasm, and — why not? — ruthlessness could do better than experience and wisdom, whether the forces of youth, in a country undermined by the process of disintegration, could play a meaningful role in the world scene. In foreign countries most newspapers commented on Mussolini with sympathy, and at home his popularity began growing at once. Increasingly large sections of the population favored him; vaster and vaster crowds cheered him deliriously; more and more young people made him their idol. When early in the morning he went horseback-riding in Villa Borghese, the largest park in Rome, young women sprang up along his path to smile at him and little children gave him the Fascist salute. When he occasionally mixed with the people in some square and patted an old woman on the back; when he helped a smith or a bricklayer in his job, saying that in the past he had been a smith himself or that he loved manual work and was envious of those who did it; when he appeared among the reapers wearing only a pair of old trousers, with his bare torso shining in the sunlight like a sturdy bronze statue, his popularity took a jump forward. Still, very few knew anything about the man himself, his traits, his abilities and shortcomings, his ambitions and intentions.

This ignorance can be explained, if not entirely justified: before the March on Rome, fascism had been a movement of moderate proportions, limited to certain regions of Italy and made up of local groups little related one to the other, each led by a man who had attained local popularity and ascendancy. In their own territories the local leaders were often better known than the duce of fascism. At any rate, Mussolini had always preferred to identify himself with his paper than with the central Fascist organization (more than once he had said that fascism could do without him, and that he was not bound to follow fascism). He ought to have been better known as the director of *Il Popolo d'Italia* than as the duce, but *Il Popolo* was not a paper of mass circulation, and though at various times it issued a Roman edition, it was read almost exclusively in Milan and its province. Apart from these justifiable reasons for ignorance, there was the political apathy of the bulk of the population, which the Italians themselves in their frequent outbursts of self-criticism had often decried but had not been able to overcome. Thus the very middle classes that, dreading bolshevism, placed their hopes of survival in fascism did not take the pains to become informed about the past of the journalist and politician whose ascent they did much to help. Nor was the king enlightened about the president to whom he entrusted his country, and as late as the eve of the day upon which he called the duce to form a cabinet he had gone around asking whether one could trust this man Mussolini (or so it is reported; and even if untrue the story would be significant as an indication of a popular state of mind, of history's judgment a posteriori).

At the time Mussolini came to power, the press did little to correct the widespread ignorance of the public. The best Italian papers, *Corriere della Sera, Stampa*, and *Giornale d'Italia*, were not in the habit of publishing biographical sketches of the persons who came into the political limelight. The biographical information about Mussolini which appeared scattered here and there at the time of the March on Rome ranged from some factual statements about his schooling and the newspapers he had directed to the deliberate misstatement in *Il Popolo* that he had obtained a university degree in Lausanne, and to such vague sentences as "the rest is known," "he is a man of great talent and courage and is a very effective orator," and "molder of the concept of the new Fascist state." The Italian people were willing to put themselves into the hands of a man whose future government would be at best a hopeful experiment and whose political talent they had no way to evaluate. The foreign press mirrored the muddled information of the Italian, and so the less attractive features of Mussolini were allowed to be buried, while the distorted picture of the great man was built up. Soon the world was to see of the Italian leader only what he and his Fascist clan wanted to show.

Mussolini had not the stuff of the statesman in him but was, and was to remain to the end of his life, a journalist at heart. As a journalist he had read voraciously, indiscriminately, and unsystematically, and whatever impressed him he absorbed, storing it in his extraordinary memory without first subjecting it to stringent scrutiny or pondering it for a time to see whether it would fit into the pattern of his previously accepted ideas: he seldom had time and inclination for much deep thinking. This casual and haphazardly built patrimony of borrowed and often undigested ideas and guiding principles gave him the false assurance that he had vast knowledge and great ability. As Count Carlo Sforza, former Minister of Foreign Affairs and, in World War II, a member of the first cabinet of liberated Italy, was once to write, Mussolini sincerely, but naïvely, believed that with the sheer force of his will he could be successful where all others had failed in correcting all that was not well in Italy. By the time he found out that the art of governing is not simple he was already the prisoner of the legend of Mussolini the all powerful and infallible ("Mussolini is always right" was one of the famous Fascist slogans).

As it proved, most of his political ideas were shallow or objectionable, or both. To him fascism was, "above all, the verb *to want* in the present tense"; and "the most formidable creation of an individual and national 'will to power' "; and "an organized, centralized, authoritarian democracy." He said: "Fascism brings back . . . color, force, the picturesque, the unexpected, the mystical; in short, all that counts in the soul of the crowds. We play the lyre on all chords:

from that of violence to that of religion, from that of art
to that of politics." His program was "simple": "We want to
govern Italy. . . . I am here [in government] in order to
defend and give power to the Blackshirts' revolution." His
guiding principles were vague: ". . . all that may make the
Italian people great, finds me favorably inclined and — vice
versa — all that tends to lower, brutalize, impoverish the
Italian people, finds me opposed. . . . There is no spiritual
and political movement that has a more solid and certain
doctrine than the Fascist doctrine. Precise truths and realities
confront our spirit, and they are: the state, which must be
strong; the government, which must defend itself and the
nation from all disintegrating attacks; class collaboration;
the respect of religion; the exaltation of all national energies."

He did not care for "the static criteria of democracy" or
"the immortal principles. . . . In democracy," he wrote,
"fascism rejects the absurd conventional lie of political
equality, the habit of collective irresponsibility, the myth of
unlimited happiness and progress." To him equality was
"antinatural and antihistorical"; representative systems belonged "to mechanics rather than to morality"; and he called
freedom "not an end but a means," which, as such, "must be
controlled and dominated. . . . Freedom without order and
discipline means dissolution and catastrophe. . . . Freedom
is not a right: it is a duty, . . . it is a conquest, . . . a
privilege. . . . The concept of freedom changes as time
passes. There is a freedom in peacetime which is no longer
freedom in wartime. There is freedom in times of wealth
which cannot be granted in times of poverty. . . . To the
intrepid, restless, harsh youths who appear in the dawn of the
new history there are other words [than freedom] that exert
a much greater charm. They are: order, hierarchy, discipline.
. . . Fascism has already walked and will again calmly walk
over the more or less decomposed body of the goddess Freedom."

His views on foreign policy were striking and often contra-
dictory: "Peace treaties, however good or bad, once signed
must be enacted. . . . Treaties are not eternal, are not irreparable. . . . To enact them means to try them out. . . . We

cannot allow ourselves the luxury of a policy of senseless altruism, of complete dedication. . . . My formula is simple: *Do ut des*, Nothing for nothing." He did not make a secret of wanting war: "Only war heightens all human energies to a maximum of tension and impresses a seal of nobility on the people who have the virtue to undertake it. . . . The Fascist state is a will to power and domination. To fascism the tendency toward empire is a manifestation of vitality, its opposite, a sign of decadence." In 1925, seven years before the publication of Aldous Huxley's *Brave New World*, Mussolini said that the idea of laboratory-created classes appealed to him, and first on the list he placed "the class of warriors which is always ready to die."

For a long time, all the same, Italy was to stay out of war. For a long time Mussolini was to declare that he did not want war itself, only the preparation and fitness for it. He may have used war and military training as a social myth, or he may have been following that much-quoted Roman dictum: *Si vis pacem para bellum* (If you want peace, prepare for war), a maxim that has proved very dangerous but which the world is still following.

Mussolini's doctrine of government could well be summed up in the words of one of those slogans of fascism which were soon to appear everywhere, in the press, on the sides of houses along main roads and railways, even in the mosaic floor of the Foro Mussolini, his stadium, where they were to create serious embarrassment to the post-Fascist generation: *Credere, Obbedire, Combattere* (To believe, to obey, to fight). Militarism and talks of war were the daily diet on which the Italians were fed. To those who believed and obeyed blindly, "to fight" became dogma, an essential part of the Fascist credo. This dogma was to enslave the nation and its duce and lead them to their ultimate catastrophe.

Along with the paucity of ideas, there were several negative traits in Mussolini: Although extremely wilful and intolerant of censure, he was, according to his associates, somewhat gullible, easily persuaded to accept another's point of view, and willing to accede to any request; aggressive, he lacked physical courage, and the only acts of daring that can be credited to him are his numerous duels, his flying lessons at a time when flying was still very hazardous, and his passion for mad driving. Although willing to condone petty theft in his subordinates and to give financial assistance to those who asked for it, he was vindictive and cruel and easily exploded in fits of wrath which terrorized his friends. His detachment from, and unconcern for, the moral rules of human behavior were so great that he has often and rightly been called completely unprincipled. Yet, despite his shortcomings, he was to remain in power for over twenty years. The questions "Why?" and "How?" have often been asked, especially after the fall of fascism and the crumbling of all the thin façades and paper castles that had concealed its true nature. The questions are still asked, and will be asked in the future by inquisitive minds, but no single satisfactory answer has been given or is likely ever to be given.

The rise of a dictatorship in any country, at any time, is almost invariably puzzling, and seldom does an analysis of its origins and causes yield fully adequate explanations. To past events some lack of logic is condoned, and the dictators who have lived in remote times are more likely to be accepted at their face value, though their spectacular careers may seem to break the common rules of history. But it appears inconceivable that anything markedly irrational may happen in our own time, and so the ascent of a modern dictator is examined more critically. The dictators of western Europe are a case in point. Hitler, the little Austrian painter, may have been a more determined, single-directed man than Mussolini and driven by the constant force of his fanaticism. The civil war in Spain and the fact that Franco was an army general may suggest readier explanations for his rise to power than for the rise of either Mussolini or Hitler. Yet, viewed against their historical and social backgrounds the phenomena "Hitler" and "Franco" are as puzzling as the phenomenon "Mussolini."

In the search for an explanation of Mussolini's rise to power it is pertinent to point out that in a speech in 1918 he himself quoted from Machiavelli's *The Prince*: "If we consider Cyrus and others who have conquered or founded empires . . . examining their acts and life we do not see that from fortune they had anything else but opportunity, which gave them the material to which they could give the shape they felt best; and without that opportunity the excellence of their souls would have died out, and without that excellence the opportunity would have failed. . . . These opportunities, therefore, made these men successful, and their excellent virtue enabled the opportunity to be fulfilled; hence their country was ennobled and became most happy." In the Italy of 1922 fortune's "opportunity" was provided by the results of that postwar psychosis that followed victory and from which the nation was still suffering: the unrest of an economically and spiritually exhausted people who wanted "pacification" with all their souls and above everything else, and forgot that the disorders were due as much to Fascist *squadrismo* as to Socialist reprisals; the fear of bolshevism, which Mussolini took great care to keep alive, even after he had recognized that the danger of bolshevism had passed; the thwarted nationalism that held together the heterogeneous groups of fascism; the continuing spiritual mobilization of a generation of young men who were still living in accordance with wartime ideals; and, perhaps more important than anything else, the fact that in Italy at that time there was not one statesman who could meet such an emergency. (Historians have castigated Giolitti for being "lazy" and not having hurried to Rome for consultations with the king, since in their opinion he could have changed the course of history; but they forget that a man of eighty has some right to be lazy.)

Mussolini's "excellent virtue" consisted in his ability to impersonate, at the most timely moment, the superman and the savior to whom, as he had said himself, "nothing is impossible"; to appear not a man whom other men could measure with their own yardstick, but the hero of a myth and a living legend. In 1922, to a population that had lost sight of its aims and will, that lacked faith in itself and was affected by a mass inferiority complex, that suffered from both real and imaginary ills, the idea of a savior capable of bringing well-being to all by the sheer force of his will was not only appealing, it was a last hope. And Mussolini, savior and superman, promised law and order, a full appreciation of victory and its worth, an Italy cured of poverty, restored to its dignity, resuming its place among the great nations of Europe, and governed by youth and youthful energy. His skill in using the spoken word, the tone of his voice, which could be solemn, prophetic, imperative, and exalting, made his impersonation convincing. He was also helped by his sensitivity to the crowds, his intuition of what they wanted, how far he could push them, how he could arouse their mystical loyalty and exert his "magnetic" attraction on them. It was perhaps what he had once read in Stirner that gave him the ability to unleash the lower instincts in his followers — callousness and cynicism, greed and vengefulness, the love of violence, of conquest and blood — and make them think that they were in pursuit of high moral ideals, evincing courage and excellence. (Soon after the end of the war, in addressing a brigade of *bersaglieri*, he said: "As you settle into peacetime, as you resume the fruitful and peaceful contests of work, you will meet again the parasites, the cowards, the war-shirkers, those who continued to be shirkers while you were dying of fire and cold, who will try to devaluate your victory, who will try to devaluate your effort, who will try to convince you that you fought for the rich, for the *padroni*, to fatten the poltroon and the lazy. Well, no. React. Use violence. Push back the insult and the insinuation into the throats of the vile. . . . You have spent good and sacred money, blood, and you have acquired certain rights. I solemnly promise you that I shall defend all that belongs to you with my pen and any other means. . . . The parasites of war will be compelled to let you precede them . . . [and] tomorrow your blood must weigh on the rights and duties of each citizen. . . . Italy is the country of the future. And the future is in your hands, in your soldierly souls.")

He was driven by a tremendous ambition, by the determination and intensity with which he wanted to be a leader. To be sure, if not periodically "rewound" he was likely to become discouraged and vacillate, to be ready too often to give up a quest when in sight of its attainment. But since he was always surrounded by men who had everything to gain by keeping him "wound up," his periods of discouragement were soon spent. The reading of Nietzsche's works had projected into his consciousness the "will to power" that had always been smoldering in his egocentric temperament — had placed it, so to say, in his hands, as a tremendously helpful tool of success. Passing moments of despondency did not quench his will to power, and indeed as time went on it seemed to become more and more imperious and unquenchable, only to collapse the more violently at the end.

Besides ambition and a will to power (which could never be satisfied and demanded ever-increasing power, a tighter and tighter grasp on men and events), besides his excellence in impersonating the superman and in handling crowds, something else sustained Mussolini through his years in government. For, like all men who can claim they have led large masses and aroused great emotions in them, he was dreaming an inspiring dream. Constantly, before the eyes of his mind, he had a grandiose vision which he strove to turn into a reality: the re-enactment of the Roman Empire. This was the moving myth of the Fascist revolution — a continuous, never-ending, daily revolution — against anything that was not Fascist and Roman, against democratic ideals, the comfortable life, the *bourgeoisie*, foreign influences and the acquisition of goods on foreign markets, and against anything and anyone who tried to check Italian expansion and prevent the Italians from doing what their great ancestors had done almost two thousand years earlier.

Benito Mussolini had not received the education of the typical cultivated Italian; he had not gone through the eight years of *ginnasio* and *liceo*, the only schools then leading to the university in preparation for the liberal professions. He had escaped the eight years of Latin that all pupils in those schools were required to take and the five years of Greek that more than half of them undertook. Yet, he had not escaped the effects of this classical pattern of culture, which influenced Italian literary expression and the interpretation of history. Even in the nonclassical schools like those attended by Mussolini, history and literature conspired in favor of the past and reminded all pupils that they were descendants of the ancient Romans who had conquered the world.

In preparing to become an adult and take his role in life, young Mussolini, like many other children, had been fascinated by the Roman legend and on the margins of his books had written the magic word *Roma*. As a young man, in the first fifteen years of the century, he was too deeply involved in his extreme political adventures and too much wrapped up in the antipatriotic role he had chosen to recognize that he and all other cultivated Italians were falling under D'Annunzio's spell; that D'Annunzio's poetry, with its vivid, sonorous imagery and emotional appeal, was turning patriotism and the cult of Rome into a rhetorical, passional mourning for the past. This consequence of a classical education that otherwise gave excellent training to the intellect was dangerous, since, measured against a glorious past, the present appears humiliating, and the contemplation of the future is likely to offer little comfort. When, at the end of World War I, Mussolini and those who felt as he did measured the Italy that was against the Rome that had been, they were sorely disappointed. By comparison with the splendor it had once reached, Italy appeared insignificant, an exceedingly poor descendant of her noble ancestors. Among the many who were deeply perturbed by this comparison, Mussolini alone was able to dispel the effects on his spirit and find sufficient faith in himself to believe that he could bring about the resurrection of the past.

It was after he had visited D'Annunzio in Fiume and seen how dead elements of the Roman culture had come to life under the breath of D'Annunzio's creative spirit that Mussolini began dreaming of a "Roman Italy," an Italy under the leadership of a man of Caesarean stature, which would "place the limits of its empire on the ocean and of its fame in the stars." (This was his own translation of Vergil's *imperium oceano, famam qui terminet astris*.) He dreamt of an Italy to whom it was "fated" that the Mediterranean sea, "our lake" and its inclosing shores, should return; and of a Rome that would again impart "its civilization, its great juridical civilization, as solid as its monuments, to the entire world." The very thought of Rome filled Mussolini with nostalgic passion, made him ask himself by what reason or prodigy a small number of peasants and shepherds had gradually ascended to imperial power and a small village of huts on the banks of the Tiber had been transformed into a gigantic city that with its legions dominated the world; by what spiritual portent Rome had transmuted an incomprehensible Oriental religion into a universal and imperial one. (It was Mussolini's notion that if it had not come to Rome Christianity would have remained an Oriental sect.) Of Rome the Immortal, Mussolini thought to make "the throbbing heart, the active spirit of the imperial Italy" of which he was dreaming, as great and magnificent a city as it had been at the peak of its greatness and magnificence. He must have marveled himself at his change of attitude toward Rome from the time of his venomous article in *Lotta di Classe,* for he once said: "There is something mysterious in this new blooming of our Roman passion. . . ."

In his vision of an imperial Italy directed by the spiritual and material power of the Eternal City, the population was one of noble warriors, moved to lofty deeds by ancient virtue and valor. As Mussolini spoke of the Italy he envisioned, the sound of his words re-evoked the cadence of the Roman armies marching along the peninsula on the well-cobbled Roman roads, and the flashing of his eyes recalled the coruscation of their blades and armor. "Italy," Mussolini said in a crescendo of intensity, giving life to his words with his forceful, incisive voice, "is a race, a history, a pride, a passion, a greatness of the past, and an even more radiant greatness in the future."

He was a modern man, and in his resurrection of the past he was not to renounce the advantage of modern innovations. To him the future Italy, "rich and free" (free from whom or what?), was to be "resounding with construction yards"; her skies and seas were to be "peopled by her fleets," and the plow was to make her soil fertile everywhere—in the marshes that he wanted reclaimed and on the sides of the steep hills that he wanted tilled, despite the strenuousness of the task and the smallness of the return.

His vision of the renewed Rome may have been too glitter-ing and lacking in depth; his intellectual sight may have not been sufficiently acute to probe into the formative elements and the institutions of the ancient Roman world; he may not have asked the whys and wherefores of Rome's success. The fact remains that the myth which sustained him through the years in power explains not only the mass choreography of Italian life — the organization of the Fascist militia with its Roman names and symbols; the Roman salute; the Roman form of address, imposed and taught in the schools to replace the customary formal "*lei*"; the huge sums spent in beauti-fying Rome; the Roman eagle placed in a cage on the Capitol; the military organization of small boys called, after Romulus and Remus, "sons of the she-wolf"; and the many other para-phernalia of a never-ending show, sometimes entertaining, often hard to bear — it explains also Mussolini's moments of great triumph, which seemed to make his dreams come true.

That the Roman passion was to pervade the national life and all acts of fascism is indubitable, but the suggestion that it could have been a main factor of stability in Mussolini's career may well appear farfetched; at this point it is offered only as a tentative interpretation. More pertinent to his im-mediate success is that while the greatest part of the popula-tion relaxed in the comforting thought that at the head of the government there was now a strong man who was to do all that needed to be done, Mussolini took steps to entrench and fortify himself in this position.

It has been repeatedly stated that Mussolini's political ac-tions of this period were dictated exclusively by empiricism and expediency, but in reality he depended upon a set of practical precepts that were handed down to him by no less authority than Niccolò Machiavelli, whom he considered "the teacher of all teachers of politics." (In 1924 he was to write that Machiavelli's *The Prince* ought to be called the vade-mecum, or handbook, of the governor of men.) Machiavelli did not intend *The Prince* as a book of rules; he meant it to be, and it is, an objective, soberly rational analysis of the political life, not as it should be, but as it was in his time — as unfortunately it still is, because, as he said, the nature of men has not changed over the generations. Machiavelli was the first man in modern times to study politics per se, independent of any metaphysical considerations or moral judgment, with cold detachment (through which here and there the author's inner fire and his passionate love of his country, break out), and it is precisely this abstraction from morality that appealed to Mussolini. With Machiavelli, Mussolini shared also a profound pessimism about men in general, similar to Nietzsche's pessimism, and faith in the excellence of the few, which made Machiavelli's prince akin to the Nietzschean superman, though a more real and practical, a much more human superman. To the prince, as to the superman, everything is permitted in order to attain his ends: it is without condemnation or criticism that Machiavelli describes, for instance, how Cesare Borgia treacherously got rid of his rivals in order to become well-established and secure in his princedom.

Several times, Mussolini stressed that he was greatly impressed by the writings of Machiavelli. In one of the many versions of his recollections, he wrote: "My father used to read Machiavelli to us in the evening, while we warmed ourselves by the last embers of the shop's fire, drinking the wine of our countryside. The impression was profound. When at forty I read the book again, it acted on me with equal force." These are romantic words. The fact is that Mussolini began quoting from Machiavelli in 1918, and that the sentence he quoted most often is: "All armed prophets won and the unarmed perished." It is not unlikely that fascism owes its early military-like features to Machiavelli, but it is in the first years in power that Machiavelli's influence on Mussolini was most evident. It was so evident that many of his close associates noticed it and remarked on it. Margherita Sarfatti, for one, said that he was "imbued" with Machiavellian thought.

Mussolini's main concern after the March on Rome, like the concern of Machiavelli's newly risen princes, was *durare*, to last — he surprised a group of Fascist leaders by remarking that the Fascist revolution might last a generation, and he warned his adversaries not to hold delusory hopes that his duration in power would be brief. In order to last, and in line with what he considered Machiavelli's dictates, he was to seek the consent of the largest possible number of citizens, but also to resort to force if necessary. Many times in his first months in power he returned to his favorite theme, Force and Consent, and he also wrote an article with this as its title, which is of Machiavellian inspiration; "Consent is as changeable as the sand formations on the seashores. . . . It can never be total. . . . Any measure taken by any government will create some discontent. . . ." Before the discontent spreads, the government must check its spreading "by using this force inexorably when it becomes necessary," because it is the duty of a party in power to strengthen itself and become entrenched in government, and it is possible that "perchance force might help retrieve consent."

To "entrench himself" in his position and to have a force at hand when he needed it, he introduced two unconstitutional elements in his government, the "Grand Council of Fascism" and the "Voluntary Militia for National Security." He announced the institution of the Grand Council at the same meeting of Fascist leaders whom he had surprised with the statement that the Fascist revolution might last a generation, and this announcement startled them even more. Among them were several members of the Fascist Party executive, but he had not consulted them, and only then did they learn that the executive was to be absorbed by the Grand Council, thus losing its independence and identity. The new organ was to include certain cabinet and party members ex officio, and other Fascist notables on Mussolini's nomination. Mussolini was to be its chief and deliberations were to be secret, though brief communiques of its activities were to be issued. It was to meet at 10:00 P.M. on the twelfth day of each month — the fixed date and its late hour conferred an air of mystical solemnity to the meetings and were part of the Fascist theatrical setup; but in practice the Grand Council met also at other times.

If Mussolini had more precise ideas on the institution he was creating and its future functions — he said they were to be consultative — he did not express them publicly. To the senate he gave a muddled description: the Grand Council was to be "the co-ordinating organ of all responsible forces," "the organ of transition for tempering fascism, . . . the most original, useful, and effective of all organs."

Several days before announcing the creation of the Grand Council, Mussolini declared that although he was the chief of government he was to remain the chief of fascism, and that "under the official clothes," which he wore only "out of duty," he would still don his black shirt. Thus Mussolini came to be the head of fascism, government, and Grand Council; the Fascist Party lost its autonomy; party and government converged, tending to fuse in the person of a single man, the supreme chief. This situation affected the balance of the government: Mussolini's first cabinet was a true coalition cabinet, and in Parliament opposition parties, Socialist and Communist, were represented. But with the establishment of the Grand Council and the accumulation of partisan powers in the chief of government, the government became much more predominantly Fascist than the slimness of Fascist representation suggested. (In Parliament fascism was still represented by the small group of thirty-five deputies elected in 1921.)

Mussolini's next move to attain his aim "to last" was dictated by his conviction that before testing "consent" he ought to secure "force." He had obtained the highest government position by promising "pacification" between Reds and Fascists, between the Socialist and Communist gangs and the squads of Blackshirts; and "normalization," that is, a return to a perfect state of law and order within the constitutional institutions. As he well knew, in order to satisfy public opinion he had to dissolve both Fascist and non-Fascist squads, but he realized that such a step was hazardous. The squads were armed (to the senate he bragged that three hundred thousand Blackshirts meant three hundred thousand rifles, and despite the exaggeration of the figure, the many rifles in Fascist hands, together with the knives, *manganelli* — clubs — and a "few glasses of castor oil," constituted a not negligible armory). If the *squadristi* and their leaders chose to refuse to stop fighting, give up glory and pay, and go home quietly, Mussolini would not be able to compel them to quit. Provoked, the squads might turn against him, overthrow his government, and replace him with another idol. Kept happy, on the other hand, they would be a source of power, always ready in case of need.

By a master stroke and to his great advantage, Mussolini succeeded in saving appearances without risking the displeasure of his Blackshirts. At its first official meeting (called at 10:00 P.M. on January 12, 1923) the Grand Council took double action: it dissolved all armed squads, regardless of the party they belonged to, and it established a "Voluntary Militia for National Security" which absorbed and incorporated the dissolved Fascist squads. These suddenly acquired a legal status, while any other fighting squads became illegal. By this action Mussolini secured another sizable gain for the Fascist Party: the considerable financial burden of supporting the squads of Blackshirts passed from the party to the nation. The militia received the king's sanction by a royal decree which openly stated that the new body was "at the service of God and the Country and under the orders of the Chief of Government." Thus the king accepted an unconstitutional army which was under Mussolini's direct control and consisted of troops infatuated with fascism and its duce, under the command of trusted officers. General Emilio de Bono was appointed commander in chief of the militia, and two other quadrumviri, Italo Balbo and Cesare Maria de Vecchi, were in its high command. In the first two years of its existence, the militia, unlike the army, did not even take an oath of loyalty to the king and could well have been called "militia for Mussolini's security and duration." (Machiavelli, indeed, recommended that the prince should not trust mercenary troops, or troops loyal to another prince, but raise his own.)

Militia and Grand Council formed the basis of an unconstitutional government that ran parallel to the constitutional, of a system which Mussolini was later to call a "diarchy," and on which he was to comment twenty years after boldly laying its foundations. About a year before his death, while at the head of the puppet Republic of Salò in northern Italy, he wrote a series of articles in the third person, which appeared, unsigned except for the last one, in the newspaper *Corriere della*

Sera.* In one article he recalled his early years in government: "The monarchy stayed, but almost immediately fascism felt the need to create institutions of its own, such as the Grand Council and the Voluntary Militia for National Security. . . . A political institution was initiated, which can be called 'diarchy,' the government by two, the 'double command.' Mussolini, sometimes an extraordinary humorist without knowing it [note that this is his own opinion of himself], said that the system was rather like a married couple's room with separate beds, a 'very bad system,' according to Honoré de Balzac's *Physiology of Marriage.*

"By and by the diarchy assumed an even more definite character, though it was not always defined by special laws. At its apex there were the king and the Duce [note that "duce" but not "king" is capitalized], and when troops marching past saluted they did so both for the one and the other. Side by side with the army, which took orders from the king, was the militia, which took orders from the Duce. The king had a bodyguard of *corazzieri,* [selected for their] unusual height, and one day Gino Calza Bini created the 'Musketeers,' the Duce's personal guard. The cabinet derived from the Constitution, but the Grand Council preceded it in importance because it stemmed from the revolution. The Hymn *'Giovinezza,'* martial and impetuous, paired the Royal March, . . . noisy and prolix, which could be played like perpetual motion. . . . Not even the military salute escaped the diarchy system: the old salute was preserved [for men wearing] caps; the Roman Fascist salute [for those] without caps. . . ."

But "at the apex" the diarchy was to be an absolute monarchy and the duce its sovereign, while the king was to be relegated to his modest throne and allowed only that dubious prerogative of constitutional monarchs, signing decrees.

The Italians did not seem to notice, or perhaps they did not mind, that the new president was taking steps to make sure he would last. Besides, the great majority of the people had faith in Mussolini. They saw the machinery of government that had long been idle begin to move again under his

* Translated into English, these articles and other documents were published in 1949 in London in Mussolini's *Memoirs 1942–1943.*

vigorous impact, and to them this in itself was a good sign. They did not care whether the machinery was set in motion gently and smoothly or forcefully, or whether it moved in the right direction. They were satisfied as long as it ran and got results, and they admired the government for its accomplishments. After almost four years of confusion, inefficiency, and civil war, the Italian people greatly welcomed the sense of security that they were experiencing. Too few had sufficient political training and interest to examine critically whether this sense of security was justified. Too many thought that government should be left to statesmen and political discussion to politicians, and that their role was to be good and honest, respect the law and the rules set by the government, and hope for the best.

To a not overly analytical eye, during the first year of the new regime the Italian situation appeared appreciably improved. Without making drastic changes in the traditional form of government, by putting into action reform programs that other men had prepared but whose drafts had been gathering dust on desks, by giving orders in a dry imperious tone that demanded obedience, by calling meetings of the cabinet and Grand Council and by daily deliberations, Mussolini created an atmosphere of efficiency of which the trains running on time were the symbol. That was not the only achievement: the national budget decreased, strikes ended, and social peace seemed to return; the population, including small children, were organized in Fascist cadres, public works programs were begun, and abroad Italy's position was improving.

Examined more closely, this period appears marked by two main facts. First, Mussolini's conscious and unconcealed effort to strengthen the state, which resulted in an enormous concentration of power in the government — he had forgotten that in 1920 he had shouted "Down with the state in all its forms and incarnations!" and had called the state a Moloch of dreadful appearance that sees everything, does everything, controls everything. Second, Mussolini's continuous alternation between threatening tones and conciliatory words, between demonstrations of force and apparent good will, alternation which is best expressed in his favorite theme of this period, force and consent. These oscillations in Mussolini's speech and behavior baffled many people, and this bewilderment was one more reason to let the "Fascist experiment" take its full course before passing judgment. At first even the opposition refrained from judging, and its criticism was mild.

As the months went by, some of the less appealing features of the new regime became evident. Especially significant was the fact that outside Rome the local leaders of fascism felt that Mussolini alone had gained from the "revolution" that they had made for him, that he had not compensated them adequately. As a consequence they tried to take the upper hand, attempted to rule in their provinces or territories according to their own will, and started a new round of physical violence. The opposition protested and became increasingly vocal, an attitude that Mussolini did not tolerate. Through the first part of 1924 the tension between the opposition and Fascists and philo-Fascists continued to grow.

14

A BODY BETWEEN HIS FEET

"I am more and more firmly convinced that
for the welfare of Italy it is necessary to
shoot, I say shoot, in the back a few dozen
deputies and send at least a couple of ex-
ministers to the penitentiary."
MUSSOLINI, May, 1915

In June, 1924, a dramatic occurrence struck fascism with
the suddenness and force of a lightning bolt and initiated a
chain of events which in the course of a few months shook
Mussolini's political edifice to its foundations, threatening his
very political survival. Then, as extraordinary luck worked in
his favor, the same chain of events so strengthened his position that he could change his government into a true and permanent dictatorship, wipe out all opposition, and set in
motion the machinery that within two years was to turn Italy
into a police state. At the roots of this occurrence was Mussolini's intolerance of censure, especially when it came from
men of higher culture and social status. Among these, his most
insistent and irksome critic was the Socialist deputy Giacomo
Matteotti.

A tall, well-built man, thirty-nine years old in 1924, Matteotti belonged to a wealthy family which owned land in the
fertile estuary of the Po River. He had studied law and criminal sociology and at an early age had embraced socialism. As
a young Socialist he had attended the congress of Reggio
Emilia in 1912, at which Mussolini had won his first national
victory, defeating Bissolati and other right-wing reformists.
Thus, Matteotti and Mussolini were old acquaintances, but

there is no record that they were ever on friendly terms. Since the early days of fascism, Matteotti had exposed its abuses and used his keen intelligence to gather and analyze proofs and data that were embarrassing to fascism and to Mussolini. He had censured fascism and the government's weak stand toward it in Parliament where the Socialist victory of 1919 had brought him. When he spoke of his adversaries his manner, always reserved, could become stern and cold and his words cutting and disdainful. Mussolini called him an "irritating and obstinate enemy."

An occasion to show again his "obstinacy" was provided to Matteotti by the first Fascist elections. In coming to power Mussolini had not dissolved Parliament, a fact of which he had boasted several times as evidence of his magnanimity toward Parliament itself and in particular toward his adversaries, whose representation was much greater than the Fascists'. Yet he had almost immediately asked one of his henchmen, the Fascist deputy Giacomo Acerbo, Undersecretary of State (who was not even a lawyer but a man "interested in economy") to prepare a new electoral law. The law, reflecting Mussolini's authoritarian tendencies, assigned two-thirds of the seats in the Chamber of Deputies to the party or coalition receiving the largest number of votes. The law was passed despite serious opposition (typically, many who opposed it refrained from voting in order not to embarrass the government and to allow the Fascist experiment to proceed). It was, however, approved by many liberals, among whom the most prominent was Giolitti. The elections took place on April 6, 1924, and were overwhelmingly favorable to the Fascists, who received about 65 per cent of the total votes cast (4.5 millions against the 2.5 millions for all other parties combined). Mussolini could well claim that the elections were the nation's a posteriori sanction of the March on Rome and the Fascist revolution.

The elections were accompanied here and there by acts of Fascist violence, and Matteotti had the moral courage to challenge them. On May 30, he delivered a speech before the Chamber of Deputies and the chief of government, amidst interruptions and shouts. He pointed out that several days before the elections Mussolini had stated that the government would not feel bound by the result of the polls but would remain in power, by force if necessary, thus invalidating the elections a priori. Matteotti went on denouncing abuses and illegal practices, which included the voting of the militia on duty and of *balilla* (children belonging to Fascist organizations), and the fact that on election day the Socialists were prevented from holding rallies and delivering speeches. (During the election campaign a Socialist candidate was killed.) He concluded with the request that the elections be declared void and a solemn plea for a return to freedom and the dignity of the Italian people.

His plea went unheard in the very excited chamber; Socialist and Fascist deputies had left their benches and were fighting on the floor. Clamor and tumult were traditional in the Italian chamber, and more than once the unleashing of anger and resentment had turned verbal debates into scuffles and the main hall and corridors of Montecitorio, the Parliament building, into an arena. This time the fight did not last long. As soon as order was re-established, a Fascist deputy spoke, calling the opposition *masnada* (a band of scoundrels). At the end of this turbulent session Matteotti turned to a fellow Socialist deputy and said: "Now you may write the eulogy for my funeral."

During Matteotti's speech, a frowning Mussolini had been sitting mute and impassive, but his wrath exploded as soon as the session was over. "That man, after that speech, should not be allowed to go around," he said, according to a later deposition of his close collaborator and friend of that time, Cesare Rossi. Rossi, who was soon to become one of the most dramatic figures of fascism, had been a revolutionary syndicalist and a writer of newspaper articles. He had first met Mussolini at a Socialist congress and had been impressed by Mussolini's handshake, so vigorous that it hurt, and by his "profound and luminous eyes." In 1914 Rossi and Mussolini found themselves working together to bring Italy into the war, and later Rossi collaborated at *Il Popolo d'Italia*. He was a Fascist of the first hour, a true *sansepolcrista*, and had held various positions in the *fasci* of Milan and in the central

organization of the party. Intelligent, prompt, violent, and
coarse, he had exerted considerable influence on Mussolini
and had been one of the most attentive watchdogs in Milan
during the March on Rome. Cesarino, as his friends called
him, was a member of the Grand Council, where his influence
exceeded his position; he was called the *éminence grise* of
fascism. Often it was he who worked out Mussolini's policies;
in his capacity as head of Mussolini's press office, he interpreted them to the public; and he acted as a link between the
president (Rossi often called him "the boss") and other Fascist leaders. He was a member of the "pentarchy" which had selected the Fascist candidates for the April elections, and he
was often seen at the president's side.

In talking about the opposition leaders to a friend after
Matteotti's speech, Cesare Rossi said: "These people are
wrong if they believe that when Mussolini pronounces threats
he is indulging in rhetoric. . . . Those who know him ought
to realize that now and then Mussolini needs blood, and that
advice of moderation will not always bring results." Cesarino
Rossi himself was in a state of strange excitement, flushed and
with bloodshot eyes, according to several newspapermen who
talked to him immediately after Matteotti's speech. He poured
out abuse and threats against the Socialist deputy and was
heard to say that with opponents of Matteotti's kind the only
thing to do was to leave the last word to a gun.

Two days later, in an article in *Il Popolo d'Italia*, Mussolini stated that the majority had been too lenient toward
Matteotti, who had made a "monstrously defiant speech, which
would have deserved something more tangible than the epithet
'*masnada.*'" And on June 6, in the course of a dispute between majority and opposition in the chamber of Parliament,
he said (very nearly summarizing an article that he had
written the previous March): "We have admirable teachers
in Russia. . . . We are wrong not to follow their example.
You would have got a charge of lead in your back. . . .
There is still time, and we shall show you sooner than you
think." (Mussolini the chief of government had not given up
the language of Mussolini the Romagnole agitator.) On June
7, however, Mussolini delivered a speech in which he talked

at length of decreased tension and the possibility of peace-ful co-existence, indeed of collaboration, between majority and opposing minority. In the following months Mussolini was often to refer to this speech as to something that neces-sarily blotted out all previous dissension, all his threats, all the acts of Fascist violence that preceded and followed it. Meanwhile, the news spread that Matteotti was working upon another speech in which he was to produce evidence against the government of such gravity that Mussolini's own perma-nence in power would be in danger.

Then, on June 10, Giacomo Matteotti disappeared. The news began to spread the next day, when Signora Matteotti came to the Parliament building and asked several Socialist deputies whether they had news of her husband, who had left home the previous afternoon and had not returned. Nobody had any information to give her, and a Socialist deputy noti-fied the police. He was surprised to learn that the police were already informed of Matteotti's disappearance. It was agreed to withhold the news from the papers for the moment, among other reasons to avoid worrying Matteotti's old mother.

The government tried to create the impression that Matteotti had gone abroad, explaining that only a few days earlier he had obtained a passport (which had previously been refused to him several times). But early police investigations revealed that upon leaving his home in a residential section of Rome along the Tiber, Matteotti had been attacked by five men. He fought vigorously, but the five attackers managed to push him into a car, which sped away while he struggled and shouted for help.

On the evening of June 12 the police arrested a certain Amerigo Dumini, an ex-*ardito*, born in the United States and well known to the police and in certain Fascist quarters for acts of *squadrismo*, for "punitive expeditions," and for having killed two persons. In Dumini's suitcase the police found Matteotti's bloodstained trousers and several scraps of blood-stained upholstery fabric that matched pieces missing from a car they had seized a few hours earlier. From the condition of the car, bloodstained and with a broken window, the police deduced that a violent struggle had taken place in it. Other arrests closely followed Dumini's. On June 13 all daily papers carried the news of Matteotti's disappearance, the next day they began talking of murder, and soon all were convinced that murder it was.

An inquiry was opened. Newspapers published the bits of information that leaked out as well as many rumors. The opposition press began piling "revelation" upon "revelation." Some of the details of the inquiry which were not published then were to be revealed at the trial of the suspected murderers and instigators in 1926. In the years that followed, the anti-Fascist press abroad published all the evidence it could gather, and more details came out when, after the fall of fascism, the new Italian government reopened the case, calling the 1926 trial a legal farce. (In 1926 the defendants were either acquitted or sentenced to short terms in prison, further shortened by special amnesty.) In the reconstruction of Matteotti's case that follows, all the evidence now available is used.

The five men involved in the abduction and suspected of the murder were all ex-*arditi*, it soon was learned; they had been in close contact with Cesarino Rossi and for some time had had free access to the press office of which Rossi was chief. Dumini, in particular, had been Rossi's close friend. The five men were said to be members of a gang which in Fascist circles was called the *Cheka* (after the Soviet secret police), or "the *squadraccia* of the Viminale," since it operated from the Viminale, the building of the Ministry of Interiors, where Rossi's office was. It had been organized with Mussolini's full knowledge and consent — some said at his order — and its task was to carry out "punitive expeditions" against political foes of fascism. Dumini was its central figure and true leader, the man whom Mussolini considered the most reliable, the only one able to plan and carry to completion what was called a practical joke.

The very existence of the *Cheka* was repeatedly denied by the Fascists, but in view of all the evidence that has accumulated over the years there can be little doubt that an organized band operated from the Ministry of Interior as an instrument of illegality in the hands of the government. In Rome, from the fall of 1923 through the spring of 1924, there were several episodes of beatings, administration of castor oil, and vandalism. One of the most publicized of such episodes was the invasion and devastation of the home of Nitti, the former prime minister. Some of the incidents were not reported to the police, and others were ascribed to "unknown criminals," who went unpunished. Only in relation to Matteotti's case did it come to light that the Fascist *Cheka* had been responsible. The *Cheka* took its orders from either Mussolini himself — who was always to deny he knew anything about it — or from one of his more violent associates, Cesare Rossi, Italo Balbo, or General Emilio de Bono. The fact that De Bono, too, was involved in the *Cheka* is the more appalling for his being the head of the Italian police. Thus he could, and did, use his immunity and his authority to screen the guilty and suppress evidence. (That Mussolini himself ordered acts of violence is proved by at least one document, which, however, is not related to the *Cheka*. It is a telegram, dated June 1, 1924, ten days before Matteotti's disappearance, addressed to the prefect of Turin, in which Mussolini urged the chief administrator of Turin and its province to "make life difficult again" for Piero Gobetti, a young liberal whose political magazine *Rivoluzione Liberale* persistently criticized the government. Life was made so difficult for Gobetti that he had to flee Italy and died shortly afterward in Paris, at the age of twenty-four.)

If Mussolini wanted an adversary chastised, he did not always need to give direct orders. His two Fascist biographers, Pini and Susmel, say: "Often, he was not aware of the formidable suggestion to violence that derived from his words and writings. We certainly cannot dismiss the possibility that the squad of the Viminale may have sometimes acted on directives given by high officials who interpreted zealously the threats that, in moments of exasperation, Mussolini expressed against his adversaries. The impunity of the authors of illegal reprisals . . . could not be explained otherwise." In other words, Mussolini had only to mention casually that somebody ought to "teach a lesson to" or "make life difficult for" a certain political opponent, and someone saw to it that the opponent got a good beating and a dose of castor oil.

At the time of Matteotti's disappearance, these facts were not generally known, at least not in any detail. But the memory of previous political crimes, the circumstances of Matteotti's mysterious abduction, the first results of the inquiry made by the police, and the indiscretions of persons who were in a position to know, were sufficient to produce, in many people's mind, the definite and shocking realization that the responsibility for the crime rested in the highest ranks of the Fascist government. The intuition of sinister scheming outside the realm of morality, in the protective shadow of the government itself, and the recognition of the deliberate ruthlessness with which these schemes were put into operation horrified anti-Fascists and even many Fascists. Public opinion pointed its accusing finger at the government and, less assuredly, at Mussolini himself.

On June 13, three days after Matteotti's disappearance and while the word "murder" had just began to circulate, the opposition refused to collaborate with the majority and withdrew from Parliament in an act of protest against the Fascist government. Two weeks later they confirmed their resolution to persist in the secession until law and order were restored. The withdrawal of most of the opposition deputies from Parliament became known as the *Aventine*, after the hill to which in ancient times the Roman plebs withdrew in protest against the abuses of the noble ruling class. The leader of the modern *Aventine* was Giovanni Amendola, a liberal deputy who the previous year had suffered an attack at the hands of the *Cheka* and who was to be attacked twice again the next year and later die in exile. Amendola was an intelligent, honest, and able man, but he lacked the strength, the initiative, and the aggressiveness required to unify an opposition composed of heterogeneous groups (Socialists, *popolari*, and some liberals), to organize it, and lead it to an effective action.

Meanwhile, Matteotti's body could not be found. And the frustrating suspense of the search for it added weirdness to an already sinister drama.

Mussolini's attitude toward the Matteotti affair was to claim at first complete ignorance, and in fact he helped spread the rumors that the Socialist deputy had gone abroad. To Signora

Matteotti, who went to see him on June 12 and asked for the return of her husband, either dead or alive, he expressed the hope that nothing serious had happened to Matteotti and the belief that he would soon be back. The same evening, addressing the Chamber of Deputies, he said that, in view of "circumstances that warrant suspicion of a crime," he had given strict orders to the police to intensify its search for the missing deputy, in Rome, in other cities, and in neighboring countries, and concluded: "I hope that Matteotti may shortly be able to resume his place in Parliament."

The reiteration of such hopes might be interpreted as an indication of sincerity, had not Mussolini been a great actor and a master in the art of dissimulation. Moreover, he was then under the spell of Machiavelli's writings, and only two months before *Gerarchia* had published his essay "Prelude to Machiavelli." Before writing it Mussolini had carefully re-read *The Prince*. There he found the suggestion that a man who comes to power should get rid of his rivals before they get rid of him and the explicit advice that he must partake of the fox's as well as of the lion's nature and learn to be "a great simulator and dissimulator." He was also told that he who deceives will always find others who will let themselves be deceived.

It is hard to believe that Mussolini was not fully informed of the murder at a time when the police were already in possession of the car in which Matteotti was abducted and were getting ready to arrest Dumini. Many witnesses have in fact testified that from the very beginning the prime minister was fully informed of the affair. Indeed, Mussolini was never entirely cleared of the unofficially repeated accusation that he was the *mandante*, the man who had given orders for the murder of the Socialist deputy. Among the many pieces of evidence pointing in this direction is the fact, disclosed in 1947, that as late as 1928 Dumini was still blackmailing the Fascist government, and the duce himself had ordered a subsidy and other help for Dumini; that some time later, at Dumini's insistence and under his threats, the government granted him a farming concession in Libya.

The question of Mussolini's direct responsibility in Matteotti's murder will undoubtedly be argued for years to come, and it will never be settled unless some new document is found (perhaps in 1995, fifty years after Mussolini's death, when now-secret archives are to be opened). One thing is certain: the man who had promised "pacification" and the restoration of order, in whom all those who had been tired of disorder and violence had placed their hopes, had created the most suitable atmosphere for the growth of violence and established an instrument of illegality in the heart of the government.

With the explosion of the Matteotti case, Mussolini's past Machiavellian schemings seemed to turn against him. After giving up all pretense of ignorance, he began to picture himself as the real victim in the Matteotti affair. On June 13, speaking again before the chamber, he said: "If there is someone in this hall who has reason to be saddened, I should say exasperated, it is I. Only an enemy of mine who for long nights had been thinking of something devilish could have put into effect this crime that today strikes us with horror and draws from us a cry of indignation. . . . The government's conscience is extremely calm." And next day he reinforced the dose and said that the crime was "barbarous, useless, anti-Fascist, and, one may say, from the political point of view, anti-Mussolinian." (In one of the newspaper articles that he was to write the year before his death, there is a casual, and bewildering, mention of Matteotti's murder: "The year 1924 was a year of serious crisis. The *regime* had to withstand the consequences of a crime which, apart from any other considerations, was — for its manner and for its time — a political mistake.")

In creating the myth of Mussolini the victim, the master simulator did not need his art. In a sense he was a victim, either of his own machinations or of his political system. Overnight his apparently secure position changed and became precarious, and his popularity touched an all-time low. His friends abandoned him, and in the streets many Fascists ostentatiously threw away their party buttons, called *cimicette* (little bedbugs). Nature had not given Mussolini great moral strength, and alone he could not face the storm. The waves of opposition battered the political structure he had erected and made it creak, while the campaign of the press was like a frightening wind that increased the fury of the storm. On the top of the creaking structure Mussolini wavered. Italy expected his downfall at any minute, and he, being extremely sensitive to the mood of the population, felt dejected. Because he had fed on a diet of success, at this serious reversal his self-confidence deserted him; used to flattery and applause, he could not face the once-crowded waiting rooms of his office, now suddenly empty, gelid, immense; he could not bear the threatening shouts of the crowd under his windows: "Give us back Matteotti's body! We want Matteotti's body!" This he could not do, for the body of this bitter foe of his, as obstinate in death as in life, had not been found.

Of Mussolini's frame of mind in those days there is little doubt. All those who have been near him, both Fascists and anti-Fascists, both reliable and unreliable witnesses, have told similar stories, to which Mussolini himself has added details. He was near panic. Unshaven, pale and wan, his eyes deprived of their usual fire, he would burst into fits of rage and re-crimination, then sit dejectedly, slumped under the load of his own silence, his elbows on his desk, his big balding head between his clenched fists. "A body was thrown between my feet to make me give up power, . . ." he said. And three months later, grown fond of his own words, as often happened to him, he was to repeat in writing: "A body was thrown between my feet. It was heavy: it made me stumble and suffer." Never before had he, the aloof, the man who had cared so little about others, yearned so much for companionship and sympathy, or felt so sorry for himself. "In the week after Giacomo Matteotti's murder I was frightfully lonely," he was to say years later. Never had the void around him been so complete and ominous. "Twenty men determined to reach me," he is reported to have said, "would not encounter the resistance of a single defender." Never had he felt so insecure. To a visitor who happened to be in his office while a hostile crowd demonstrated under his windows, he said: "If this mob advances, I'll shoot."

In those days Ugo Ojetti, a man of letters and an acute observer of men and events, neither a Fascist nor an anti-Fascist but reflecting the opinion of certain intellectuals, noted in his *Taccuini* (*Notebooks*): "Really, there are two dead men, Matteotti and Mussolini. And Italy is divided: those who mourn for the death of the one, and those who mourn for the death of the other."

Those who mourned for Mussolini's death could have spared themselves the pains. Despite his deep distraction, the man whom Fate had in turn exalted and chastened still had enough vitality to take initiative. If he could not produce Matteotti's body, he could try to placate the mob by throwing a few scapegoats at it. While the police made many arrests — about seventy, it was estimated — he chose the main scapegoats, perhaps inevitably, from among his closest collaborators, the men who had been with him for years and having pushed him up along the steep road of his ascent had been rewarded with high positions. The most tragic figure in the drama, second only to the dead deputy with his unfound body, was Cesare Rossi. Because of his familiarity with Dumini and the role of the press office in the whole affair, not proven at that time but strongly suspected, public opinion accused him of being the instigator, the one who had planned the murder. Mussolini asked for his resignation. Rossi fought for his position, protested his innocence, and yielded only after a violent quarrel with the president. On June 14, Mussolini "accepted" Rossi's resignation in a three-line letter in which he did not even thank his former friend for his far-from-negligible services. Afraid for his life, Rossi went into hiding from which he wrote threatening letters to the president: "Your cynicism, of which you have already given appalling proofs, is now aggravated by your complete loss of self-control at this moment when you should master a situation which is entirely of your own making. . . ." Rossi prepared a memorandum of incriminating revelations, which was kept secret for a few months, and whose publication was to spark a Fascist reaction.

A warrant was issued for Rossi's arrest, and on June 23 he gave himself up to the police. After many months in jail, he was released while awaiting trial, evaded police surveillance, and escaped to France. But this was not to be the end of his calvary. About three years later, he was to be lured near the Swiss-Italian border, seized by Italian Fascists, taken across the Swiss waters of Lake Lugano, and sentenced to thirty years in jail for his anti-Fascist activities abroad. Ironically, after the fall of fascism he was to be arrested and jailed again, this time for his role in the Fascist regime and the part he was suspected to have taken in the Matteotti affair. Eventually the judges at the 1947 trial were to acquit him, more out of pity for a man grown old and broken in spirit than because any piece of evidence decisively cleared him. They felt that he had expiated his crimes with his sufferings.

On June 14, besides Rossi's resignation, Mussolini accepted that of the Undersecretary of the Interior, Aldo Finzi. A flyer with D'Annunzio in World War I, a Fascist of the first hour, and a Fascist deputy in the chamber since 1921, Finzi had been, like Rossi, one of Mussolini's watchdogs in Milan during the March on Rome and had acted as Mussolini's envoy in certain political negotiations. Finzi was never accused of a direct connection with Matteotti's murder, but Mussolini insisted that Finzi show his loyalty and resign in the hope of appeasing public opinion (which had accused Finzi of improper financial dealings) and of diverting attention from himself, an aim that seems to have been his topmost concern in those days.

After Rossi and Finzi it was De Bono's turn to tender a forced resignation, and his case is indicative of the low moral standards Mussolini sought in his collaborators. Immediately after Matteotti's murder, public opinion accused De Bono of having favored the murder in various ways — in particular, by giving Dumini a passport which the leader of the *Cheka* might have used to leave Italy had the event gone according to plan. It is not surprising, therefore, that De Bono should have given up his post as head of the police. In Mussolini's mind, however, the slur that these accusations cast on the general's moral figure must have seemed irrelevant to the leader of a military body; he did not ask De Bono to resign his post as head of the Fascist militia until the following fall, when a journalist was publicly to accuse the general of complicity in Matteotti's murder. In June, 1926, both a pro-Fascist senate commission and a high court acquitted De Bono for lack of evidence. He was then named governor of Tripolitania and left for Africa, kicked upstairs to be sure, still in a prominent and trusted position. Later, in the first months of the Ethiopian war, Mussolini again gave him a leading role.

On the day De Bono resigned as head of the police, Mussolini himself surrendered the Ministry of Interior to Luigi Federzoni, then Minister of Colonies, a founder, with Corradini, of the Nationalist Party in 1910 and a most devoted and loyal subject of the House of Savoy. Although the press explained Mussolini's move as one that would allow him more time for his other duties, including those as Minister of Foreign Affairs, it was often repeated that in this instance the king had imposed his will on his prime minister.

Two weeks after Matteotti's disappearance Mussolini received an overwhelming vote of confidence in the senate. He promised return to political normality and "pacification" within the frame of the Italian constitution. He took this opportunity to remind the senate that Fascist organizations, "in all corners of Italy," were strong. All indications are that the senate's vote of confidence was motivated by that much-too-widespread mover, the fear of a shift to the left. Had Mussolini fallen at that time, the next government would have been dominated by the Socialists; and the senate, like most of the middle class, decidedly disliked this prospect. (According to at least one report, in a moment of deep dejection Mussolini himself prepared a letter of resignation addressed to the king in which he suggested Turati as his successor. If ever written, the letter was not delivered.)

The vote of confidence gave Mussolini grounds for reasserting his will to last, but it did not change public opinion. There was, in his own words, "a resumption in great style of antifascism at home and abroad." In fact, antifascism abroad was spotty and limited to Italian exiles. The foreign press was rather sympathetic. When Ramsay MacDonald, then the British prime minister, approved a condemnatory resolution against Mussolini's government, the antigovernment press criticized him and charged him, according to the *New York Times*, with "adopting an amazingly offensive attitude." The *New York Times* felt the need to declare: ". . . nobody questions Mussolini's integrity and honesty, and his determination and ability. . . ." According to this usually well-informed paper, there was "not a breath of suspicion against Mussolini himself."

But at home the wave of antifascism was very strong, and the campaign of the opposition kept passions alive. Yet, the opposition missed its chance to overthrow Mussolini, to win a full victory, and change the course of Western history.

Several times in this period Mussolini himself analyzed the tactics of the opposition. By staying away from the Chamber of Deputies, the opposition leaders prevented the functioning of a branch of government established by the Italian constitution, and thus offered the king a pretext for constitutional action against the Fascist government. With their unrelenting, persistent campaign in the press, they kept public opinion aroused and hoped to tire Mussolini, place fascism in an untenable position, disrupt the parliamentary majority, and attract into the sphere of the opposition entire groups that had been solidly pro-Fascist. The opposition was later accused of timidity, yet its tactics might have brought decisive results had not a number of prominent liberals supported Mussolini and his government. The former prime ministers Giolitti, Salandra, and Orlando, and the philosopher Benedetto Croce, faced with alternatives, to draw a new government from the strongly Socialist opposition or to reinforce the existing government, chose the latter course. (They were to withdraw their support of fascism months later, when it was too late, and then their action seemed an ineffectual gesture.) Giolitti and Croce were men of great ascendancy and had many followers. Since they and the majority of senators were favorable to Mussolini, the king had no reason or justification for a constitutional action under pressure of the opposition. It is said that when a member of the opposition presented him with a document containing incriminating evidence against Mussolini, the king covered his eyes and stopped his ears, saying:

"I am blind and deaf. My eyes and ears are the chamber and the senate."

Under these circumstances, the rest of the year was marked by uncertainty, vacillation, and small victories scored in turn by Mussolini and his foes. Early in July Mussolini gave a first small turn to the screw that was to block freedom in Italy: he enacted decrees that subjected the press to political authority and gave to the prefects the right to confiscate newspapers at their discretion. The immediate effect of these decrees was a new wave of criticism both from anti-Fascists and liberal pro-Fascists. At this time Mussolini also received proofs of renewed support. The Matteotti affair had not affected the provinces as deeply as the capital, and in many zones of Italy the Fascists were still loyal and zealous. Leaders in the provinces had been watching the situation and hoping for a prompt change for the better, through use of force if necessary. After almost two months of waiting, they began to fear that Mussolini's inaction would bring on a disaster into which they would be dragged. For their own sake, they tried to "rewind" Mussolini, they called mass rallies, and they led parades that were displays of Fascist might. They dispatched groups of Blackshirts to march in the streets of Rome — once a group of 156 Fascists in military array marched straight into Mussolini's office without meeting any resistance in the deserted halls.

The duce of fascism began to regain assurance. His speeches became firmer. He produced some of those remarks which were to become the slogans of the Fascist regime: "A German philosopher said: 'Live dangerously.' I should like this to be the motto of young, passionate, Italian fascism. . . ." Commenting on Fascist "sins of vanity," on the too-numerous honorary titles distributed among Fascists, he said: "It should have been a matter of pride for us, to arrive naked at the goal."

Slowly, the opposition press lost some of its aggressiveness. This mild slackening proved to be deceptive. The storm broke out again, furiously, and the clamor of the opposition reached its peak on August 16 when a country guard discovered Matteotti's naked body in a shallow grave on wooded grounds some fifteen miles north of Rome. A wood file, never satisfactorily explained, was in the grave. It had been the guard's dog which had guided his master to the grave, but why had not the dog scented the body before? The wildest rumors spread throughout Rome. Matteotti's body had not been in that grave; it had been hidden somewhere else; it had been kept in a hospital. All manner of sinister machinations were suspected. The explanation may be simpler. The guard and his dog had been alerted by the discovery, a few days earlier, of Matteotti's suit coat, hidden in a nearby ditch. Before that discovery there had been no reason for a search in that part of the country.

At the trial Dumini was to testify that he and his accomplices had not planned to kill the deputy only "to teach him a lesson"; that Matteotti had been accidentally killed in the struggle, and the killers had then lost their heads and driven madly through the countryside until dark, when they stopped in a lonely place to bury the body. What they said may be true. If not, if the murder had been premeditated, still the facts would not have been incompatible with the mad drive, of which the police had found ample evidence in the car they had seized. One question remains. It is probable that not even the instigators of the crime knew where the body lay. After it had become evident that it was a case of murder, they had nothing to gain by not having the body "discovered" promptly. But then why did they not know, why could they not find out where the body was? One possible answer is that the murderers had not been able to describe or to find again the place they had chosen at night under the excitement and strain of their deed.

To the renewed battle of insults and vituperation Mussolini added his personal touch: a threat. As a platform from which to launch it he chose not Rome but the slopes of Monte Amiata, in Tuscany, at a safe distance from cities and possible foes. There he told a group of local miners: "The day when [the members of the opposition] pass from their irksome vociferations to concrete deeds, on that day we shall make

them the litter of our Blackshirts' camp." (Mussolini may
have meant that his opponents would be strewn before him
like the straw used underfoot in muddy army camps, but his
words are more stunning than clear. He was proud of them.
According to Ojetti he once commented: "These sentences are
my *chic* as an orator. I thought and meditated over [this
speech] for three hours before delivering it.")

Although meant as a threat, the sentence did nothing more
than arouse a certain amount of indignation. Despite the increasing tension, the political situation might well have
dragged on without reaching a climax, had the opposition not
published two more incriminating documents, a letter which
Balbo had written over a year earlier and the memorandum
that Cesare Rossi had prepared before his arrest. In a letter
addressed to the secretary of the *fasci* in Ferrara, Balbo had
ordered acts of violence and stressed: "Since I am writing from
Rome [where Mussolini was], it means that I am quite sure of
what I am telling you." (After the publication of this letter,
Balbo, who had succeeded De Bono as head of the militia, was
excused from his post, but he remained one of the most influential members of the Grand Council.)

Rossi's memorandum accused Mussolini of having established the Fascist *Cheka* and assigned to him the moral and
political responsibility for the acts of violence that had preceded the Matteotti affair. The president's moral complicity
in the murder itself was not specifically stated, a fact that was
differently interpreted. The Fascists maintained that Mussolini was innocent or Rossi would have accused him explicitly;
but their opponents contended that Rossi could not have accused Mussolini without incriminating himself and that Rossi's memorandum did not disprove Mussolini's guilt. At any
rate, the revelations were so serious that many people thought
that the king would demand Mussolini's resignation. Instead,
the publication of Rossi's memorandum precipitated a strong
reaction from Mussolini. The memorandum was published on
December 27; two days later, speaking before a meeting of
Fascist journalists, Mussolini announced an imminent resumption of Fascist initiative to gain decisive victory. On
December 31 a wave of violence accompanied several of the

Fascist rallies called in many parts of Italy; on the same day, a deputation of militia "consuls" went to see Mussolini and demanded that he take "full responsibility for the [Fascist] revolution"; many opposition papers were seized.

On January 3, 1925, before the Chamber of Deputies, Mussolini delivered a speech which marked the end of constitutional government and the beginning of dictatorship in Italy. The opening words set the tone: they linked the speech to other words which he had pronounced on November 16, 1922, when, addressing the chamber for the first time after the March on Rome, he said: "With 300,000 well-armed young men ready for anything and most mystically prepared to [obey] any order from me, I could have punished all those who have defamed fascism and tried to throw mud at it. I could have turned this deaf and gray hall into a bivouac for [our] maniples." By alluding to this threatening sentence, Mussolini conditioned his listeners' spirits and prepared their mood for the defiant question he then asked: was there a deputy who would like to take advantage of his constitutional privilege and accuse him before the high court of justice? Since the opposition deputies were still on the *Aventine*, the chamber broke into applause and shouted "We are all with you!" and "Long live Mussolini!" Mussolini had won his battle before it had begun. From this position of sudden strength he disclaimed any complicity in either Matteotti's murder or the acts of violence that had preceded it and yet assumed for himself "the political, moral, and historical responsibility for all that has happened." Mussolini continued: "If fascism has been nothing but castor oil and *manganello*, and not a superb passion of the best Italian youth, it is my fault. If fascism has become a criminal association, I am the head of this criminal association. If all violence has been the result of a certain historical, political, and moral climate, mine is the responsibility, because I created this political, historical, and moral climate through propaganda that spread from our intervention in the war to this day." And he ended: "Italy . . . wants peace, wants tranquillity, wants industrious calm. This tranquillity, this industrious calm we shall give her with love if possible, with force if necessary. Rest assured that in the next forty-eight hours the situation will be clarified. We all know that what is in my heart is not a personal whim, it is not lust for government, it is not ignoble passion; it is simply a boundless and mighty love for the *patria*."

The speech of January 3 has been called an act of force which was not met with force. The government at once mobilized the militia. Within three days many politically suspect gathering places were closed, many groups and organizations were dissolved; innumerable searches of homes and offices and numerous arrests were made; local authorities were authorized to repress antifascism; and the seizing of opposition papers became a daily event. The last liberals in the government resigned, and the *Aventine* passed an ineffectual resolution against the government. In the year that followed these hurriedly taken measures were translated into a permanent set of *Leggi fascistissime* ("*most* Fascist" laws), according to Mussolini's principle that action must come first and doctrine or legislation should be based on the results of action. Freedom of the press and freedom of assembly came to an end. Individual freedom and safety became subject to the discretion of Fascist officials.

After the speech of January 3, Mussolini was not only the president of the cabinet of ministers, first among equals, but the chief who stood high above his ministers, the dictator with full executive powers. He alone was responsible to the king; and the king, having submitted to a first violation of the constitution in 1922, no longer had the will or the strength to stand up and fight in defense of it. The constitutional parliamentary system, and democracy had fallen into a state of coma that was to last some two decades. Mussolini was well aware that the king did not like this state of affairs, and in the series of articles published in 1944 he was to comment: "While in the second half of 1924 the king had resisted the maneuvers of the *Aventine* with a certain determination — even when he had been called to play a more or less direct role — he did not seem very pleased with the action of January 3, through which, with the suppression of all parties, bases were laid for the totalitarian state."

In January, 1926, Mussolini took a further step for his own protection: he suppressed all opposition in the chamber. Until then, most *Aventine* deputies had remained firm in their secession, and only the Communists had returned to the chamber. But early in January the dowager queen, Margherita of Savoy, died. She had been a charming and intelligent woman, whom poets had sung and the entire population adored; although she had shown a marked sympathy for the Fascist movement and for Mussolini himself, she was mourned by Fascists and anti-Fascists alike. The day she was commemorated in the chamber, a group of secessionist deputies appeared at the ceremony. When Mussolini saw them he could hardly contain his wrath, and on the grounds that there was "a moral question to be liquidated" he reconvened the chamber for the next day. He then dictated his conditions for the return of the *Aventine* deputies: they must recognize the Fascist revolution, repudiate the *Aventine* campaign, and sever communications with anti-Fascists abroad. Only three deputies accepted these drastic conditions, but despite their act of submission they were later forced out of office.

At the end of October, 1926, the screw rapidly tightening on the Italian people received another turn. The occasion was an attempt on Mussolini's life, the fourth since November 4, 1925. In the first attempt, according to plan, Mussolini was to be killed as he spoke from the balcony of Palazzo Chigi, the Ministry of Foreign Affairs, by Tito Zaniboni, a former Socialist deputy, who had set up a high-powered gun in a hotel room across the street. But the police, warned in advance, arrested Zaniboni minutes before Mussolini appeared.

In the second attempt, Violet Gibson, a sixty-two-year-old Irishwoman later described as "mentally unstable," wounded Mussolini in the nose with a pistol shot as he stepped out of a palace on the Campidoglio where, by coincidence, he had just opened an international meeting of surgeons. (Taken back into the palace for the surgeons' care, he reappeared shortly afterward and was photographed in a velvet-collared frock coat and bowler hat, with binoculars in hand and a monstrous piece of adhesive tape on his nose.) A few days later he commented: "Pistol shots pass; Mussolini stays on." On this occasion he received a decoration created *ad hoc* for "a wound of the Fascist revolution."

In a third attempt, a young anarchist, Gino Lucetti, threw a bomb at the car in which the chief of government was riding; the bomb bounced back and exploded after the car had passed.

The fourth attempt took place in Bologna and is one of several Fascist mysteries that have never found satisfactory explanation. In Bologna, on October 31, the duce spent a day which may be considered representative of his official activities in that period. He was celebrating the March on Rome four days' late, having been busily celebrating in other places. In the morning, on a handsome horse, in the gala uniform of the highest rank of the militia, bespattered with decorations and wearing a huge white panache on top of his black, fezlike cap, he inaugurated the new city stadium and inspected units of the militia and armed forces that had convened in a spectacular display of Fascist strength. In the afternoon, no longer on horseback but still in the splendor of his uniform and decorations, he opened a scientific meeting. ("I don't believe," he said among other things, "that science will ever be able to succeed in explaining the why of phenomena, and there will always remain a zone of mystery, a closed wall before which the human spirit must bend its knees and write . . . one word only: God." This is how current newspapers reported his speech. In an edited and official version of his speech the human spirit lost its bending knees but retained its writing hand.) He left the meeting in an open car, which proceeded toward the railroad station under a rain of flowers thrown from many windows, while on both sides of his path an acclaiming crowd insistently and frenetically shouted "*Alalà*."

Suddenly a pistol shot cut the air above the moving car. Straight in his seat, Mussolini brought his hand to his head first, then to his neck. He was not wounded. As the car stopped for a brief moment he said loudly: "They did not get me!" and remained calm and smiling — according to the chronicle of that day — as the car started up again. Smiling, unaware that behind him a savage scene was enacted. . . . Zealous Fascist officials grabbed a fifteen-year-old boy, Anteo Zamboni, and the crowd lynched him. The body bore fourteen knife wounds, a bullet hole, and traces of strangulation when later examined. The dead boy was clothed in a dark brown suit and a Fascist black shirt, but when the duce himself, questioned by the police, made his deposition he said that he had clearly seen "a young man of average height in light-colored clothes and a soft hat." He was on the side of the car opposite that on which the boy had stood. Ensuing speculations ranged from the hypothesis that there had actually been two men, both with pistol in hand and both ready to shoot at Mussolini at exactly the same time, to the suspicion that the Fascists themselves had staged the attempt on Mussolini's life as a pretext for passing a set of restrictive laws that had been drafted some time earlier.

The reason for this suspicion was the promptness with which the government presented, and Parliament passed almost without debate, a number of laws and regulations "for the defense of the state." They included the suppression of all antigovernment papers and parties; the establishment of the *confino*, or compulsory residence, for political offenders, and of a political court of justice similar to a wartime military court, with military judges and without right of appeal; the introduction of capital punishment for civilians; and the organization of a secret branch of the police. Through their acts and the fear they aroused, the *tribunale speciale* (the new court of justice) and the secret police, later known as OVRA, were to play important roles in Italian life.

Briefly reviewing these events in the series of articles he wrote in 1944, Mussolini commented: "This exacerbation of the policies of the *regime* in the totalitarian direction did not go unobserved in [royal] court circles. From that moment the people began to talk of a monarchy that was prisoner of the party and to pity the king, relegated from then on to a secondary plane, by comparison with the duce." If the king was unhappy, Mussolini had reason to be pleased. No longer did he need to worry: he was going to last.

The measures and laws for the safety of the state brought the long-sought-for social peace to Italy. The opposition was stifled, rendered utterly impotent, and for lack of active foes fascism gave up its open aggressiveness, although still fighting occasional battles underground. Law and order appeared restored, and the nation did not seem to care that they were not the traditional law and order of constitutional Italy. In the mind of the young people of Italy the duce resumed the prominent position that he had held before the Matteotti affair, and again he was the idol of the crowds, the man to whom small children addressed their prayers and slightly older children presented their guns, while their parents smiled proudly and indulgently.

15

THE CATHOLIC

"... whether at the head of the Church there
is the Jesuit or the modernist, we always see
in it the typical organization for the exploitation of consciences, the constant ally
of the boss, the nucleus of all reactionary
forces."

MUSSOLINI, August, 1914

T HE month of February, 1929, was one of the coldest remembered in Europe. Even in Rome, where the climate is
mild and temperatures seldom drop below the freezing point,
icy winds from the north brought spells of inclement weather;
it snowed, an unusual event, and, even more unusual, the snow
on the ground did not melt at once; mains froze; pipes burst;
and the Romans did not always keep warm in their homes. But
February 11 was a relatively mild day. In the morning the
sky was overcast, and a light, thin rain, little more than a mist,
fell over the Eternal City and covered it with a damp gray
coat.

At about 11:30 that morning Mussolini, arriving in the
wide Piazza San Giovanni in a black car, noticed that the rain
had not deterred a large crowd from gathering around the
low, square bulk of the Lateran Palace. The usual cordon of
carabinieri, present whenever he went on official missions,
divided the crowd in two wings and left a wide passage for the
cars. The size of the crowd must have surprised him, since
the reason for his visit to the Lateran Palace had been kept
strictly secret. It seemed probable that the many priests and
other clergymen, and the large groups of *seminaristi* whom he

could tell at a glance by their black frocks and red sashes, had been informed by the church hierarchies about his business at the palace. The rest of the crowd had gathered there because the presence of *carabinieri* and photographers had attracted the attention of the curious and idle, and word had spread that some important event was in the making.

That day the duce neglected the opportunity to seek communion with the crowd, to be uplifted by his own words to them, or to listen to their exalting ovations. His car drove through the square, entered the open portal of the Lateran Palace, and stopped at the arcade in the courtyard. As he stepped out, better groomed than usual in a morning coat and top hat, and began climbing the wide stairway, his mind must have been filled with the importance of his mission. The stairs were inclosed between walls covered with worn epitaphs in Greek and Latin on stone slabs taken from cemeteries, but he paid no attention to them. In a few minutes he was going to see the culmination of over two years of patient effort, the achievement of a feat which many statesmen in the past had unsuccessfully attempted, the settling of differences that had lasted sixty years: in short, the solution of the "Roman Question."

As he reached the second floor, Mussolini entered the halls of the Missionary Museum where with greater lavishness than taste a wealth of objects of ethnical interest from missions all over the world was crowded in showcases and upon tables. All this — the precious ivory and gold, the stones and jade, the Chinese vases and Indian statues, the marbles, the ancient bronzes, and the hand-woven cloth — was the property of the church. And so were the grounds on which the Lateran Palace and the Church of San Giovanni were built; sixteen centuries earlier, the Catholic convert, Emperor Constantine, had donated this land to the African-born Pope Melchiades. But what were these belongings in comparison with the lands the church had lost to Italy in the years of the *Risorgimento*? During the ten centuries before the *Risorgimento* the church had been not only a spiritual but also a temporal power, and the popes had ruled over a good portion of Italy. But then, as the ideals of the *Risorgimento*, liberalism, freedom, and the right of peoples to their independence, conceived by the exiled Giuseppe Mazzini, spread to the shapers of Italian unity, as small Piedmont took it upon itself to reunite Italy under the House of Savoy, the temporal power of the church was threatened. And since that time the great dilemma known as the Roman Question had been present in the minds of Catholic and liberals alike: for the fulfilment of the ideals of the *Risorgimento* and the unification of Italy it was essential that the popes renounce their sovereignty over the papal territories, especially over Rome, which had always been the beacon of Italian civilization and had become the only city that the patriots could regard as the capital of the nation they were dreaming of. But the church had long taken the stand that its temporal power was necessary for the preservation of the popes' freedom and independence, and particularly necessary to the popes was Rome, which for so many centuries had been both the spiritual capital of the Catholic world and the political capital of the popes' civil principate. How was it possible to reconcile these opposite needs?

Early discussions and negotiations between Piedmont and the Vatican had led nowhere, and after 1859, one by one, the papal territories, Romagna, Marche, and Umbria, passed from Pius IX to Victor Emmanuel II of Piedmont and by plebiscite were annexed to the new kingdom of Italy. Cavour, the great Piedmontese statesman who was the political architect of Italian unity, made another attempt to settle the Roman Question in 1861, but failed. Finally, in 1870, Rome fell to the Italian armies, and Italy had the capital for which her sons had fought and died.

If, in crossing the halls of the Missionary Museum, Mussolini was preparing in mind for the ceremony ahead and thinking back to these events, he could not but feel the enormous pride in the return of Rome to the Italians that most Italians shared, both those of 1870 and those of 1929. His own dream of reliving the old Roman glories was a measure of what Rome meant to the Italians, of how indissoluble the ideas of Rome and Italy were in their minds. He certainly had little sympathy with the dismal view taken in 1870 by Pope Pius IX, who, considering himself to be dispossessed and "usurped" (with Victor Emmanuel the usurper), had refused to recognize the very existence of Italy and to exchange diplomats with the royal court. Thereafter he called himself a "prisoner" in the Vatican and did not set foot out of it. The Italian government had passed a law for the protection of the pope's person and interests, which became known as the law of the guarantees. One of its terms was the provision of a financial indemnity for the lost territories. As all Italian govments accepted it, and Pius IX and his successors stubbornly closed their eyes to its very existence, the law of the guarantees remained a one-sided treaty. The yearly payments of the Italian government to the Vatican accumulated in the Bank of Italy, and the Roman Question found no solution.

Not until February 11, 1929. On that day the dissension that had crystallized in 1870 was to be solved in a solemn ceremony, which fittingly was to take place in the *Sala dei Papi* of the Lateran Palace. It was a vast hall with a pink marble floor and gilded ceiling, with a number of showcases as crowded and no more attractive than those in the other halls. As Mussolini entered, he met his host, His Eminence the Most Reverend Cardinal Pietro Gasparri, secretary of state to His Holiness Pope Pius XI. An inner satisfaction lit the face of the short, stocky cardinal; heightened by the habitual benevolence that marked the prelate's relations with his fold, it seemed an expression of warm friendliness. The same satisfaction and pleasure were reflected in Mussolini's coarser features and softened to a degree his innate stiffness and assertiveness. At forty-five, after years of sedentary tasks, Mussolini had lost some of his statuesque looks. His face had grown heavier, the hairline was fast receding, and the weight of his chin spoiled the famous square jaw. The muscles of which he was so proud, had begun to soften. As he bowed a little to shake hands with Cardinal Gasparri, his slightly rounded shoulders strained his formal coat. All the same, he radiated power and virility and had an imposing appearance despite his average height. His host, at seventy-seven, was plump and vigorous. The handshake between His Eminence the Cardinal and His Excellency the Prime Minister was a firm and prolonged clasp of two strong hands.

The old cardinal had been in the palace three-quarters of an hour, for if time is precious to a dictator, who must constantly guard himself against the tricks of men and fortune, three-quarters of an hour is nothing to those who think in terms of eternity, who belong to an institution issuing from an everlasting God rather than a changing fate. The ceremony did not begin until twelve noon. Then, the men in the hall, church dignitaries and members of the Italian government, took their places on one side of a long table — the cardinal in the center and Mussolini at his left — and the presentation of credentials began. Cardinal Gasparri was so moved that he could not finish reading his accrediting letter and had to pass it to the secretary of the Sacred Congregation for Extraordinary Ecclesiastical Affairs, who read on in a steadier voice.

As soon as the credentials were approved, the cardinal and the prime minister began signing documents as representatives of the Holy See and the Italian monarchy. They signed a political treaty, a financial agreement, and a concordat. Thus the pope acquired sovereign powers over the minuscule Vatican state, which had an area of just over one hundred acres and comprised little more than the Vatican, the Basilica of St. Peter, and the monumental square in front of it; diplomatic relations between the newly created state and the kingdom of Italy were established; the Roman Catholic church was compensated for the loss of territories; and the status and practice of the Catholic religion in Italy were regulated. Cardinal Gasparri closed the ceremony by presenting a gift to Mussolini, the gold pen used to sign the documents.

When the crowd learned that the Lateran treaties were concluded, a wave of enthusiasm swept the square and loud cheering resounded outside the palace.

Although it had transpired that both the Italian government and the Roman Catholic church were seeking a solution of the Roman Question, the progress of the negotiations, the place where the consultations were held, and the names of the persons involved had been kept strictly secret. The opinions of the Italians were divided, and while some thought that the dissension was too deep to be composed, others had been conditioned by Fascist propaganda and believed that nothing was impossible to the duce — not even a solution of the Roman Question; but nobody had expected it so soon. Four days before signing the Lateran treaties, Cardinal Gasparri announced to a much bewildered body of foreign diplomats accredited to the Vatican that the Roman Question would be settled, but he gave no details and made no comments. Foreign newspapers speculated on the possible terms of the agreement, but inside Italy the Fascists controlled the press so efficiently that the secret did not leak out. On February 11, the news of the reconciliation between church and state came as a great surprise.

From Piazza San Giovanni the wave of enthusiasm spread throughout the Eternal City and extended to the rest of the world. Catholics everywhere hailed the reconciliation as one of the most significant events in the modern history of the church, and they looked upon Mussolini, planner and shaper, with sincere admiration. Among non-Catholics also the reactions were most favorable, and the words "Mussolini Solves the Roman Question" appeared in huge type, in many languages, on the front pages of the newspapers of the world; even many of Mussolini's enemies conceded that he had had a remarkable success. There seems to be little doubt that of all the duce's actions and achievements this was the one that was received with the widest approval. It marked the high point of his career.

Gaetano Salvemini, in his book *Mussolini diplomatico*, says that the reconciliation was Mussolini's greatest publicity stunt and points out that, rather than a molder of events, Mussolini was an opportunist taking advantage of very favorable circumstances. Despite the popes' firm and intransigent stand, things were not as bad as they seemed; the passage of time had shown that the dissension between church and state was more formal than real; the Holy See was much better off without the burden of a territory that the popes had administered poorly, driving the liberal section of its population to rebellion (and sowing the seeds of that stubborn anticlericalism which had been so prominent in Mussolini's father); for years the religious and earthly authorities in Italy had been living side by side — though ignoring each other — and had thrived; undisturbed, the popes had been able to exert their spiritual leadership with the same old splendor and with undiminished prestige, while the kingdom of Italy flourished, emerged much strengthened from its infancy, and took its place in the society of great European nations. Thus, time and the Italians' common sense achieved a *modus vivendi*; the reconciliation between church and state had been in process for years, though not officially recognized. At this historical moment Mussolini let the world believe that he had achieved a most arduous feat, which in fact was no feat at all.

To a certain extent, this view is valid. With his fine flair for publicity, the ex-journalist could well plan and time the spreading of an unexpected piece of news in order to obtain the greatest possible effect. He could foresee the front-page headlines with his name in inch-tall letters, the paper boys shouting the news in many languages, and the sensation that would ensue; he could easily anticipate the sweet taste of suddenly enhanced fame, the world-wide acclaim, the glory that the artfully advertised achievement would bring to him. Yet to say that the reconciliation was nothing more than a publicity stunt does not explain why Mussolini succeeded where statesmen before him had failed. An attempt to analyze the elements of this success brings forth a question: had the once blasphemous son of the atheist smith become a true believer, the sincere supporter of the Catholic church? Two days after the signing of the Lateran treaties, Pope Pius XI commented: "We have also been favored. A man was needed like the one that Providence has placed in Our path. . . ." And from various sides many had echoed: ". . . the man of Providence . . ." Was the duce of fascism really a man of Providence? And if so, what special attributes that might serve the Catholic cause had Providence detected in him?

In his profession of atheism and his antireligious stand, the young man Mussolini had gone far beyond the demands of his Socialist belief. Marx is said to have once remarked that religion is the opium of people, and accordingly most European Socialists abstained from religious practice, but, as Vandervelde said in his Lausanne lecture at the time of young Mussolini's unfortunate debate with him, to many Socialists religion remains "a private affair, an affair of conscience." In denouncing this point of view, Mussolini advanced the arrogant and contemptuous ideas elaborated in his booklet "Man and Divinity." At that time he was little more than twenty years old, and one may think that, as it often happens to the very young, he had overshot his target and found himself in a position from which he was either too shy or too proud to withdraw. But his gross attacks on religion in general and on the Roman Catholic church in particular outlasted his early youth. As a teacher of French in Oneglia, writing in the local Socialist paper under the pen name "True Heretic," he had indulged in no less foul and shocking language than he had used in Switzerland: when the Catholics asked for religious instruction in public schools, invoking the principle of liberty, he denounced this "black liberty" and accused the priests, whom he called "black germs as fatal to mankind as the germs of tuberculosis," of trying "to poison the people's children with Christian teaching." Of Holy Communion, which to him was "a religious conscription," he had written: ". . . at the time when the good Jesus, somewhat drowsy after the Lenten rest, is about to reawaken . . . the priests conscript all children of religious families. . . ." The child's soul is then "purified by the swallowing of a farinaceous host." Having "eaten Christ" man cannot sin, and if he does, this means that Christ "has been evacuated. . . ."

Later, when he was editor of *Lotta di Classe*, he pursued his one-sided attack; using a Sorelian metaphor, he called the priests "professional liars" and asserted that "calumny is still the sovereign weapon of priests," that "Christ is dead and his teachings moribund," that "the Gospels and the so-called Christian morality are two cadavers"; and he repeated an assertion in "Man and Divinity," that the man of religion shows "atrophy of the reasoning powers" and the "religious debasement pushes man back toward animality."

Even after he abandoned socialism, Mussolini professed strongly antireligious feelings. The first program of the *fasci*, published shortly after the founding of the movement in 1919, called for the confiscation of all ecclesiastical property, and as late as January, 1920, Mussolini proclaimed: "Today two religions are competing for the domination of the soul and the world: the black and the red. Today encyclicals are sent off from two Vaticans, from the one in Rome and from the one in Moscow. We are the heretics of both religions." (Not long before he had said: "We detest from the depth of our souls all Christianity, from Jesus' to Marx's.")

But then he had one of his sudden changes of mind, the origin of which is hard to trace. It may have been due to a flash of intuition — to his intuition and flair he always attached great importance — or it may have been the result of a casual remark that he had heard or read and made his own; or perhaps the slumbering mysticism of his childhood, when he was under the influence of his religious mother, awoke abruptly in the mature man. He began talking in favor of the church, and it is likely that from the very inception of this new attitude, in his most ambitious moments he nursed the unuttered hope, undoubtedly vague at first, of earning for himself the glory due to the Italian who would settle the Roman Question. In May, 1920, he told a startled national Fascist congress that the Vatican represented "four hundred millions of men scattered the world over," and that in intelligent politics one ought to use "this colossal force" for one's own ends rather than antagonize it. From then on he consistently stressed the spiritual importance of the church in Italy and that Catholicism was the only universal living ideal of ancient Rome. In his maiden speech in the Chamber of Deputies he had the courage to mention the Roman Question — which for decades no one had dared to mention in Parliament — and to profess himself in favor of its solution. In his maiden speech as prime minister, he again broke the tradition of the Chamber of Deputies by invoking God and asking His help.

Between his first speech as a deputy and his first as chief of state, an event of significance to the Catholic world took place, the death of Pope Benedict XV, in January, 1922; and the unusual circumstances that surrounded it may have affected Mussolini's later actions. For the first time since 1870 and the capture of Rome, the Italian government officially acknowledged the pope's death and ordered flags to half-mast, in token of mourning. To the pontifical throne ascended the archbishop of Milan, Achille, Cardinal Ratti, who became Pius XI, and for the first time since 1870 the newly elected pope appeared on the outer loggia of St. Peter's to bless the Romans gathered in the square, thus resuming an ancient tradition that all "prisoner popes" had wilfully disregarded. It seemed as if the Holy See and the Italian monarchy were exchanging signals and telling each other that dissension was obsolete and their stubborn stand was absurd.

Mussolini, duce of fascism, but not yet in power, viewed the events in the light of his extraordinary intuition of men and circumstances and could not but conclude that the times were ripe for a reconciliation. It was evident that the new pope wished it. In the dry square face of Pius XI, in the small twinkling eyes and deeply set features, in the physical vigor of the old pope whose favorite sport had been climbing the Alps, Mussolini could detect a purposefulness and a determination that gave a special weight to his actions. If the pope had come out into the loggia to bless the crowd, he had not done so without strong motivation, and with his presence he seemed to say: "I am here to wipe out past offenses and to compose differences. I am offering a helping hand to the Italian statesman who is willing to go along with me." Mussolini was willing, and when a few months later he became prime minister he let the Vatican know that his intentions toward it were friendly indeed.

His pro-Vatican policy was the result of a well-thought-out strategy, and there are no sure indications that it involved his conscience. It is significant that only in one instance, on a visit to Switzerland, did he dare to say: "My spirit is profoundly religious." He well knew that to Italian ears these words would not ring true. After the March on Rome, he had his children hurriedly and quietly baptized, and three years later he and Rachele, who had been married in civil rites, arranged for a religious ceremony, so that no formal flaw was left in his family's religious status. But never in his life did he show any genuine signs that the hand of God had touched him;

never did his actions or words reveal a basic change of attitude toward moral and spiritual values. He called fascism "a great religious phenomenon," but fascism had in common with religion only the mystic appeal to the masses that defies rational analysis, the rituals that satisfy fantasy — so sensitive and demanding in Latin people — and bring uplifting experiences into an otherwise drab existence. If fascism was a religion, it was one of violence and individualism, which stressed the passing moment over eternity, the personal act of valor over the strife of the spirit, ambition and pride over humility and resignation; a religion which to the masses preached the surrender of the individual will not to God in Heaven but to the omniscient and all-powerful on earth.

Mussolini made no effort to appear a devout Catholic. He did not go to church and did not observe the church's holy days; in his many talks and articles he gave no hint that he had scruples or qualms, that his conscience was troubled by those problems and uncertainties, those occasional agonies of indecision, that mark the conscience of religious men. Indeed, he seldom gave indication of having a conscience. And yet, with his great ability as an actor, had he wanted to impersonate the Catholic he could have succeeded easily. But as Arturo Carlo Jemolo, a Catholic writer and an independent thinker, remarks in his book *Chiesa e Stato negli ultimi cento anni* (*Church and State in the Last Hundred Years*): "The image of the devout son, of the penitent, of the son in prayer, was not an image of himself that he could accept; his intuition told him also that it was not an image of himself that he could show to his faithful: the most sincere and trustworthy [were] barbarian warriors."

Not until three years after the reconciliation was Mussolini to pay his first and last official visit to His Holiness, and since the pope grants audiences but does not solicit them, the late date of the visit seems to indicate procrastination, perhaps reluctance, on the duce's part. When at last he did pay his visit, he was careful to let it be known that he had been excused from the custom of kissing the pope's hand (did he recall, and dread, the daily kissing of the director's bony hand at the Salesian school?); and when at the end of the visit to the pope he could not shun the ceremonial prayer at St. Peter's tomb, he entered the pew and knelt only after making sure that all photographers had been sent away; as Jemolo remarks, photographs of Mussolini kneeling in prayer were inconceivable.

If, then, Providence had placed the man Mussolini in the pope's path, it was not because the duce's heart had been touched and he had embraced the true faith. There were other reasons. In the particular political and diplomatic climate of that time, a Mussolini at the head of Italy could not but be viewed with a certain favor by the church, as represented by its pope. Before becoming Pius XI, Achille Ratti had been papal nuncio to the new republic of Poland, and during the Bolshevist siege of Warsaw had courageously and untiringly aided the defenders. He had seen with his own eyes what the Bolshevists had done. Moreover, he was a most devoted son of Italy and remained so after his ascent to St. Peter's throne. To him an Italy turned Bolshevist would have been the greatest calamity that could afflict his church and his country, a calamity that Mussolini, who had indulged in a pose as the protector of Christianity, claimed he and his Fascists had staved off. Upon his return to Italy, Achille Ratti, then archbishop of Milan, allowed the Fascists to enter the cathedral in their warrior-like garb, with their flags and standards, and attend the celebration of the anniversary of the Italian victory on November 4, 1921.

Pius XI dreaded not only bolshevism but socialism for its stand against religion, and, in line with the millenary tradition of the Roman Catholic church, he was against most forms of liberalism. So was Mussolini. The pope appreciated this trait in the duce and said so explicitly at the time he linked him with Providence. The full sentence, from which only a few words have been quoted, reads: "A man was needed like the one that Providence has placed in Our path; a man who should not share the preoccupations of the liberal school, to whose members all those laws, all those ordinances, or rather disordinances, We say, were so many fetishes, and as fetishes were held the more inviolable and venerable, the uglier they were and the more deformed." Mussolini, six years earlier, had applied the term "fetishes" to the ideals of freedom and democracy, to the liberalism that had sprung from the French Revolution and which the pope deprecated. Mussolini had then declared that he had no fetishes, that he had no regard for the great democratic principles. An authoritarian like Mussolini, whose achievements at that time still appeared constructive to many, had greater appeal than a liberal to the highest authority of the church.

In Mussolini the pope must have seen another reason to hope for the settlement of the Roman Question. As Mussolini himself was to reveal a few months after signing the Lateran treaties, the last previous negotiations between the Holy See and the Italian government had been opened in 1919 under Orlando's premiership. Shortly afterwards Orlando's government had fallen over the peace settlement of Versailles, and the negotiations with the church had been interrupted. The solution of a question that had remained unsolved for sixty years required time and sustained efforts, but in the years before the ascent to power of fascism all cabinets had appeared unstable, offering no grounds for renewed negotiations. In 1926, when the first views upon the Roman Question were exchanged between the Vatican and Mussolini's government, the duce was already a full dictator, well-intrenched in his position; it was evident that he intended to last. He gave that sense of stability and authority without which the negotiations would have led nowhere. Besides, he had eliminated from the chamber many of the deputies who might have opposed the ratification of an agreement with the church and, in particular, he had dissolved the Socialist Party.

Both the pope and the duce took a personal interest and an active part in the negotiations. The Vatican lawyer Francesco Pacelli, brother of the future Pius XII, acted for the church and was received 129 times in private audience by the pontiff for discussions of specific points in the agreements. Domenico Barone, councilor of state, who had held high positions in pre-Fascist governments, was the negotiator for the Italian side and reported frequently to Mussolini. Early in January, 1929, after a brief illness, the old councilor died. Mussolini, who did not trust anyone to step into the negotiations at such a late stage, resolved to pursue them himself. For over a month Pacelli paid frequent visits to the duce at his private residence. "Our talks," Pacelli is said to have later recalled, "began at 11 P.M. and often lasted until 1:00 in the morning. I used to look with infinite admiration upon the man who sat before me, and to whom neither day nor night brought rest, but only continuous passionate work, at the service of his nation."

Many drafts of the treaties were drawn, many corrections made. And thus the reconciliation came to be.

¶

That Salvemini was right at least in part in calling the reconciliation Mussolini's greatest publicity stunt is proved by its timing. The duce engineered his show in such a way that between the signing of the Lateran treaties in February and their ratification in May there were "popular elections" at the end of March. Undoubtedly he thought that the enthusiasm over the reconciliation would help the "plebiscite," or rather it would help to explain the almost unanimous consent that he anticipated.

The Chamber of Deputies that he had dissolved at the end of 1928 was the last elected in Fascist times by different and competing parties: in the March elections, according to a new law, the voters were presented with a single list of four hundred candidates chosen by the Grand Council from lists previously suggested by authorized organizations, mostly confederations of workers and employers. Thus the new law reduced the elections to voting for or against an official ballot prepared by the government itself. Under the circumstances the mere thought of an electoral defeat was ludicrous. (In the chamber the new law passed with 216 votes in favor and only 15 against, "in perfect Fascist style, without debate, with absolute discipline," as the official bulletin of the Fascist Party commented.) All organized opposition had been swept away, and in the Fascist police state any attempt to organize an opposition was doomed to fail; castor oil and *manganelli* were still available to the Blackshirts and occasionally used.

The memory of the 1924 elections was still vivid, especially in anti-Fascist minds, and Mussolini himself had kept it alive by often repeating that he would get what he wanted by force if he could not have it by consent. No one could hope that if the voters at the booths met with coercion and other irregularities, a Matteotti would rise in the chamber to challenge the validity of the elections. To the many anti-Fascists who kept police and jails busy, it must have seemed pointless to vote at all.

As for the duce, he had no doubt that he would obtain a great success, and in the days preceding the elections he more than once spoke of them as if they had already taken place and he knew their outcome, with an assurance that proved in advance the futility of any protest. "The new electoral law . . . *has functioned* excellently," he said. "The new chamber *is* rising. . . . All forces *have been* represented. . . . We vote for an idea, *for a regime*, not for men. . . . The regime *will be* more totalitarian tomorrow than today." (The italics, of course, are not Mussolini's.) He also called the candidates "deputies," either inadvertently or purposefully.

The elections did not belie Mussolini's words. According to official figures, over 89 per cent of the voters went to the polls; they cast over 8,000,000 votes in favor and only 136,000 against the regime. But the figures seem odd. That almost 90 per cent of the voters had actually turned up on election day is highly unlikely. The "no" votes were too few to seem valid in the light of previous arrests, of actions of the special tribunal, and other repressive measures that showed the existence of an appreciable, if disorganized, opposition; they seemed too many under the prevailing circumstances; for in many places ballots were opened, and an eye was kept on each voter (on leaving the polling place the dissenting voter may have heard the question "Are you sure you haven't made a mistake?"). It is reported that after the elections some Fascists said laughingly that at the last moment they had been ordered to vote "no" to spare the elections a unanimity that might have had too strong a totalitarian flavor.

It would be a distortion of the truth to deny that in 1929 the Fascist regime was popular in Italy; possibly the majority of the people would have voted for Mussolini even if free to vote against him. But the probable tampering with the ballots marks the establishment of a practice which was to be the doom of Fascist Italy: the juggling of data in order to please and to fulfil "expectations in high places."* And the expectations were to grow steadily, after the easy success of the plebiscite. The success was easy, for it was obtained with little actual compulsion and hardly noticeable pressures, with a thorough organization, a shrewd system of propaganda, the abolishing of a freedom that was not yet missed, the lulling of the people with dreams of grandeur. The electoral success was in fact a part of Mussolini's publicity stunt.

¶

In this atmosphere of consent and applause, in a chamber elected by this plebiscite, the Lateran treaties came up for debate in the second week of May. The debate was to last only two days, because, as Jemolo remarks, in times of Fascist efficiency everything had to proceed with the rhythm of a triumphal march. Then Mussolini was to illustrate his point of view. After the chamber voted, the bill was to go to the senate. The Fascist chamber was more prepared to acclaim than to debate, and it was likely that, according to already established practice, the duce had determined in advance the length and terms of all discussions, the points to be stressed and those to be slurred over. The most important thing was to show that Mussolini had succeeded where the great Cavour had failed and to impart solemnity to the ratification, which otherwise might have appeared perfunctory. Mussolini could have limited his speech to a few sonorous words and would have received the desired acclamation. Instead, he chose to give an address that lasted almost three

* At a time when revelation of the juggling of data was still a shock to most Italians, the author heard a physicist tell of the following incident. The physicist had gone to see a chemist friend in a laboratory at the University of Rome and asked him what he was working on. "I am determining the content of manganese in the rocks around Rome." "What? Do you mean to say that extracting manganese from these ores is an economically feasible process?" asked the physicist. "It is so wished in high places," the chemist answered noncommittally and went on with his work.

hours and fills forty-seven pages in his collected works; he also chose to use words and expressions that the pope was to call "harsh, crude, drastic" and "heretical or worse than heretical on the very essence of Christianity and Catholicism."

The fact is that, along with the wide applause for the reconciliation, there had been some criticism, and not solely in foreign countries. The most anticlerical of those in the inner circle of Fascists were asking whether the state had not made too great concessions to the church. The pope himself had given validity to their concern. In the speech in which he had called Mussolini "the man that Providence had placed in Our path," Pius XI had also said that the concordat, if not the best possible, was certainly one of the best, and thus he let it be known whom he considered the winner in religious matters. If to Mussolini an image of himself kneeling in prayer was inconceivable, also unthinkable was an image of himself making concessions without even realizing that he had done so. In his speech before the Chamber of Deputies, he tried to redress the balance, or rather to make it bend in his favor, and appear as the man who had achieved the reconciliation in spite of "the popes' intransigency, . . . always immutable," and who had also obtained the best possible terms for the state.

His speech was a sequence of dry, peremptory assertions, alternating with a lengthy and detailed, if not always accurate, exposition of events, which covered the history of the Roman Catholic church, its temporal power, and the origins and development of the Roman Question. This show of erudition was meant to document and give weight to his assertions, whether these were valid or somewhat distorted. Although it was evident that he had carefully planned the historical and erudite tenor of his speech, he could not refrain from making his main point — that he was the winner rather than the loser in the deal with the church — at the very beginning, and he opened his address with some of the words to which the pope was to object.

Cavour's formula in seeking an agreement with the Vatican had been "a free church in a free state," and in the previous debate some of the deputies had indicated that the formula was now a fact. But Mussolini refuted this point of view by asserting in his opening sentences that "in the state the church is not free and not even sovereign." Some other "harsh, crude, drastic" words were disseminated in this speech. "We have not revived the temporal power of the popes, we have given it enough ground for its burial" (this is as newspapers reported the sentence; edited versions have "we have buried it"). "The concordat concluded with the Holy See is the best from the point of view of the state. . . . Rome is sacred because it was the capital of the Empire. . . . But then it is sacred *also* because it was the cradle of Catholicism. . . . There has been talk of right of sanctuary. If a criminal flees into a church, the *carabinieri* will run after him and grab him. . . . In three months I have confiscated more Catholic papers than in the previous seven years. It was the only way of leading them back to the right tone. . . . The Fascist state fully claims for itself its ethical quality: it is Catholic but it is Fascist, in fact, above all, exclusively, essentially Fascist."

The words that the pope called "heretical or worse than heretical" were part of the duce's analysis of the origins of Catholicism, with which he opened his lengthy historical review: "This religion was born in Palestine, but became Catholic in Rome. Had it remained in Palestine, very probably it would have been one of the many sects that flourished in that seething environment, as for example those of the Essenes and the Therapeutae, and very probably it would have died out without leaving any trace behind."

Mussolini's speech on the Lateran treaties had enormous repercussions. Not only did it irritate Pope Pius XI; on the one hand it allayed the concern of the many anticlericals in Italy and warned those who had hoped for an application of the concordat favorable to the church. On the other, it gave matter for learned studies of Mussolini's stand toward religion, for attempts at reconciling some of his apparently discordant views and interpreting the thought behind fine points of the concordat. Now, many years after the reconciliation and Mussolini's death, these scholarly studies seem vain and absurd, and the only conclusion that seems valid and explains all inconsistencies is that Mussolini did not care about these matters, that he was concerned solely with himself, his great performance, the light in which this performance put him.

and the satisfaction it could give to his greed for power. Margherita Sarfatti recently related that in speaking of the reconciliation the duce remarked: "People say that I change opinions. Did you ever see a sailor at the helm of a boat? He gives the rudder a pull to the right and one to the left, but if you look behind the boat, its wake is straight." Indeed, his course of action was a straight line, the most direct road to more power, greater recognition and praise, louder acclaim. And his intuition told him when and in what direction he should move the rudder. Thus, although in his speech before the Chamber of Deputies he erected his own arch of triumph, Mussolini did not push further his drastic stand and, despite papal rebuke, he pronounced in the senate a more moderate and conciliatory speech, a speech in which, as far as he could do so without losing face, he tried to tone down some of his statements in the chamber and remove the sting from them.

In the chamber none spoke against the treaties, and the bill was passed, 317 to 2. In the senate, the old philosopher Benedetto Croce expressed reservation not for the agreement per se, but for the way in which the concordat was drawn. In the early days of fascism, Croce had been a sympathizer and had admired the duce, but the Matteotti affair had opened his eyes, and in early 1925 he drafted the "intellectuals' manifesto," in which some forty men of culture proclaimed their faith in liberal ideals. Mussolini harshly rebuked Croce in the senate for his criticism of the concordat and accused him of being one of those who, unable "to produce an event, namely to make history before writing it, take their revenge afterward by diminishing it, often without objectivity, sometimes shamelessly." Croce's honest stand proved futile — so futile, as everyone realized, that it marked the last open opposition in the senate — and the treaties were approved with 316 votes in favor and only 6 against them.

The ratification of the Lateran treaties in June, 1929, did not put an end to the skirmishes between Pius XI and Mussolini. One of the fundamental points of dissent, probably the most essential, was the fact that both church and Fascist government claimed the right to educate youth. In the encyclical *Rappresentante in terra*, devoted to the Christian education of youth and published at the end of the year, Pius XI stressed the educational mission of the church; its right to judge any other form of human teaching insofar as it is helpful or contrary to Christian education; its privilege to keep vigil on the education of the faithful in all schools. Mussolini, on the other hand, could not renounce "the totalitarian principle of the education of the young," which had been applied since 1926, when the *Opera Nazionale Balilla* came into being. It organized all children, even the very young, into military-like formations, in Fascist uniforms; it made the children march, perform athletic exercises, taught them how to become "good Fascists," and turned small boys into minuscule soldiers, according to the slogan *Libro e moschetto, fascista perfetto* ("Book and musket, perfect Fascist").

The pope could not but disapprove of this thorough Fascist indoctrination received by children before they had learned to think — an indoctrination which, in Mussolini's words, gave them "the sense of virility, of power, of conquest." And the pope strove to retain his hold on the young through Catholic education.

The conflict between the Holy See and the Fascist regime reached a peak in the spring of 1931, when a bitter dispute arose over *Azione Cattolica*, a lay organization with a social and educational program, working directly under the ecclesiastical authority. The regime challenged its functions and accused it of interfering and being incompatible with Fascist activities. In several cities the official propaganda against *Azione Cattolica* resulted in violence directed against Catholic organizations and clubs, in beatings, desecration of the cross and holy images, blasphemous language, and shouts of "Down with *Azione Cattolica!*" and, in a few instances, "Down with the Pope!" Although Pius XI reacted promptly and firmly in the encyclical *Non abbiamo bisogno*, the conflict was destined to subside, for neither the pontiff nor the duce had any interest in straining their relations to the breaking point. Soon an agreement was reached, and the Fascist regime pledged itself to respect most, if not all, of the privileges that *Azione Cattolica* had so far enjoyed.

Some conflict between the Church and fascism was to flare up again in 1938 over the Fascist promulgation of anti-

Semitic laws; some clauses of these laws restricted the freedom of family relations and marriage, the sanctity of which
the Church considered of its own competence Apart from
these skirmishes, however, the relations between Pius XI and
Mussolini were in general not devoid of sympathy and sometimes tinged with signs of mutual admiration. Both the pope
and the duce were authoritarians, and though the authority
of the pontiff was consecrated by a tradition of millennia
spent at God's service while Mussolini's had been forcefully
acquired, their respective authoritarian stand was a link
between them.

16

VILLA TORLONIA

"Family. *See* Fascist state."
                    Mussolinian Dictionary

In the preface to his book *Vita con mio padre* (*Life with My Father*), published in 1957, Mussolini's oldest son Vittorio states that his father "did not belong to his family" and implies that the reason for this was to be found not so much in his heavy and time-consuming duties as in his very nature: a solitary man whose full confidence no one enjoyed, who in his entire life had only a few friendships and no lasting ones, for, "having known men and their pettiness, he felt toward them not only a psychological but also a physical intolerance." It is clear that the man whose son could write these words was still as self-centered and lacking in outgoing affection as in his youth. Under no circumstances could Mussolini have been a family man, and it would be futile to look for meaningful and warm expressions about children, women, and the family in general in the thirty-four volumes of his collected speeches and writings.

In children he saw only the material out of which he could mold future generations of Fascists and soldiers, the little robots he was to train in the use of both "book and musket," who, in the uniform that effaced their individuality, marched and drilled before him. He could praise the beautiful show of order and obedience that they gave, but he could evince no understanding of their nature. Once he defined women as "a pleasant parenthesis" in the life of man, but otherwise held them in low esteem, considered them "incapable of synthesis"

and therefore unable to achieve "great spiritual creations";
he considered women, physically, intellectually, and morally,
beneath men, and he did not believe that any great man had
ever been inspired by a woman. (In accordance with these
views, suffrage for women, which had been in the program of
the *fasci*, was first shelved, then dropped entirely.)

Not being a family man, Mussolini adapted easily and
willingly to a bachelor's life. In October, 1922, when he
marched on Rome and assumed power, he left behind him his
family (at that time he had three legitimate children, Edda,
Vittorio, and Bruno, twelve, six, and four years' old), thus
repeating his pattern of behavior in 1912, when he moved to
Milan to be director of *Avanti!* and left Rachele and Edda in
Forlì. In 1912 the "leaving behind" had lasted only a few
months, but the separation begun in 1922 was to continue for
seven years. In Rome, after staying some time in a hotel and
not liking it — too often people crowded into the lobby to see
him, and either he felt the lack of privacy or, as some critics
suggest, he was afraid for his personal safety — he settled
comfortably in an apartment in Via Rasella, in the heart of
the city, not far from the Ministry of Interior in the Viminale
and the Ministry of Foreign Affairs in Palazzo Chigi. Margherita Sarfatti helped him find a good housekeeper, Cesira,
who ran the place efficiently and became very jealous of her
rights as the only woman caring for the personal needs of the
chief of state. Benito Mussolini resumed the life of a bachelor,
and in his apartment he entertained a few men of consequence
and many lady admirers.

In his first year in power Mussolini had several occasions
to go to Milan and see his family — often hurriedly, sometimes for as little as an hour. (When he was in Rome, he
talked daily to Rachele on the telephone.) In the spring of
1924, during the electoral campaign, he spent several days in
Milan, but on the pretext that he was to work late at night and
preferred to sleep at the office, he did not stay with his family.
When Rachele learned that he was spending his nights at the
home of Margherita Sarfatti, who had recently become a
widow, she was so incensed that she left Milan and sought
refuge with a sister in Forlì; but soon the breach was patched

up through the good offices of family friends. (For a few years longer Margherita Sarfatti was to remain the duce's favorite and exert a decided influence on his tastes. She also influenced Fascist art by contributing art criticism to *Il Popolo* and *Gerarchia* and by organizing exhibitions of modern painting. In 1930 she fell into disfavor and was barred from these activities.)

Mussolini and his family came to follow a more regular pattern of mutual visits. For his birthday Benito met his family in Romagna, usually at the Rocca delle Caminate, the old ruin that had been the goal of his childhood expeditions and which had been rebuilt and presented to him for use as a country home. In Romagna he liked to mingle with the people and pretend that he was one of them; he attended farmyard dances and, according to his local admirers, he waltzed at top speed like a young man. His family spent several weeks each summer at Riccione, a resort on the Adriatic, and there he often visited them. It is said that when he lifted little Bruno in his arms, all the mothers on the shore were moved to tears; and when he went for a dip and a swim, numerous ladies plunged into the water after him, often in such excitement that they forgot they were in street clothes. More than one lady was rescued on the point of drowning.

The children, with Rachele, spent Christmas vacation in their father's apartment in Rome. The bachelor's flat was then transformed into a family home, and the bachelor himself tried to become the benevolent father — he was shy with his children and preferred to let Rachele rule the family with a firm hand. Before the family's arrival, a Christmas tree was set up in the living room, although Christmas trees were neither in the Catholic tradition nor often seen at that time in Italy. The presents were always small, since throughout his life Mussolini affected an ignorance of the value of money and a taste for thrift. Even later, when living in great comfort if not in luxury, he neither carried money himself nor handled it directly, and he delegated to others all financial transactions, however small.

Of the apartment in Via Rasella, Vittorio Mussolini recalls, besides the Christmas tree, a huge white porcelain eagle perched on the grand piano in the living room and a live puma tied to a leg of the piano. These were the years when the duce liked to display fondness for wild animals and familiarity with them. The puma, a Christmas gift from one of his admirers in Argentina, a tired animal upon arrival, had seemed harmless to Mussolini; but as soon as it regained its liveliness and untamed roar, the duce hurriedly dispatched it to the zoo. There, in another cage, was a lioness, Italia, once allowed to roam Mussolini's apartment. When the lioness was still a cub, he used to take her riding in his open Alfa Romeo along the wooded avenues of Villa Borghese, so that the strollers in the park would see the daring man and his pet and talk of them to others. After she had grown too big to be kept at home, he often went inside her cage at the zoo to feed her, play with her, or shake her paw — before an enthusiastic photographer.

Early in 1925, in the apartment in Via Rasella, Mussolini suffered a sudden collapse, caused by a duodenal ulcer. In the past he had complained about his stomach, although he was moderate in his eating habits and long before had given up tobacco and wine. The strain of the Matteotti affair intensified his symptoms, and the crisis came a little over a month after he had victoriously closed that episode with the speech marking the beginning of total dictatorship. The best doctors and surgeons were summoned, and after consultations and X rays they decided not to operate but ordered complete rest and a strict diet for their illustrious patient. The nature of Mussolini's illness was withheld from the press, and even Rachele was not told the true state of things and was discouraged from coming to Rome in order not to alarm the population.

Hiding the true nature of Mussolini's illness caused much speculation both then and later, and many rumors about his state of health were circulated from time to time. According to the most persistent rumor, the duce had syphilis, and in late 1938 many persons believed that in the duce they recognized a loss of mental power and an erratic behavior which they associated with the venereal disease. In the light of his own hints in "My Life" and what Angelica Balabanoff has written about him, it seems certain that as a young man he suffered from syphilis. Later, several doctors denied that they had detected any signs of it in the duce, but the possibility that they were protecting his reputation cannot be entirely disregarded. At any rate, there is no doubt about the nature of the duce's illness in 1925. Throughout his life he was to have recurrent stomach pains which required an even stricter diet than the vegetarian regime he usually followed. In the winter of 1925, after a few weeks in bed, he resumed his regular activities.

In September, 1927, Benito was called to Milan for the birth of his third son. Romano was born almost ten years after Bruno, the youngest of the other children, and about ten months after the duce had launched his "demographic" campaign to increase the Italian birth rate by the imposition of a tax upon bachelors between twenty-five and sixty-five years of age. The proceeds of this tax were to go directly to the National Organization for the Protection of Mothers and Children. In announcing the new tax, Mussolini pointed out that the state would be insured a contribution from those men who, having come of age, abstained from creating a family. Unmarried women were exempted, he said, because often their failure to marry was not a choice they had made. Romano Mussolini's birth may thus be considered an example set by the duce for the sluggish population; and the birth of Anna Maria, in September, 1929, may have been a further example. With five children the Mussolini family could enter the contest of *belle famiglie italiane,* for which Mussolini himself had established prizes.

The reunion of the family, which took place in November, 1929, may have been decided in the same exemplary mood. But it may also have been a concession to Mussolini's recent role as "man of Providence" and "good Catholic" in achieving the reconciliation with the church. The architect of this holy feat, on whom innumerable Catholics were looking with profound gratitude and reverence, could no longer live in a bachelor's apartment with his family over four hundred miles away. For some time Mussolini had asserted that he wanted to have his family with him, blaming the separation on the difficulty of finding suitable living quarters in Rome. But for several years Prince Giovanni Torlonia had offered his villa on Via Nomentana to the duce and his family, and Mussolini had used it as a summer residence and for occasional official receptions in winter. (Among the persons whom he had entertained at Villa Torlonia was Ras Tafari, the future Negus Haile Selassie of Ethiopia.)

Villa Torlonia was an old house of classical style with columns and a triangular tympanum of white marble on its front, in the fashion of a Greek temple. As if realizing that so much classicism appeared pretentious in modern days, the villa hid among the old pines and oaks of a vast park. The park was further screened by a high wall, and the passers-by could only peek through the bars of the gate. The Mussolinis went to live behind that wall in the green seclusion of the park, under the protection of the many *carabinieri* and plainclothesmen who paced the sidewalks outside.

Inside the park Rachele raised her chickens and Benito his pets — young lions, an eagle, and many horses, most of them thoroughbreds, gifts from many parts of the world. The children had cats, dogs, turtles, and two ponies. Early in the morning Benito used to go horseback riding in the park with his teacher of equitation. Gradually, with stubborn determination, he learned to jump obstacles of increasing height. At other times he rode a bicycle along the green alleys or played soccer with his sons. Riding, fencing, tennis, and soccer in Villa Torlonia; swimming near the shores of Romagna; skiing (or pretending to ski: all photos show him holding skipoles, but on foot) on the Terminillo, the mountain he had discovered near Rome and made accessible for winter sports; these were his favorite relaxations, or at least those in which he wanted the public to believe he was engaged. He took great pride in his sturdy build and physical fitness, and if a rumor happened to spread in Italy or abroad that he was in poor health, he hurriedly summoned reporters and photographers to Villa Torlonia, the seashore, or the mountains and let them see with their own eyes the marvelous shape he was in and his skill at sports. (Yet in most of the photos showing him so engaged he looks tense and tired. This is true both of early photos, as one taken after a flying lesson in 1920, and of later ones where he is on horseback, swimming, or doing farm chores.) Having followed the duce while he performed, one by one, what he claimed were his daily exercises, some reporters asked themselves when he had time for the cares of government.

In Villa Torlonia Rachele was the queen. A queen who helped the maids and tended her vegetable garden, but also took advantage of an official car and chauffeur for long rides with her children. A queen in a certain isolation, for she set herself in a room separate from her husband's — history does not say at whose advice or instigation. Thus she gave proof of her wisdom, which was no less admirable for being primitive and simple. When in the gossipy circles of Roman society the news had spread that Donna Rachele was going to live in Rome and resume her place at her husband's side, many had gleefully smiled in anticipation of the blunders she would make and the poor figure she would cut at official and social affairs. But Rachele disappointed them and with rare common sense almost always stayed at home. The few times when she was seen at a party, at a dinner at the royal court — the queen of Italy was fond of her — at the theater, or in the stadium watching a parade with her children, she showed herself for what she was: a plump, still pleasing woman, cheerful, retiring, a typically good mother who would offend no susceptibilities. She is said to have been somewhat more of a problem in her native Romagna, where she liked to play the role of important person and dispense favors to friends and relatives. Later she occasionally wanted to have her say in certain political matters, acting impulsively and with obduracy. But her doings were never among the worst ills of fascism.

Villa Torlonia was Mussolini's private residence, and only rarely was it used for official receptions. Members of his family recall two such occasions. The second, a concert in the largest hall of the villa in December, 1931, would have been forgotten if the guest of honor, the Mahatma Gandhi, had not startled the company by making his entrance with a small goat on a leash. In April of the previous year a ceremony of greater significance to the family was held in Villa Torlonia: Edda's wedding reception. Edda was a girl of stubborn and capricious temperament who had earned the affectionate nickname of "mad filly." The year before she had fallen in love with a Jew, thus greatly upsetting her father. Mussolini's sister Edvige, in whom he confided, remarks that at that time there was no talk of anti-Semitism, and yet it was clear that such a marriage would have caused much clamor around the duce of Catholic Italy, the chief of government who had signed the Lateran treaties. In a letter to Edvige, whose co-operation he enlisted in persuading Edda to give up her love, Benito asserted that nine out of ten mixed marriages are not successful and swore that Edda's marriage, a "true and real scandal with the aggravating circumstance of unhappiness," could not and would not take place.

Concerned about the kind of son-in-law that Edda, if left to herself, might give him, Mussolini resolved to take the matter in his hands and find her a suitable husband but not feeling up to this task, he asked his brother Arnaldo to make discreet investigations. Edvige writes: "Arnaldo had a good inspiration and turned to a Sicilian deputy, a friend of his, who had recently married an Italo-Brazilian young lady of excellent and wealthy family, and who had a detailed and at the same time panoramic view of the political and social circles of the capital. . . ." He suggested Count Galeazzo Ciano, the son of Admiral Costanzo Ciano who had led the famous *Beffa di Buccari*, planned by D'Annunzio. The elder Ciano, regarded as one of the great war heroes, had been made a count in recognition of his war record. An early Fascist in the days of the March on Rome, he had shuttled between Rome and Milan in carrying out negotiations between Mussolini and other hopefuls, especially Salandra. Mussolini proved his gratitude by appointing Costanzo Ciano Undersecretary of the Navy and, later, Minister of Communications. The president of the cabinet and his minister, who never wavered in his loyalty to fascism, not even after the Matteotti affair, became good friends. When Costanzo's son Galeazzo was suggested as a possible husband for Edda, Mussolini more than welcomed the suggestion.

It is strange but revealing of Mussolini's character that while both Rachele and Edvige claim that Costanzo Ciano was Benito's "close friend," Mussolini had not heard of Ciano's son and had to be told of him by someone "with a panoramic view" of Roman society. Galeazzo Ciano was a bright and handsome young man at the beginning of a diplomatic career, and his outgoing and friendly manners made an excellent impression in the first encounter with Edda. She fell in love, and the match was settled. (Between the dismissal of the Jewish suitor and Galeazzo's appearance on the scene, another young man, son of a businessman of Romagna, briefly courted Edda, but the romance was shattered suddenly when the young man asked the duce what dowry Edda would have. The mention of a dowry aroused the duce's fury, and he shouted "She has nothing, and neither do I!")

Despite the duce's professed poverty and love of simplicity, Edda's wedding reception was sumptuous. Villa Torlonia was flooded with precious gifts and white flowers — so many flowers that Donna Rachele sent four carloads of them to the ossuary of the war dead in a Roman cemetery. According to Vittorio Mussolini, more than five hundred guests crowded the park. In addition to most of the Roman aristocracy, the guests included high prelates, whose red robes looked like huge flowers in the wooded park, foreign diplomats, wealthy businessmen, Fascists of high rank, relatives, and friends. The ladies wore splendid clothes and jewels of great value. Caterers served the refreshments under Rachele's supervision, and Benito, in a sociable mood at the wedding of his favorite child, introduced the young couple and lingered to speak amiably to the guests. But after the company had left he turned to Vittorio and Bruno and said, "Boys, when you get married it will be without so much fuss. Today's ceremony is enough for me."

In later years Galeazzo Ciano came to be regarded as the dauphin of the hereditary dictatorship that Mussolini was thought to have founded, and there is no doubt that Ciano expected to become his father-in-law's successor. It was evident by then that Vittorio and Bruno lacked the intelligence, the strength of character, and the ambition that are required for positions of responsibility. Galeazzo, with a prompt if somewhat superficial intelligence, with more refined manners, and disarmingly friendly toward all, appeared much better suited than his brothers-in-law to the subtle ways of politics. Later, appointed foreign minister at the age of thirty-three, he showed that he could orient himself in complicated situations but lacked the maturity or the strength of will to steer events. Enormously impressed by the importance of his position and the duce's confidence in him, he became Mussolini's admirer and imitator. At official ceremonies he assumed as straight a posture as the duce himself, wore the same frowning expression, expanded his broad chest, and when Mussolini thrust out his chin, Ciano thrust his own half an inch farther. Only too late, when the harm done to Italy was irreparable, did he attempt an independent stand and oppose the duce. But in spite of his shortcomings, Ciano, perhaps more than any other European diplomat of his time, performed a lasting service: in the six years he was foreign minister, he kept diaries and wrote minutes of the duce's conversations with statesmen and diplomats. These form the most unique individual body of documents of that period on European history behind the scenes and contain a most vivid series of snapshots of the totalitarian mind at work.

The next family event was a sad one: the death of Benito's brother, Arnaldo, on December 21, 1931.

As small children in Predappio, Benito and Arnaldo were good playmates who shared games and escapades, but they were early separated, when nine-year-old Benito was sent to the Salesian school in Faenza. For a few more years the two brothers, who always attended different schools, spent their summer vacations together; but then their paths parted altogether. Arnaldo went to Switzerland a few months before Benito left it, then returned to Italy and eventually settled in Friuli, a region of northeastern Italy that was invaded by the enemy after the defeat at Caporetto. When this happened, Arnaldo, compelled to leave his home, joined the Italian army. At the end of the war he accepted a position in the administration of his brother's *Il Popolo d'Italia* in Milan. Benito had little interest in administrative questions; during this period the two brothers saw each other rarely, and there is no record that they kept in touch by correspondence. Benito felt closer to his sister Edvige, to whom he wrote letters and postcards that she has preserved. In October, 1922, when Benito went to Rome to become prime minister, he left the direction of his paper to Arnaldo. From that time on, through visits, letters, and the habit of long-distance telephone calls, a steady collaboration developed between the two brothers, and this brought them closer to each other.

In his physical appearance Arnaldo somewhat resembled Benito, although his heavier build and rounded shoulders, the softer features further softened by a pensive expression, the chin trained to rest on his chest and not to jut forward, gave him the look of a preacher rather than of a man of action. In temperament he was very different from Benito: meek, soft-spoken, and retiring, he was profoundly religious, and to his collaboration with his brother he brought common sense, a serene detachment, and humility. Through his brother Arnaldo, Benito retained his grasp on the paper, from which not even the premiership could tear him away, since journalism was what he was born for and the smell of printed paper was to him the most fragrant scent. On Arnaldo he imposed his strong will — and not only in matters concerning the paper. Arnaldo made frequent trips to Rome to discuss with Benito the policies of the paper and the stories to be covered in it. If Benito disliked a recent article, the point of view or the political interpretation, his loud objections were heard outside the office, but Arnaldo took the scolding in his stride and remarked that his brother barked but did not bite. Before accepting an appointment, a new task, or an honorary position, Arnaldo dutifully consulted his brother, and thus Benito was able to prevent Arnaldo from coming too much in the public eye, for the star of a second Mussolini, though a small one, might have marred the splendor of the first. Arnaldo, uncomplaining, went on quietly with his work and performed the unpleasant tasks that others in the family shunned: he dealt with the relatives of Benito's illegitimate son Benito Albino and made arrangements for the boy's education; he looked for a suitable husband for Edda; he gathered information about political suspects; and he sifted publications and inventions, applications for interviews with the duce, requests for financial help from the deserving and undeserving and for mercy from political offenders.

Humbly and quietly, Arnaldo went on helping Benito, keeping an eye on him and his family like an older brother, trying, unsuccessfully more often than not, to be a moderating influence in politics, until death came to him. At the funeral in Romagna Benito followed the casket a few paces ahead of the other mourners, straight and proud in his loneliness, his chin thrust forward, a long deep furrow between contracted brows. Upon his return to Rome, on Christmas Day, he wrote the first pages of *Vita di Arnaldo* (*Arnaldo's Life*), a book published the following year and intended to honor his brother but in which he erected one more monument to himself.

Of Arnaldo he had little to say except to stress Arnaldo's devotion to him: "Arnaldo proved that he knew the intimate and tormented battles of my spirit. . . . Arnaldo was always aware of his responsibility as director of a newspaper which was founded not by his 'brother' but by the man whom he was proud to obey as a simple soldier. . . . He brought daily his stone to my edifice. . . . He had an extraordinary respect for my work. . . . I felt him omnipresent, but in the shadow. There was the most ample and reciprocal 'confidence,' but in him there was also the devotion to the chief." To fill the slim booklet and give a rough outline of what Arnaldo's life had been, Benito Mussolini was compelled to quote Arnaldo's own diary of his army service, an account of his activities as a soldier sent to Benito by Arnaldo's commanding officer, and excerpts from Arnaldo's articles in *Il Popolo d'Italia*. These excerpts appear to have been selected according to the amount of praise they contain for Fascist achievements and the duce himself. "The Duce, in his complex work that has no pause, had never doubted the wisdom of the people. . . . Benito Mussolini, with his great prestige as leader, political man, inspirer, has clarified the Italian political and spiritual position. . . . The Duce must be present only in manifestations, we dare to say, of historical character. And now . . . the Duce must resume his ascent of history." From Arnaldo's letters Benito quoted passages containing such sentences as these: "God protects you, the Italians venerate you. . . . I beg you to excuse me for having dared to advise you. . . . Your appointment . . . has been . . . the most luminous thing. . . . This morning I read your speech. No need to say that I liked it very much. . . ."

Mussolini ended his book with the statement that he felt the grief for Arnaldo's death as "a secret fire" and with the promise that the Fascist ideals, in which his brother also believed, would triumph and outlast him.

After Arnaldo's death Benito asked his sister Edvige to come live in Rome. Edvige, a woman of common sense and of more even temperament than the fiery Rachele, was married and had several children. Her husband held a position controlled by the Fascists, and it was easily arranged that he move to Rome. In many respects Mussolini's relations with his sister appear to have been the most normal that he was to have with any human being, and the letters that he wrote to her in wartime could have been written by any soldier to his sister. Yet a few sentences reveal a cold unconcern that pierces like a spike of ice: after the retreat from Caporetto, Edvige's husband, Michele Mancini, was listed among the missing, and for two months the Red Cross had no information about him. To Edvige, who had begun to despair, Benito wrote a letter that was meant to comfort her: "It is a very sad thought . . . that Michele may have died — and not even of the fine death that gets you in a battle; but who knows how, during a retreat due to the irresponsibility of the government and to the treason of the Germans in Italy. . . . As long as I am able, I shall do everything necessary for you and your little girls. . . . Rome is full of shirkers! What a shame!" Shortly afterward, having learned that her husband was a prisoner in Germany, Edvige tried to obtain his release through the Red Cross and asked Benito to inquire what had become of the application she had filed. Mussolini reported to his sister that the man he had sent to find out had been told that "through the Vatican the application would move at a faster pace," but, Mussolini wrote, *"I forbade him* to turn to that side for help. . . . If our Michele is a prisoner . . . it is due to those responsible for the obscure and infamous defeat, and the Vatican is first among them. Precisely. Be patient, my dear, and wait. . . ."

There is no record of Edvige's reaction to this lack of sympathy, but in the long run the feelings between brother and sister appeared unchanged. After the war their correspondence dwindled and stopped almost completely. Occasionally Benito consulted Edvige about family matters, or enlisted her help, as in the case of Edda's infatuation for the young Jew.

In Rome, Edvige took up charitable work. Getting money for charities from her brother was at first her main task, but soon she also came to act as go-between for the families of political offenders in jail, at the *confino,* or sentenced to death. Many have remarked that Benito was usually generous with these people, and willing to commute a death penalty, reduce a term in jail, and assist the families of prisoners. (He easily gave in to pressures, only occasionally reversing himself once the persuader had gone.) Fewer have stressed that the duce always placed as a condition to his generosity that the prisoner give tangible signs of having reformed and formally repudiate his previous political conviction. Because Edvige was known to have influence, she soon fell into the net of political intriguers, men who wanted to advance their careers, and adventurers of all sorts; and she had neither the discernment to recognize them at first sight nor the ability to disentangle herself once she had been enmeshed. The fact that the well-meaning Edvige should become an instrument of corruption is a clear example, and may be regarded as a symbol, of what fascism was doing to the Italians.

Among the toilsome tasks that Arnaldo humbly performed for his brother, the most amazing is the preparation of Benito's

autobiography for English readers. The idea that the duce
write his memoirs at this time was suggested to him by his
staunch admirer, Richard Washburn Child, the United States
ambassador to Italy from 1921 to 1924. Already there were a
number of biographies of Mussolini written by others, and
he seemed to have forgotten that, when his friend Torquato
Nanni had written the first full biographical sketch of him in
1914, he had urged that it not be published, asserting: "Biographies, so long as I live, never!" Having forgotten this, he
not only gave biographers a free hand but went so far as to
suggest that Margherita Sarfatti write his biography; he
assisted her by providing documents and suitable parts of
"My Life." He was pleased with the finished product, *Dux*
published in 1925, a highly romantic and not always accurate
portrait as seen through the eyes of an adoring woman; and
he wrote a preface in which he said that he detested all
biographers but was "perfectly resigned" to his fate as a
public figure.

When Ambassador Child pointed out that no biography
could take the place of an autobiography, Mussolini agreed.
Child made all the arrangements, and Mussolini's *My Autobiography* was published in 1928, first as a series of articles
in the *Saturday Evening Post* and shortly afterward in book
form in both the United States and England. On the jacket
were these words in Mussolini's hand: "There is no other
autobiography by me." In the preface to this book Ambassador Child wrote: "So he began. He dictated. I advised that
method because if he attempts to write in longhand he corrects
and corrects and corrects. It would have been too much for
him. So he dictated. The copy came back and he interlined
the manuscript in his own hand. . . ." Thus a number of lies
and near-lies were presented as facts to the English-speaking
public.

Mussolini's book was not really "by me," since Arnaldo
took care of it; and in stating that no other autobiography
existed Mussolini was forgetting his youthful and truly autobiographical "My Life," which the French literary weekly
Candide had republished only four years earlier. Child's assertion that Mussolini "dictated" the new book is decidedly

ot true, and false is the impression he gives (without actually
saying so) that he himself took the dictation. In *Vita di
Arnaldo* Mussolini himself explained how the autobiography
was written at Ambassador Child's suggestion: "We decided
with Arnaldo that I would give him the outline, the elements,
and documents and that he would relieve me of the task of
writing it. The preparation of my autobiography is his. He
put a great zeal, a great diligence into it, he put much time
into it, and he translated the events of my life not in a resounding, but in simple, frank prose, as the Americans
wished." This statement is confirmed by many letters that
Arnaldo wrote to Benito concerning the writing, the financial
arrangements, the pressures from Child to hurry the book.
Arnaldo sent the drafts of each chapter to Benito, who made
his corrections in longhand, as can be seen in the preserved
originals of two drafts.

In the United States the book was received with reservations. The comments ranged from criticism of the translation
that was indeed very poor and awkward, to the regret that
Mussolini had chosen to "declaim" his book rather than write
it, with the result that his prose was more rhetorical than the
Anglo-Saxon ear was used to — to Mussolini, accustomed to
his own rhetoric, Arnaldo's prose had seemed simple; from
the complaint that Mussolini's book was self-exaltation at the
highest pitch, to the remark that he had failed to document
the unjust condemnations that he had piled upon the shoulders
of his opponents.

Yet *My Autobiography*, despite its shortcomings, its having
been ghostwritten, and its many factual distortions, is a vivid
portrait of a man and a regime. Mussolini emerges as a superman, long accustomed to be considered, and to consider himself, all-powerful and infallible; the man who does not need
to qualify his words, for they have come to be accepted at
face value; the naïve egocentric, genuinely convinced of the
greatness of his achievements, which he claims entirely for
himself, as if he had never had collaborators and supporters
but had done everything singlehanded; the ambitious, spurred
on by the thirst of power, yet believing that the motive for his
actions was love of Italy and the Italians, and admiring him-

self for this great love; the man who despised all theory except
the theory of violence and relied entirely on his intuition
(". . . as if a revelation had come to me. . . . I suddenly
understood. . . . Up leaped the idea. . . ."); the man who
occasionally, in the state of excitement in which addressing a
crowd always placed him, improvised "some declarations of
principles" that later he used as a "guide" in all his political
actions; the candid ignorant who was not ashamed to reveal
his childlike approach to difficult problems. (In 1922, when
he was still a journalist, he decided to attend an International
Conference at Cannes. Arnaldo, asked to change 10,000 lire
into French money, brought back "no more than 5,200 francs.
. . . This little personal experience made a deep impression.
It made me realize an angular fact; the Italian currency had
lost half of its value in comparison to French currency! It
was a grave symptom. It was a humiliation. . . . Up leaped
the thought that this situation must be cured by the vital
strength of fascism." He had already said, in commenting on
the failure of a large Italian bank, "For the first time I
found myself squarely challenged by the gigantic problem
of public finance. For me it was a new airplane — and there
was no competent instructor anywhere in the field.")

Possibly because it was so candid and revealing, *My Autobiography* was published in Italy only after Mussolini's death.

In considering biographical and autobiographical material
on the Mussolini of this period, one cannot disregard *Talks
with Mussolini*, by Emil Ludwig, a book which was published
in twelve languages in 1933. The German writer specialized
in "humanized" biographies with a decidedly psychological
slant, and he was well known for his books on Goethe,
Wagner, Bismarck, and Napoleon. Before beginning to write,
Ludwig spent much time in imaginary conversations with his
subjects, asking them questions and working out their replies.
He now applied the dialectical method that he had used with
the dead to the study of Mussolini's character. Ludwig's initial feelings toward the Italian dictator, whom he had watched

in action for many years, was one of mistrust, but on recognizing traits reminiscent of Nietzsche's teachings he became open-minded and sympathetic. The writer had two interviews with the dictator in 1929, but at that time he was unable to interest the duce in a biography. He had better luck in the spring of 1932 when the duce consented to be "studied" and was willing to grant Ludwig numerous interviews.

The talks between Ludwig and Mussolini, across the desk in the duce's office, were like a game between two wary cats: the German, who did most of the talking, realized that he must humor the dictator at all costs and keep him in a good mood. He avoided direct attacks; smoothed down a few touchy questions by referring to historical parallels, comparing Mussolini in turn with Caesar, Goethe, Faust, Napoleon, Byron, Lenin, and Trotsky; and ably led the duce to simple answers, which went unchallenged. Quicker in thinking, prompter in adapting to changing situations, the Italian was on guard without showing that he was. Acting was second nature to him, and with ease he acted the part of the man who has nothing to hide and can speak the few necessary words between the long, roundabout questions with full candor and in perfect friendliness. The interviews were to the advantage of both men: to Mussolini, this was a unique chance to be written up by a famous author, a liberal and pacifist, who specialized in the study of the great; for Ludwig it must have been a unique financial proposition, if it is true that twelve editions in twelve languages were paid for by the Italian government at the expense of the taxpayers.

Ludwig, who like so many before him came at once under the dictator's spell, questioned the duce in Italian, and after each interview wrote his notes in German. Shortly after the closing of the interviews he sent the German manuscript to Mussolini for his approval. The duce changed a few words, struck out a few sentences, and authorized translations into Italian and other languages. When the Italian publisher sent him the galley proofs of the Italian translation he made many more corrections and told the publisher that Ludwig was an ass and, at least in one case, had attributed to him foolish beliefs. The fact that he had not made these corrections in the

German manuscript indicates, as Salvemini points out, that although Mussolini claimed to know German well he was only superficially acquainted with the language.

At any rate, Mussolini authorized the publication of the Italian translation as corrected, and the official Fascist news agency *Stefani* announced publication. The publisher sent the first printed copies of the book to the duce and almost immediately received an irate telephone call from the duce's press office; the book was not to go on sale. Mussolini's secretary and then Mussolini himself added their recriminations over the telephone. The publisher pointed out that he had included all the duce's corrections and that he had the duce's authorization to publish the book, but to no avail. A police agent was sent to confiscate the galleys bearing Mussolini's own corrections, but not before the prudent publisher had secured a photographic copy as proof of his contentions.

In a further change of mind Mussolini and his press office authorized the sale of the 20,000 copies already in print, since the German edition was already on sale and the French translation was soon to be published; but the preparation of the second edition was postponed until the Ministry of Propaganda had time to go over the text. The corrections that were then made chiefly concerned Mussolini's religious views, not dissimilar to those that had irritated Pope Pius XI a few months after the reconciliation with the church. Thus expurgated, the second edition of Ludwig's *Talks with Mussolini* was approved and appeared on the market.

When Ludwig's book came out in the early thirties, very few people in Italy and in other countries knew much about the dictator, his past, his "true" ideas, and his future intentions; they saw him only at official functions or reflected in the stories that the press office was instructed to give out. Consequently, *Talks with Mussolini*, this candid portrait of the dictator, was of considerable interest. In our day, seen against the background of all the material that has since been published on the duce, Ludwig's portrait loses its appeal. Yet many Italians still remember one of Mussolini's statements: "Anti-Semitism [he said to Ludwig] does not exist in Italy. Italians of Jewish birth have shown themselves good citizens, and they fought bravely in the war. Many of them occupy leading positions, in the universities, in the army, in the banks. Quite a number of them are generals. . . ." The Italian Jews, who interpreted this assertion as a pledge, were stunned when, suddenly and without warning, the anti-Semitic laws were promulgated in 1938 — and *Talks with Mussolini* was withdrawn for good from circulation.

17

PALAZZO VENEZIA

"There is something Roman and warrior-like rather than militaristic in all our attitudes. Nor is the pageantry or the picturesque side lacking. To me this side is very important. I do not understand sullen and gloomy politics . . . ."

MUSSOLINI, May, 1921

UNTIL September, 1929, Mussolini occupied offices both in the new Palazzo del Viminale, the Ministry of Interior, and in the old Palazzo Chigi, the Ministry of Foreign Affairs. But he could not be satisfied with the modest space that democratic Italy allocated to her chiefs of government, and he made provisions for his own headquarters in the historical and grandiose setting of Palazzo Venezia. The palace is in the heart of Rome and surrounded by the monuments of greatest significance for those who have made a cult of ancient Roman glories: the Tarpean rock and the Capitol Hill, the imperial forums, Trajan's marketplace, Nero's tower, and Marcellus' theater. It was built by the popes in the second half of the fifteenth century and later ceded to Venice, from which it passed to Austria. It remained the property of the Hapsburgs until expropriated by the Italian government during World War I.

Palazzo Venezia is in the fashion of a medieval castle, with battlements and a low tower, of a warm brown, the color of the old horses stationed with their *carrozzelle* on the far side of the vast square before it. The windows on the second floor (the noble floor) are a distinguished feature of the façade: they are tall and wide, taller and wider than those of other old Roman palaces, and a big stone cross cuts their openings

in four. The center window is taller than the rest and opens
on a narrow stone balcony. At the time Palazzo Venezia was
returned to Italy, it was in a sad state of repair, and the government ordered extensive restoration. After the duce decided
that he would take over the palace, the restoration was
promptly completed and the interior refurnished. (The work,
costing millions, was of course paid for by the taxpayers, as
was the remodeling of the Rocca delle Caminate, the duce's
private plane and cars, the many "presents" from the population, and all the other paraphernalia of his position that
enabled him to live sumptuously and still be able to tell
Edda's suitor that he owned nothing.)

For his own office the duce chose the largest of the very
large halls on the second floor, the one with the tall window
opening on the balcony. This hall, called *Sala del Mappamondo* after an ancient map of the world displayed there, is
about 66 feet long and 43 feet wide; it is two stories high and
has two rows of windows — the top row originally belonged
to rooms on the third floor that were done away with to make
the hall on the second floor higher. The architectonic effect of
the columns and the decorations painted on the walls makes
the hall seem more enormous than it is. From the center of the
ornate ceiling hangs a heavy chandelier with innumerable
lights, and on the floor is the inscription in mosaic "Anno V"
(Fifth Year), for Mussolini had ordered that years be counted
from the day of the March on Rome. The huge hall was left
unfurnished except for a desk and three chairs beside a monumental fireplace in the corner farthest from the entrance hall.
This is all Mussolini required for his official life: a desk on
which to lay the few papers he was working on (or pretending
to work on, as the teasers and the maligners claimed); a
chair for himself and two others for occasional important
visitors, but none for his collaborators or for Fascist leaders
who in his presence were always required to stand; and the
balcony from which he harangued the crowd. For his unofficial life, a small door by the side of the fireplace led to a
private apartment, of whose furnishings there is no record
available.

When Mussolini moved into his new quarters in September,

1929, people commented that now he had his *reggia*, his royal palace, which was counterpart to the king's Quirinal. It was a tangible expression of what the duce later called "diarchy," the government by two. Palazzo Venezia came to be the symbol of the Fascist regime in its strongest period and one more proof of Mussolini's love for the dramatic: many visitors have described the awe they experienced when the chief usher opened the massive door into the Sala del Mappamondo and they were left to cross the more than twenty yards to Mussolini's desk in the distant corner; the perfect stillness — Mussolini seldom raised his head from his work and rarely got up to greet a visitor; the majestic solemnity of the hall; and the man, small at a distance and half-hidden behind his desk, yet filling the space with his mere presence. Very few visitors were not overpowered by this perfect staging, and one of the few was the U.S. Undersecretary of State Sumner Welles. Welles, however, visited Mussolini at a later time and under exceptional circumstances: in February, 1940, when World War II had begun but was still in the phase of the "phony war," Roosevelt, who still hoped to reverse the course of events and re-establish peace, sent Sumner Welles to explore the European situation. Welles's mission was of such importance that Mussolini did not abide by his usual practice and met his visitor at the door. While walking to the desk with the dictator, Welles did not notice the hall so much as the change in Mussolini, who looked "fifteen years older than his age."

Palazzo Venezia was visited by many illustrious guests: the Mahatma Gandhi of India, Chaim Weizmann of Palestine, Ramsay MacDonald and Neville Chamberlain, Pierre Laval, Maksim Litvinov, and others. Mussolini was always willing to discuss international issues with other chiefs of government, but on condition that they come to Italy — after two brief trips, to Switzerland and to London, in his first months in government, he did not travel outside Italy until 1937, when he paid his first visit to Hitler in Germany. Germany was a strongly policed country where the duce felt as well guarded and protected as in Italy, but elsewhere his personal safety might have been at stake. He went into the free world for the last time in February, 1923.

In Palazzo Venezia Mussolini received not only foreign statesmen and the high Fascists in his government but also more humble people, people who helped him wage his peaceful battles inside the country: the "battle of the lira" — for the revaluation of Italian currency; the "battle for wheat" — to produce more and import less; the "battle to reclaim the marshes"; and the "demographic campaign." (Demography is the statistical study of populations, but with characteristic disregard for accepted definitions Mussolini used the words "demographic campaign" to indicate the government's efforts to promote a higher birth rate through legislation and propaganda.)

Typical in this respect was the celebration of the first Mother's and Child's Day in Palazzo Venezia, on Christmas Eve, 1933, when Mussolini was host to the ninety-three most prolific women in Italy — one from each Italian province. These country women with lined faces, worn out by childbearing, these ninety-three mothers who together had given birth to over thirteen hundred children, came to the capital in their Sunday best, wearing their black shawls and scarves, and all day they were kept busy and on their feet. Guided by a special committee of Roman women, the ninety-three visitors were given a Fascist tour of the city. At 9:30 they visited the Exhibit of the Fascist Revolution, opened the previous year. They paused before the Shrine of the Fascist Martyrs, where they bent devoutly to kiss the glass of the case containing the bloodstained handkerchief that Mussolini had pressed to his nose after Violet Gibson's unsuccessful attempt on his life. They went to place a wreath in the Fascist Martyrs' Chapel in the Littorio Palace. They received medals and diplomas in the offices of the National Organization for the Protection of Mothers and Children; and at last, before going to the Augusteum for the closing ceremony, they stopped at Palazzo Venezia and were introduced into the presence of the dictator.

Mussolini could always find the chord that touched the hearts of the humble, and with the ninety-three "best" mothers of Italy he was affable, praised them warmly, and to each gave a "practical" offering as the tangible expression of the pride he took in them. On the marble floor the tired feet (many of the women were unaccustomed to shoes) felt less tired for a short while. The prematurely aged faces cheered up. The women got their reward for the long and crowded day. They, out of the millions of Italian women, had been singled out, given the privilege of being near the duce, of filling their eyes with the sight of him and their hearts with his kind condescension, of actually touching his hand when he gave them his gift.

Later Mussolini was to recognize officially the part that fathers played in the production of children and honor not the most prolific mothers but the most prolific couples. He was also to give personal directives on the action to be taken by the Fascist Union of Numerous Families "in order to increasingly develop the demographic consciousness needed for the quantitative and qualitative development of the Italian people."

Other ceremonies went along with Mussolini's demographic campaign. In November, 1933, in a Lictorian Ritual of Weddings, 2,620 couples were married in Rome, and each got a present from the duce. He, in his turn, received messages announcing "a *balilla* within a year" as a gift to Fascist Italy or the promise of a prompt increase in progeny. At about the same time free tickets were made available for wedding trips to Rome, and shortly afterward another new practice was established: the priest celebrating a wedding gave each couple a government insurance policy offering a prize for fecundity, together with Pope Pius XI's encyclical *Casti connubi.*

Mussolini's concern for the Italian birth rate acquired the intensity of a true fixation. As a young man and a Socialist he had been in favor of the reduction of births, but having once changed his mind he went to the opposite extreme, with incredible naïveté. He noticed that although the Italian birth rate was still increasing, the increase was not as great as it had been in the past, and he began to worry: "What are forty million Italians compared to ninety million Germans and two hundred million Slavs?" he asked the Chamber of Deputies in May, 1927. "What are forty million Italians compared to forty million Frenchmen plus ninety million inhabitants of the [French] colonies, or compared to forty-six million Englishmen plus four hundred and fifty millions in the [British] colonies?" Mussolini's answer to his own question was that the forty million Italians ought to become sixty millions by mid-century, and thus he set the country the preposterous aim of increasing the population by 50 per cent in twenty-three years. Along this line of thought, another slogan was added to the many Fascist slogans: "The strength of a people rests in its numbers," and women meeting Mussolini for the first time introduced themselves by saying: "Five children," "Eight children," "Ten children."

In a country that was already as overpopulated as Italy a "demographic campaign" was risky and entirely out of place. In spite of Mussolini's "demographic whippings" to the nation, the first of which was the tax on bachelors, the increase of the birth rate continued to decline slowly but steadily. But the demographic campaign, however absurd, was not without certain beneficial consequences. It brought about a long-overdue social program that included free medical assistance for the needy and the distribution of free meals and clothing, summer camps for children, protection of unmarried mothers, and a vigorous attack upon several social diseases, of which the greatest killer was tuberculosis.

It is probable that Mussolini undertook his successful "battle for wheat" because of "demographic" considerations. For one thing, he believed that the drift of country people into the cities was the main cause of the sluggish birth rate, although French statistics suggested that the opposite was true. Besides, the rapid increase in population that he hoped for would require the production of more food, especially bread and *pasta*, the staples of Italy. But Italy had always produced much less wheat than was needed and bought the rest on foreign markets. The expenditure for wheat accounted for a substantial part of total imports. In 1925 Italy imported over two million tons of wheat.

Mussolini sent letters to specialists in all parts of Italy asking whether they thought it possible to increase the yield of wheat in the areas where it was already grown, and when they replied in the affirmative he decided that since it was possible it ought to be done. In 1925 he launched the battle for wheat, to which farmers and landowners responded with zeal, and in the following years the production of wheat was increased as much as one-third. The duce took care to keep good will alive by yearly celebrations at which he personally handed out prizes to the best wheatgrowers, whom, in his fanaticism for everything Roman, he called the "velites [foot soldiers] of wheat." Now and then, when he could escape his official duties, he joined the peasants of Romagna or those of the land around Rome and helped them tend the wheat, sow, reap, and thresh. Then, it is said, he accepted the wages due to him as a farmhand. Several photographs show him as he handled the golden wheat, immersed in a golden sea, his torso bare and bronzed, his head covered by a wide-brimmed hat against the merciless rays of the sun. There is, as well, an incongruous photograph of Mussolini sowing grain with a stiff rather than a sweeping motion of his arm, and wearing a black fez and a regulation black coat so long that it brushes the ground. Around him a number of men in Fascist uniforms are raking and, behind them, long-faced, bona fide farmers look on with unhappy eyes.

A few years after the launching of the battle for wheat, more land was made available for agriculture. In the most grandiose and truly lasting "realization" of the Fascist regime, marshy lands, especially the Pontine marshes, were reclaimed. Many rulers, from the days of ancient Roman to modern times, had attempted the reclamation of the Pontine marshes, but although occasionally considerable success was obtained, it had never been permanent. Water had again swamped the land, and malaria had driven away the few inhabitants. To insure lasting achievement, Mussolini, who had the advice of an exceptionally fine expert, Arrigo Serpieri, undertook a program of "total reclamation." Along with the drainage of the land, the program provided for roads and towns, the bringing in of earth fill, the planting of trees, and the selection of the most suitable new farm crops. Helped by modern advances in technology and science, employing thousands of workers for some fifteen years (thus also reducing unemployment), and with the expenditure of huge sums, Mussolini was successful where others had failed. Malaria was extirpated, the marshy lands turned green and fertile, and healthy towns sprang up.

The reclamation of lands all over Italy enlarged the Italians' living space and thus favored the demographic campaign. In 1932, when inaugurating the first new town, Littoria, on what had been the Pontine marshes, the duce could say proudly: ". . . once, in order to find work, it was necessary to go beyond the Alps or cross the ocean. Today the land is here, only half an hour away from Rome. It is here that we have conquered a new province. It is here that we have waged and shall wage true war operations. This is the war that we prefer."

Unrelated to the demographic campaign, the "battle [for the revaluation] of the lira" was the outcome of Mussolini's experience in 1922 when he realized how much the value of the lira had dropped. It was then that "up leaped the thought" that something had to be done to remedy this humiliating state of affairs, and to this thought he returned in 1925 after he had consolidated his position in power. He then began to work for the revaluation of the lira. Foreign countries saw an active and energetic Italy determined to follow her leader and accepting financial sacrifice without protest. This determination appeared so encouraging that foreign banks were willing to assist the Fascist regime. The lira was stabilized at a higher value than it had had in the past. A lot of paper currency went up in a bonfire, and circulation was greatly curtailed. It was a mixed blessing that brought advantages to the wealthy, while the working classes had to submit "spontaneously" to a cut in their already meager wages. Eventually the forced value of the lira upset the balance of foreign trade.

Of all home policies of the Fascist regime, these battles and campaigns were the dearest to the duce. To other achievements attributed to him he gave only passing attention.

Neither the important guests nor the impersonal (to him, faceless) visitors — the prolific mothers, the farmers whose progenitors had tilled the same land for generations, the winners of athletic contests, the numberless *federali* (block or area captains), the widows of war heroes, and many others — filled more than briefly the emptiness and the solitude of Palazzo Venezia. When his loneliness became acute, the duce went out on the narrow balcony and shared the life of the square below. He watched the strollers, perhaps wondering how many of them were plainclothesmen, and the loafers in the busy café across the square; he watched the traffic that converged upon Piazza Venezia in a confused pattern from many streets and became miraculously orderly as it went around the policeman on duty in black uniform, helmet, and huge white gloves, who agitated his white club with the jerky motion of a marionette.

At other times, from his balcony, Mussolini supervised the work that was going on near Piazza Venezia: excavations and reconstructions in Trajan's Forum; the opening of a new, grandiose street among ancient monuments, from Piazza Venezia to the Coliseum; the renewal plan that was to give a new look to the Capitol Hill. If he thought that the workers were slack, he immediately sent down a man to speed them up. All the work that was being done under his eyes and further away was to change Rome into Mussolini's Rome, the *Urbs* in which all ancient monuments came back to life and some medieval landmarks disappeared.

The balcony gave him much deeper satisfaction, dissipated his loneliness more thoroughly, when a crowd was assembled in the square and he could seek communion with it. He loved the "oceanic gatherings," the packed sea of men in black shirts who pressed toward Palazzo Venezia like surf toward the shore. Their roar, like the resounding cadence of swelling waves, was sweet to his ear, for in it he recognized the single two-syllable word, "Du-ce, du-ce, du-ce," repeated over and over. He responded with a formal talk or with a few words, happy to receive this huge demonstration by the people of Rome. It is not known whether he realized that this "spontaneous" display of enthusiasm was at least in part due to efficient organization. In these gatherings there were certainly many persons who did not need incitement and found rallies an uplifting pastime, but others were present because they had received one of the red postcards sent out by the *federali* to all registered Fascists, and they knew that if one absence went unpunished, two or three would call for reprimand, the loss of a job, or other punishment. To go to a rally may have been a nuisance, but later the red cards were to bring a more dreaded message, first a summons to "volunteer" for the Ethiopian war, then for the Spanish.

The pageantry in Piazza Venezia varied: the usual crowds listening to Mussolini's speeches alternated with military parades, tourists calling for the duce to come out on the balcony, university students from all over Italy (to whom Mussolini gave the watchword "book and musket," symbolizing thought and action), flyers returning from flights across the Atlantic, and other groups. But the most superb spectacle of all was that of the *avanguardisti* (thirteen-to-eighteen-year-old boys belonging to the youth organizations). Once a year they came to Rome and performed perfectly disciplined physical exercises, moving supple limbs and bodies in precise rhythm and harmonious synchronism. Younger children also, the eight-to-thirteen-year-old *balilla* and *piccole italiane*, and the *figli della lupa*, under eight years of age, occasionally paraded and performed simple exercises before the duce. The younger the children, the greater was their pride in their uniforms and their love for the duce, to whom some teachers made them address their prayers and for whose smile they would have attempted the impossible.

The physical training of youth was admirable, but other aspects of Fascist education were not as good. Even Mussolini's pro-Fascist biographers, Pini and Susmel, admit that "the moral and cultural formation of youth was less harmonious and perfect [than the physical]. Social ideas and political and international views were less clear. Too much rhetoric was the basis of the conformists' orthodoxy; too much conservatism snarled the revolutionary impetus; and too many residual moral insufficiencies nestled in the souls. . . ."

The "School of Fascist Mysticality" that Arnaldo Mussolini founded in Milan could do little to illumine young, confused minds. In Fascist parlance, "mystics" were those who gave everything and asked nothing in return, who relinquished their will and were ready to "believe, obey, and fight" blindly, out of a pure passion in which intelligence and understanding found no place. The youth of Italy, as Mussolini would have had it, were a mystic group who surrendered its thinking powers even before learning how to use them. In a few instances an "old-fashioned" family environment tempered the influence of Fascist education — in Italy the family was a strong unit, abiding by its own customs, rules, and traditions — but otherwise the young drew little inspiration from the example of their elders. By the early thirties the plethora of Fascist rhetoric and adulation swamped the regime and stifled the finest expressions of Italian culture. One piece of Fascist prose, chosen at random, the written statement of a deputy in Parliament who had been Undersecretary for Public Education and was president of the National Confederation of Professionals and Artists, will provide an illustration of how supposedly well-educated persons had come to think and write: "The National Council of the Corporations . . . expresses to its President, Chief of Government and Duce of Fascism, its unshakable faith in the future of the Nation and of the regime; affirms that the corporative organization, created by the Duce, and enacted, in its institutions and spirit, by the action of leaders and followers, is, in its function of harmonic synthesis and of social forces and interests, the cornerstone of the Fascist political system; declares that it wants to be an increasingly effective instrument of the [Fascist] revolution, both in the social and economic field, so that all productive forces may collaborate, under the Duce's guidance, to the benefit of the Fatherland."

In his attempts to escape the solitude of the Sala del Mappamondo, the duce gave himself more and more frequently to an activity that he had always enjoyed: inaugurating "realizations of the Fascist regime." As Fascist rhetoric spread, any new cornerstone, construction, excavation, school, institution of higher education, airline, piece of reclaimed land, street, stadium, and whatnot became a "realization" of the regime.

Realizations were so timed that each year Mussolini could inaugurate a batch of them on or about October 28, during the celebration of the anniversary of the March on Rome. The most elaborate and showy celebration was the one of the *decennale* or tenth anniversary, when for more than a week the duce alternated public addresses, full of Roman and Fascist passion, and inaugurations. He began on October 25, and on that day at the head of a column of five hundred cars he drove from Turin to Milan, thus inaugurating the new *autostrada*. In Milan he dedicated two buildings and a school, and then he left for other cities and other inaugurations. The celebrations reached their most glorious height on October 28, in Rome, when he opened the grandiose athletic center *Foro Mussolini*, among whose features were a stadium surrounded by sixty marble statues of athletes and a fifty-five-foot-high obelisk, made of a single piece of marble, bearing the word DUX in huge carved letters. Its pointed top was supposed to be solid gold, but according to rumors the unscrupulous builder had used gold foil instead. (The many Fascist slogans in a mosaic floor created embarrassment for the organizers of the 1960 Olympic Games in Rome. Some wanted to cover the mosaic floor with dirt, but others remarked that fascism, an unfortunate, shameful episode, could not be so easily hidden from history.)

On the same day, October 28, the duce, on horseback and in his most resplendent uniform, with a white panache on his fez, cut the ribbon across Via dell'Impero, thus opening a grandiose artery, half a mile long, running straight through a typical and unforgettable Roman scene of sunbaked ruins and umbrella pines. (After the conquest of Abyssinia, Mussolini had three marble maps hung in Via dell'Impero; one showed the boundaries of the ancient Roman Empire, the other two the extent of Italian territories before and after the Ethiopian war.) The day before, in Rome, the duce had inaugurated the Exhibit of the Fascist Revolution: two daring architects had concealed the front of an old exhibition hall behind a stunning modernistic façade in which three huge, stylized *fasci del littorio* seemed immense axes ready to swing down and chop off the heads of the people as they

entered. Inside, the show itself did not match the imaginative-
ness of the façade, and the many newspapers clippings, the
eerie pictures, and gory trophies formed an excellent self-
caricature of the regime and what it stood for.

For several days thereafter Mussolini went on "inaugurating" in other cities and towns, at the same fast pace. Oblig-
ingly, in Littoria, where the first settlers had arrived on October 27, the first baby was born before the celebration of the
decennale was over.

The Sala del Mappamondo was Mussolini's private office, and
government business was carried out in other halls of Palazzo
Venezia. One hall was reserved for the Grand Council, and
when the council was meeting, the *moschettieri*, Mussolini's
personal guard, were on duty, as at other formal ceremonies
and receptions, dressed in black uniforms with skulls and
crossbones as their insignia. A few years later another Fascist
institution, the National Council of the Corporations, over
which Mussolini usually presided, began holding its sessions
there.

About the Fascist corporative state much has been said and
written, for it was the feature of fascism that aroused the
greatest and longest-lasting interest abroad, although its
ideological aims were never attained. The failure is due in
large part to the inherent weaknesses of a totalitarian regime
in which a chief and a hierarchy interfere in affairs about
which they know too little. After giving "inspiration" to corporativism, Mussolini apparently lost interest in it and left
its realization in the hands of his legislators, who by and
large were competent, and to others he appointed to leading
roles, who in general proved not to be up to the task. From the
time he abandoned orthodox socialism, Mussolini advocated
class collaboration instead of class struggle, because he
thought that only from harmony between capital, technology,
and labor could production increase and bring wealth to the
country. He claimed that the seed of corporativism was contained in a speech he had given in 1919, on the occasion of

his unfortunate electoral campaign, when he said: "We believe that one of the necessities of modern life that cannot be postponed is to give the largest possible place to technical competence and that the state organism should be transformed through the institution of national technical councils, elected by trade and professional organizations and by cultural associations."

The legislators gave form to Mussolini's inspiration in the labor charter promulgated in 1927 and, more specifically, in what may be considered its central article: "In the collective contract of work there is the concrete expression of the solidarity between the various factors of production, through the conciliation of opposed interests of employers and workers, and their subordination to the superior interests of production." In accordance with this principle, the corporations were established. Each corporation consisted initially of workers' and employers' representatives. Later, members of the Fascist Party were included in each corporation, in a sort of political supervisory capacity which in itself represented undue government interference. Corporations became protectors of workers who held party cards against those who did not; employers' representatives managed to tip the scales in most decisions so that the balance between capital and labor was never achieved; pressures and intrigues to obtain leading positions were so great that the corporations soon became one of the largest areas of patronage; at their head were men appointed directly by Mussolini for reasons other than their technical competence.

Evidence of Mussolini's loss of interest in corporativism are the vague generalities that he uttered on the subject. "Fascism establishes true and deep equality of all individuals in respect to the nation. The difference is only in the degree and amplitude of single responsibilities. . . . The objective of the regime in the economic field is the realization of a higher social justice for the entire Italian people. This means assured work, adequate wages, a decorous home, the possibility of promotion and constant growth." In 1934 he said: "This is an imposing assembly — the most imposing perhaps, in Italy's history . . . . [It] is a revolutionary assembly, one, that is, which acts with method and enthusiasm in order to foster — in institutions, laws, and habits — the political and social transformations that have become necessary to the life of a people. . . . An organization that should gradually and inflexibly shorten the distances between the largest, smallest or nonexistent [*sic*] assets of life." Of Mussolini's numberless utterances about corporations and the corporative state the most "sculptorean," most assuredly pronounced and insistently circulated, was: "The Fascist state is either corporative or it is not Fascist."

Nominations made "high up" (by Mussolini himself) to positions that ought to have been elective (as originally planned) account for much in the failure of corporativism, but were not characteristic of the corporations. It was as if the lonelier Mussolini became, the greater he felt the urge to do everything himself. In time, he went through a frenzy of nominating, transferring, and dismissing men in the Fascist hierarchy. The verb "to resign" was used in a peculiar way: Mussolini "resigned [*dimissionava*]" his ministers and collaborators, and the persons so "resigned" often learned from the newspapers that they were no longer in office. When dismissals and the shifting of responsibility took place on a large scale, they were called the "changing of the guard" and occasionally were held in Palazzo Venezia with the formal introduction of the new set of officials to the duce.

None of his activities relieved Mussolini of the sense that something was amiss, that he was not enjoying life as he should; and to one of his biographers he complained that he felt a prisoner of his office. From the man who had been an inmate of the Rocca of Caterina Sforza this was an appalling admission.

1925 *"Farmers and landowners responded with zeal when he launched the battle for wheat. Now and then, he joined the peasants of Romagna or those of the land around Rome to help them sow, reap, and thresh."*

1925 *"In another cage was the lioness Italia, once allowed to roam Mussolini's apartment. He often went to the zoo to feed her, play with her, or shake her paw — before an enthusiastic photographer."*

1931 "With five children the Mussolini famil
could enter the contest of belle famiglic
italiane, for which Mussolini himself
had established prizes."

February 11, 1929 "Church dignitaries and members of the government took places at a long table — the cardinal in the center,
Mussolini at his left. Cardinal Gasparri was so moved that he
could not finish reading his accrediting letter and had to pass
it to the Secretary of the Sacred Congregation for Extraordinary Ecclesiastical Affairs."

1935 *"In Pontinia, one of the new cities built on land reclaimed from the marshes, Mussolini received the wedding rings. In Rome, the ceremony was staged before the tomb of the unknown soldier on the dazzling white monument to Victor Emmanuel II. The proud and stately Elena, queen of Italy, was the first Roman woman to throw her ring — and the king's — into the crucible above the incense-burning flame."*

18

THE FOUNDER OF AN EMPIRE

> "Imperialism is the eternal and immutable
> law of life. All considered, it is only the need,
> the wish, and the will to expand that each
> individual, that each lively and vital people
> carries in itself."
>
> MUSSOLINI, January, 1919

IN the splendid isolation of Palazzo Venezia Mussolini indulged in dreams of grandeur and saw visions of himself
ascending to greater power, dominating expanding territories,
as a true Caesar and builder of empires. The Roman passion
was still burning in him and flared up in his speeches, which
seldom failed to sound a hosanna to Rome, her culture, her
doctrine, her profound wisdom. It appeared also in his actions;
driven by it, he strove to make Italy the direct continua-
tion of the Roman Empire, to turn the young people and manhood of Italy into an array of "Romanly virile" cohorts, to
revive Roman names, titles, myths, and customs, both for the
militant Fascist and for the lay public in its daily life; pouring
over Rome, which to him was still the *Urbs* of the Latins,
amounts of money to make other cities jealous, he beau-
tified her with parks, brought back into the light her forgotten
monuments, and built new ones to compete with the ancient in
splendor and costliness, if not always in artistry. But when this
was done, he had not yet conjured up the Roman Empire.

Over this Empire he brooded in his solitary hours in the Sala
del Mappamondo, and to bring it about he made solitary decisions, seeking no advice. His empire was to be colonial, at
least in the beginning, for only as such would it fit his "demo-

graphic campaign" and be justified in the eyes of the world: a colonial empire, he thought, would fall into the pattern of conquest that all mighty nations had followed in the past and would therefore be morally justified; it would redress the injustice perpetrated at Versailles, where, though a victor, Italy had been robbed of her share of the spoils, and would cure the Italians of the sense of frustration they continued to feel; finally, it would provide a much-needed outlet for Italy's growing population. To Mussolini, the modern Caesar, it would bring glory and the awed recognition of the world.

Mussolini frequently spoke in vague terms of "the empire," without defining it either in space or time, saying that to achieve it the existing "eight million bayonets" ought to multiply, the population must increase. "If we decrease [in numbers], gentlemen," he once explained to the Chamber of Deputies, "we do not build an empire, we become a colony."

In Mussolini's reasoning, logic and muddled thinking were always mixed. It was true that civilized nations in the past had conquered lands and earned wealth by subjugating backward peoples; yet, after World War I — the war to end all wars — the building of empires had been forsworn, colonial exploitation was going out of fashion, and the trend was rather toward the independence of existing colonies than the seizing of new ones. It was also true that Italy aroused a certain amount of sympathy for the ill-treatment she had received at Versailles; and it was generally recognized that the Italian colonies, Libya, Eritrea, and Italian Somaliland, were no asset, no more than a collection of deserts. All the same, this did not mean that more successful empire builders would consider Italy morally entitled to acquire forcefully new colonies in Africa. Italy's emigration problem was already unquestionably acute: the United States, Canada, and Australia had passed stricter immigration laws after World War I. Mussolini could well argue that a colonial empire would absorb the surplus population without the loss of nationals to foreign countries. Yet, the need for an empire could hardly be a reason for encouraging an increase in population.

At first the dictator planned his empire entirely by himself. He turned his eyes to Africa and fixed them on Abyssinia, the only African country that had preserved independence from white rule. It was a vast country, impenetrable for lack of roads and railroads, with no access to the sea except by way of the only railroad from Addis Ababa, the capital, to the port of Djibouti in French Somaliland; a country in which enormous stretches of torrid deserts and barren and stony plateaus alternated with green and luxuriant lands; where lions, leopards, hyenas, lynx, and wolves grew large and fierce; of whose vast mineral deposits much was said and very little was definitely known; a country whose main exports were coffee and hides. Yet Abyssinia was the logical object of Mussolini's imperialistic ambitions. It bordered upon the Italian colonies of Eritrea to the north and Somaliland to the southeast; for decades it had been recognized as in the Italian sphere of influence by European colonial powers. When Menelik became Negus of Abyssinia in 1889, he signed a treaty of friendship with Italy, a treaty he soon denounced to attack Italian troops stationed on soil annexed from Abyssinia. In the battle of Adowa that ensued, the Italians were defeated by a native army eight times their strength; and the Abyssinians perpetrated the most barbarous atrocities on Italian prisoners.

This happened in the year 1896. Benito Mussolini was thirteen years old and at school; the news of the Italian defeat was a severe blow to his impressionable mind. Of his feelings at that time he was to write in "My Life" while serving his term in the Rocca of Caterina Sforza for his efforts to prevent the war in Libya: "That day [of the defeat at Adowa] I was ill. At about 10:00 A.M. one of my school friends . . . ran to me in the dormitory with an open newspaper, shouting: 'Read! Read!' I grabbed the paper. . . . From the first page to the last it talked of nothing but the disastrous battle — ten thousand dead and seventy-two cannons lost. Those figures are still hammering in my skull. The next day, crouched on top of the wall surrounding our school, we saw an interminable parade of country people who were going to the city to protest."

If the child Mussolini could long nurse a grievance, the dictator had the means for revenge. He had signed treaties with England and France, pledging to preserve the status quo in Abyssinia and defining the spheres of influence of each country; with Abyssinia he had signed a twenty-year treaty of amity called the Pact of Friendship, Conciliation, and Arbitration. But treaties were not brakes to his actions. He was always ready to enter into agreements with any willing country, to sign friendship, or trade, or mutual security pacts, because to do so enhanced his sense of his own importance in the world. Yet the countries entering into agreements with him were blind and deaf, for repeatedly he stated that treaties were not eternal but bound to be "revised," which in his mind meant that they were subject to change, including complete violation. The memory of the Adowa defeat was longer lasting and more impelling than any treaty provision. "The great account opened in 1896," as Mussolini was to call the Italian defeat, had to be settled at all costs. Then the Roman dream would become reality.

Other considerations may have come to his mind: his determination to leave a deeper imprint in history than any great Italian ever had; his belief that a large empire might truly prove economically advantageous, especially since the world depression had begun to threaten Italy's always precarious economy and, together with the forced, artificial value of the lira, had caused foreign trade to decline; and the fact that he had run out of "stunts," ideas for new roles for himself and entertaining activities to keep the Fascists happily busy and perpetually acclaiming him. On the enormous stage that Fascist Italy had become, no great performance had been given since the reconciliation with the Vatican. Now the actor was ready to extend his stage deep into Africa and play his role of empire builder before the entire world. He could also play another role, that of the bearer of the true faith to the tribes of Abyssinia belonging to the Coptic church. In this role, Mussolini rightly surmised, he would please the Vatican and obtain, if not its blessing, its support. Thus in the early thirties he talked of peace and prepared for war.

In the mind of Mussolini the importance of the colonial

enterprise slowly grew out of all proportion and became his sole concern. He usually saw only one side of any question, and he let the colonial campaign overshadow the troubles of Europe, the rise of nazism with its threat to the world, the advantages that Italy might obtain from good relations with England and France, and the Italian pledge to abide by the rulings of the League of Nations. He forgot the lofty words he had pronounced in his own defense at the Forlì trial in 1912 against another colonial expedition, the applause he had then received, and the admiration of his judges. Nor did he remember the dire consequences of the Libyan war, the economic exhaustion in which it left Italy, and the unpreparedness of the army and the nation when Italy entered World War I. In his one-sided stubbornness he did not stop to consider the enormous cost of a war fought at such a distance and at an accelerated (and hence more expensive) pace, and he did not realize, or refused to take into consideration, that a colony is a long-term investment unlikely to bring returns within the life span of an already mature man. He had made up his mind and was not going to change it.

Shortly before the opening of hostilities in Abyssinia, Mussolini declared: "*Noi tireremo dritto* [We shall go straight ahead]," and made it clear that ahead he would go, even if this meant war with England. It was not a bluff but a resolution made in full awareness, under the threat of the British fleet in the Mediterranean.

Yet, in the early thirties Mussolini had not pushed this far his plans to conquer Abyssinia.

Benito Mussolini was an armchair Caesar. In early 1932 he summoned General Emilio de Bono, the aging quadrumvir of the March on Rome, one of his most trusted followers, certainly among the most loyal and devoted. At the time of the Matteotti affair, the duce had requested the general's resignation for his alleged complicity, but De Bono had not fallen into disgrace as Cesare Rossi and others had done; instead, he continued to be appointed to important posts, a fact that may explain his devotion. In 1932, when Mussolini summoned him for a private talk, he was Minister of Colonies.

The duce asked De Bono to go to Eritrea and report on existing conditions. As early as 1925, Mussolini had directed an earlier Minister of Colonies to place Eritrea on a good defensive footing against possible attacks from bordering Abyssinia, and De Bono was to see how Mussolini's orders had been carried out. Of this mission De Bono was to write: "I left in March of that year and remained in the colony only long enough to get a positive idea of all the needs, which were many. Governors and military commanders used all their competence and good will to push progress; and progress was achieved miraculously, considering the very limited financial resources. Upon my return I gave a succinct report to the chief of government, plainly representing the state of affairs, but in an optimistic spirit."

De Bono's mission went unnoticed in Italy and in other European countries, which thus failed to receive a warning. In further private conversations, Mussolini instructed De Bono to increase the military efficiency of Eritrea and build a network of roads. (Proudly De Bono was to report that in the autumn of 1933 he and the duce were the only two persons informed of plans for military operations in East Africa.)

In preparing for the invasion of Abyssinia, it was Mussolini's policy to pour into Eritrea many times the money and supplies that his experts thought necessary; and during the last months he increased the contingent of Italian troops destined for service in Africa. He could hope that he would not need the great amount of supplies he was sending into Africa or the numerous divisions set aside for the campaign; he could hope that as soon as the invasion began the heterogeneous Abyssinian empire would collapse. In Mussolini's mind this belief was further strengthened by knowledge of clandestine diplomatic activities designed to win over some of the dissident rulers and their tribes.

In December, 1934, an incident at Wal-Wal provided Mussolini with a pretext to prepare openly for war and gave a dangerous twist to the course of history. Wal-Wal was a watering place in the desert near Italian Somaliland and well inside Abyssinia according to all maps; but the border between the

Italian colony and the Abyssinian empire had never been de-
limited. At Wal-Wal there was a garrison of some 150 Somalis
in the service of Italy and an unspecified number of armed
Ethiopians. The only neutral who had any knowledge of the
state of things was a certain Colonel Clifford, an Englishman
who headed a commission to demarcate the frontier of Somaliland. Clifford went to Wal-Wal at the end of November, 1934,
for reasons that have not been explained, and found the two
opposing groups facing each other at a short distance, shouting
insults, with loaded rifles in hand; he thought best to leave that
place. Ten days later, according to the Italian version, Abyssinian troops armed with machine guns attacked the Italian
Somalis; according to the Abyssinian version, Italian Somalis,
with two tanks and three airplanes, attacked the Ethiopians.
Italy immediately demanded apologies and reparations, but
the Negus, who had yielded in several earlier incidents, this
time took a step that broke all tradition in the pattern of relations between European and African peoples: he appealed to
the League of Nations.

Abyssinia had been a member of the League since 1923,
when her membership was supported by both France and Italy.
England opposed it on the ground that Abyssinia was not a true
state and the reigning empress, Zaiditu, was a self-appointed
ruler who had dethroned the previous emperor and imprisoned
him in chains. Besides, England maintained, Abyssinia was not
a civilized nation and the slave trade was still flourishing there.
Why Mussolini's Italy supported Abyssinia's admission to the
League is a matter of speculation, unless the thesis of the apologist Luigi Villari is accepted. According to Villari, the Italian
move may have been prompted by the suggestion of the *West-
minster Gazette* that Great Britain be given a mandate over
Abyssinia — a mandate surely contrary to the interests of Italy.

At any rate, on January 3, 1935, Haile Selassie's government sent a wire to Geneva denouncing the Italian action at
Wal-Wal. The League began to study the case, a difficult one
since there were no neutral witnesses. (After long study the
arbitration commission failed to fix responsibility for the incident and returned some sort of verdict of not guilty for lack of
proof.)

The Wal-Wal incident did not disrupt the negotiations that

Mussolini had undertaken with the French foreign minister, Pierre Laval, over several colonial questions. Indeed, only two days after the Abyssinian protest to the League, Laval arrived in Rome and after two days of conversations with the duce reached an agreement extremely favorable to France. Because of this, it was generally assumed (although officially denied) that Laval had promised that France would give Italy a free hand in Abyssinia; but an exchange of letters between Laval and Mussolini, long kept secret, proves that although the familiar expression "a free hand" was used, Laval had not agreed to Italian military operations in Africa. The price Mussolini had to pay was renunciation of the hope that at some future time Tunisia would pass from France to Italy. This hope was justified by the fact that Tunisia is the closest African territory to the Italian peninsula and its European population at least as much Italian as French. Mussolini also agreed to the gradual loss of the special privileges that Italians enjoyed in Tunisia, among which was the right to preserve their nationality for themselves and their descendants. Thus, another example of inconsistency, the dictator who bid for an empire so that Italians would not have to lose their nationality in foreign countries was willing to give up some 100,000 Italians in Tunisia; but the agreement did not go into effect.

In April the Ethiopian affair took another puzzling turn: Ramsay MacDonald, the British prime minister, Pierre Flandin, the French premier, and their foreign ministers, Simon and Laval, met for four days with Mussolini without broaching the subject of Abyssinia. The place of the meeting was Stresa, on Lake Maggiore; the occasion, Hitler's announced intention to rearm — a threat perhaps sufficient to put Abyssinia out of mind; the outcome, the short-lived Stresa front, born when the three countries pledged themselves to keep Germany in check, preserve Austrian independence, and maintain peace in Europe.

To Mussolini, the pledge of peace in Europe did not preclude war in Africa. And the British and the French also carefully avoided any mention of Ethiopia, a subject that might have clouded the excellent relations at Stresa. Laval, satisfied with his agreement with Mussolini, had no interest in reopen-

ing the question before the British at Stresa. The British themselves were of two minds: they enthusiastically embraced the
new principles of internationalism and collective security
through the League of Nations and sought disarmament, arbitration, and the punishment of aggressor nations. But strong
pro-Italian and anti-League currents had developed, especially
among Catholics, conservatives, and businessmen. And so
MacDonald and Simon, who expected an election within a
year or so, may have preferred to let matters rest.

Two months later Great Britain entered into a separate naval
agreement with Germany, inflicting the first blow upon the
Stresa front and the League of Nations and in effect showing
that each country could go her own way.

At the end of June, Anthony Eden, then Minister for League
Affairs and a symbol of English interest in the League, paid a
visit to Mussolini to propose a peaceful settlement of the Ethiopian question: Great Britain would give Abyssinia a corridor
to the sea, and in exchange Abyssinia would relinquish a part
of the Ogaden territory to Italy. Mussolini disliked Eden at
sight, found him cold, conceited, obtuse, importunate, and disdainful, and went out of his way to be impolite. It was said that
their talks were stormy, their encounters punctuated by reciprocal threats. Not without justification, Mussolini felt that
Ogaden would add one more desert to Italy's already vast collection. He considered Eden's proposal unacceptable.

A few days after this unfortunate meeting Great Britain published the results of a "peace ballot," a poll promoted by the
League of Nations, which indicated that British public opinion
was in favor of applying economic sanctions against aggressors.
With some reason, Mussolini had never taken into consideration the possibility of sanctions: when Japan had attacked
Manchuria in 1932, the League had proved impotent, thus giving the impression that aggression outside Europe would go
unpunished. The "peace ballot" and the opinion of lesser
European nations now put sanctions in a different light. Mussolini considered withdrawing from the League, as Germany
had done in 1933, but realized that Italy had nothing to lose
and much to gain by a display of formal courtesy toward other
nations. By this time, however, the Stresa front was completely

shattered, the traditional good relations between England and
Italy were over, and the clouds on the horizon of Europe were
swiftly darkening.

By mid-September the war in Africa appeared inevitable
even to inveterate optimists. Pessimists believed that Mussolini's provocative acts, combined with the presence of the British home fleet in the Mediterranean, might produce the spark
that would set off a European war. Mussolini was sending division upon division to East Africa and at the departure of each
pronounced valedictory speeches of increasing aggressiveness.
In speeches and in interviews with the foreign press he condemned the policy of Great Britain, whose strength came from
her empire but who, he contended, opposed an Italian empire
in order to safeguard her interests in the Suez Canal.

In England, in view of the coming elections, the "peace ballot," and public opinion, the government embraced an all-out
policy in favor of the League of Nations and the imposition of
economic sanctions on aggressor nations. At the end of September Winston Churchill spoke in London and "tried to convey a
warning to Mussolini," as he recalls in *The Gathering Storm*:
"To cast an army of nearly a quarter-million men, embodying
the flower of Italian manhood, upon a barren shore two thousand miles from home, against the good will of the whole world
and without command of the sea, and then in this position em-
bark upon what may well be a series of campaigns against a
people and in regions which no conqueror in four thousand
years ever thought it worthwhile to subdue, is to give hostages
to fortune unparalleled in all history."

It is tempting to speculate what effect these words may have
had on Mussolini, if he read them, as Churchill believed he
did. The chance seems negligible that at this late date, committed as he was to the Ethiopian war by both the fatalistic drive
of his own determination and the amount of money he had spent
in the undertaking, Mussolini would have allowed this warning
to dissuade him. (To an interviewer from the *Morning Post*, he
said that the cost of preparation was already 2 billion lire —
100 million prewar dollars — and asked "Can you believe that
we have spent this sum for nothing?") Coming from Churchill,
who as a young man had fought in colonial wars and was still

an exponent of British imperialism, opposing any abdication of power in India, the warning must have seemed another proof of British policy, holding fast to her empire and grudging a colony to Italy. But Churchill's words might well have had another effect on the dictator, for they were, unwittingly, exalting his coming colonial feat. In his own mind the duce was an empire builder, and Churchill made him view himself as a "conqueror" facing enormous difficulties, who would push two thousand miles from home to achieve a feat that no conqueror in four thousand years had achieved, thus accomplishing something "unparalleled in all history." To a man almost certain that he could obtain the victory and achieve that feat, Churchill's words must have been a further incitement rather than a deterrent.

Negotiations for a peaceful settlement of the Ethiopian question were continued by an *ad hoc* committee of the League even after the African campaign began, and they were to culminate in the Hoare-Laval plan that called for the partition of Abyssinia, giving to Italy somewhat more territory than she had by then occupied. (To both Mussolini and British public opinion the proposal was unacceptable.)

While taking up a position against the Ethiopian war and for the League's policies, Great Britain was unofficially assuring France that she would try to water down the sanctions on Italy, if imposed, and connived with France in an embargo on arms to Ethiopia through the control of the port of Djibouti, the only access to Abyssinia from the sea. It is said that Haile Selassie, placing pathetic confidence in traditional British justice, could not understand why it was so difficult to procure the modern arms and equipment he needed and was trying so desperately to buy. But then, during the war, the unofficial embargo was lifted, in part at least.

After the Ethiopian war ended there was much speculation about the conditions under which war might have been averted and at what moment Mussolini would have accepted a peaceful compromise. Not unreasonably, many Englishmen, with their keen sense of responsibility and conscience, have blamed their government for its wavering stand; for letting Abyssinia remain virtually unarmed and giving Italy the impression — or even saying outright—that she was free to act as she pleased, provided certain British interests were respected in the region of Lake Tana and the waters that run into the Nile; for having ignored Mussolini's preparations, only to react uncompromisingly when it was too late. The sense of guilt evident in some books about the Ethiopian venture, like Arnold Toynbee's *Survey of International Affairs for 1935* and Geoffrey T. Garratt's well-documented *Mussolini's Roman Empire*, might seem justified in view of the duce's ostensible indecision and apparently sincere—perhaps occasionally truly sincere— attempts to find a peaceful solution of the Abyssinian question.

On closer scrutiny, Mussolini's indecisiveness proves to be due to his irresolute temperament, which caused him to reverse any decision from hour to hour. But hidden behind this habit of mind was the tremendous driving power of an insatiable ambition. If his line of conduct zigzagged between yes and no, between acceptance of compromise and preparation for conquest, still its main progress was always in the same direction, unavoidably pointing toward an Abyssinian empire over which he was to have absolute authority and control.

The Ethiopian war was decided and carried out by the will of a single man: the dictator Benito Mussolini. Even before the Wal-Wal incident brought his intentions to the fore, he was so committed in his own mind, his imperialistic ambitions had gathered such momentum, that it is hard to conceive how anything could have stopped him.

It has been said that Mussolini could plan his war of imperialism because he knew that he had the Italian people behind him, that in fact the Ethiopian conflict was a popular war. This statement requires some qualification. A well-considered evaluation of public opinion is always difficult in a country under dictatorship, and the insider has few more elements on which to base his judgment than the outsider, for a distorted press, an efficient propaganda machine, and repeated, "well-organized," spontaneous demonstrations blur the true picture. Yet some assumptions can be made with a certain confidence that one will remain within the bounds of probability. The majority of Fascist youth, raised in the belief that war is good in itself, drilling in military exercises, sensitive to the point of touchiness in their national pride, and taught to worship the duce as a demigod, could not but be behind the dictator, await with impatience the chance to show their valor, and fight for their own and Italy's glory. But others did not want war. The German-speaking Tyroleans did not feel the appeal of "more land" and did not see any need to fight in Africa; white-collar workers as a rule preferred their desks to the fortunes of war in the tropics; many intellectuals who had preserved the power of independent thinking feared the consequences of an unjust and expensive colonial war that at best would give Italy territories of little or no economic value. The summer and fall of 1935 marked a low spot in the popularity of fascism. For the first time since the Matteotti affair, Italians grumbled openly and openly criticized Mussolini's actions. Only three years later, when giving vent to opinions at variance with the official, Italians in private homes avoided rooms with telephones, which they feared might be tapped, and carefully closed doors before speaking. But in late 1935 grumbling was heard everywhere, in the street, in offices. There was talk of revolution, of an army pronouncement and a coup d'état. The grumbling and talk of great changes were sedate and resigned, as if those who opposed Mussolini felt conscious of their helplessness in the face of a well-organized police state and the unshakable will of its chief. Discontent increased with the opening of hostilities on October 3.

What dispelled a large measure of the discontent and rallied the Italian people around the duce was the imposition by the League of Nations of economic sanctions, which went into effect on November 18. Sanctions were applied according to the principle of gradualness; many countries disregarded them; oil and coal, the commodities Italy most needed for the war, were not included. As imposed, the sanctions were to prove ineffectual, but to the Italian people, ignorant of the intrigue behind the scenes, exposed only to the Fascist viewpoint, the very idea of sanctions, of the unfairness, if not injustice, of sanctions, was a heavy blow. It reawakened the sense of injury the Italians had experienced at the end of World War I, and again they felt rejected by the society of great powers, betrayed in their aspirations to a just share of living space. If Mussolini's rule was too demanding; if some Italians were tiring of him and his unforeseeable moves; if an empire might prove a disastrous expense for a country like Italy; all these, the Italians felt, were internal questions in which other governments had no right to interfere. Sanctions had never before been decreed, and in choosing Italy as the first case, in calling her an aggressor and thus favoring "barbaric Abyssinia," the nations imposing sanctions were committing an unforgivably unfriendly act.

Italy was indignant, and the duce, supported by his smoothly working propaganda machine, exploited the indignation to the utmost. He entrusted the Association of War Widows and War Mothers with the task of finding ways by which the effects of the sanctions could be counterbalanced. Foreign products were to be boycotted, and the campaign for "autarchy" (self-sufficiency), already begun, was to be energetically pursued. The war widows and mothers began collecting gold, silver, and copper for the war effort, and when among the gold they found a few wedding rings the duce took the hint and staged the most mystical mass performance Italy had ever seen. On December 18, one month after the sanctions were decreed, the married women of Italy offered their gold wedding rings and those of their husbands, receiving in exchange steel rings with the inscription "Gold to the Fatherland."

The offering of wedding rings was not the first in history. Frenchwomen had responded to a similar appeal from the leaders of the French Revolution in 1792. At the end of World War I, when inciting the Italians to financial sacrifice, Mussolin had quoted a page from Michelet's *History of the Revolution* which relates that event; and from Michelet he undoubtedly took inspiration in 1935. But after going through the mill of his sense of drama, the ceremony in Italy became a huge pageant that surged to heights of solemn dedication. In cities, towns, and villages Italian women formed processions and marched to collecting points; bishops and other members of the clergy blessed the rings; large braziers burned to melt down the gold. In Pontinia, one of the cities built on land reclaimed from the marshes, Mussolini himself received the wedding rings from the inhabitants. In Rome the ceremony was staged at the "Altar of the Fatherland," before the tomb of the unknown soldier, on the dazzling white monument to Victor Emmanuel II. The proud and stately Elena, queen of Italy, was the first woman of Rome to throw her ring (and the king's) into the melting crucible over the incense-burning flame. (Wealthy Italian women hastily bought new rings for the offering and hid their prized ones; none dared be seen in public wearing a gold wedding ring.)

The "spontaneous sacrifice" — there had been no coercion except propaganda and the unmistakable "expectations in high places" — opened the hearts of the Italians and prepared them for further deprivation. The imperialist war became popular.

Mussolini did not visit the scenes of battle, did not accept the Abyssinian emperor's challenge to meet him on the field; yet he insisted on being the chief strategist for all Ethiopian operations. In early 1935 he sent 10,000 Italian workers to build roads and military installations. In his book on the campaign, General de Bono admits that at that time Eritrea was not ready to accommodate so many, lodgings were insufficient, and most workers had to be housed in tents. In desert land the climate was unhealthy, and many died. A secret telegram from Mussolini to De Bono reveals that two shiploads of men who had contracted malaria were sent back to Italy. Not for the sake of Italian men, but for fear of public reaction, Mussolini advised De Bono to use only native workers in the lowlands during the summer months.

In March, 1935, the duce wrote De Bono: "You are asking for three divisions by the end of October: I am resolved to send you ten, I say ten. . . . We lost Adowa for lack of a few thousand men. I shall never commit that error. I want to sin by excess rather than by default." He did not stop to consider the overcrowding of Massawa — the landing port in Eritrea —

the problems in logistics, and the difficulties of transporting to the interior over three times as many men as had been planned for. But there was little that the old general, the duce's subservient acolyte, could do. "Answer with a monosyllable," the duce once requested, and De Bono, after each order, wired "Yes."

To Mussolini time was a factor of prime importance, and impelled by the preposterous demands of the time-pressed dictator the Fascist workers and militia achieved miracles. Toynbee has this to say: "Of all Europeans who were concerned in the African war of 1935–36 the most respectable were the Italian workmen, who performed prodigies of labour in building motor-roads at an extraordinary pace over an intractable terrain. Even the Italian soldiers, who submitted to being mobilized and sent to march and climb over trackless Ethiopian mountains under a tropical sun, deserve their meed of praise. . . ."

In the preface to a book by Marshal Badoglio, De Bono's successor, the duce was to explain his need for haste, for the rapid pace he set for the preparation and conduct of the war: "The categorical imperative of the African war, as of all wars, was this: we had to win; but in the Ethiopian war to this imperative circumstances added another, no less categorical imperative: *we had to win and fast.* Never did a war in general and a colonial war in particular take place under more singular conditions: Italy was not only compelled to attack and defeat, on the Ethiopian plateaus, an enemy prepared by European instructors and equipped with modern weapons,* but she had also to fight on two other fronts, the political and the economic, as a consequence of sanctions . . . applied by the League of Nations for the first time and only against Italy. Thus some kind of speed race was set in motion between Italy and the League of Nations which, if the vicissitudes of war had not been favorable to Italian arms, would have probably passed to the application of more drastic measures. . . . The factor 'time' was therefore a resolutive element."

Because of the time factor, Mussolini ordered De Bono to

---

* This statement, which seems preposterous, is a reference to the Abyssinian use of dumdum ammunition, of which more later.

anticipate the opening of hostilities. As originally planned, the war was to start (possibly through a staged provocation ostensibly Ethiopian; otherwise, on Italian initiative) at the end of October. But on September 29 the duce wired De Bono: "We must absolutely cut short any temporizing. I order you to begin advancing in the early hours of October 3, I say 3. I am waiting for immediate confirmation." The confirmation did not fail to come.

Mussolini kept De Bono under a constant fire of instructions, orders, requests, letters, wires, and telephone calls, usually many in a single day. On October 6 Adowa fell into Italian hands; on November 9 another "sad memory" was wiped out when Italian troops recaptured the fortress of Makallé, which had also been lost to the Ethiopians at the time of the Adowa defeat. But under Mussolini's orders, General de Bono had acted against his best military judgment, spending an enormous effort to obtain a small gain. To Mussolini he explained the need for a halt in order to reorganize the front and the supply lines. Mussolini agreed — and then replaced General de Bono with Marshal Pietro Badoglio.

Badoglio was an ambitious and somewhat unsavory character. He had distinguished himself in the Libyan war and early in World War I, but at Caporetto his army was the first to be defeated, and his critics say that he fled and abandoned several divisions to the enemy. Whatever his behavior at Caporetto, he was named marshal of Italy by the king, who also bestowed upon him the title of marquis, reportedly at Badoglio's request. In addition to this title, he was to ask for and obtain the hereditary title of duke of Addis Ababa at the end of the Ethiopian war. He had been chief of the armed forces in Mussolini's cabinet and governor of Libya, although, according to Fascist sources, Mussolini had been warned that Badoglio was not trustworthy. The marshal gradually acquired a reputation for holding more than one remunerative position at a time. But Mussolini chose to ignore Badoglio's shortcomings and saw in him only a more energetic general than De Bono, and one likely to speed up the pace of the war.

In agreeing to succeed De Bono as "high commissioner of Italian East Africa," Badoglio requested that full responsibility for military operations be left to him; the duce agreed. But the impatient dictator could not refrain from keeping Badoglio, and General Rodolfo Graziani on the southern front, under the same barrage of orders and instructions he had fired at De Bono. Giving orders excited him, gave him a feeling of vicarious participation in the war; as if he smelled the burning gunpowder and saw the streaming blood, he became war-crazed and was seized by the frenzy revealed in his innumerable letters and telegrams to military commanders: "I authorize you to drive away the Swedish missionaries." "I authorize you to use gas as the last resort to overcome the enemy's resistance and in case of counterattack." "I authorize the summary shooting of . . . suspects." "It is all right to use gas if . . . necessary for the supreme reasons of defense." "I authorize you to use gas, even on a large scale."

Thus Badoglio used poison gas, even mustard gas, against the Ethiopians, in direct violation of the Geneva Convention of 1925. Mustard gas, sprayed or dropped in bombs, burns the skin and causes intense pain; if not treated at once, the burns spread and ultimately cause gangrene. Terrorized by the burning rain, the native troops would disperse. The Ethiopians filed a complaint with the League of Nations, listing this and other presumed violations of the rules of war, the most incriminating of which was that the Italians had deliberately bombarded Red Cross units.

Pertinent to this report is a wire that Mussolini sent General Graziani, commander of the southern front, on January 1, 1936: "The news of the bombing . . . of a hospital of the Swedish Red Cross has aroused in that country . . . and in the rest of Europe a great sensation of which our enemies take full advantage. . . . No one is more in favor of a harsh war than I . . . and in this sense I have given you recent instructions; but the game must be worth the candle. . . . Give strict orders to have Red Cross installations diligently respected everywhere." The duce may have later reversed his orders, or his orders may have been disregarded. The fact is that Red Cross units were later bombed and that, perhaps unknown to Mussolini, on March 4, 1936, his own son Vittorio participated in the bombing of a British Red Cross unit where a Dr.

John Melly was treating burns caused by mustard gas. (Melly did not survive the war, but he lived long enough to give an account of the episode.) Vittorio, a volunteer pilot at nineteen, relished "the magnificent sport," and his own account, *Flying Over Ethiopian Mountain Ranges*, reveals a callousness delighting in cruelty: ". . . one group of horsemen gave me the impression of a budding rose unfolding as the bomb fell in their midst and blew them up."

If the Ethiopians accused the Italians of many violations of the League's conventions, the Italians missed no chance to bring charges against the Ethiopians. These barbarians, the Italians said, commit atrocities (an accusation that was probably well-founded, in view of tribal tradition in the treatment of prisoners); they mutilate the bodies of the dead; they use Red Cross emblems to camouflage military supplies and troops. The accusation that Italy made most insistently was that the Abyssinians fired the type of explosive bullet called the dumdum, which had been outlawed by the League.

At home Mussolini made no references to the Italian use of poison gas but dwelled upon the Abyssinian use of dumdum bullets with great emphasis, arousing the indignation of the Italian population. The indignation increased when the press reported that a large stock of these bullets had been found to bear the trademark of a British firm. The British denied the allegation that they were supplying Ethiopia with such ammunition, and the League of Nations engaged in a study of the various allegations, the charges and countercharges, and the testimony of neutrals in Abyssinia, who were generally Ethiopian and British sympathizers. Meanwhile, the Italian armies advanced, the war approached its end.

On the afternoon of May 5, 1936, seven months and two days after the start of the war, Marshal Pietro Badoglio made a spectacular entrance into Addis Ababa at the head of his victorious columns. He was preceded by a row of protective tanks, and with him rode Italian journalists. Behind came the Eritrean *askaris*, tall, handsome, and fast-running, wearing their characteristic fezzes and waving curved swords. Last came the Italian troops, tired and dirty but unabashed as always by the test of endurance they had gone through under the tropic sun. Along the passage of the conquering army were the Ethiopians; and among them many arms were raised in the Fascist salute. All afternoon and evening the tanks and trucks and armored cars rolled on. There were some three thousand motor cars, the "formidable mechanized war unit the like of which had never appeared on the battlefields of Europe during the great conflagration," of which Mussolini had boasted a few days before.

Two days after the occupation of Addis Ababa, General Graziani entered Harrar. Haile Selassie had fled to Djibouti and had sailed for England on May 3.

The conquest of Abyssinia crowned Mussolini's most ambitious hopes since the "heroic vigil" of fascism that preceded his ascent to power. It was his triumph. To announce that Italy had her empire, he let it be known that he would speak from the balcony of Palazzo Venezia at 10:30 P.M. on May 9.

In the evening Rome appeared in its most glittering attire under the multicolored lights that matched the red, white, and green of countless flags proudly deployed. The illuminated squares and ancient monuments were as bright as day; concealed lights magically transformed the water of many Roman fountains into cascades of pure, sparkling gems; the pine trees, darker than the night, absorbed some of the glare from the lighted ruins over which they towered. More dimly, thousands of lights were shining in the windows of Rome. Piazza Venezia seemed packed with more people than it could contain, and the crowd flooded Via dell'Impero and other neighboring streets, climbed over the monument to Victor Emmanuel II, and perched on balconies and rooftops. Squares and streets resounded with the rumble of expectant crowds. From a high platform on which he stood as straight and motionless as a statue a militiaman extended a long trumpet and sounded three loud blasts. In the square the noise subsided. On the small central balcony the stocky figure of the dictator appeared. He placed his square hands on the marble parapet, leaned forward, and spoke in his full, deep voice: "Officers! Noncommissioned officers! Soldiers of all the armed forces of the state in Africa and Italy! Blackshirts of the Revolution! Italians in the Fatherland and in the world! Listen!

"With the decisions that in a few moments you will learn . . . a great event is accomplished: Today, May 9, of the fourteenth year of the Fascist era, the fate of Ethiopia is sealed.

"All the knots were cut by our shining sword, and the African victory stands in the history of our Fatherland whole and pure as the fallen legionnaires and those who survived dreamed it and wanted it. At last Italy has her empire. A Fascist empire, because it bears the indestructible signs of the will and might of the Roman Lictor, because this is the goal toward which for fourteen years the disciplined energies of the young and lusty Italians were driven. An empire at peace, because Italy wants peace for herself and for everyone and resorts to war only when compelled by the imperious, ineluctable necessities of life. A civilizing empire, humanitarian toward all the peoples of Ethiopia.

"This is in the tradition of Rome, who, after winning, allowed the [defeated] people to share her destiny.

"Italians, here is the law that closes one period of our history and opens another, like an immense passageway to all future possibilities:

"1. — The territories and the peoples that belonged to the Ethiopian empire are placed under the full and whole sovereignty of the kingdom of Italy.

"2. — The title of emperor of Ethiopia is assumed by the king of Italy for himself and his successors.

"Officers! Noncommissioned officers! Soldiers of all the armed forces of the state in Africa and Italy! Blackshirts! Italians!

"The Italian people has created the empire with its blood. It will fecundate it with its work and defend it against anyone with its arms.

"Legionnaires! In this supreme certitude raise high your insignia, your weapons, and your hearts to salute, after fifteen centuries, the reappearance of the empire on the fated hills of Rome.

"Will you be worthy of it? [The crowd answered with a single, resounding 'Yes!']

"Your cry is a sacred oath that binds you before God and men, for life and death!"

As soon as Mussolini finished speaking, the jubilant crowd broke out in an ovation unparalleled. In the loud rejoicing only one word could be distinguished, repeated with increasing warmth and appeal: "Duce! Duce!"

The dictator stood silent on the balcony, as if incapable of moving or of further words. He knew by intuition that the nation was united around him as never before; the exultation in Rome, in the entire country, was genuine, as it had not always been in the past. Surely he felt that he cut a more heroic figure than any contemporary European statesman — even Great Britain must recognize this. Perhaps he knew that he was at the moment of his greatest glory. But he did not realize, and for several years was not to realize, that from that moment his descent began — a steady descent to his ruin and death.

The Abyssinian war was disastrous for Mussolini, Italy, and all Europe. Inside Italy it had deleterious and insidious consequences. Under the tension of preparing for war at all costs and at the swiftest possible pace, those who were responsible for preparations did not screen the scrupulous from the unscrupulous, practiced favoritism, and allowed dishonesty to flourish. A new crop of profiteers sprang up, and the sight of their easy profits encouraged speculation, monopoly, and corruption; business scandals multiplied. Political interference in economic life and the disproportionate expansion of bureaucracy foiled any attempts to stifle the spreading dishonesty. The conformity of the Italian press was by then complete, and not even the mildest dissent found expression, except in the futile complaints of the upper middle class and the intellectuals. Corruption was not denounced; speculators took for granted their impunity. When financial scandals were brought to the duce's attention, he replied: ". . . only the petty pilfering of the housemaid who snatches from the grocery money a few lire for herself. . . . There is nothing one can do against rats in the granary. . . ." Coming from the superman who claimed all the achievements of his regime for himself, this attitude of condescension was equivalent to connivance. At the same time, adulation and flattery spread, as they are bound to spread in any regime where all authority is vested in one man. But in Mussolini's case they were especially dangerous, for, while the vacuum which he had created around himself favored his detachment from reality, adulation and flattery inflated his own opinion of himself. More and more, he imposed his blind will on others; less and less did he tolerate contradiction. It was as if he had reverted to that state of extreme egocentrism only natural in childhood, which he had never outgrown, all the more dangerous and vicious in view of the power that he had acquired and the machinery he had established to exert that power. The password among high-ranking Fascists became "Tell Mussolini what he wants to hear." A story that circulated at that time is significant: Mussolini once inaugurated a factory with great pomp and fanfare, as was his habit, but the factory was poorly planned and defective, and, unknown to him, it was never put into operation.

The mesh of deceit in which he was wrapped became so thick that it concealed truth. Eventually he was to recognize that he was surrounded by professional optimists intent on presenting a much too rosy picture of the state of things, but it was then too late, and he had lost control of events.

The consequences of the Ethiopian war for the history of the Western world were more dramatic than those strictly limited to the internal affairs of Italy. To say that the African venture was the direct cause of World War II would be an exaggeration and distortion of the facts: Hitler was so determined to carry out his program of expansion and conquest and his fanaticism was so compelling that it is difficult to imagine circumstances under which he could have been checked and the war avoided. Yet there can be little doubt that Mussolini's campaign in Abyssinia and the ineffectual sanctions imposed on Italy favored the conditions that led to the great conflagration.

The main concern of all members of the League of Nations in applying sanctions upon Italy was to avoid a European war.

They decided against military sanctions because Mussolini had declared that to military sanctions he would answer with military actions. England and France, which led the other countries in the application of economic sanctions, wanted to save the principle of collective security by penalizing the aggressor but were afraid of unduly weakening Italy — France had much to gain from a strong Italy on the Austrian border, and England would have welcomed a solution that did not jeopardize friendship with Italy. On the eve of Mussolini's declaration of war on Abyssinia, Churchill wrote to Austen Chamberlain: "I am very unhappy. It would be a terrible deed to smash up Italy, and it will cost us dear. How strange it is that after all these years of begging France to make it up with Italy, we are now forcing her to choose between Italy and ourselves! I do not think we ought to have taken the lead in such a vehement way. . . ."

As a result of the mixed feelings of France and England toward Italy, economic sanctions were a half-measure: the embargo on weapons had little effect, since Mussolini was already well-stocked with those he would need; an embargo on oil and coal — Italy produced scarcely any — would have been effective and very likely would have made it impossible for Mussolini to pursue the war. It was the fear of this embargo, which the League took into consideration, that induced Mussolini to undertake his race against time, spurring on his generals faster and faster.

The ineffectual manner in which the sanctions were imposed facilitated the outbreak of World War II in two different ways. On the one hand, it showed to both existing and would-be dictators that the League's system of collective security had neither the means nor the power to halt aggression. While the fight was going on in Africa, Hitler occupied the demilitarized zone of the Rhineland, established by the Treaty of Versailles, and then made conciliatory advances, saying that Germany had no further territorial ambitions. Other countries seemingly accepted his words at face value, he went unpunished, and his insatiable greed grew enormously. Two months after the conclusion of the Ethiopian war, Francisco Franco prepared to cross the sea from Tangier into Spain to establish a third Fascist dictatorship in western Europe. He sought the help of Abyssinia's conqueror, and Mussolini, though he had just declared that he wanted ten years of peace in which to develop his new territories, sent the first clandestine volunteers into Spain. Mussolini may have acceded to Franco's request because he feared, as he said, the threat to Italian fascism of a Red regime in the Mediterranean, or he may have been lured by the appeal that the idea of action always held for him. Certainly he was sustained by the conviction, springing from his success in Africa and often loudly professed, that he could win any war in a few months. Spurred by Mussolini's example, Hitler also sent volunteers to Spain. The dictators had reason to believe that they were stronger than the democracies.

On the other hand, the imposition of economic sanctions upset the alignment of European powers. Before the African war, Hitler stood alone, surrounded on the west and south by guardians of collective security, England, France, and Italy. In the hope of checking Hitler's ambitions, Mussolini had sponsored a four-power pact in 1933. Great Britain, France, Italy, and Germany had pledged themselves to preserve the equilibrium of Europe by the peaceful revision of the least-fair clauses of the Treaty of Versailles. Mussolini had also chosen to be the champion of Austrian independence, which Hitler threatened, and at Stresa pledged himself to keep Germany in check.

If only in respect to Hitler's growing assertiveness, Mussolini had been on the side of the angels. But with the African war he lost France's and England's friendship; the smarting rancor caused by the sanctions dimmed any hope of patching things up. Mussolini, like Hitler, stood alone, and the inevitable happened: Italy fell into Germany's outstretched arms.

PART 4

A LASTING FRIENDSHIP

19

THE QUARREL OVER AUSTRIA

"Neither for Germany, nor with Germany, but
at the side of Germany."
MUSSOLINI, April, 1940

An attempt to explain events of world significance in terms
of the acts of individuals may be deemed unjustifiable or at
least an oversimplification. Yet Mussolini's and Hitler's pre-
ponderancy and the control they held over their countrymen
were so great that in several instances the most plausible
interpretation of the history of their two countries rests on
their personal relations and attitude toward each other.

There is little affinity between the Italian and German people, and in Fascist times little love was lost between the two.
Indeed, over the generations and through the study of history
in books presenting only a nationalistic point of view, most
Italians had come to look upon Germany and German-speaking Austria as "traditional enemies." Germans and Austrians
were the villains of many tales that old women told young
children at bedtime. Even when carrying out diplomatic
skirmishes with France and England, the Italians looked for
trouble from Germany and Austria; at each European crisis
they strengthened the defenses of the Brenner Pass, not of the
passes into France. (Nevertheless, the popular feeling did
not always affect foreign policies and it did not prevent the
Triple Alliance before World War I.)

A long chain of historical facts seemed to justify the
Italians' attitude toward the Germans. German tribes settled

in the Roman Empire had been a first disintegrating element of it and a threat to Roman civilization; it had been under the repeated attacks of invading German hordes that the Western Empire had fallen, and Germans — Goths and Lombards — had established kingdoms over all or parts of Italy. German were the emperors of the Holy Roman Empire who claimed their right to rule over Italy, overran her soil, and sacked her cities. (Around the most famous of these emperors, the ruthless Frederick Barbarossa, an epic saga grew in Italy, mourning the wounds he inflicted, extolling the heroic resistance against him; and Italian children were expected to memorize the poems of this saga.) Ethnically, German was the Austrian Empire, which sprang from the ashes of the Holy Roman Empire and dominated large parts of Italy.

During the *Risorgimento*, the wars of independence provided fuel for the Italian animosity against German-speaking people. Before World War I, intellectuals decried Germany's economic invasion of Italy as an especially unpleasant aspect of Pan-Germanism. Popular sentiment against Germany and Austria grew so strong in 1914 that the Italian government chose neutrality rather than to go to war at the side of the two Central Powers. The war further exacerbated the Italians' animosity, and Germany and Austria remained Italy's traditional enemies.

Stronger than the factual reasons for the enmity was the less definable conflict of temperaments. The Italians, easygoing and fatalistic, quick-witted, individualistic by nature, with qualities of pliance and resilience that made them adjust to the most difficult situations and bounce back from any stresses or reverses of fortune, could not appreciate the seemingly humorless drive and meticulousness of the unbending Germans, their taste for pompous formality and strict discipline, and their frequent lack of tact. In Mussolini's time personal contacts between Italians and Germans were limited, and the only Germans that the great majority of Italians came to recognize were the tourists with the most pronounced characteristics: those Germans who came with little money to spend but behaved as if they owned the country, called the Lago di Garda *Gardasee*, renamed many Italian places, did not conceal their contempt for the "natives," and boasted of the time when they would be at the Brenner Pass.

In short, the want of confidence between the two peoples was not conducive to friendship. But neither were the personal traits of the two dictators: Mussolini and Hitler exemplified the most extreme characteristics of their peoples, and the differences between them were more antithetical than the average differences between the Italians and the Germans. Yet in time the duce submitted to the fuehrer's enticements and fell under his spell; the two dictators became united by a strong personal bond, akin to friendship, in the name of which they committed the most tragic follies and shaped the destiny of the Western world. To explain how this came to be, the steps in the relations between Mussolini and Hitler must be closely examined.

Adolf Hitler had taken Mussolini as his political model upon hearing of the duce of fascism, shortly before the March on Rome, and in *Mein Kampf*, which he began to write the following year while in prison for an unsuccessful *Putsch*, he had shown how he meant to apply fascism to the problems of Germany. When he became the German chancellor in January, 1933, he said that he wanted only as much power as Mussolini had acquired right after the March on Rome, and there were echoes of Mussolini's voice in the speeches in which Hitler told the German people to hold up their heads, regain their old pride and self-confidence, and help rebuild a united Germany that would regain the position she deserved in the world. Hitler's admiration for the Great Man of Italy was unfeigned and in time it was to turn into personal attachment; for, together with his cold insensitivity and unsurpassed cruelty, Hitler preserved, in that melting pot of contradictions, the soul, a streak of romanticism and sentimentality. Blended with his single-mindedness and fanaticism, it made him capable of an occasional tenacious friendship.

Admiration had played no part in Mussolini's early attitude toward Hitler. To him the German had been a man little known in politics — when he received Hitler's request for an autographed photo he flatly refused — an insignificant imitator of Fascist doctrines and practices; and later, simply an obstreperous advocate of a strong Germany, who was likely to make trouble in Europe. It is, therefore, harder to explain Mussolini's friendship for Hitler than Hitler's for Mussolini — the more so because in the Italian there was none of the German's hysterical romanticism, and the span of emotions, from love to hatred and cruelty, was much smaller. The friendship, in fact, was very slow to develop, and even when in full bloom it was to be tainted in turn with resentment, suspicion, envy, jealousy, and anger. At times, in fact, Mussolini was to strive to free himself from the yoke of Hitler's influence. Yet he came to consider Hitler his true friend and directed his actions to please him. The main reason for Mussolini's yielding to Hitler's display of affection may well be the crucial moment at which the affection was displayed. Mussolini was then no longer young, or aging well, for his health had begun to give reason for concern. No less burdensome than physical illness was the splendid isolation in which he had placed himself after the building of the empire. As he came to feel that perhaps not all was well and he might be losing his grip, he further stressed his role as demigod, but the resulting vacuum around him became oppressive. Loneliness and premature old age went hand in hand.

He complained of his lack of friends, but he had himself to blame. Of the men who stood by him in the days of the March on Rome, Cesare Rossi had been abducted out of Switzerland and lay in prison at Mussolini's order for knowing too much about the Matteotti affair. Aldo Finzi, whom he had forced to resign, never reappeared on the Fascist political scene. Michele Bianchi had died in 1930; and Mussolini kept the three surviving quadrumvirs at a safe distance, whenever feasible, in order to avoid competition. De Bono and De Vecchi had spent much time in Africa as governors of Italian colonies, and after the conquest of the empire De Vecchi was shipped to Rhodes to govern the Dodecanese; by then De Bono was too old to cause concern.

Balbo had been and still was a great problem: thirteen years younger than Mussolini, physically attractive and probably the most intelligent of Fascist leaders, he had soon be-

1937 "Mussolini could always find the chord that touched the hearts of the humble."

938 "The younger the children, the greater their pride in their uniform, the greater their love for the duce."

1938 *"In time the duce fell under the fuehrer's spell, and the two dictators became united by a bond akin to friendship, in the name of which they committed the most tragic follies."*

1938 *"In children he saw only the matter out of which he could mold future generations of warriors, he saw only the uniform that effaced all individuality."*

1944 "In the puppet Republic of Salò, Mussolini seemed a powerless old man. His eyesight weakened, and to read the papers he wore glasses and flooded his room with light."

1945 "Mussolini was urged to leave Milan for Como, accompanied by a small body of German and Fascist troops. Thus his ultimate odyssey began. . . ."

come very popular. He was outspoken, an independent thinker and a *frondeur*, and had a wide range of friends, including army men, Blackshirts, and famous beauties, as well as lukewarm Fascists and anti-Fascists. In his post as Minister of Aviation, which he had held for several years, he had not done well by the Italian air force, for he lacked the technical background, but had excelled as a pilot. His several flights over the Atlantic had added the aura of hero to his charms and extended his popularity to the other side of the ocean. According to persistent rumors, he aspired to the duce's succession and therefore was dangerous. Upon his return from a transatlantic flight to North America in 1933 and an enthusiastic welcome in Chicago, where he landed during the Century of Progress Exhibition, Mussolini hugged him with great warmth, spoke solemn words in his praise, made him marshal of Italy, and shortly afterward appointed him governor of Libya. But Balbo's voice made itself heard even at such a distance, and the duce, becoming incensed by the young man's criticism, threatened to send him to a *confino* or deal with him even more severely.

One man Mussolini could have called his friend, had he taken the pains to cultivate the friendship before he felt the need for it: his former rival, the soldier-poet Gabriele d'Annunzio. Since the advent of fascism, D'Annunzio, old and shriveled, much less fiery but still gallant, had behaved as if he had forgotten that Mussolini had betrayed him in Fiume, stolen his plans for a march on Rome, pushed him aside, and imitated the pageantry of his own Regency of the Carnaro without giving him credit for it. Indeed, the poet had showered the once clumsy and unrefined journalist with letters, telegrams, messages, congratulations, professions of solidarity and admiration, gifts, and invitations to his villa, calling him "Dear Companion," "Companionable Companion," "Young Brother," "Benito," or simply "Ben." Only a few times had the duce accepted an invitation to visit D'Annunzio in the crowded disorder of the villa on Lake Garda, where works of art in bad taste and war trophies of all sorts provided the poet with what he called a spiritual environment. To Mussolini and other visitors the expensive confusion appeared to be a dismal stage for the shadow that the once-picturesque actor had become. To be sure the poet, spendthrift and penniless to his last hour, expected favors from his powerful friend — not least among these the monumental publication of his collected works and the bow of the ship "Puglia," which he set up on the shores of the lake and equipped with cannon; but this fact did not alter the warmth of his friendliness for a man he had once disliked.

When D'Annunzio died in March, 1938, Mussolini's young foreign minister and son-in-law Count Galeazzo Ciano noted in his diary that the duce did not appear moved. In the lengthy trip through the countryside toward D'Annunzio's villa at the time of the funeral, Mussolini did not turn his thoughts to the dead man but took stock of the amount of scrap iron he saw here and there that could be reclaimed for war purposes. Only a few days later did he remark that he felt the emptiness that D'Annunzio's demise had left behind. Though it seems unlikely that he experienced any specific regret at the poet's death, the very word "emptiness" may well be the key to his attitude toward Hitler: to him the fuehrer's friendship came as a promise of a more and better filled life at a time when he felt lonely. Later, as his health failed and exerting his will became an effort, Mussolini submitted entirely to the fuehrer and did what he was told to do, even when it was contrary to his best judgment.

A closer examination of the various stages in the two dictators' relations reveals failure and coldness at the onset. Mussolini and Hitler met for the first time in June, 1934, in Venice. Until that time the duce had opposed the resurgent Pan-Germanism in the Nazi regime, and Hitler's advisers pressed him to seek a better understanding. From the very first moment Mussolini had the upper hand. Self-assured and vigorous in his martial uniform and hat, he went to meet his guest at the airport. When Hitler came down the plane he looked pitifully pale and sickly. He was wearing a brown raincoat and patent leather shoes and revolved a soft gray hat nervously in his hand. Mussolini grumbled to the nearest man: "I don't like him." The chancellor's attire was more conspicuous than his physical traits: he was thin and flabby — the duce set a great value on muscles, his own and others' — with small, nondescript features, and his bulbous gray eyes lacked luster, except when he went into a trance or a fit of hysterics. His black hair was slick and fell down in long stiff strands over the left side of his forehead, while his short mustache completed the comic look that not even Charlie Chaplin could fully recapture in his film "The Great Dictator."

Hitler was at a great disadvantage: Mussolini had been in power almost twelve years, was approaching the high point of his career, and had many achievements to his credit. He had played host to numberless statesmen, and his intuition told him how to deal with each of them. In 1934 Hitler, who had been in power only a year and a half, was not so much a guest to be treated with deference or consideration as an admiring pupil who was avowedly striving to imitate his teacher and who in the presence of the Great Man could not keep his nervousness in check. Hitler was on his first trip abroad; the unsuccessful Austrian painter of cheap water colors had previously crossed only the border between Austria and Germany, two countries that in his mind were one. The one language he spoke was German, while Mussolini liked to pose as a linguist (as a part of his pretense that he could do anything and do it well). In Venice the two dictators had no interpreter, and their conversations were entirely in German — Mussolini's only disadvantage. They had their first talks and spent their first night in Stra in an old villa, long in disuse, that had been hurriedly made ready for the illustrious guests. But in the humid heat of the June day the mosquitoes were untractable, and at night, it was rumored, Mussolini was disturbed by the ghost of Napoleon, who had once stayed in the same villa. They moved to Venice the next day and went on with their talks. Little is known of what the two said to each other. Hitler, as often happened to him, could not stop talking. In his memoirs Von Papen expresses regret for not having been present, claiming that he could have stemmed the flood of Hitler's words and diverted its course. Mussolini, who in all probability understood only a small part of what Hitler said, later related that the German chancellor had recited to him long passages of *Mein Kampf* (a book the duce had never been able to finish reading) and had lectured him on the superiority of the German race.

Mussolini patronized his guest, and in Venice all applause was for the duce, who received the usual ovation when he appeared on a balcony in Piazza San Marco, while the crowd ignored the little chancellor who was listening from another balcony. Mussolini summed up his impressions of Hitler by calling him a *pulcinella*, buffoon. The visit in Venice gave grounds for the misconception that Hitler was Mussolini's imitator on a small scale and more to be laughed at than feared. Yet Hitler was by far the stronger and more dangerous of the two dictators, and the twists in his personality — his subtle viciousness and refined cruelty, his sadistic inventiveness that allowed for the most brutal methods of torture and extermination — were so enormous that by comparison Mussolini's streak of cruelty, his aggressiveness and violence, pales and appears less significant. Within little over a month the *pulcinella* was to begin to show his cards.

Although no communiqué was issued about the encounter in Venice, and despite the duce's glib remarks about it, the two dictators undoubtedly discussed an issue that was bringing increasing friction in the relations between Italy and Germany, namely the independence of Austria. Being born a German Austrian — one of those Austrians in whom German nationalism was very strong and who regarded the division between Germany and Austria as a crime — Hitler advocated the inclusion of Austria in a Greater Germany. He said so in the opening pages of *Mein Kampf*, and since he had become chancellor he had exerted influence on Austrian Nazis, placed his own henchmen in command, and organized a relentless propaganda campaign, accompanied by widespread terrorism.

These Nazi activities could not but displease Mussolini, who feared the resurgence of Pan-Germanism and wanted to put brakes to Hitler's actions. An *Anschluss* between Germany and Austria would bring the Germans to the Brenner Pass and be a threat to Italy, especially if Hitler were to carry out the program of militarism and expansion expounded in *Mein Kampf*. To prevent an *Anschluss*, Mussolini became the advocate of Austrian independence and strongly supported Chancellor Engelbert Dollfuss. He forgot the old traditional enmity and strove to establish a stable satellite Fascist regime in Austria. By the time he and Hitler met in Venice, Dollfuss was little more than a tool in the duce's hands.

Dollfuss had become chancellor in 1932, but Mussolini's efforts to promote fascism in Austria had started earlier: since 1930 he had given money and arms to the Austrian Fascist formations, the *Heimwehr*, and had remained in touch with their leaders. After Hitler came to power in January, 1933, Dollfuss, to counteract the assertiveness of the Austrian Nazis, sought the help of the *Heimwehr* and thus identified himself with fascism.

Between April and July, 1933, Dollfuss paid three visits to the Italian dictator, and in these encounters, and through long letters, the duce undertook the Austrian's education in the arts of dictatorship and the display of authority. His pupil was receptive. At first the lessons seemed to have only an educational purpose, but soon Mussolini began to stress, with increasing urgency, the need for action. He advised an open attack on advocates of socialism on the grounds that their defeat would win many Austrian Nazis to Dollfuss and would result in a weakening of Hitler's influence over Austria. Under further pressure from Italian diplomats speaking for Mussolini, Dollfuss resolved to take decisive action against the Socialists. In February, 1934, after four days of street fighting in Vienna in which Socialist workers were massacred and casualties ran in the hundreds, Dollfuss accomplished his coup d'état and instituted a clerico-Fascist dictatorship. But Mussolini, with his old fear of bolshevism and the Reds, had misjudged the consequences of an attack against the Austrian Socialists. If there was to be fascism in Austria, the Socialists came to think, they preferred the German anticlerical type to the Italian and Catholic-inspired type which Dollfuss had embraced, and they turned to Hitler.

After these events in Austria the relations between Italy and Germany deteriorated, and it is against this troubled background that Mussolini's and Hitler's first encounter must be viewed.

Two weeks after the talks in Venice, Mussolini was to learn with a shock of what barbaric actions and what thoroughness in executing them his apparently timid imitator was capable. On June 30 Hitler personally led a great purge in which he ordered killed many of the men who had helped him gain power, among them his friend Ernst Roehm, the leader of the Nazi S.A. formations, the Brownshirts. The brutal-looking Roehm and his Brownshirts were accused of widespread homosexual practices, and there is no doubt that in many instances the accusations were justified. The reason for the purge, however, was a different matter. Under Roehm the Brownshirts had gained great strength and aroused rivalry in the regular army. Unable to check this rivalry by peaceful means, Hitler decided to suffocate it in blood. On the probably unfounded pretext that Roehm had prepared a coup and was ready to carry it out, Hitler had Roehm arrested and executed without trial. The same fate befell Roehm's chief lieutenants. The massacre spread to many parts of Germany, and was not confined to the high ranks of the Brownshirts. According to later estimates from neutral sources, 401 persons perished in the purge, including many Jews, the victims of an anti-Semitism that flared up wherever acts of violence were committed.

In Italy Mussolini was indignant, according to members of his family, but he did not react publicly against the purge and its perpetrators. Soon another event, coming in the wake of the first, excited his wrath and drove him to take concrete measures.

By this time, the summer of 1934, Mussolini and the Austrian chancellor had reinforced their ties and were what may be called "good friends." The duce had invited the Dollfuss family to spend their summer vacation in a villa in Riccione, and Frau Dollfuss and the children were already there on July 25, when the chancellor himself was due to arrive. The two chiefs of government were to take this opportunity to discuss the Austrian situation; Dollfuss, who had been warned of Nazi intrigues and Nazi infiltration in the heart of his own government, planned drastic countermeasures, but first he wished to have Mussolini's advice.

He never got it. On July 25, the day he was expected in Riccione, news arrived that he had been murdered in the Austrian chancellery. Upon Benito and Rachele Mussolini fell the sad task of bringing the news to the wife of Dollfuss, and Mussolini's disinclination for this sort of duty augmented his feeling that the assassination of his friend was a personal outrage. Dollfuss was killed in an attempted *Putsch* led by a group of Austrian Nazis disguised in the uniforms of the Austrian army. The circumstances under which the *Putsch* occurred, together with Hitler's elated behavior when the first news of the assassination reached him, left little doubt as to the identity of the instigator.

Enraged, the duce sent four divisions to the Brenner Pass, ready to march into Austria if Germany made any move in that direction. He wired to the Austrian vice-chancellor, Prince von Starhemberg: "The independence of Austria, for which he [Dollfuss] fell, is a principle that has been defended and will be defended even more strenuously by Italy." To the world he declared: "*L'Austria non si tocca* [Hands off Austria]," and he let the strictly controlled Italian press go up in arms against the Germans. Not long afterward, he visited a summer camp for Austrian youths on the seashore near Rome with Prince von Starhemberg; after attending a commemoration of the late chancellor, he spoke with agitation to the prince: "It would mean the end of European civilization if this country of murderers and pederasts were to overrun Europe. . . . Hitler is the murderer of Dollfuss. . . . A horrible sexual degenerate, a dangerous fool. . . . The abominable and repulsive spectacle that Hitler showed the world on June 30 would not have been tolerated by any other country in the world. . . ."

Mussolini's vehement rancor against Germany was still

fully alive the following September when, in a formal speech, he said: ". . . thirty centuries of history allow us to look with supreme pity upon certain doctrines advocated beyond the Alps by the progeny of a people who did not know how to write and transmit the documents of its life at a time when Rome had Caesar, Vergil, Augustus."

The duce was not yet ready for friendship with the fuehrer, but the assassination of Dollfuss did not really work against it. Indeed, it was a turning point. Mussolini had hoped that France and England would follow up his military action at the Brenner Pass with an equivalent, tangible expression of disapproval. Instead, they remained aloof and trusted that Hitler, having burned his fingers once at the expansion game, had learned his lesson and would make no further attempts. The disappointment that the duce experienced shook his never-strong faith in the Western democracies and initiated the process of isolation of Italy which culminated during the Ethiopian war and drove the two dictators unavoidably together.

The first steps toward a close partnership between Italy and Germany were taken a few months after Mussolini's proclamation of the empire, while Italian and German troops were fighting on the same side in Spain, and resulted in the Rome-Berlin axis. It was Mussolini who with his colorful use of words gave the name to the Rome-Berlin axis, but it was Hitler, the shrewder dictator, who engineered the rapprochement between Italy and Germany. On November 1, 1936, in a speech in Milan in which he made a sweeping survey of the international horizon, the duce touched on the relations with Germany and pronounced these words: ". . . these agreements that have been consecrated in appropriate papers and duly signed, this vertical line Berlin-Rome, is not a diaphragm [*sic*], it is rather an axis around which all the European states may collaborate that are animated by a will for collaboration and peace." Perhaps because it was born so unidiomatically the expression "Rome-Berlin axis" was destined to be long-lasting.

Hitler's contribution to the axis, more than Mussolini's, stayed within the tradition of international politics. In *Mein Kampf* Hitler had stated that the only two countries with which Germany could ever enter into an alliance were Great Britain and Italy. With the passage of time and the trend of British foreign policy, a partnership between Germany and Great Britain appeared more and more problematic. Since 1934, on the other hand, the question of Austria had alienated Fascist Italy from Germany and seemingly strengthened the alignment of Great Britain, France, and Italy against Hitler. The fuehrer stood by himself, at the head of his country, without foreign supporters. When the Ethiopian war began, he foresaw the isolation in which Italy was to find herself and became as wary as a cat watching her prey. In early March, 1936, while Italy was fully engaged in Africa and not likely to move to help France, Hitler sent his troops to occupy the Rhineland.

At this juncture Hitler must have had a foretaste of the peace of mind that he would enjoy if the Italian threat to the Brenner Pass were removed once and for all, and he made up his mind. The Ethiopian war was by then moving rapidly toward its conclusion, and Italy, already with several military victories to her credit, promised to be a worthier ally than at any time since World War I. Hitler offered to assist Italy in the Ethiopian war as soon as Germany was better prepared, and in Rome it was said that Hitler had sent a message to the Italians: "Resist only a few months longer and we shall be able to help you." But the war ended before Germany made any formal commitments. The following September, through his minister Hans Frank, Hitler sent out feelers to the duce about a closer collaboration and offered to recognize the Italian empire, a move that cost him nothing and pleased Mussolini, who was very touchy on this subject and angry at the majority of European countries, which had refused recognition.

Before sending out these feelers, Hitler had taken another step, ostensibly aimed at settling his differences with Austria and allaying Mussolini's fear of a German drive for the annexation of that country. In July, 1936, he had concluded an agreement with Austria, which seemed to improve relations between the two countries and safeguard Austria's full sovereignty. Mussolini had not been entirely reassured. He knew that Hitler was much too shrewd to enter into an agreement which was not to the Nazis' advantage; and he probably guessed that beside the published clauses there were secret ones that would allow Hitler to pursue his propaganda and promote Nazi infiltration in the Austrian government. Nevertheless, the agreement formally removed the last stumbling block to a rapprochement between Italy and Germany.

In the final shaping of the axis, Galeazzo Ciano had his part, his first important assignment: from October 20 to October 25, 1936, the thirty-three-year-old foreign minister was in Germany, where he talked with Joachim von Ribbentrop, the fuehrer's special adviser on foreign policy, and had a long conversation and lunch with Hitler at his villa at Berchtesgaden. Von Ribbentrop, the son of an army officer, was a handsome, well-groomed man of the Nordic type, and soon to become Hitler's foreign minister. He owed his brilliant career to his knowledge of the world, for he had lived abroad several years, including a stay in Canada, and spoke English fluently. Listening to Von Ribbentrop's inexhaustible tales of distant men and lands, to his glowing plans for imperialistic conquests, Hitler came to experience the "fascination of the universe." Von Ribbentrop's words gave form and substance to Hitler's unformulated dreams and stimulated his instinct as world prophet; Von Ribbentrop's ability to scheme and prepare the ground for action facilitated Hitler's task in carrying out his program of expansion.

In their first encounter, as in the many that followed, Von Ribbentrop and Ciano spoke English, for Ciano knew no German but, like Von Ribbentrop, spoke English fluently. In their many contacts the cold, thorough, calculating German and the pleasant, superficial, and ambitious Italian came to know each other well, to dislike, and, at the climax, to hate each other. But the first meeting was very cordial.

Hitler's welcome must have filled the young foreign minister with pride and flattered his vanity. The fuehrer played the charming host, said he was glad that Ciano had come to visit Germany, and professed himself greatly touched by the greet-

ings that Ciano conveyed to him from the duce, whom Hitler
called "the leading statesman in the world to whom none may
even remotely compare himself." (Not much later Hitler was
to modify this sincere opinion of the duce and demote Mussolini from Superman No. 1 to Superman No. 2, second only to
the fuehrer himself.) The fine points of the collaboration between the two countries were worked out while Ciano was in
Germany, and the viewpoints of the two dictators were carefully examined. The report that Ciano gave Mussolini upon
his return to Rome was satisfactory, and five days later the
duce made his unidiomatic announcement of the Rome-Berlin
axis.

Yet despite the axis and the repeated, mutual professions
of friendship, the relations between Mussolini and Hitler remained strained and tinged with a certain suspicion for a
while longer. The two men had not met again after their
unhappy encounter in Venice, and the bitter memory of its
failure could not but affect some of their thoughts and actions.
After each of his assertive moves Hitler was attenuating the
picture in the duce's mind of the nervous man in the brown
raincoat; in this picture he was shedding the raincoat and
donning a resplendent military uniform, while replacing
nervousness with assurance and competence. Mussolini, on his
part, undoubtedly still nursed a deep resentment against the
flabby chatterbox who had tricked him within a few weeks of
the Venice meeting by revealing a perverse, cruel drive and a
Machiavellian ability to scheme.

Thus at first around the axis rotated uneasiness and the
shadows of mistrust. Duce and fuehrer closely watched each
other's diplomatic activities, the attempts of each to reach an
understanding with Great Britain, the pressures each exerted
over Austria; and Mussolini took easy offense at remarks
slighting the martial qualities of the Italians. But then Mussolini's feelings changed as the result of a visit to Germany, any
reservations that he might have had about Hitler's good faith
were dispelled, and he plunged into a friendship that was to
tie him to Hitler until his own death, seven and a half years
later.

The visit had been long in the making. In September, 1936,

when the German minister Hans Frank opened the consultations which ended in the creation of the axis, he also expressed to the duce "the fuehrer's desire to receive him in Germany at the earliest possible moment, not only in his capacity as head of the government but also as founder and duce of a party with affinities to National Socialism." The duce, who had not set foot out of Italy (and the Italian colonies) since 1923, replied that insofar as a visit to Germany was concerned it was his wish to undertake it. "It must, however, be well prepared, so as to produce concrete results. It will cause a great stir and must therefore be historically important in its results." Hitler took the hint wholeheartedly, setting out to surpass the duce's expectations, and a year later, in Sepember, 1937, he gave Mussolini a spectacular reception, the like of which no other statesman had ever received in Germany. It was a carefully staged reception, meant to flatter and impress. It is said that the apartment for the duce was made ready by two experts, one in charge of hanging pictures, the other arranging flowers, and that the fuehrer had told them: "I want the reception of my teacher to be perfect."

The duce arrived in Munich, his first stop in Germany, on September 25, 1937, accompanied by ministers and other members of the Fascist hierarchy, including that younger image of himself, the solemn Ciano of official occasions. Hitler was at the railroad station, grabbed Mussolini's hands, and led him down a double line of busts of Roman emperors toward a packed square, dominated by a gigantic M perched on top of a column in the center. S.S. troops marched past the dictators in a ceremonial parade. In the first conversation between the two dictators, the duce appointed the fuehrer "honorary corporal of the Fascist militia," the rank he himself held. The next day the Italian party was taken to witness a display of military power at the army maneuvers in Mecklenburg, where they saw new German artillery and other new weapons and planes. On September 27 the Italians were taken to visit the Krupp steel foundries in Essen, and Mussolini was duly impressed by the tremendous output of guns of all kinds. In the evening they arrived in Berlin. For the final fifteen minutes of the trip the separate trains on which Mussolini and

Hitler rode were running parallel, their engines aligned, moving at exactly the same pace, "as if they signified the parallelism of the two revolutions," in the words of *Il Popolo d'Italia.*

Of the arrival in the German capital, Ciano in his diary has only one word to say: "Triumphal." Banners in the German and Italian colors reached from roofs to sidewalks; emblems of the *fasci* and golden Roman eagles glowed in the night; crowds aligned on both sides of streets roared a welcome to the Italian dictator. In the car in which he rode with Hitler, Mussolini stood up to let himself be seen and receive well-organized ovations at his passage; the fuehrer remained seated, drawing back a little, to let his guest enjoy the full glory of the moment. The festivities reached a peak on the following afternoon when both dictators addressed a crowd of "over a million men" — according to Hitler — who had gathered to hear them. The steady rain did not spoil the ceremony. Hitler spoke first, calling Mussolini "one of those lonely men of the ages on whom history is not tested but who themselves are the makers of history," and proclaimed that the forces of the two empires, the Italian, created by the duce's constructive power, and the one Germany had become owing to her policies and military might, were the strongest guarantees of peace in Europe. Then it was Mussolini's turn to climb the podium and prepare to speak. In front of him thousands upon thousands of German arms rose in the Roman salute. The bands played *Giovinezza* and the Royal March, while from the darkened skies the rain fell with greater strength. "My visit to Germany and her fuehrer," Mussolini said, "and the speech that I am to give before you constitute an important event in the life of our two peoples and also in mine. . . . The fact that I came to Germany does not mean that tomorrow I shall go elsewhere. . . . It is above all in my capacity of chief of a national revolution that I wanted to give a proof of open and clear solidarity to your revolution. . . . Fascism and nazism are two manifestations of that parallelism of historical positions which unite the lives of our nations.

"My trip to Germany has no recondite ends. Here we do not scheme to divide Europe. . . . To the people throughout the world who anxiously ask themselves what may come out of the Berlin encounter — war or peace — the fuehrer and I may answer together, in a loud voice: Peace."

The rest of Mussolini's speech was a review of past events, the awakening of Germany through the Nazi revolution, the common aim of defeating bolshevism, Germany's friendly stand during the Ethiopian war, and the birth of the axis. The speech ended with a heavy stress on the 115 million Italians and Germans and the need for them to unite "in one single unshakable determination."

In the course of this speech the duce pronounced the memorable sentence: "Fascism has its ethical principles, to which it intends to be faithful, and they are also my morals: to speak clearly and openly, and, if we are friends [sic], to march together to the end." This was Mussolini's most sincere declaration of principles. The faithfulness between countries, at which he had often scoffed as something nonexistent or necessarily giving way to national expediency, became his norm in the case of Germany even though he did not always "speak clearly and openly." The great change was due entirely to his German visit. Not only was he flattered by the deference with which the creator of the new and powerful Germany treated him, but he was also thoroughly impressed, altogether dazzled by Germany's display of strength and capability, by her perfectly fitting military garb and smoothly functioning organization. To him Germany appeared as the most promising, the best-prepared country in the world, the conqueror of the future. He had no element of comparison, for he had not been out of Italy or her colonies for many years, and he did not know the Anglo-Saxon world. Once, in his first months in power, he had spent three days in London but had seen little more than what lay between Claridge's Hotel, where he stayed, and Downing Street, where a conference on war reparations was held. Of American idealism he, the materialist, had no clear conception. Little did he understand the heritage of democratic aspirations of a people who had come from many countries in search of freedom, individual dignity, and liberty and equality for all. Even less could he understand that these people wished to share their heritage with the countries from which they had come. The effect that Wilson's European mission had on Mussolini's nationalism is clear evidence of this lack of understanding. In Germany, on the other hand, Mussolini was not presented with ideas but with facts and things, tangible, desirable, enviable things. His German visit sealed his friendship with Hitler and snapped the lock on the chain that bound him to the fuehrer.

It was after Mussolini's return from Germany that the pattern of friendship between duce and fuehrer emerged distinctly and in its final shape. To Hitler friendship was a simple and personal feeling, exclusively directed toward its object, as linear and enduring as a steel wire. He could keep it in a separate compartment, and it never affected his political actions. If expedient for the greatness of Germany as he saw it, he acted against the obligations of friendship, breaking promises and pledges. But the anxiety and the fear of his friend's reactions seized him; he sought reassurance and strove to patch up any possible cracks in the friendship. In Mussolini, in whom single-directedness was not strong and often disrupted by circumstances, the friendship for Hitler was a complex tangle of feelings. There was, first of all, the pledge of loyalty to Germany and his determination to remain faithful to the pledge, a determination in which the belief that Germany was absolutely invincible certainly played its part. There was also a sense of inferiority that drove him to appear self-assured, unaffected by Hitler's offenses; and there was a spirit of emulation, which made him postpone recriminations or a breach in the friendship — to a time when he could do so from a strong position. There was a fatalism, a resignation to whatever destiny brought, which, tenuous at first, increased with the progress of his illness and his growing mental inertia.

The sense of inferiority revealed itself in some of his actions immediately after his return from Germany. He compared the Italians he knew with the Germans he had seen and came to the conclusion that Italian military men were not as efficient, as hard and tough, as the Germans, that the Fascist performance was not as perfect and stupendous as the Nazi. To remedy this condition became one of the duce's fixed ideas. He said repeatedly that he must change the Italian character, and he accused the Italian bourgeois of being cowardly and lazy, of liking to live in peace; he resolved to "Prussianize" Italy. To this effect, in December, 1937, he made the "historic decision" to lead Italy out of the League of Nations, under pressure, it was said, from Hitler, who had taken the same step over four years before. More closely related to the "Prussianization" of Italy were some measures aimed at reforming the character and "style" of the Italians, measures that were long remembered for their nuisance value. They included the "abolition" of handshakes, which in his opinion were an indication of softness, and the order to use the Roman salute in all forms of friendly greetings; the substitution of the traditional *lei* in formal address with either the Latin *tu* or the more respectful *voi*; and the introduction in the army of an unnatural and tiresome parade step which the duce called the Roman step. It was an awkward imitation of the German goose step used in Munich by the S.S. who had paraded before him, but he considered it his own creation and was enormously proud of it. "The parade step," he said, "symbolizes the force, will, and energies of the young Fascist generations, who are enthusiastic about it. It is a step in a difficult and hard style, which requires preparation and training. For this reason we want it. It is a step that sedentary men, corpulent men, morons, so-called duds, will never be able to do. For this reason we like it. Our adversaries proclaim that the parade step is the most genuine expression of authentic militaristic spirit. We are glad of it. For this reason we have adopted it, and in a little time we shall execute it perfectly. Because the Italian people, when willing, are able to do anything."

The best illustration of the pattern of friendship between the two dictators, at about this time, is provided by their reciprocal behavior in the last phase of their quarrel over Austria. German intrigues to promote the Nazification of Austria had not ceased, and ruthless incitement to violence and fraud had kept Austria in a state near civil war. In vain had the courageous Kurt von Schuschnigg, Dollfuss' successor, appealed to European countries for help and support. Even Mussolini appeared to have lost his once-strong interest in Austrian independence as a result of axis policies, and in a conversation with the Austrian chancellor in Rome in the spring of 1937 he had advised Austrian co-operation with Germany, and though stating that his attitude toward Austria had not changed, he had carefully avoided making any commitments. Von Schuschnigg was left to fend for himself against the Nazi's increasing arrogance.

Indeed, Mussolini's indifference to the Austrian cause was most noticeable in November, 1937, when he was still in the euphoric mood in which his visit to Germany had left him and ready to do anything to please his friend and partner Adolf Hitler. At that time he told Von Ribbentrop that he was "tired of mounting guard over Austrian independence," especially if Austrians no longer wanted it. He explained that with the empire and the war in Spain, Italy's interests centered in the Mediterranean. In short, the duce was willing to wash his hands of Austria, with only one condition: neither Germany nor Italy would take any further step without consultation. The condition was fair, and Von Ribbentrop readily accepted it.

In February, 1938, without informing Mussolini, Hitler summoned Von Schuschnigg to Berchtesgaden for secret talks that were to have far-reaching consequences. A full account of this meeting was published only after World War II, in Von Schuschnigg's own book *Austrian Requiem*. The story that he tells and others confirm is appalling. With Von Schuschnigg Hitler was incredibly callous. He launched into a vehement attack against the policy of the Austrian government, calling the history of Austria "one uninterrupted act of high treason," to which he was determined to put an end. In his characteristic way he worked himself into a rage, poured abuse on the Austrian chancellor, who had no chance to speak in his own defense, scolded, threatened, and boasted that he could be in Vienna overnight and no one could stop him — not France or England, nor Italy, with whom there was "the closest friendship." In the end he presented Von Schuschnigg with a set of demands amounting to the complete Nazification of Austria and her army and to German penetration of the Austrian government. It was an ultimatum, and Von Schuschnigg was requested to sign on the spot. "Unlike Mussolini," Hitler said in the course of the meeting, "I do not go in for much talk or prenotification." Under the pressure of Hitler's repeated fits of wrath, and the strong hint that if he did not comply he would be imprisoned, Von Schuschnigg eventually signed the "agreement." (Hitler is said to have also dropped the hint that Austria could write off any help from Italy, for in his view a German army of 100,000 men could keep the Italian forces in check.)

These "conversations" at Berchtesgaden were kept strictly secret in Germany and even the Austrian legation in Berlin was kept in the dark. But sufficient information reached Rome, probably from Vienna, to make Mussolini realize that the *Anschluss* was by then inevitable. Mussolini was hurt. What hurt him was not so much Hitler's accelerated pace in the drive to annex Austria in spite of pledges to preserve Austrian independence, nor was it the unfair treatment that Von Schuschnigg had received, but the fact that he, Mussolini, had not been consulted or informed of so momentous an event as the meeting at Berchtesgaden. He made it clear that in the future Germany would do well to abide by the pledge not to do anything concerning Austria without consultation, a pledge to which Italy had strictly adhered. But Hitler was to ignore this reminder.

In this mood of resentment Mussolini resumed and intensified diplomatic activities to bring forth an agreement with Great Britain. He also sent a verbal message to Von Schuschnigg approving his visit to Berchtesgaden and shamelessly reasserting his own personal friendship for the Austrian chancellor as well as Italy's unchanged attitude toward the Austrian cause.

Mussolini described the time after Hitler's and Von Schuschnigg's talks as the intermission between the fourth and fifth
acts of the Austrian affair, and he wondered when the fifth
act would begin. It began sooner than he expected. On March
9 Von Schuschnigg, in a last attempt to save Austria's independence, announced that four days later, on Sunday, March
13, he would hold a plebiscite in which the Austrian people
would have a chance to declare whether or not they wanted a
free Austria. The announcement of the plebiscite gave Hitler
the pretext that he had been waiting for, and he prepared to
carry out his plans for an *Anschluss.*

"The hot day for Austria," as Ciano called it, was March
11. Once again, in spite of previous agreements, Hitler failed
to consult Mussolini, and the duce learned of the fuehrer's
move from Vienna. "The news over the telephone," Ciano
wrote, "has confirmed, from hour to hour, the mobilization at
the Bavarian frontier and the German decision to attack. At
about noon Schuschnigg accepted the postponement of the
plebiscite, but the Germans did not consider it sufficient
and wanted his resignation. He asked us through Ghigi [the
Italian minister in Vienna] what to do. I conferred with the
Duce several times. From here we cannot take the responsibility of advising him in either direction. Therefore he must
act according to his conscience. On orders from Paris the
French chargé d'affaires asks to see me in order to consult
about the Austrian situation. I answer that we intend to consult with no one. . . ." (This disdainful reply, speciously
implying a firmness of stand and irrevocable decision, was a
part of the Fascist façade that masked the paucity of ideas,
the superficial policies, and the mental inertia of the Fascist
leaders.)

"6:00 P.M. Von Schuschnigg resigns [Ciano continued in
his diary], Seyss-Inquart takes his place.* Independent Austria no longer exists."

---

* Artur von Seyss-Inquart was a "fifth columnist," the chief instrument of
German infiltration and machinations in Austria.

At last, at about 9:30 the same evening, Mussolini received a letter from Hitler, brought by a special messenger, Prince Philip of Hesse. The prince, a nephew of Kaiser Wilhelm, had been a lieutenant in the Hessian dragoons and the Prussian cavalry. His marriage to King Victor Emmanuel's second daughter, Princess Mafalda, in 1925 created the first bridge between official enemies of World War I. Prince Philip then became a Fascist and Nazi sympathizer. His political bent and his Italian connections, his reputation as an adventurer and the aura that being a king's son-in-law conferred on him, earned him the role of personal link between the German and Italian dictators, a role in which Hitler made ample use of him. Hesse, who frequently flew from Berlin to Rome, became known as "the winged messenger" and "Hitler's mailman."

The letter that on March 12 Hesse brought to Mussolini opened with a sentence which is most significant in a study of the dictators' relations: "In an hour fraught with destiny I turn to you, Excellency, to give you the news of a decision which appears to be imposed by circumstances and is by now immutable." Only after the decision had seemingly become "immutable," only at the end of the "hot day for Austria," after Hitler had ordered his troops to move toward the frontier, was the fuehrer's letter delivered to the duce. Only then did the duce receive, in Ciano's words, "explanations of what had happened and a precise declaration on the recognition of the Brenner as an Italian frontier." The "explanations" so shamelessly distorted the Berchtesgaden meetings and the ensuing happenings in Austria that Hitler could call the German invasion of Austria an "act of legitimate defense." But the duce did not seem to mind either the lateness or the distortion of the report, for Ciano writes: "The Duce is pleased and tells Hesse to inform the Fuehrer that Italy watches the events with absolute calm."

The enormity of Mussolini's betrayal of the Austrian cause is best appraised in the light of Hitler's own behavior. Hitler, the arch-breaker of promises, expected something better from the Great Man south of the Alps, a straighter line of conduct, sincerity, and loyalty to friends. At the moment he and his troops were on the point of crossing the border into Austria, he worried about Mussolini's possible reprisal. The encounter in Venice, Mussolini's action upon Dollfuss' death, his repeated request that nothing be done to change the status quo in Austria without prior consultation, must have come insistently to Hitler's mind.

The fact is that the fuehrer, while still in Germany, while his move was not yet irrevocable although he had written to Mussolini that the decision was immutable, was anxiously waiting for a word from his "mailman." When Hesse called Berlin, it was the fuehrer himself who answered. The record of the conversation speaks for itself:

"Hesse: I have just come from Palazzo Venezia. The duce accepted the whole thing in a very friendly manner. He sends you his regards. . . .

"Hitler: Then please tell Mussolini I will never forget him for this.

"Hesse: Yes.

"Hitler: Never, never, never, whatever happens . . . As soon as the Austrian affair is settled, I shall be ready to go with him, through thick and thin, no matter what happens.

"Hesse: Yes, my fuehrer.

"Hitler: Listen, I shall make any agreement — I am no longer in fear of the terrible position which would have existed militarily in case we got into a conflict. You may tell him that I thank him ever so much; never, never shall I forget.

"Hesse: Yes, my fuehrer.

"Hitler: I will never forget, whatever may happen. If he should ever need any help or be in danger, he can be convinced that I shall stick by him, whatever may happen, even if the whole world were against him.

"Hesse: Yes, my fuehrer."

In fact, Hitler was never to forget, and his personal bond with Mussolini was greatly reinforced. The next day he sent a telegram to the duce: "Mussolini, I shall never forget him." After a few hours of probably mixed feelings the man never to be forgotten coolly replied: "My attitude is determined by the friendship of our two countries consecrated in the axis."

After the *Anschluss* Mussolini's popularity in Italy took a dip that at least equaled the one immediately before the Ethiopian war. A great number of Italians had viewed the birth of the axis with misgivings that within a year and a half were fully justified by the *Anschluss*. The Italians had known very little about the diplomatic dealings between Italy, Austria, and Germany or, in particular, about the duce's and fuehrer's pledges to each other. Yet they immediately recognized that Hitler's seizure of Austria had come as a surprise to the duce. This surprise was revealed when for several hours after news of the *Anschluss* neither press nor radio commented on it. As the Italians well knew, usually all information media in their country received precise directives on the release of important news, the official "interpretation," the details to be stressed, the space or time to be allotted, even the size of the headlines; and the omission of comments made them realize that for a while Mussolini was uncertain whether to show himself as much outraged as they felt he must be, or, for the sake of friendship and the pledge of faithfulness to Germany, get the most he could out of the *fait accompli*. The second course — submission to Hitler's will — was the easier of the two, and soon the press and radio burst out in praise of the fuehrer who at last had united two countries always wanting to be one.

A few days later Mussolini, addressing the Chamber of Deputies, tried to hide his frustration under a thin veil of historical justification for the *Anschluss* and sought to demonstrate that the *Anschluss*, far from being detrimental to Italy as some people claimed, had reinforced the axis. Besides, "when an event is fated to happen," he said, "it is better that it be made with you rather than in spite of you, or, even worse, against you." The Italians were not reassured. They were the more shocked by Mussolini's acquiescence in Hitler's deed for his having never retracted his famous words: *L'Austria non si tocca.*" Many Italians sent anonymous letters of protest to Mussolini and Ciano; many Italians wistfully hoped that Hitler's return visit to Italy, which had been set for the beginning of May, would be canceled as a result of his action in Austria. But they were soon disappointed.

🚩

The preparations for the fuehrer's visit revealed the spirit of emulation in Mussolini's relations with Hitler: he wanted to give his friend at least as impressive and grandiose a reception as he had received in Germany. Along the railroad from the Brenner Pass to Naples all houses that could be seen from the train were whitewashed and trimmed with Fascist slogans and welcoming sentences in brilliant black letters; greenery and flowers were planted around railroad stations; in Rome a new station was built to receive the illustrious guest; Rome, Florence, and Naples were augmenting the power of their illumination, modernizing store fronts, manufacturing banners, *fasci*, and swastikas to be hung along main streets and squares; the navy and air force were preparing spectacular demonstrations; militia and youths were drilled.

The fuehrer and his suite arrived in Rome on May 3, in four well-filled special trains — Mussolini and those in attendance during his trip to Germany had been easily accommodated in a single train, but the Nazi bosses' love of Italy and what she might offer in a spirit of gala hospitality explain their large number. Rome was not in its best mood, and gave the Germans a cool, almost hostile, reception. It warmed up a little only toward the end of the visit, when Hitler called Italy "the most glorious soil in the history of humanity" and proclaimed that after two thousand years, through the historic efforts of Benito Mussolini, the Roman state was resurrected. He solemnly declared: "It is my unalterable will and my bequest to the German people that it shall regard the frontiers of the Alps, raised by nature between us both, as forever inviolable."

The king insisted on monarchic protocol and did not surrender to the duce his prerogative of playing host to a chief of government. This caused some annoyance to the men concerned: the king did not like the German upstart, whose manners were plebeian; Hitler did not feel at ease in the stifling, antiquated atmosphere of the royal palace; and Mussolini resented having to play second fiddle to the king. According to a story that Ciano says he had from the king, the fuehrer created a great stir when in the middle of the first night at the royal palace he asked that a maid be sent to him, because he could not go to sleep unless he saw a woman arrange his sheets. According to the king, Hitler took drugs and other stimulants and, according to the duce, covered his pale cheeks with rouge.

From Rome Hitler was taken to Naples, where he was duly impressed by the Italian fleet: cruisers and battleships left the harbor in perfect formation, and as each ship passed the royal tribune the many voices of the crew fused in one loud, vibrant salute: "Long live the king!" Submarines dived in and out of the water like schools of young dolphins, guns roared, and above the fleet airplanes droned in the deep-blue sky. Hitler's visit ended in Florence, where the once-thwarted artist dragged along the reluctant son of Predappio's smith to visit galleries and admire masterpieces. (It was Hitler's love of Italian art that induced the Germans to pillage museums and private collections after the fall of Mussolini.) The duce, who had never indulged in gallery tours, followed the fuehrer with a bored expression and later admitted that looking at pictures tired him.

In the little time left for diplomacy, Von Ribbentrop offered Italy a pact of military assistance. Though nothing came of it immediately, the offer was the seed of the "Pact of Steel" which was signed a year and a half later. Hitler was charmed by his visit to Italy, and by Tuscany in particular. When the two dictators parted at the station in Florence, the duce said, according to the omnipresent Ciano, "No force can part us any longer," and the fuehrer's eyes filled with tears.

20

THE CRIMINAL MADNESS

> "We must get into our minds that we are not
> Hamites, we are not Semites, we are not
> Mongols. And then, if we are none of these
> races, we are evidently Aryans . . . of Med-
> iterranean type, pure."
>
> MUSSOLINI, October, 1938

IN the summer of 1938 Mussolini, pursuing the "Prussianization of Italy," doggedly pushed an anti-Semitic campaign,
modeled on the Nazi pattern.

Until then there had been little anti-Semitism in Italy.
There were approximately 50,000 Italian Jews, little more
than one out of every thousand of the population, and in
modern times they had never constituted a problem. Mussolini had often publicly recognized this fact and paid tribute
to the many Italian Jews who had rendered great service to
their country — most conspicuously he had done so in his
interviews with Emil Ludwig, which spread his reassuring
word far afield. The launching of a policy of racial discrimination came as a surprise and antagonized not only the Jews
and their friends but the Vatican and the monarchy as well: the
Vatican, both because the Catholic doctrine is universal and
open to all races by definition, and because the restrictions on
mixed marriages and other clauses of the racial laws in-
fringed on the holy institutions of marriage and the family;
the monarchy, because anti-Semitism was against the spirit
of the constitution, which insured religious freedom to all
Italian citizens.

The anti-Semitic campaign was officially launched on July
14, 1938, with the publication of the *Manifesto della Razza*,
a pseudoscientific document signed by five university profes-

sors and several younger "scientists." Only after World War II was it revealed that Mussolini himself had compiled the largest part of the manifesto; indeed, only Mussolini could have so shamelessly put together so many absurdities and tried to drown them in rhetoric and verbosity. The existence of human races, Mussolini asserted, is not "an abstraction of our mind, but corresponds to a material, phenomenal reality, which our senses can perceive." Great and lesser races exist (according to the manifesto), and the concept of races is purely biological. Since for several centuries there has been no influx of other races in Italy, "there exists *by now* [italics added] a pure Italian race. . . . The conception of racialism in Italy must be essentially Italian and with a northern-Aryan direction. . . . This means elevating the Italians to an ideal of higher consciousness of self and greater responsibility." In a paragraph more directly concerned with the Jews, Mussolini chose to distinguish between Jews and Semites: "*Jews do not belong to the Italian race.* Of the Semites who through the centuries landed on the sacred soil of our country, nothing is left. Also, the Arab occupation of Sicily has left nothing except a memory in a few names [he overlooked the Arabic features of many Sicilians and southern Italians]; anyhow, the process of assimilation is always very rapid in Italy. The Jews represent the only population that can never be assimilated in Italy, because they are constituted of non-European racial elements, absolutely different from the elements that gave origin to the Italians." After the publication of the manifesto the campaign swiftly gathered momentum, supported by a newly founded magazine *La Difesa della Razza* (*The Defense of the Race*) and by the daily press, which mercilessly hammered at the faults of Italian Jews and the crimes of "international Jewry."

When the Italian Jews asked themselves the probable causes of the anti-Semitic campaign, the answer that most readily came to mind was that Mussolini had made a deal with Hitler. Perhaps he had agreed to the campaign in return for Hitler's promise that he would not annex the South Tyrol or insist on the transfer to Germany of the German-speaking minorities who lived there. This hypothesis seemed likely, for the *Anschluss* had not only extended Germany to the border, but it had also intensified the nationalistic unrest that, in a mild form, already existed in the South Tyrol. As a result, there had been almost daily agitation, symptoms of intolerance, and demonstrations, all of which the Italians had blamed on Hitler's propaganda. They had surmised that Hitler would soon demand a plebiscite or offer the Germans in the South Tyrol the option to resettle in Germany. The unrest, however, subsided without an apparent cause, and for this reason Italian Jews assumed that the anti-Semitic campaign was the price that Hitler had exacted from Mussolini. But all subsequent evidence points against this assumption: the files of the Italian embassy in Berlin eventually revealed that in 1938 Nazi propagandists in the South Tyrol had been temporarily halted under strong pressure from the Italian government, but that no compensation was asked; and that Mussolini himself, afraid that the German minorities might create a pretext for the annexation of the South Tyrol, had suggested to Hitler a transfer of South Tyroleans to Germany. (This was actually undertaken in 1939.) The South Tyrol question proved to be unrelated to the artificial upsurge of Fascist anti-Semitism.

The tragedy of the Italian Jews was due to little more than a whim of the Italian dictator, to his spirit of emulation which drove him to imitate his great friend Hitler, and to his consequent desire to Prussianize Italy. There is reason to believe that Mussolini himself did not attribute any greater importance to the anti-Semitic campaign than to other measures directed at reforming "the Italian style," the introduction of the Roman step or the abolition of handshaking and the formal *lei*. In October, 1938, in a "very important speech," not published at the time, Mussolini told the national council of the Fascist Party that he had "given several mighty punches in the stomach to the Fascists' enemy, the *bourgeosie*." (The *bourgeosie* could not but be an enemy of fascism because Mussolini defined it tautologically by attributing to it all possible anti-Fascist traits.) "The first punch," he was to say, "has been the Roman parade step. . . . The introduction of the Roman step had an enormous repercussion

throughout the world, as an expression of moral strength.
. . . Another small punch: the abolition of *lei.* . . . Another punch in the stomach has been the racial question. . . .
To me the racial problem is a most important conquest, and it
is most important to have introduced it in the history of Italy.
. . . The racial laws of the empire will be rigorously enforced, and all those who act against them will be expelled,
punished, imprisoned. . . ."

At other times he tried to link racialism with the newly
created empire and stressed the necessity of avoiding the possible contamination of the "pure Italian" race with natives in
Africa and Jews at home: "Without a clear, definite, omnipresent race consciousness it is not possible to keep an empire.
This is why certain problems that were once in a shadow zone,
since October 3, 1935, have become of burning actuality."
(But he had let this actuality burn for almost three years.)

The lack of good reason, or even a good pretext, for the
anti-Semitic campaign raises the question whether, in spite of
his statements to the contrary, Mussolini did not nurse personal feelings against the Jews. As far as it can be ascertained,
he first encountered a definite expression of anti-Semitism in
Nietzsche's works, which he read when he was twenty-five. His
review articles in *Pensiero Romagnolo* indicated that he had
been strongly impressed by Nietzsche's view that the Jews had
brought about an inversion of spiritual values; and that this
had made the rabble triumph over the proud and strong, over
all that was intrinsically Roman — in the Jew, Rome had seen
its very counternature. This early seed of anti-Semitism did
not fall on fertile soil. In Predappio and the small towns
where Mussolini had studied there had been no Jews, for they
generally lived in the large cities and not in villages and
towns. In the family and at school he had not met anti-Semitism, and many of the persons with whom he had later associated were Jews (among them, Angelica Balabanoff and Margherita Sarfatti). Nietzsche's words could not have awakened
latent antipathy. But soon Mussolini evinced those vague apprehensions and misapprehensions about the Jews which are
a sign of ignorance and on which anti-Semitism is often built.
He said more than once that the Jews themselves created anti-

Semitism by being too conspicuous and invasive, altogether too-Jewish, and he condemned those Italian Jews who participated in the Zionist movement. Of "international Jewry" he was more openly critical, and as early as 1919 he accused the great Jewish bankers of London and New York of supporting the Jews of Moscow and Budapest in their revenge on the Aryan race; in Nietzschean fashion he called bolshevism the vengeance of Judaism upon Christianity. Later he repeatedly attacked "Jewish international finance," which in his mind was the chief cause of hostility to fascism in foreign countries.

The first to suffer from this vague anti-Semitism, as wavering as many of Mussolini's opinions, was his daughter Edda, when she had fallen in love with a young Jewish suitor. Yet, until the time of the alliance with Germany, Mussolini's anti-Semitism was not dangerous and belonged rather to his cumbersome baggage of superstition than to his political beliefs. With the birth of the Rome-Berlin axis a slow, insidious change set in, of which the public could not be aware. Significant in this respect is one of the directives issued to the Italian press by either Mussolini himself or his inner circle. Dated December 26, 1936 (three and one half months after the announcement of the axis), the directive reads: "Do not show interest in anything concerning Einstein."

Albert Einstein was by far the most prominent German Jew, and before the advent of nazism his theory of relativity was regarded as one of the highest expressions of German abstract speculation. When Hitler came to power, almost overnight Einstein's theory became the sterile product of a necessarily sterile — insofar as Jewish — mind and a threat to German science. His villa was searched, his belongings were confiscated, and his papers on relativity were burned in a bonfire on the square before the state opera house in Berlin. Anti-Einstein sentiment in Nazi Germany was indeed so strong that Mussolini's order to suppress any comment on Einstein and his work might have been interpreted as an act of courtesy of one friend to another. There were reasons for this interpretation: prominent Italian mathematicians who had worked with Einstein could go on teaching Einstein's theories undisturbed, and Italy was then granting asylum and the possibility of resettlement to many German Jews who had fled Nazi persecution. But less than a year after the restrictive directive about Einstein, Mussolini's attitude toward the racial question appeared changed, gradually becoming active and aggressive. The industrious Ciano, recording facts and bits of conversation, traced the path that Mussolini followed to reach this new goal. A goal it was, because Mussolini seemed intent on working up anti-Semitic feeling in himself and emulating his friend Hitler in the tenacity of his hatred.

As early as September, 1937, Ciano heard the duce talk venomously and absurdly of the Jews, saying, for instance, that America was in the hands of Negroes and Jews; that the Jews were a disintegrating element who did not want children because they feared pain; that in future only Italians, Germans, and Japanese would play important roles in the world, while other nations would be destroyed by the acid of Judaic corruption. On November 6, 1937, the duce told Hitler's special envoy Joachim von Ribbentrop: "We are conducting a very determined and increasingly intensive anti-Semitic campaign." No racial campaign was underway at that time, and the duce's remark reveals both wishful thinking and his eagerness to show Von Ribbentrop he had embraced Hitler's most cherished cause.

In February, 1938, Mussolini seemed to have changed his mind again and given in to more moderate views. He wrote a note on the Jewish problem for "Diplomatic Information," a new and semiofficial column appearing in *Il Popolo d'Italia*, sometimes written by Mussolini and sometimes by Ciano. In this note, in his deftly muddled way, he distinguished between the international Jewish problem, which in his opinion could be solved by the creation of a Jewish state, and the Italian problem, which did not exist; and he stated that the Italian government had no intention of taking measures against the Italian Jews as such, provided that they were not against the regime. But Ciano commented in his diary: "The duce himself has defined this piece, which in form is almost conciliatory, a masterpiece of anti-Semitic propaganda." Shortly before the publication of the *Manifesto della Razza*, Mussolini told Ciano that Jewish writers and newspapermen would be banned from further activity. "The revolution," he said, "must by now impress its mark on the Italians' customs. They must learn how to be less *simpatici* and become hard, implacable, hateful: masters." In August he took the stand that since the Jews represented about one-thousandth of the Italian population they should participate only in that ratio in the over-all life of the state. In October he told Ciano: "Anti-Semitism has now been injected in the Italians' blood. It will go on circulating and developing by itself. Besides, although this evening I am conciliatory, I shall be most harsh in the preparation of the laws." In November Ciano found him "more and more aroused against the Jews. He approves unconditionally the reactionary measures taken by the Nazis, and he says that under similar circumstances he would go even further." (A round of pogroms in Germany was at that time horrifying the free world.) Later the same month the duce appeared indignant because the king had indicated that he felt "infinite sympathy for the Jews."

Two sets of laws against the Jews were passed, in September and November. Mussolini was to say that the Italian racial laws were much worse on paper than in practice, that they were not strictly enforced, and that Italian Jews fared much better than the German. As far as Mussolini's own campaign is concerned, there is certainly some truth in this claim. In Germany anti-Semitism had been prevalent even before the advent of Hitler; in Italy it had not existed, and the Italian people did much to alleviate the Jews' plight. Yet Mussolini's campaign brought deep and widespread suffering, the loss of positions, the expulsion from public schools and universities of both teachers and students, many restrictions and limitations upon certain activities, the humiliation that accompanies flagrant discrimination, and, above all, the separation of families. The young and fit, those who could hope to start a new life outside Italy, went to England and France, Palestine, the Americas, and even the Far East, leaving behind them relatives, parents, and children. The foreign Jews who had found sanctuary in Italy were now obliged to leave, shed their briefly held sense of security, and resume their wanderings. The suffering was to turn into tragedy after the fall of Mussolini, when the campaign in Italy passed to Hitler's control. Then the machinery of

Fascist racial legislation facilitated the endeavor of the Nazis to persecute and exterminate the Italian Jews — more than 8,000 Italian Jews were deported to German concentration camps and gas chambers; only a little over 600 returned to Italy at the end of World War II. Because many others had left the country, the Jewish population in Italy was then about two-thirds what it had been before the anti-Semitic campaign.

Early in January, 1939, a little less than five years before the Nazi occupation of Italy in September, 1943, President Roosevelt sent a message to Mussolini proposing that the duce sponsor the settlement of European Jews in a part of Ethiopia. Mussolini replied that, while he favored a Jewish state, he felt that only three countries, the United States, Brazil, and Russia, were materially able to support such an undertaking on their own soil. A few months previously Mussolini himself had hinted at the possibility of opening some regions of Ethiopia to Jewish immigration, and his reply to Roosevelt must have been dictated by the fear, on second thought, that helping the people whom Hitler persecuted would displease the fuehrer. Thus, out of loyalty to a friend who was the incarnation of cruelty and perversion, Mussolini missed a unique opportunity to win the sympathy of the world.

Mussolini, preoccupied with the opinion Hitler had of him and of Italy, was losing whatever sense of proportion and moral discernment he had had. In the summer and fall of 1938, together with racial legislation, he issued laws, rules, and directives to limit the careers of bachelors and women and to prohibit marriage between Italians and foreigners of any race; he imposed the Fascist uniform upon white-collar workers in the civil service; he tried to change the "Italian style" by devices as trivial as the launching of the "fashion of the new women's hairdo" or the issuing of a new Fascist uniform. He placed on the same plane the persecution of 50,000 Jews, the penalization of those who went against "demographic" principles, and regulation of style. This distorted perspective, this absurd issuing of laws upon laws, directives upon directives, aroused a deep concern among Italians (including many once-ardent Fascists). They felt that a person in his right mind would not act so irresponsibly, that Mussolini was not in his right mind but becoming insane.

Mussolini's behavior in another field might have created similar concern, had the Italians known more about it: the conduct of the Spanish Civil War. The duce had sent the first help to Spain in the hope of drawing much glory from Franco's speedy victory. But as the war dragged on inconclusively and Franco suffered frequent setbacks, the duce grew impatient. Without the slightest regard for actual conditions or the difficulties Franco faced, he showered the *generalissimo* with letters and telegrams urging him to fight on at all costs at a faster pace, to obtain the victories that were necessary to his own prestige. Of one such letter, Ciano wrote: "[It is] an excellent, virile document which reinforces our commitments if Franco will fight but which leaves the door open to our 'unfastening' if the generalissimo insists on a war of nerves." Nor did Mussolini refrain from sending direct orders to his own troops and air force in Spain, without conferring with Franco or letting him know what he had done. The bombardment of Barcelona, due to one such order, resulted in great devastion and many casualties. But Mussolini did not cease meddling if he thought the game worth the candle.

An entirely different example of his extraordinary conduct is furnished by his treatment of one of his army officers. In the morning, speaking directly to the man and praising him for his deeds, the duce announced that he was to be made a general; in the afternoon he annulled the promotion, having learned that the man was a bachelor. "A general," Mussolini said, "must be the first to realize that without men one cannot make divisions."

Mussolini's conduct in the Spanish war was not public knowledge at the time; but other symptoms were sufficient to make the Italians surmise that he was in an abnormal state of mind. On the causes of his presumed mental condition there were two schools of thought: some believed that the duce had never recovered from the blow inflicted at the time of the *Anschluss*, when he realized that he was only the junior partner in the Rome-Berlin axis; and that he felt both a desire to ingratiate himself with his senior partner and a need to assert his will madly and at random. Others were sure that the duce was suffering from syphilitic infection and his state was a symptom of that disease. Rumors of Mussolini's incipient insanity were so persistent that not even the great success he was to obtain at Munich in September, 1938, could halt them.

Mussolini was not insane, at least not in the strict sense of the word, but he showed definite signs of intellectual and physical decline. In his isolation he did not see many people, and it is therefore the more remarkable that several impartial observers should comment on his condition. William Phillips, the U.S. ambassador, relates that on the day before Munich he conveyed to Mussolini a message from Roosevelt appealing to him to intervene to save the peace. Phillips reports that he "read the message very slowly, *as Mussolini was beginning to lose his English*" (italics added). Two years earlier, on the occasion of his first interview with the duce, which lasted ten minutes, the ambassador had remarked: "[Mussolini's] knowledge of English, while limited, was certainly sufficient for this conversation." (According to Margherita Sarfatti, Mussolini began to learn English in 1923 after meeting George Nathaniel, Lord Curzon and his wife. Lord Curzon, then the British foreign secretary, was in Lausanne to preside at an international conference which Mussolini attended. In parting, Mussolini said to Lady Curzon: "Today I'm not able to write you a letter in English, but I will be in a month; and I promise to let you have one"; and kept his promise.)

Early in 1939, the new French ambassador, André François-Poncet, is reported to have remarked that the duce was "in a period of intellectual decline." In March of that year, the secretary of the Fascist Party, who had not seen Mussolini for two months, found him looking tired, as if aged many years. Doormen and attendants commented on his state of constant agitation. Later in the year, it was evident to his collaborators that he was suffering from a recrudescence of his stomach pains. Shortly after Christmas the chief of police, Arturo Bocchini, told Ciano that the duce ought to undergo treatment for syphilis, which Bocchini considered the cause of the duce's psychological state. It was shock at the dictator's aged appearance and sluggish behavior that prevented Sumner Welles from noticing the impressive staging in the Sala del Mappamondo in 1940. Ambassador Phillips, who accompanied Welles, confirms that the duce's appearance had changed since he had last seen him. "His eyes seemed to droop and there was an expression of fatigue when his face was in repose." Welles himself told Chamberlain that Mussolini may not have suffered a stroke, but he looked very tired and seemed perturbed. And there were many reports that Mussolini was taking morphine to relieve pain.

It was an incredibly tragic fate that, through the eventful months leading to Italy's participation in World War II, an entire country should be guided and dominated by the will of a man ill in mind and body; by one whose thinking was founded less and less on reason; one to whom action, however unplanned, however vicariously experienced, held the greatest attraction; one who closed his eyes to reality, the appalling state of military preparedness and national finance, the opposition of the population and of even his collaborators, rather than put to the test his alleged ascendancy over Hitler and risk the loss of Hitler's esteem; a man who changed his mind from hour to hour, whose decisions, affecting a whole hemisphere, hinged on such irrelevant factors as who had had the last word with him or how incensed he was about the laziness and lack of fighting spirit of the people he himself had molded during the Fascist revolution; a man who was so firmly established in power, so completely (if resignedly) accepted, that no one dared to contradict him, let alone attempt to overthrow him.

Yet, at first, Mussolini was a moderating influence in the complex, rapidly deteriorating political scene, a brake to the precipating crisis of World War II.

21

COMPANIONS IN FOLLY

"It is a matter of pride for us to participate in
this struggle of giants, destined to transform
the world geographically, politically, spiritually."

MUSSOLINI, December, 1942

FIVE months after Hitler's visit to Italy the friendship between the two dictators sustained an international test from
which it emerged victorious, becoming the instrument of a
compromise that delayed the outbreak of World War II. Mussolini was hailed as the savior of peace, and his waning popularity once more flared briefly. The compromise that was then
achieved is now remembered as "the tragedy of Munich":
it gave Hitler time to occupy more land and become better
prepared to attack and to defend himself in the conflict that
he was to unleash.

Although in the Munich crisis all nations involved committed mistakes, the direct responsibility for the tragedy that
it brought forth rests entirely with Hitler. Mussolini may be
blamed for the indirect effect of his past actions and over-all
conduct in government, the installation of the first twentieth-
century totalitarian regime in western Europe, and the example that he had set for Hitler, as well as his alliance with
Hitler's Germany and his strange loyalty to it. The democratic
countries made a fatal error of judgment, trusted Hitler's
word, and did not recognize that the aggressive steps he had
taken in the past, first rearmament, then the military occupation of the Rhineland and the annexation of Austria, formed

a pattern which would be repeated again and again unless the free world took strong measures to check it.

The annexation of Austria was Hitler's first move in an ambitious scheme to reunite all Germans into a greater Germany, absorb German minorities living in other nations, and enlarge his country's living space by an eastward drive. While he was working for the Nazification of Austria, Hitler used the same propaganda machinery and the same methods of intimidation to encourage agitation among the Sudeten Germans, the German minority in Czechoslovakia. After the *Anschluss*, the relations between Germany and Czechoslovakia deteriorated rapidly; and at the beginning of September, 1938, they took a turn for the worse. Hitler began pressing openly and loudly for the surrender of the Sudetenland. But the president of Czechoslovakia, Eduard Benes, a man greatly respected and with an international reputation, courageously refused to yield, although aware that refusal might mean war with Germany. Since France was Czechoslovakia's ally and Britain allied with France, the crisis over the Sudetenland threatened to spread over most of Europe.

From the middle of September Mussolini was engaged in echoing Hitler's point of view and supporting Hitler's demands. Not unreasonably, he chose to stress that Czechoslovakia was an artificial state, created at Versailles and including groups of many different nationalities. He formulated this theme of his many discussions in a speech at Treviso, in northern Italy, on September 21: "If today Czechoslovakia finds herself in a situation that might be called delicate, it is because she was not — by now one may say 'was' — simply Czechoslovakia, but Czecho-Germano-Polono-Romanio-Slovakia." He had already called this complex nation "a counterfeit state, monstrous also in geographic configuration," and "a No. 1 mosaic state." Mussolini's stand on the Czechoslovakian question was broader than Hitler's, and while the fuehrer was demanding the Sudetenland — his last territorial claim in Europe, as he asserted — Mussolini asked for plebiscites in each of the national groups in Czechoslovakia, thus fostering the dismemberment of that country.

In the last week of September the situation was so tense that a European war seemed inevitable. Mussolini commented: "It would be really absurd, I should say criminal, if millions of Europeans threw themselves at one another simply in order to preserve Benes' sovereignty over eight different races." The British prime minister, Neville Chamberlain, flew twice to Germany for conciliatory talks with Hitler, but each time he was confronted with stiffer terms. Czechoslovakia first, then France, mobilized, and shortly afterward the British Admiralty issued orders for the mobilization of the fleet. Mussolini held consultations with his general staff, planned to send troops to Libya, and called a small contingent of men to the colors. Hitler had given an ultimatum to Czechoslovakia, asserting that he would march against her on October 1 unless she surrendered the Sudetenland three days before that date, but then he shortened the time and declared that the German army would move on September 28 at 2:00 P.M. Ciano wrote in his diary: "This means war. May God protect Italy and the Duce."

At 10:00 A.M. on September 28, four hours before the expiration of Hitler's ultimatum and the expected outbreak of hostilities, a series of diplomatic moves to avoid a catastrophe aroused hopes and relaxed the enormous tension. At that hour the British ambassador in Rome, Lord Perth, went to see Count Ciano to convey Chamberlain's personal appeal for the duce's intervention to save peace and civilization. Ciano rushed to Palazzo Venezia, where he had no difficulty in persuading Mussolini to accept the part of mediator. The sudden shift from spectator to actor was all Mussolini needed to regain his old self-assurance. At once he spoke on the telephone to the Italian ambassador in Berlin, Bernardo Attolico, and his purposeful tone was not a sham: "Go immediately to see the fuehrer," he told Attolico, "and, assuring him first that I shall stand by him in any eventuality, tell him that I advise him to delay for twenty-four hours the beginning of operations. In the meantime, I shall study and decide what must be done to solve the problem."

Ambassador Attolico was a remarkable man. His devotion to his country matched his dedication to duty and the self-abnegation with which he untiringly performed his tasks. He had proved his diplomatic ability in Moscow, where though a representative of Fascist Italy he had made friends among the Communists; he was held in high regard in Berlin, where he had been since 1935, becoming one of the best-informed and wisest foreign diplomats. At first he had worked for rapprochement and an easing of tension between Italy and Germany, but, once he became aware of the true intentions of the Germans in high command, he resolved to save Italy from the Nazi madness at all costs and against all odds — not least of these, his failing health. At the first definite signs of war he was to do all in his power to try to bring about the "unfastening" of Italy from Germany that many Italians passively wished for. To this end, courageously, he was to take responsibility and initiative that went against the directives from Rome; but in vain. Mussolini's and Ciano's nearsightedness and obtuse ignorance were to thwart his efforts.

Mussolini's order on September 28 pleased Attolico. An hour later he called back: he had hastened to the Reich chancellery, where he had interrupted Hitler's conference with the French ambassador, François-Poncet, on an arbitration proposal offered by France. Attolico had then shown to Hitler his notes on Mussolini's telephone call, which he had translated into German en route from the Italian embassy. After only a slight hesitation Hitler acceded to the duce's request. By 3:00 P.M. Mussolini, Chamberlain, and the French premier, Edouard Daladier, had agreed to meet with Hitler the next day in Munich; shortly afterward, President Roosevelt also sent an appeal to the duce; and at 6:00 P.M. Mussolini and Ciano left Rome. Early next morning Hitler met them at Kufstein on the old German-Austrian border. There they boarded his train for the rest of the trip to Munich, and Hitler, with maps of the Sudetenland and of western fortifications, explained to Mussolini his plan to "liquidate" Czechoslovakia because that country kept his hands tied and did not allow him the freedom to act against France.

The meeting opened in a conciliatory atmosphere. It started very early that afternoon (September 29) and lasted until 1:30 A.M. the following day. Mussolini was pleased with the turn of events, the role he could play at the conference, the fact that the Italian delegation was treated with greater friendliness and deference than were the other delegations. He was the most at ease of the four main actors in the drama and at an advantage because he could speak French, some German (with a pronounced southern accent), and could claim that he knew English; neither Chamberlain nor Daladier spoke German, and Hitler knew no language but his own. The duce evinced efficiency and foresight when he took from his pocket a memorandum containing proposals which he offered as the basis for discussions. In reality the proposal was not his own; it had been elaborated in Germany by one of the two rival factions in Hitler's entourage, secretly placed in Attolico's hands, and received by the duce in Rome the evening before. By presenting it as he did, allowing no time for other proposals, Mussolini defeated the rival German faction. His influence on the meeting was not limited to this. That day Hitler seemed to submit entirely to Mussolini's ascendancy and did not leave his side: if the duce smiled, he also smiled; if the duce frowned, he also frowned. The French ambassador who observed this phenomenon of adaptation was under the mistaken impression that Hitler always would be entirely under Mussolini's influence.

For lack of organization the meeting, so hastily called together, dragged on inconclusively for several hours, often breaking down into smaller groups that argued special points, and suffering from the difficulty of communicating in four languages. Mussolini began to show his annoyance and paced the room like a lion in a cage, but not without stopping now and then to dispense advice, participate in an argument, draw the conclusion of a discussion. At last a document was drafted and signed: it provided for the evacuation of the Sudetenland in five stages, starting on October 1 (by the time the agreement was signed October 1 was "tomorrow") and to be completed within ten days. An international commission was to determine the new border. Thus Germany got 11,000 square miles of Czechoslovakia, and, along with these, great industrial and strategic advantages. The Czechs were not consulted. Hitler had categorically refused to admit their delegation to the meeting, and they waited to hear their fate in a Munich hotel.

The exceptional welcome that Mussolini received upon his return to Italy, the acclaim of the people who spontaneously (this time the word has no second meaning) rushed to see him pass in his train; the king's unexpected appearance at the station in Florence to congratulate him on his success; the triumphal arch of green leaves through which he rode upon his arrival in Rome; the general rejoicing — all this irritated rather than pleased Mussolini. It gave him a measure of the Italians' preference for compromise over drastic, direct action and their deeply felt aversion to be dragged into a war at the side of Nazi Germany. It seemed to defeat the sixteen years of Fascist revolution and all his efforts to turn the Italians into a tough, warrior population, ready to fight at any time and under any circumstances, and able to conquer as the ancient Romans had done.

Despite his disappointment in the Italian lack of military fervor, this new wave of popularity flattered his ego, and he did nothing to repress it. Upon his arrival in Rome he went directly to Palazzo Venezia, and when the large crowd packed in the square acclaimed him the savior of Europe, he appeared several times on the balcony, like a prima donna responding to curtain calls, and then pronounced the words that his intuition told him the crowd wanted to hear: "You have lived memorable hours. In Munich we have worked for peace with justice. Is this not the ideal of the Italian people?"

As soon as the first enthusiasm for the averted danger subsided, a more objective evaluation was made of the price that had been paid in moral values, the surrender to aggression and the betrayal of a country that had felt itself protected by treaties and powerful allies. In Italy, as elsewhere, the sobered people began to ask themselves whether Munich had saved the peace or contrived appeasement. And Mussolini's popularity waned again.

But Mussolini served as a moderating influence on other occasions. After the *Anschluss*, Ciano wanted to square accounts
with the Germans by annexing Albania; after Hitler's visit
to Italy, the Germans again proposed a military alliance
which in official parlance was to tie formally and solemnly
National Socialist Germany and Fascist Italy (and in the less-
official language of Hitler's interpreter was meant to chain
Italy to Nazi Germany). In both cases, Albania and the military alliance, Mussolini temporized.

He let Ciano write reports on the feasibility of his schemes,
make plans which, in the tradition of Machiavellian princes,
at one time contemplated the assassination of Albania's King
Zog; and continue with preparations for the peaceful seizure
of that country; but for a long time he put off action to a
politically more suitable moment and held in check Ciano's
youthful impatience. In reply to the German proposal, he
argued that the solidarity of the two regimes had been so
often and so obviously displayed that a formal alliance was
not necessary and might even prove harmful. Again after
Munich, under the psychological effect of his success and the
regained sense of superiority over Hitler, Mussolini refused
the alliance. If the alliance were to be defensive, he said, it
was neither necessary nor urgent, as no nation was in a position to attack the much stronger totalitarian states. If the
alliance were to be offensive, then the aims of the allying
states ought to be clearly defined and agreed upon. But then
he reversed his stand on both issues and thus helped defeat the
compromise reached at Munich.

In January, 1939, he sought the alliance with Germany in
view of the action he was planning in Albania and of a possible conflict with the democracies. Difficulties arose in other
quarters. At that time Hitler envisaged a tripartite military
alliance which was to include Japan (a signatory, with Italy
and Germany, of an anti-Comintern pact). But the Japanese,
who had agreed in principle, were not yet ready to sign a
treaty and raised all sorts of objections and reservations about

the pact as drafted by the Germans, advancing counterproposals and altogether following dilatory tactics.

Irritated, the duce suggested a return to the original idea of a bilateral agreement between Germany and Italy, without Japan, at least for the moment. The Germans demurred. They did not want to renounce the military alliance with the Japanese. They were concerned with world-wide as well as European politics, with the future as well as with the present, and in view of a possible major war it was of great importance to them to tie to their side the most powerful and aggressive nation in the East. Mussolini, on the other hand, was prompted by his immediate European ambitions, and was not planning ahead. To obtain concessions from France (in Italy there was organized agitation for the acquisition of Corsica, Nice, Savoy, and Tunis) and to swallow up Albania in a single bite, an alliance with Germany, strengthening his position, would be essential; but the inclusion of faraway Japan in that alliance was immaterial. To plan ahead, to preserve a wide perspective, to weigh consequences, had never been the forte of the Fascist regime and were even less the forte of Mussolini in his state of decline, in his detached self-centeredness. After suggesting the bilateral treaty he took no direct initiative with Hitler, he did not work on a draft proposal, but sat back and waited for the German reaction to his suggestion, and for whatever piece of confidential information the Germans were willing to drop in his lap.

While the duce was waiting, and inconclusive diplomatic consultations were going on, Hitler sprang another surprise that stunned the whole world and brought World War II a step closer.

For some time Ambassador Attolico had been reporting German pressure on Czechoslovakia and other symptoms that gave reason for concern. But nothing could shake Mussolini's conviction that the German aspirations were of a purely national character: Hitler had repeatedly asserted that he did not want one single Czech inside his frontiers, and Mussolini believed in his sincerity. Moreover, Attolico could not always report specific facts to justify his apprehensions, for Von Ribbentrop and other German officials carefully avoided him, fearing his perspicacity and ability to deduce the truth from the most tenuous indications. Hence Mussolini refused to worry about the clouds that were gathering over Czechoslovakia, and as late as March 13 Ciano could write in his diary: "Nothing of particular importance for us, inasmuch as the duce does not intend to give any special significance to the Slovak crisis, which is developing and assuming disquieting proportions."

But in the next two days Mussolini learned through diplomatic channels that Hitler, after a conversation with the president of Czechoslovakia reminiscent of the one he had had with Von Schuschnigg a year earlier, had sent troops into Bohemia and shortly afterward followed them into Prague. There, on March 15 he proclaimed the establishment of the protectorate of Bohemia and Moravia, territories which, he said, "for a millennium had belonged to the *Lebensraum* of the German people," from whom "violence and stupidity tore them away arbitrarily." At the same time he set up Slovakia as an independent state and promptly sent German troops to "protect" her independence. By mutual agreement between Germany and Hungary, Ruthenia went to Hungary. Of the Czechoslovakia of the Munich crisis nothing remained.

On March 15, after German troops had entered Czechoslovakia, Hitler's "winged messenger," Prince Philip of Hesse, arrived in Rome. Two days earlier Attolico had foreseen Hesse's trip and interpreted it as an ominous sign: having seen Hitler with the scowl he wore on great occasions, Attolico had desperately tried to obtain information. Germans in high position were all tight-lipped. As a last resort, Attolico called Hesse's residence on the pretext of inquiring about Princess Mafalda's health. He was told that Hesse had been urgently summoned to Berlin. The "winged messenger" was being kept at hand, and from that moment Attolico had no doubts that matters were very grave.

This time Hesse did not carry even a letter for Mussolini,

simply a verbal message relaying the fuehrer's thanks for Italy's unshaken support and an explanation of his coup. The Czechs, Hesse said, had not abided by the decisions made at Munich, and they had, in addition, mistreated the Germans in their territory.

Mussolini was thoroughly upset. For the next three days he appeared "unhappy," "depressed," "anxious," "gloomy," and wavering, uncertain what course he was to take. His first concern was the figure he would cut should the Italians learn of Hesse's visit ("The Italians would laugh at me; every time Hitler occupies a country he sends me a message"). He was aware that Italy was swayed by a wave of utter indignation against the Germans and could not but know that he himself was to blame. As Mario Donosti (the penname of an Italian diplomat) says in his book on Mussolini's foreign policy, *Mussolini e l'Europa*, "The snake that Mussolini had warmed in his bosom had become so huge that he no longer had either the force to strangle it or the courage to thrust it far away. To reverse his position, abandon Germany, attract to himself the wrath, by now very dangerous, of Berlin before having won the sympathies of London and Paris was a very difficult enterprise. It was much more consonant with the methods of the Fascist government to close one's eyes to the danger and intoxicate oneself with other apparent successes in order to forget the real failures."

To procure "an apparent success," the occupation of Albania was once more considered, and once more it was postponed. It could not counterbalance, in world opinion, Germany's annexation of a territory as rich as Bohemia. Besides, it might have shaken the precarious balance in Yugoslavia and precipitated a new crisis. There was talk of German pressure on Yugoslavia, where the Croatians were agitating for independence; there were rumors that they might appeal to Berlin for aid in carrying out plans for autonomy; and these rumors aroused Mussolini's fear that the Germans might cross the Croatian mountains and come to the shores of the Adriatic. "In such a case," Mussolini said, "these are the only alternatives: either to fire the first shot against Germany or to be swept away by a revolution which the Fascists themselves will bring about. No one would tolerate the sight of a swastika in the Adriatic."

This was an appalling admission of his own ineptitude, of the futility of the seventeen-year-old Fascist revolution — and he had no intention of firing on the Germans. By March 18 he had convinced himself that Hitler had done the right thing, and he outlined an editorial to that effect for *Giornale d'Italia.* On March 20, through the German ambassador, he received Hitler's assurance that the Germans had no interest in the Adriatic; and the next day the news that the Western powers contemplated a "democratic bloc" hardened the duce in his philo-German policy. He spoke in this sense to the Grand Council, in an address which Ciano called "marvelous, . . . argumentative, logical, cold and heroic." Balbo, the inveterate *frondeur,* is reported to have said to the duce: "You are shining Germany's boots."

Mussolini's arguments in favor of loyalty to Germany were shallow: "We cannot change politics because after all we are not prostitutes," and "The period of waltz tours, if it ever existed, is now decidedly closed." (He alluded to accusations that in the past Italy had been flirting with one great power after the other; and he overlooked the part that he himself had played in possibly the most serious "waltz tour" in 1914.)

In private conversations he was more critical of the Germans than in public; he recognized the need to define aims and objectives, to establish zones of influence and action for Italy and Germany; he admitted that Hitler had not played fair with him and once expressed his intention to write a personal letter to the fuehrer — a characteristic reaction to a crisis affecting the world — to say that certain events were blows to his personal prestige and could not be overlooked. But this letter was never written; instead, he received one from the fuehrer.

Hitler, taking the opportunity of the celebration of the twentieth anniversary of the foundation of fascism, poured praise upon the duce: praise for the duce's stand against bolshevism, for the example he had set to the world, for the regeneration of twentieth-century Europe, which was due to him. The fuehrer also reasserted his own and his people's immutable friendship: "You must see in this friendship not only a sign of platonic adhesion," he said, "but you must regard it as the unshakable decision to draw, if needed, even in the most difficult moments, the extreme consequences of this solidarity." (Hesse, in his verbal message, had said that the fuehrer and the German people would be willing to help Italy in any circumstance, even in a war with France, but the duce had sharply retorted that in that case the Italians would fight alone, without accepting a single man from Germany.)

It is not easy to say whether Mussolini was pleased by the letter. It is reported that upon reading it he became "extremely talkative." He hinted that in a scheduled speech the next day he would assume a more conciliatory tone toward France. Indeed, the next day he mentioned only the Italian demands in Africa — Tunis, Djibouti, Suez — omitting Corsica, Savoy, and Nice. At the same time he warned Germany that "geographically, historically, politically, militarily," the Mediterranean was "vital to Italy" and that when he said Mediterranean he meant to include also "that gulf which is called the Adriatic."

This warning to Germany, coming less than a week after Germany's official reassurance in regard to the Adriatic and the day after Hitler's letter full of praise and promises, shows that at heart Mussolini was realistic and did not trust the loyalty of his German friends. With realism went also the habitual bluff, for Mussolini was convinced of Germany's military strength and realized that he would not be able to stop a German thrust to the Adriatic if Hitler was resolved to make one. But the bluff had one positive result: it restored the self-assurance of the bluffer. And at the moment the duce greatly needed self-assurance.

In those days he had at last given in to Ciano's old desire and was preparing for the occupation of Albania in order to counterbalance German annexations and strengthen the Italian end of the axis. The warning to Germany gave him the feeling that he had done all that could be reasonably expected to protect himself during the Albanian attack and to place Hitler in the moral position where he could not retaliate with a move in Yugoslavia. In this confident frame of mind, less than two weeks after his speech and warning, he ordered his troops to land in Tirana. The landing began on April 7, Good Friday, a holy day in Catholic Italy.

Of the Balkan states Albania is the most important to Italy, for it lies on the eastern side of the Strait of Otranto at the entrance to the Adriatic Sea. Possession of Albania means control of the strait and therefore of the Adriatic. But Albania was already *de facto*, though not *de jure*, an Italian protectorate or vassal state, and its conquest by Italy was not essential. King Zog I was indebted to Mussolini for the protection he had received since his days as prime minister and, a little later, as the rebel who had overthrown the legal government to put himself on the throne. Under the cover of several political and military treaties with Albania, the Fascists had acquired strong financial interests in the land, above all the exploitation of Albanian oil. The Fascists had not, however, used their position to develop the country systematically, had not promoted education, built good roads, helped Albanian agriculture, or supplied the army with modern weapons. In 1939 Albania was still a primitive country whose sparse population was in large part constituted of fierce tribesmen living in the mountains in a seminomadic state and whose society was loosely organized under an almost feudal system. At the top of the system was King Zog, a mediocre ruler, unpopular among the tribesmen, to whose needs he was insensitive.

For a year Ciano had planned to take advantage of this unpopularity in order to overthrow Zog and tie his own name to a glamorous adventure. At the end of March, 1939, as soon as Mussolini gave the "go" sign to the Albanian expedition, Ciano ordered the Italian minister in Albania to intensify pressure upon dissatisfied chiefs and tribesmen, a pressure which had been exerted ever since Ciano had first conceived his coup. The disorder and rebellion that followed gave Mussolini a pretext to occupy the country and restore the order that his own men had disrupted. The occupation, initiated on April 7, was considered a success by the Fascists the next day when King Zog fled to Greece with his Hungarian wife Geraldine and their two-day-old child. Several days earlier Ciano had written in his diary: ". . . it seems probable that King

Zog will give in. There is, above all, a fact upon which I am counting: the coming birth of Zog's child. Zog loves his wife very much as well as his whole family. I believe that he will prefer to insure to his dear ones a quiet future. And frankly I cannot imagine Geraldine running around fighting through the mountains of Unthi or of Mirdizu in her ninth month of pregnancy."

The reaction of the Western democracies to the Albanian coup was mild, as was to be expected after the moderate reactions to German action in Bohemia and Moravia. Mussolini took upon himself the task of reassuring Greece and England. In his early years in government he had once shelled and occupied the island of Corfu. Now both Greece and her ally, England, feared that the occupation of Albania meant a second occupation of Corfu, if not an invasion of Greece. Furthermore, the British thought the occupation of Albania a breach of promise, for with a gentlemen's agreement in January, 1937, and an Easter pact in the spring of the following year, Italy and England had pledged to respect the status quo in the Mediterranean. The foreign office, however, seemed to be satisfied with Mussolini's explanation that since Albania had been in the Italian sphere of influence for many years, occupation had not changed matters at all.

For the sake of France and England Mussolini tried also to bring to light the anti-German character of the Albanian action, and instructed the Italian embassies in Paris and London to see that some newspapers interpreted the occupation of Albania as a move to impede German expansion in the Balkans. But toward the United States the duce acted with a levity and a lack of discernment which may be attributed in part to his ignorance of faraway countries and in part to the opinion he had formed of Americans at the time of Versailles, when he was convinced that Woodrow Wilson had betrayed the Italian cause. On April 15, a week after the occupation of Albania, Roosevelt sent a message to Mussolini and Hitler asking them to offer a ten-year non-aggression pledge to thirty-one states, which he listed. In return, the United States would help to find a solution to the disarmament problem and the question of access to raw materials.

When Ciano brought the message to the duce, Mussolini at first refused to read it, then read it but dismissed it lightly, saying that it was "a result of progressive paralysis." The same day he had occasion to discuss it with Marshal Hermann Goering, who had come to Rome to expound Hitler's views on the European situation. Goering thought Roosevelt's proposal a symptom of mental disease and believed that Hitler and Mussolini should not demean themselves by answering it directly; the press could reply in the strongest terms.

On April 20 the duce spoke before the organizers of a universal exhibition, or world's fair, that was being planned for 1942. On this occasion, implicitly answering Roosevelt, he stated that the plans for the exhibit were a proof of his peaceful intentions; that he had no desire to attack anyone. He affirmed that the policies of Rome and the axis were "inspired by the criteria of peace and collaboration" a fact of which Italy and Germany had given many concrete proofs. "Anyhow," he said, "we do not let ourselves be affected by press campaigns, convivial vociferations, or Messianic messages, for we feel that we have both a clean conscience and the men and means for defending, along with ours, everybody's peace."

With the occupation of Albania Mussolini could lull himself into the delusion that he had attained equality with Hitler, and from this position of regained self-confidence he again pushed negotiations for a military alliance with Germany. By this time his irritation at Hitler's unexpected move in Czechoslovakia had subsided and given way to the fear that unless he concluded the alliance Italy would find herself isolated between a hostile democratic bloc and a dynamic Germany. Meanwhile, the Japanese had made it clear that they were not yet ready for a tripartite pact, and Mussolini, more pleased than disappointed, pressed again for a bilateral treaty. Though Von Ribbentrop hesitated, always hoping to include Japan, Hitler gladly took this opportunity to tie Italy to his cart. The "Pact of Friendship and Alliance" between Italy and Germany was signed on May 22, 1939. Mussolini, always looking for the dramatic, changed the cumbersome name to "Pact of Steel," though it is reported that he would have preferred to call it a "Pact of Blood." Both designations were pertinent; the first was descriptive, the second prophetic.

The draft of the pact had been left almost entirely to the Germans; it had been tentatively formulated when the tripartite alliance including Japan was under consideration. After the coup in Albania, a meeting between Ciano and Von Ribbentrop took place on May 6 and 7 in Milan, at Mussolini's request, but neither the duce nor his foreign minister had thought it necessary to undertake the burdensome task of drafting an Italian proposal. Mussolini jotted down a set of instructions for Ciano's benefit, the opening and closing sentences of which are extremely interesting; Mussolini began: "It is my firm opinion that the two European powers of the axis need a period of peace lasting no less than three years. It is only from 1943 on that a war effort can have the greatest expectations of victory." And he concluded: "*General attitude*: to talk of peace and to prepare for war." (Between these two sentences he explained that he needed the period of peace in order to mobilize and arm Libya and Albania, pacify Ethiopia, complete the reconstruction of six warships, replace obsolete artillery, improve the Italian economy, and strengthen the relations between the Italian and German peoples; he then made a brief survey of foreign and economic policies of the axis.)

The two foreign ministers seemed to be in full agreement on one point: both countries wished a long period of peace. Mussolini was to stress again the need for peace until 1943 in a memorandum that he sent to Hitler right after the alliance was concluded; thus he created the belief that the alliance contained a secret clause specifying that Italy would not enter a war until that date. But such a clause did not exist, and the period of peace was not mentioned in the text of the pact. In Milan, at any rate, Ciano and Von Ribbentrop did not examine a draft of alliance but agreed that Von Ribbentrop would have one prepared, to be discussed through the usual diplomatic channels.

At this point, before the details of the alliance were worked out, before the Italian people had seen the proposed pact, Mussolini insisted on a public announcement of this "indissoluble communion of the two states and the two peoples." A month had passed since the landing in Albania, and the duce needed another glamorous achievement, another handful of dust to throw in Fascist eyes. He was also aroused against the French press, which had spread rumors of anti-German demonstrations in Milan and now made the comment — valid, indeed — that Mussolini's pro-German policy did not represent the will of the Italian people. A further reason for the announcement was the fact that the British were on the point of signing an Anglo-Turkish pact "of Mediterranean protection," which the duce considered directed against Italy.

Not for six days after the announcement did Ciano see the German draft. "I've never read such a pact," he commented in his diary; "it contains some real dynamite." But the duce was pleased. Like the drafts that had been prepared for the tripartite alliance, this one contained a brief clause for reciprocal consultations and several clauses spelling out in detail the obligations of each party, should the other become involved in conflict, "to come immediately to the side of the threatened party as an ally" and to assist it "with all its military forces on the ground and sea and in the air." In the hands of a government as unscrupulous as the German the pact was a terrible instrument against a government as inept as the Italian. Yet neither Mussolini nor Ciano gave it a serious thought, nor did they have it examined by their legal advisers. The Fascist had always boasted of "straight lines," of not turning to look behind them, of "unmistakable policies." Any attempt to make the pact more reasonable by softening some of its clauses would have been against the Fascist mentality and Mussolini's sense of honor. Only two modifications were introduced in the final draft: Mussolini asked that the pact have a time limit and proposed a ten-year period, with possibility of renewal; Ambassador Attolico pointed out that Italy had at least the right to request a guarantee of the Brenner frontier, and Mussolini added a sentence to this effect.

Two days before the signing of the military alliance, Musso-lini said: "A bloc of 150 million men will be formed, against which nothing can be done. This bloc, a formidable array of men and weapons, wants peace, but it is ready to impose it should the great conservative and reactionary democracies try to stop our irresistible march."

To attempt to discern Mussolini's intentions in his jumble of words about peace and war seems hopeless. To protect peace and to "impose" it, he wanted the Italians "to arm more and more powerfully." He said: "There are knots in the European policy, but to untie these knots it is perhaps not necessary to make use of the sword. All the same, these knots must be resolved once and for all. . . ." And: "The doctrine of fascism is clear, and my will inflexible. . . . We shall march with Germany in order to give Europe that peace with justice that is the profound desire of all peoples. . . . Whatever may happen, I declare to you, with absolute certainty, that all our goals will be reached."

These do not seem the words of one who truly wants peace. Yet the study of documents and the testimonies of collabora-tors and diplomats indicate that Mussolini badly needed and wanted at least three years of peace, as he had instructed Ciano to tell Von Ribbentrop; and in all his talk of war and loud threats against the democracies one must recognize habit, bluff, and the excitement that talking to acclaiming crowds about future glories always aroused in him. Besides, he trusted that the Germans also desired a long period of peace, as they had asserted. But the peace the Nazis would have welcomed was not Mussolini's total peace; it was the avoidance of a large-scale conflict, peace that did not exclude a German thrust against Poland or an Italian move against France. In fact, on the day after the signing of the alliance, while Mussolini and Ciano were rejoicing, Hitler convened his top military men and held a secret conference at which he said that an expansion toward the east was essential to insure adequate food supplies in a war against the democracies; therefore he had decided to attack Poland at the first suitable opportunity, certain that he would be able to limit the conflict and avoid the intervention of the Western democracies. Since secrecy was necessary for success, Hitler added, German aims must be kept secret from Italy and Japan.

On this frightful insincerity was based the alliance of Germany with Italy.

Hitler had always propounded German expansion toward the east, and his behavior was consistent. But Mussolini's conduct is less easy to understand at first glance. After seventeen years spent in preparing the men and youth of Italy for war, of talking war and creating a warlike atmosphere, why did he want and need three more years of peace? The explanation is that, after closing his eyes for years on Italy's military unpreparedness, he had suddenly opened them and seen the appalling condition of the armed forces at the end of 1938. He could blame himself, the system of deception and greed that he had allowed to spread, and the immense cost of the Ethiopian and Spanish wars for the great shortage of war materials and the pitiful state of the men in service, poorly trained and miserably outfitted. His own policy of "autarchy," aimed at turning Italy into an independent and self-supporting economic unit, had wrecked the Italian economy, which had never flourished and had been shaken badly by the world crisis in the early thirties. Autarchy, by which only home products and materials were used, enormously raised prices and cut down exports. Foreign currency and gold reserves became exiguous and were rapidly dwindling. The Italians were repeatedly asked to tighten their belts.

Mussolini complained that in the matter of armaments and preparations he had been cheated, and on the basis of this deception all his apologists have cleared him of any responsibility, as if as chief of state, holding the three portfolios of the armed forces, he should not have retained at least part of that omniscience in all aspects of government of which he had so often prided himself.

Among his apologists, his wife, in her naïve attempt to exonerate her husband, wrote one of the most incriminating paragraphs: "For the sake of truth, I must report that I then tried personally to help my husband to see more deeply, beyond the reality that was shown to him. . . . Once the Undersecretary of Aviation came to *Rocca delle Caminate* to report and was asked to visit the Caproni aircraft factory, located near Predappio. The undersecretary paid his visit, promised to furnish materials for a few hundred airplanes, and after some time it was announced that hundreds of this new type [of plane] were already built and equipped. Instead, at Predappio the materials for two, I say two, planes had arrived. The inquiries that followed my charges [of fraud and incompetence] always confirmed what I had uncovered. In the irritation that seized him after revelations of this sort, Benito used to exclaim: 'Ninety-nine times out of a hundred, Mother is right!' "

The chief of police of that period, Carmine Senise, also tells of some incredible episodes: "His [Mussolini's] gullibility encouraged everybody to let him believe one thing for another. Once, for instance, he was taken to see an aviation field on which over a thousand planes were lined up to be shown off. Proudly Mussolini admired that superb display of force and never knew that only a few of those planes could rise from the ground and fly." Senise also relates that when there were military parades the army borrowed armored cars from the police, painted them gray-green, and restored them to their former color afterward. Mussolini himself was aware of at least some of these almost incredible deficiencies and once told Senise: "Do you want to have an idea of how far matters have gone? In Albania [Italian] soldiers wear shoes with cardboard soles: imagine those shoes in the mountains and snow!"

Yet he must have thought himself free from blame. It is reported that at a cabinet meeting in the spring of 1939 he asserted that army administrators were inefficient, their statistics were never accurate, and insofar as guns were concerned he had been deceived: the artillery was old and insufficient. Ciano comments in his diary: "The Duce is very much dissatisfied. . . . He has the feeling, and he is right, that beyond appearances, which are more or less put on, there is little underneath. . . . The military make a big ado with a lot of names. They multiply the number of divisions, but in reality these are so small that they scarcely have more than the strength of regiments. The ammunition depots are lacking in ammunition. Artillery is outmoded. Our antiaircraft and antitank weapons are altogether lacking. There has been a good deal of bluffing in the military sphere, and even the Duce himself has been deceived — a tragic bluff. We will not talk about the question of the air force. Valle [General Giuseppe Valle, Undersecretary of Aviation] made the statement that there were 3,006 first-class planes, while the information service of the Navy says that they amount to only 982. A gross exaggeration. . . ."

Though his eyes were opened, Mussolini could not hope to remedy swiftly the appalling state of affairs in the armed forces. The economic condition of the nation did not permit it. Rather than admit defeat, Mussolini contrived the project of a world's fair in 1942, and to this end he began building a set of extremely modern buildings on the outskirts of Rome. He hoped that the exhibition, attracting foreign tourists, would bring the much-needed flow of currency into Italy. Hence he set 1943 as the earliest possible time for his participation in a war. The plan was naïve, and Mussolini certainly underestimated the cost of a war. Besides, it is very doubtful whether in his slothful mental state he would have been able to take energetic action had he had the financial means to do so.

In confirming the "disastrous" condition of the army, Ciano writes: "But what is the Duce doing? His attention seems to be spent mostly on matters of form; there is hell to pay if the 'present arms' is not done right or if an officer does not know how to lift his legs in the Roman step, but he seems to concern himself only up to a certain point about the real weakness, which he certainly knows very well. In spite of my formal charges in connection with. . . the efficiency of our aviation, he has done nothing, absolutely nothing. . . . Does he fear the truth so much that he is unwilling to listen?"

Whether or not the duce might have rallied by 1943 and taken vigorous action to improve conditions in the armed forces will always remain a matter of speculation, since Hitler upset Mussolini's timetable and did not give him a chance to follow the program he proposed.

No sooner had Hitler wiped out Czechoslovakia than he began to advance claims upon the free city of Danzig and the Polish Corridor. In April, 1939, Great Britain, resolved by then not to let aggression go unpunished, pledged to assist Poland with all her might should Poland's independence be threatened. Hitler immediately denounced his previous non-aggression pact with Poland, which dated from 1934. In the next few months he again used the tactics that had been so successful in Austria, the Sudetenland, and the rest of Czechoslovakia: he provoked Poland in various ways, making preposterous claims and starting a propaganda campaign against the alleged mistreatment of the German minorities in Poland. For the fourth time in little over a year the pattern was repeating itself.

Yet Mussolini did not recognize it, or if he did he gave no signs that it worried him. Taking at its face value Germany's professed conviction that when the moment came England and France would not fight for Poland's sake, he reiterated to Hitler his expression of solidarity in the Polish question. He did not feel that danger was imminent: the Pact of Steel provided for consultations before any military action, and in the absence of official communications the credulous duce felt confident and optimistic.

At the beginning of July, France declared her interest in maintaining the status quo in eastern Europe and in doing so initiated a true "war of nerves." Ambassador Attolico was one of the first to see the unavoidable crisis approaching, and he began to shower Rome with pessimistic reports, which Ciano received with unbelieving skepticism. Attolico was devising ways to bring about the "unfastening" of Italy from Germany, but Mussolini, firm in his loyalty to Hitler, refused to consider any breach or attenuation of the military alliance.

Instead, he conceived a plan for a new Munich, a large conference at which he would again be the mediator and hero.

Though he had always thought of himself as a victor of wars, he was not disinclined to be once more a victor of peace. But Hitler showed little interest in mediation. Finally, under Attolico's alarmist bombardment about the Nazis' war preparations, Mussolini sent his foreign minister to Germany for talks with Von Ribbentrop. Still in an optimistic mood, the duce personally drafted a communiqué which stressed the identity of views of the two foreign ministers, stated their common will to resist encirclement and aggression, and expressed their opinion that the difficulties threatening Europe's life could be peacefully solved through diplomatic negotiations.

The conversations took place in Salzburg from August 11 to August 13, but the outcome did not fulfil Mussolini's expectations. .He realized that things were not going well when Ciano, in Germany, refused to talk about the meeting over the telephone. When Ciano returned to Rome, Mussolini learned that Hitler was stubbornly determined to attack and destroy Poland, and that nothing would deter him. Ciano had talked to both Von Ribbentrop and Hitler. They had repeatedly said they were certain that France and England would not intervene. But, Ciano felt, they were in bad faith, for Hitler asserted also that the big war against the democracies should be fought while fuehrer and duce were still young. Ciano reminded Von Ribbentrop that the Nazis had recognized the need for two or three years of peace, but Von Ribbentrop replied that the situation had changed. Neither he nor Hitler paid any attention to the Italian's arguments in favor of delay and possible peaceful solutions. In fact, they treated Ciano with such a lack of consideration that he felt thoroughly humiliated and was still in a rage when he returned to the duce.

Mussolini was no less irritated and no more prepared to take a firm stand than Ciano had been in Salzburg. At this point Mussolini could have denounced the Pact of Steel, for the Germans had not abided by the clause providing for consultation and were planning a military action against the wish of their ally. Both Attolico, in Berlin, and Ciano urged him to terminate the military alliance — in the following months

Ciano, anti-German after Salzburg, was to work with unsuspected vigor and pertinacity to keep Italy out of the conflict. Mussolini was well aware that Hitler was committing a folly and might well unleash a second world war with disastrous consequences, especially for Italy. And yet, to stay out of the war, to renounce fighting after having asserted so often the need to fight, meant the negation of all he had advocated for seventeen years, the negation of the whole Fascist doctrine, and the breaking of a young alliance based on this doctrine. It meant a repetition of Italy's "betrayal" of Germany at the time of World War I and the certain loss of Hitler's friendship. "If there had not been the precedent in 1914," Mussolini is reported to have said, "I would tear up the alliance."

Divided between the dictates of his reasons and the demands of his ambition, between the fear of disaster for Italy and himself and the allurement of the idea that once more he might make war speeches, announce victories, and appear on the world stage as an invincible leader, Mussolini entered one of his worst periods of indecision. He wavered, in turn gave in to Ciano's pressure, reacted and reasserted his will to march all the way at Hitler's side; he changed his mind from day to day and from hour to hour, giving his associates the impression that the final choice between war and peace was going to be left to the turn of a coin rather than to a well-pondered analysis of facts and circumstances.

It was a week after Ciano's return from Salzburg before Mussolini learned that Germany and Russia were on the point of signing an agreement of friendship and non-aggression. The Germans had again failed to consult the Italians before this move, which was against Fascist doctrine and the anti-Comintern pact, but which insured Germany protection from the rear in case of war with the Western democracies. On August 25 the duce received a message from Hitler which made it clear that he was ready to march at once on Poland. Yet the fuehrer was obliged to pause briefly, and it was Mussolini who made him pause. Caught between a peaceful and a belligerent mood, the duce replied that the Italians were not ready to go to war but would do so if the Germans were to supply equipment and raw material. In return, Hitler asked for a list of Italian needs. At this point Ambassador Attolico and the German ambassador in Rome, Hans Georg von Mackensen, took the initiative in the hope to save the peace. Von Mackensen told Ciano unofficially that the fuehrer had temporarily halted mobilization, waiting to see what the Italian requests would be, and the ambassador advised that the list of demands be made very extensive. On the following day Attolico made his move. He transmitted to the fuehrer Mussolini's message containing the asked-for list, hastily compiled after consultations with the chiefs of staff. ("It is enough to kill a bull — if a bull could read," Ciano wrote of this list.) Hitler asked Attolico when the Italians expected the delivery of the goods requested. Seeing his chance, Attolico did not hesitate a second. "Immediately," he replied. (The list, according to Ciano, involved "seventeen million tons, which would require seventeen thousand cars for their transportation.")

Mussolini's message read:

"Fuehrer:

"This morning I convened the Chiefs of Staffs of the Army, Navy, and Aviation, with Minister Ciano and the Minister of Communication also attending, and here is the minimum that the Italian Armed Forces need, in addition to what we have, in order to sustain a *twelve-month* war:

Coal for gas and metallurgic industries	six million tons
Steel	two million tons
Lumber	one million tons
Copper	one hundred fifty thousand tons
Sodium nitrate	two hundred twenty thousand tons
Potassium salts	seventy thousand tons
Rosin	twenty-five thousand tons
Rubber	twenty-two thousand tons
Toluol	eighteen thousand tons
Spirits of Turpentine	six thousand tons
Lead	ten thousand tons
Tin	seven thousand tons

Nickel	five thousand tons
Molybdenum	six hundred tons
Tungsten	six hundred tons
Zirconium	twenty tons
Titanium	four hundred tons

"Food and textile requirements will be met by resorting to rationing.

"In addition to the raw materials as above, you know that our entire war industry is in the quadrilateral Turin-Genoa-Milan-Savona and along the Tyrrhenian coast, that is, half an hour's flight from Corsica. In order to protect these industrial plants, the destruction of which could literally paralyze our war effort, an immediate shipment of [antiaircraft] batteries with the corresponding ammunition is necessary.

"General Keitel is in possession of the list of machinery items that are indispensable to speed up our war production.

"Fuehrer,

"I should either have not sent you this list, or the list would have contained a smaller number of entries and much smaller figures, had I had the time foreseen by mutual agreement to accumulate reserves and accelerate the rhythm of autarchy.

"Without the certainty [*sic*] of these supplies it is my duty to tell you that the sacrifices which I should ask the Italian people, sure of being obeyed, might be in vain and compromise your cause along with mine.

"If you think that there still might be any possibility of a solution [through negotiation], I am ready to give you, as on other occasions, my full solidarity and take whatever initiative you may consider useful to this purpose.

"Mussolini."

To send this message was to swallow a bitter pill. Ciano wrote: "The Duce is really out of his wits. His military instinct and his sense of honor were leading him to war. Reason has now stopped him. But this hurts him very much."

Although Mussolini "immediately" clarified Attolico's misunderstanding, Hitler had to admit that he was in no position to furnish all the material requested and courteously, if begrudgingly, he allowed Italy to give political support without actually fighting. In the course of the correspondence between the two dictators in that thunderous month of August, Mussolini explained that "forces superior to his will" prevented him from giving his partner his "positive solidarity in the moment of action." He praised Hitler's "superb realizations" and foresaw "a new, incontestable success." The two friends exchanged pledges of solidarity, expressions of "understanding," and thanks for past and future support in terms that reveal their disingenuity and lack of candor. They reveal also where the greater ability was, for, in confessing Italy's weakness rather than insisting on the consultation clause of the Pact of Steel, Mussolini placed himself in a subservient position from which neither his own actions nor Hitler's continued personal deference were to raise him.

On September 1 Hitler "liberated" Danzig and began military operations against Poland, and two days later England and France entered the war.

22

AT WAR

"War is the most important thing in a man's life, as maternity is in a woman's."
MUSSOLINI, January, 1943

To Mussolini, the man of action, the nine months in which Italy took no active part in the conflict were a torment, a period in which he felt an outcast from the world scene. Neutrality was humiliating, and he coined the term "non-belligerency" to explain Italy's position. He was not a neutral, but a man at the window, a chief of government obliged by circumstance to bide his time. The constraining circumstances were not his people's vehement sentiment against war or the mounting distrust and hatred of the Germans, to which he gave no weight and which he did not take into consideration, but the lack of arms and the money to buy them.

Toward the Germans, who were carrying out so ruthlessly plans made without consulting him, who by refusing to consider any diplomatic solution were depriving him even of the glory of a second Munich, Mussolini experienced an irritation that Ciano took care to fan. When Ciano spoke against the alliance, the duce always seemed to sway, uncertain on what side to join the conflict, for join it he eventually must. But Mussolini was dazzled by Hitler's easy victories in Poland, and at times seemed so envious, so bitter, that he wished Hitler dead. Early in November, 1939, when Hitler escaped unharmed an attempt on his life in Munich, Mussolini sent him a telegram of congratulations but, according to Ciano, felt no great joy. Yet Hitler, very much alive and conquering, exerted a great fascination over the duce even at a distance. No matter what Mussolini might say one day to Ciano, the next day his admiration and strange loyalty for his ally would come to the fore and he would express what he really felt: full solidarity with Hitler. The question of the point of honor returned: he would fight on the German side because honor so dictated. This was a decision he made again when confronted with Hitler's victories — and all those around him sensed that there would be no going back on it.

Restless, feeling himself condemned to inaction, he gave himself up to his much-too-frequent wishful thinking. Preparations went well, in his opinion, at a sure and rapid pace. By spring he would be ready to give rather than receive help. He would requisition copper from the Italians, even from the churches ("The churches do not need copper but faith"), and give 3,500 tons of it to Germany. He continued to refuse to see the discontent, the economic straits, the shortage of food, the intolerance for the Nazi regime with which the Italian people prepared to face almost certain participation in the war. When the English stopped their shipments of coal, the duce said he was pleased: this was a whipping to the Italians, who thus would learn to rely only on their own resources. He disregarded the fact that the ensuing scarcity of coal would slow down industry. He covered his ears when some of his collaborators tried to tell him the truth about the state of finances and the military output. (He said that a state falls because of internal instability or military defeat, never for economic reasons.) Again and again he expressed the humiliation he felt at having "to remain with our hands folded while others write history," at being "the laughingstock of Europe."

But there he was wrong: outsiders were not laughing at him. The world at large still took him seriously, still hoped that he might throw his weight in the balance to achieve a compromise peace. In the winter of 1940, after Hitler's blitzkrieg in Poland had given way to the "phony war" and nothing seemed to happen in the front lines, a new desire to avoid the real war and a new optimism spread over the world. Typical of this attitude was the mission on which President

Roosevelt sent Undersecretary of State Sumner Welles at the end of February, 1940. Welles was to visit the capitals of the democracies and of the axis powers and report to the President on the possibilities of establishing a just and lasting peace, but he was given no power to make proposals or negotiate. His first stop was Rome, where he saw Mussolini (and was shocked by the dictator's physical appearance).

The relations between Rome and London had deteriorated shortly before, for Mussolini had refused to sell war materials to England, and in turn England had ordered the confiscation of the coal carried to Italy on German ships. Yet the Germans, too, appeared dissatisfied with their ally who had expressed eagerness for war but refused to fight when the time for war came. Top Nazi officials like Goering and Von Ribbentrop were openly venting their distrust. The President of the United States still thought that there was a chance to keep Mussolini out of the conflict, even perhaps to negotiate a compromise peace in Europe, and that the chance, though small, should not be overlooked.

In his conversation with Sumner Welles, Mussolini strongly supported the German point of view, but he did not exclude the possibility of a negotiated peace, provided it were concluded promptly while the belligerents' armies were still inactive, and provided certain concessions — too great to be accepted as they were asked — were made to the axis powers. Welles then proceeded to the other capitals for other informal discussions, and then stopped again in Rome on his way back to the United States. It was the middle of March, and the atmosphere had changed: afraid lest Mussolini be persuaded by American arguments, Hitler had sent his foreign minister, Von Ribbentrop, to Rome to tell Mussolini in rather strong terms that Italy's place was at Germany's side. A meeting of the two axis leaders was arranged.

On the eve of his departure to meet the fuehrer, Mussolini saw Welles. Although the undersecretary reported to the duce that in London and Paris he had found moderation and reasonableness rather than inflexibility, and that everywhere he had met with appreciation for the duce's efforts to

preserve the peace, he found Mussolini firm in his attitude
of solidarity with Germany. Von Ribbentrop had succeeded
in defeating the plea of President Roosevelt.

The meeting between the two dictators took place on March
18 at the Brenner Pass, the great gate to Italy, through which
the Teutonic invaders had descended upon the peninsula and
through which in a little over three years the Teutonic invaders would descend once again. It was snowing heavily.
The small lake, the few sparse fir trees, the rounded domes
and craggy peaks were nearly hidden. Mussolini, waiting for
Hitler in his train, was in high spirits: the night before he had
had a dream "which tore away the veil from the future," and
although he did not describe the dream, he said he knew well
what he wanted to tell Hitler.

The duce and the fuehrer had not met since the time of the
Munich conference, and if Mussolini expected to find Hitler
in the same submissive mood, waiting for hints and words
from him, watching all his moves, mimicking his expression,
he was in for a disappointment. It was a self-confident fuehrer
who allowed himself to be escorted to the duce's car, cordial
as usual and deferential in manner, but very much the master,
the senior member in the axis partnership. He began talking
calmly enough, making few gestures, but uninterruptedly, in
an endless monologue. He analyzed the causes of the war,
stressed the swiftness of the Polish campaign, described the
preparations for attack in the west, exalted the strength of
the German armies, enormous German production, and the
formidable fortifications already completed, and said that he
would defeat France and England sooner than they thought.
Mussolini was smothered under a flood of words and statistics
— of casualties, of recruits, of reserves, of guns, tanks, infantry weapons. Hitler concluded by telling Mussolini, suavely
indeed, that he was not going to ask anything of Italy, but
that he was firmly convinced that the fates of Germany and
Italy were indissolubly linked. (In an entry on the Salzburg
meeting Ciano had sadly remarked: ". . . as far as the

Germans are concerned an alliance with us means only that
the enemy will be obliged to keep a certain number of divisions facing us, thus easing the situation on the German war
fronts. They care for nothing more. . . .")

In the little time that was left, and as dazzled by Hitler's
military power and prowess as he had been in Germany in
1937, Mussolini stated that Italy's honor and interests demanded her intervention in the war. Unrealistically, he spoke
of the ever-growing power of Italy's war potential and of the
excellent morale of Italian troops, but then he damped his
statement with the admission of a financial situation which
would not allow Italy to wage a long war. Hence Italy would
enter the conflict at the decisive hour, as soon as German
operations created a favorable situation.

Of the need to enter the war as soon as a glorious end was
in sight, and thus not to miss the "jump into history," Mussolini became more and more convinced in the weeks after the
meeting at the Brenner Pass. In those weeks he withdrew more
and more into his shell of illusions and delusions about conditions at home — he would "galvanize" the Italians when
the moment came — the responsibilities and wicked intentions of the Western democracies, the territorial gains that he
could obtain by his intervention in the war at the appropriate
occasion. To everything else he closed his eyes and ears.
(Balbo, for one, then governor of Libya, is said to have informed the duce of the sad condition of troops in Libya, the
shortage of supplies, sufficient only for a very short conflict.
Mussolini did not heed him. ". . . the 'old man' has gone
crazy," Balbo reportedly told his friends. "I talk of military
cadres, of materials that I need, and he tells me that he cannot
delay his appointment with history!")

Hitler's swift conquest of the neutral countries, of Norway
and Denmark early in April, of Belgium, Holland, and Lux-
embourg a month later, whetted Mussolini's appetite. He began
to visualize revised maps of Europe, Africa, and the Near
East on which the Italian colors spread further and further.
The pressures that the Western democracies put on him to
keep him out of the war, and the offers of substantial concessions that both England and France were unofficially advanc-

ing, made no impression on him. In the fateful weeks that preceded Italy's entrance in the war, President Roosevelt, who was resolved not to leave a stone unturned in order to limit the conflict, sent three messages to Mussolini. They were full of idealism, of solemn words and concepts. "Forces which slaughter, forces which deny God, forces which seek to dominate mankind by fear rather than reason, seem at this moment to be extending their conquest, . . ." said Roosevelt in one of his messages. "I make the simple plea that you, responsible for Italy, withhold your hand, stay wholly apart from any war and refrain from any threat of attack. So only can you help mankind tonight and tomorrow in the pages of history."

But the duce could not be won to idealistic causes and had little use for the lofty prose of others. His materialistic ambitions had grown enormous; control of the Mediterranean Sea and domination of the Adriatic were no longer enough; Italy had to have "a window on the ocean." In reply to Roosevelt's first message the duce told Ambassador Phillips: "Italy must have freedom of outlet into the Atlantic, and this cannot be done under the guns of Gibraltar."

Yet territorial ambition was not the sole motive underlying Mussolini's actions, the reason for his entering the conflict. "Italy is and means to be Germany's ally, and Italy cannot remain absent in the moment when the future of Europe is at stake," he wrote Roosevelt. Italy — or rather he, Mussolini — could not be absent. This was the crux of the matter. The duce wanted, *needed* to fight; he *must* fight. And in this frame of mind, fighting was much more vital than winning.

Hitler took pains to confirm Mussolini in his resolve to fight, to keep him under a spell, and to this end wrote him long-winded letters explaining motives, reporting advances, analyzing situations; he wrote frequently, in pompous, cordial, and always deferential terms. He never failed to state his understanding of Italian nonintervention ("I am of your opinion, Duce, that under the existing circumstances it was a good thing that Italy did not become involved at once in the war, at our side"); he never failed to flatter him ("What these operations mean to me . . . is understood by only one other man in the world, and that man is you, Duce"); he never failed to thank him for his diplomatic and material assistance. But neither did he fail to hammer on and on that the fates of the two countries were united, that their aims were common, and the outcome of the war would affect both equally; he always took care to mention "us" ("To men like us it should be possible . . . one way or other to put an end . . . to the terroristic blockade of these democracies"; "Our two regimes will not only determine the physiognomy of the new Europe, but will also, above all, be sufficiently strong, together, to insure and preserve the results of the struggle for a long time").

These letters, Ciano said, went to the duce's heart.

Mussolini's state of mind at this time was the product of many discordant elements. His great wish to fight was contrasted by his inability to act, his abulic avoidance of objections and contradictions; the fatalism that kept him tied to Hitler reinforced his egocentrism; and though he spoke in behalf of millions he took into consideration only one, himself. Instead of carefully preparing his ground, winning others to his point of view, and striving to secure approval, he reached lonely decisions, and to avoid having them questioned he shunned all the human contacts he could shun. For a long time the Grand Council, which included Fascists "of the first hour," had been the one body where a semblance of freedom of speech had been preserved and some habit of advice-giving tolerated. But Mussolini became intolerant of the advice of the Grand Council, and in order to prevent an expression of anti-German and anti-war sentiment, he stopped calling meetings after 1939. Cabinet meetings went on, but they became little more than gatherings at which the other members approved without discussion the proposals that the duce advanced in his multifarious capacities as the head of many ministries.

Even the high commands of the armed forces could only obey. As early as March, 1938, Mussolini had announced that in case of war he would take upon himself the supreme military command. (Less than two months before, Hitler had assumed the command of all the armed forces of the Reich, and Mussolini had warmly congratulated him on the move.) The duce's announcement was unconstitutional, and in the spring of 1940 the king put up an unexpected fight for his prerogatives, which included leading the nation in time of war — but eventually capitulated and agreed to "delegate" the command to his prime minister.

Thus on his own initiative, without consulting or notifying his cabinet, on June 10, 1940, Mussolini declared war on France and England. France was being rapidly conquered by the German armies; victory seemed to be in sight. The favorable moment that Mussolini had been impatiently awaiting had come at last. To the Italian population, still against war but somewhat softened in view of Hitler's fantastic victories, the duce said: "An hour marked by fate strikes the sky of our country. The hour of irrevocable decisions. . . . If today we are resolved to meet the risks and sacrifices of a war it is because our honor, interests, and future impose it in an iron manner; for a great people is really great if it considers sacred its obligations and if it does not avoid the supreme tests which determine the course of history. . . . This gigantic struggle is no more than a phase in the logical development of our revolution; it is the struggle of poor and countless people against the starvers who ferociously hold the monopoly of all the riches and all the gold of the earth; it is the struggle of fertile and young people against people who have become sterile and are in process of decline; it is the struggle between two centuries and two ideas. . . . The password is only one, categoric and compulsory for everybody. It is already flying over us and lighting the hearts from the Alps to the Indian Ocean: To win! And we shall win, in order at last to give a long period of peace with justice to Italy, to Europe, and to the world.

"Italian people!

"Take up arms and show your tenacity, your courage, and your valor!"

Then Mussolini set himself to lead his nation in the tremendous conflict, taking as his supreme guide his "animal instinct": he was convinced that when he followed his instinct he was always right and when he followed the advice of his fellow men he was almost always wrong.

But his instinct led him to his ruin.

The war punctured the inflated balloon that was fascism and made it clear that Mussolini was more deft with words than deeds, that Italy as an invincible nation existed only in his imagination, and the great war machine of which he had boasted was only a prop to enhance his showmanship on the stage of the world.

From the start the axis operations lacked unity. Mussolini did not make precise arrangements with Hitler on the conduct of the war, and no real co-ordination was established between the two countries. The duce wanted to fight "not with Germany, but at the side of Germany," and wage his own independent, "parallel" war. Thus he kept free to make his own decisions, on the spur of the moment, whenever he saw the mirage of easy successes that would heighten his own prestige and allay the smarting jealousy he felt at Hitler's sweeping victories. He foresaw a war of short duration — he told his chief of staff, Badoglio, that it would be over by September — that promptness of action and determined aggressiveness would make up for deficiencies in military preparation.

The power concentrated in his person was enormous, for he was chief of government, supreme commander of all war operations, and minister of war, of the navy, and of the air force. He took full advantage of this power to improvise strategy and tactics, make decisions against the advice of his generals, change his mind with incredible frequency, give orders to subordinates (bypassing their superiors), press for speed, and request impossible victories when the morale at home was low. These were the practices that he had followed in the Ethiopian campaign, and he must have thought that they would be successful again. He did not perceive that the problems of a conflict which threatened to become world-wide were very different from those of a colonial enterprise and its difficulties enormously greater. Nor did he see that he was confronted with these magnified problems and difficulties at a time when he was in a phase of mental and physical decline.

In fact, no responsible chief of government would have led a nation into a war in the condition in which Italy was. Mussolini was well aware of the military unpreparedness which in the last few years had been repeatedly brought to his attention. The men who could be put in condition to serve were only two or three million, a far cry from the "eight million bayonets" that at the height of his demographic campaign he had promised to the nation. And the men in service were ill-equipped. Clothing was inadequate, and after mobilization there were not enough uniforms to go around. It is reported that at the beginning of the war there was sufficient ammunition for a single month of fighting. The heavy artillery was obsolete, the same that had been in use in World War I, and only late in 1938 had the duce seriously undertaken its replacement. In 1939 industries for the manufacture of modern armaments were being developed, but their production, necessarily slow at first, was further hampered by a chronic shortage of raw materials. (A symptom of this shortage was the requisition of iron fences and gates that Mussolini ordered shortly before entering the war.) The effects of production, once belatedly begun, were hardly felt by the Italian armed forces, for until the spring of 1940 Mussolini went on exporting newly produced armaments, even to France and England, in order to obtain sorely needed foreign currency.

The Fascist press had constantly extolled the greatness of the air force, and the Italian people had come to believe in it. But many planes had been lost in the sky over Spain, and at home there were only about a thousand in condition to fly. They were neither modern nor especially good, and their pilots were inadequately trained. Lack of reconnaissance craft prevented the efficient protection of ports and the fleet. The navy, proud in the past and worthy of its millennial tradition, was in better shape, but its supply of fuel was scant. Indeed, in time the shortage of oil was to become one of the major factors of defeat: it caused ships to be idle in ports and motor transport to be abandoned in the African desert. Italy did not have aircraft carriers, since Mussolini had proudly announced that Italy herself was a huge aircraft carrier extending into the Mediterranean. The deficiencies of the navy and air force were to become more tragic when the Allies began to take advantage of radar.

Afraid lest peace break out before he had "the few thousand dead" he needed "in order to be able to sit at the peace conference as a belligerent," Mussolini rushed into the war when an easy victory seemed in sight and the French army was disintegrating under the impact of the Germans' swift advance. Yet he met with difficulties at the very start. At his own order, the troops along the French border were in defensive position; suddenly he ordered them to attack. Badoglio replied that in a mountainous region, without good roads, it would take twenty-five days to shift troops and artillery into an offensive position. Mussolini insisted on a prompt attack, as the French had meanwhile asked for an armistice and he saw the prospect fade of glory on the battlefield.

The weather was bad up in the mountains, and it was snowing. The troops arrived at the front insufficiently equipped, many still in the light clothing and cardboard shoes they had been wearing in the plains. They were unable to overcome French resistance to an effective degree, and underwent serious losses: many froze to death, and many more suffered severe frostbite. The armistice with France spared Italy probable severe reverses, but it did nothing to fulfil expectations: for reasons that are not clear even today, Mussolini withdrew his claim on Nice, Savoy, Corsica, and Tunisia, demanding only the small territory that his troops occupied.

The French misadventure should have taught Mussolini to check his sudden impulses, listen to the voice of reason, and concentrate his forces, as Hitler advised, where they were most needed: the Mediterranean. His avowed objective in the war was to gain access to the oceans, and he planned a sweeping campaign in North Africa to push the British out of Egypt and conquer the Suez Canal. By directing all efforts to this aim he might have attained it. He met with easy success at first and so came to believe that he could win the African war with the men and materials at hand in Libya.

But Libya was as poorly prepared for an offensive as was the mother country, and Balbo, her governor, had repeatedly asked for well-trained troops, more armored cars, tanks, planes, and other supplies. He needed all this, and seven months to prepare, before he could launch the attack on Egypt. Mussolini disregarded Balbo's advice and ordered him to keep ready for the attack, but on June 28, the very day he received the duce's order, Balbo died in a plane crash over Tobruk, shot down — accidentally, it is believed — by Italian antiaircraft. (Mussolini received the news of Balbo's death while on a tour of the French front and did not appear to be moved. Badoglio, who was with him, comments: ". . . perhaps the disappearance of the only one of the Fascist hierachy who had dared to challenge his supremacy was not altogether unwelcome.") In Balbo's place Mussolini sent Graziani, one of the victors of the Ethiopian war, who was known for his cruelties toward the Abyssinians. Like Balbo, Graziani did not feel prepared for an offensive, but Mussolini wanted at least one encounter with the British before a German invasion of England, which Hitler said was imminent, put an end to the war.

Graziani attacked on September 12, met no resistance from the British, who had not expected an attack from Libya, and reached Sidi Barrani, well inside Egyptian soil. Mussolini was "radiant with joy" for the success which afforded Italy "the glory she has sought in vain for three centuries." But this success (as well as previous gains in East Africa) was not conclusive. Graziani was obliged to stop at Sidi Barrani, in a precarious position, his supply lines greatly overstretched, any further advance made impossible by the scarcity of armored vehicles — in his foolish conceit, Mussolini had refused German offers of armored units, wanting to prove to Hitler that he was able to win the African war by himself.

It was evident that only by concentrating in Libya all available men and materials could Mussolini hope to gain a decisive victory in Africa. Instead, he spread his forces thin. What Hitler really wanted of his ally was workers for his factories, and in fact hundred of thousands of Italians were sent to Germany over the war years. This humble task behind the scenes could not satisfy the duce, and in a spirit of emulation he successively sent planes to bomb England, attacked Greece, participated in the German occupation of Yugoslavia, and sent an army to fight in Russia.

The engagement directed against England was limited and of little consequence. Soon after the armistice with France, Mussolini, anxious to get his share of glory, offered to furnish men and aircraft for the invasion of Great Britain. Hitler turned down his offer, then changed his mind, and by the end of October Italian planes were participating in the bombing. Toward the end of the year Italian participation, which had not been very effective, ceased altogether.

The Greek adventure was one of Mussolini's most disastrous moves. In October, 1940, Hitler occupied Romania without informing his partner beforehand. The duce was indignant: "Hitler always presents me with a *fait accompli.* This time I am going to pay him back in his own coin. He will hear from the papers that I have occupied Greece. In this way the equilibrium will be re-established." These remarks, reported by Ciano, are of October 12, and on October 28 Italy attacked Greece.

The invasion was not entirely the result of pique, and Mussolini himself said that his decision had ripened over the months. Ciano, as greedy as the duce for booty and honors, for some time had added his incitement to the duce's schemes. Both men regarded Greece as an easy quarry, a weak country that would capitulate at the first blow. Ciano spoke of "complete collapse within a few hours." And Mussolini said that he would hand in his resignation as an Italian if anyone objected to fighting the Greeks.

In August, 1940, plans for the invasion of Yugoslavia and Greece had been underway, but the Germans put a stop to them on the grounds that all efforts had to be concentrated against England. Mussolini submitted to Hitler's will without protest and toward the end of September he even began demobilizing — for this absurd order he gave no explanation to his dumbfounded generals. Three hundred thousand men had been sent home by the time the attack on Greece began.

Mussolini, as always, had listened only to the advice that

best fitted his delusions: he belittled the information of his intelligence service on the strength of Greece and gullibly accepted Ciano's rosy reports on that country's internal weakness and the results of Italian underground activities. His chiefs of staff were against the campaign and stressed that the forces available were insufficient, that the landing in shallow Albanian waters would be precarious, and the action would exhaust already meager Italian resources. Mussolini criticized his generals before the chamber, accusing them of overestimating the enemy and not wanting to wage war. He listened eagerly to General Visconti Prasca, the commander of Italian forces in Albania, who asserted he was ready for the campaign and confident of a speedy victory.

In choosing the date for the attack the duce followed his sense of the histrionic, for October 28 was the anniversary of the March on Rome. Yet it was sheer irresponsibility to start a war in the mountains of Greece in mid-autumn — even the sanguine Visconti Prasca advised against it, but the duce curtly replied that the campaign could not be postponed.

About warning Hitler of his intentions he changed his mind and on October 19 sent him a letter in which, buried in a flow of lengthy considerations about France, Africa, and Spain, was the announcement that he would attack Greece very soon. Since Hitler was then on a tour of France, the message was delivered with some delay. The fuehrer at once summoned Mussolini to a meeting in Florence on October 28. By the time the two dictators met, the attack on Greece had begun, and Hitler could only express his solidarity, although he had hoped to halt this ill-considered move, as he later made clear in a letter to the duce.

The poorly equipped Italian troops met with stiff resistance and bad weather and within a few days were retreating along the entire front. Mussolini, who had taken upon himself the full responsibility for the attack, now blamed Visconti Prasca and replaced him with Marshal Cavallero. Soon afterward he recalled Badoglio as chief of staff. But neither these changes, nor his continuous telephone calls and telegrams to the new commander in Greece, Cavallero, urging him to action and victory, nor his order that all ministers and top party officials enlist and fight in Greece substantially improved the situation. The British occupied Greek bases from which they could bomb the Italian fleet and Romanian oil wells; and Franco, who had considered entering the war with Hitler and Mussolini, found one more reason for deciding against it. The fortunes of war changed in favor of the axis only when the Germans came to the rescue the following spring and conquered Greece. After this, Hitler and Mussolini occupied Yugoslavia, and Mussolini further spread his forces in order to hold Croatia and Dalmatia.

The early reverses in Greece were followed by others elsewhere. In November a single British bombardment at Taranto put out of action half the Italian fleet — Mussolini, according to Ciano, did not seem to realize the full gravity of this blow. In December the British launched a counteroffensive in Africa, and Graziani began a ruinous retreat, in the course of which 100,000 men were taken prisoners. Graziani's nerves were badly shaken, and he proved incompetent, yet he was not wrong in blaming Mussolini for the defeat, saying that for lack of adequate armored units he had been obliged to fight the battle of the flea against the elephant — General Wavell had fewer divisions than Graziani, but they were superbly equipped. Instead, the armored cars, tanks, and planes that Graziani had requested as indispensable to the war in the desert had not materialized. Italy did not have them.

In Africa, as in Greece, the situation improved after German intervention. In February, 1941, General Rommel took over the African campaign, although he was nominally under Italian command. In March the axis' troops reached Egypt once more. Rommel, however, did not direct operations in East Africa, and there the Italians were defeated: Eritrea, Somalia, Ethiopia fell to the British one after the other. Mussolini lost his empire five years after conquering it.

The war in North Africa proceeded with heavy losses and sharp changes of fortunes. In late June, 1942, after several advances and retreats, Rommel seemed to be headed for the delta of the Nile and a spectacular victory. The duce, incapable of checking his impatience, flew to Africa where he planned a triumphal entry into Alexandria, his "Napoleonic" goal. It is said that he had taken along an Arab horse and the "sword of Islam," a gift he had received from two thousand Libyan Arabs after the conquest of the empire. But Rommel, finding British resistance stiffer than expected, had to stop at El Alamein, and Mussolini, having waited three weeks, returned to Italy. In the fall of 1942 the Allies landed in Algeria and Morocco.

Long before the landing in North Africa, Hitler's most costly miscalculation had decided the course of the war. On the morning on June 22, 1941, the German ambassador in Rome transmitted to Ciano a letter from Hitler to Mussolini. Thus the duce learned that Hitler had broken his treaty with Russia and was attacking her. In the fuehrer's own words, this was the gravest decision of his life. Mussolini should have realized how truly serious the decision was when he received a second message, dated June 30, in which Hitler admitted that Russian resistance was exceeding all expectation: "For eight days we have attacked, defeated, or destroyed one armored brigade after the other, and yet no decrease in their number or aggressiveness has been noticed. . . . The Russian soldier fights with truly stupid fanaticism."

Mussolini was caught unaware — he had received only the vaguest hints of German plans against Russia — in the midst of diplomatic activities for a commercial treaty with the Soviets. There is no evidence that he asked himself whether it was not extremely dangerous for Germany to open a second front that Hitler himself had taken care to avoid before starting the war in Poland; or whether in the long run England might not benefit from the acquisition of a strong ally. Foremost in his mind was his own participation in this new campaign, which the Germans thought they would win in eight weeks. Again in a hurry lest he miss the fruits of victory, he sent an expeditionary force to the Russian front. His staff was against this new burden, and even Hitler would have gladly done without it. (He wrote to the duce that he was in no hurry for Italian assistance in Russia, and added: "You may always give decisive help by strengthening your forces in North Africa.")

Late in July Mussolini insisted to his staff that more troops be sent to Russia and the expeditionary corps be increased to form an army — the duce's reason was that Italy's contingent could not be smaller than Slovakia's. According to General Mario Roatta, some 250,000 men were sent to the eastern front over a period of three months carrying only enough supplies to last a month. Theirs was a tragic fate. They fought bravely and, despite tremendous odds, gained early victories. But as the war continued the Russians displayed unsuspected strength. At the end of 1942 they launched a tremendous offensive, and by early 1943 half the Italian forces on the eastern front were lost, made prisoner or dispersed. If the same force had been sent to Africa, the 250,000 men might have tipped the scales in favor of the axis.

Throughout this period the duce's mood was variable, changing sharply and swiftly with events — or in spite of them. The war reverses might leave him calm, serene, and confident in the ultimate victory, or detached and lulled by illusions, or indignant and pessimistic, even hoping for Germany's defeat. ("Note in your diary," he once told Ciano, "that I foresee unavoidable conflict arising between Italy and Germany. . . . I feel this by instinct, and I now seriously ask whether an English victory would not be more desirable for our future than a German victory.") Small successes elated him disproportionately, but when they did not bring an immediate change in fortune he was quickly deflated. More and more frequently he burst out into invectives against the Italian people who, in his opinion, did not measure up to the standards he had set — but had not been able to enforce.

His complaints were bitter. He lacked suitable material, he said; even Michelangelo needed marble to make statues; had

Michelangelo had only clay he would have been no more than a potter. The Italian race had to be strengthened. Reforestation of the Apennines, Mussolini wildly suggested, would make the climate more rigorous and eliminate the weaker stock. The Italians of 1914 were better than those of 1940, he said once in what was perhaps the severest condemnation of his two decades in power. At the first bomb that destroyed a work of art the Italians would lapse into a fit of sentimental weeping and surrender. After the war there would be a "third wave" of totalitarian measures. He was secretly preparing lists of those who would be eliminated. The Italians were a race of sheep.

The people of Italy did not deserve such harsh criticism. They fought hard for their country in spite of immense difficulties, but they could not bring themselves to collaborate effectively with the Germans. As the war proceeded and they had more frequent occasions to come in contact with their ally, their traditional antipathy increased. They were especially shocked by the German display of cruelty. There were rumors of incredible mistreatment of Italian workers in Germany; both Mussolini and the king received reports to this effect. Soldiers returning from the front related that in Africa as well as in Russia the Germans took for themselves all means of transport and left the Italians to retreat on foot. Many saw with their own eyes the way the Germans treated vanquished populations and persecuted the Jews.

The duce shared this aversion for the Germans, and to the outbursts against his own people he added others against Italy's ally. He called the Germans disloyal because they had concluded an armistice with Greece, leaving him out of it; he accused the Germans of recognizing on paper Italian rights in Yugoslavia but in practice throwing him only "a little heap of bones." "They are dirty dogs, and I tell you that this cannot go on for long," he told Ciano. And another day: "I wonder if at this time we do not belong among the vassal nations. And even if this is not so today, it will be so on the day of total victory for Germany. They are treacherous and without sense of restraint." He bragged that he was building fortifications in the *Vallo Alpino* for the time when Italy would be at war with Germany; since this war would certainly come, it was a good thing that the British bombed German cities by day and night. When the Germans took for themselves Romanian oil that Italy greatly needed, he called them highway robbers. German soldiers in Italy were presumptuous, quarrelsome, and drunken. Not even Hitler escaped his wrath: "Personally, I have had my fill of Hitler and the way he acts. These conferences called by ringing a bell are not to my liking; a bell is rung when people call their servants. And besides, what kind of conferences are these? For five hours I am forced to listen to a monologue which is quite fruitless and boring."

Hitler summoned Mussolini to frequent meetings, often at the last minute, usually by telephone — hence Mussolini's resentment of the "ringing of a bell." Mussolini meekly complied and flew to Salzburg, Munich, the Brenner Pass, or the fuehrer's headquarters near the Russian front. Sometimes he tried to delay an encounter if he had met with military reverses and was concerned for the figure he would cut in Hitler's eyes. (This happened, for instance, after the debacle in Greece, but Mussolini did not know that Hitler too had an uneasy conscience for not having undertaken the much advertised invasion of England.) In these meetings Hitler was always in command; he did all the talking and seldom gave the duce a chance to make a point, advance requests, and speak as he had intended. Under a coat of politeness, Hitler always let the duce feel his superiority. "Hitler has been courteous, friendly, understanding," the duce allegedly said of the meeting after the reverses in Greece. "Even too much. That man is hysterical. In telling me that no one had shared my distress more than he, he had tears in his eyes. All this is an exaggeration. He makes me feel too much his goodness, his generosity, his strength and superiority. . . ." Hitler, on the other hand, is reported to have said: "My conversations with the duce never lasted more than an hour and a half, as the rest of the time was dedicated to ceremonies. The only instance in which our talks lasted almost two days was when things in Albania went badly, because then I was obliged to bolster the duce's morale."

That Mussolini gradually lost initiative and became entirely subservient to Hitler is evident from the lengthy letters exchanged between the two dictators. They made sweeping surveys of their situation, exchanged views, and professed their mutual friendship. To Hitler's opinions Mussolini always agreed. "I am sorry that my letter of October 19 has not reached you in time to allow you to express your opinion on my planned action in Greece, an opinion which, as in other instances, I would have followed carefully." After Hitler's surprise move against Russia the duce wrote: "In the light of what you have made known through your appeals to the German people, I am convinced that it would have been dangerous for our cause to delay and postpone to another time this by now inevitable and logical solution. . . . Here too the abscess had to be cut out." Repeatedly Mussolini made insistent requests for raw materials and especially oil, the shortage of which was slowly turning into a major cause of disaster. Hitler often left the requests unheeded.

Mussolini's — and Italy's — complete subservience to Germany began when Hitler, in a letter dated April 5, 1941, commenting on the need for the co-ordination of Italian and German military action, wrote: "To this end I would like to propose to you, Duce, that you be willing to agree that I send directly to you, in the form of 'recommendations' and 'wishes,' the general points of view needed for the totality of the operations. Then you, Duce, as supreme commander of the Italian army, would . . . give the necessary orders." And Mussolini answered: "I completely agree with you concerning the unified conduct of operations according to the formula you propose." Thus by Mussolini's consent the fuehrer became the supreme strategist of the war. Soon he sent dive bombers to Sicily and military and civilian units into Italian cities, so that gradually all strategic and sensitive Italian positions were supervised by Germans. Germans were seen and felt everywhere. Taking advantage of their favorable rate of exchange, they bought all they could, imposing a serious drain on Italian resources.

The presence of the Germans, the military defeats, and the scarcity of food as well as of other necessities fanned public discontent. Although Mussolini sent glowing reports to Hitler on Italian morale (he always referred to it by the German *Stimmung*) and their unquenchable desire to be on the battlefield, the Italian people were increasingly dissatisfied and exhausted. They saw less and less sense in Mussolini's adventure. (In the past he had been "always right," now he was always in the wrong, and responsible for all the Italian sufferings.) The people yearned for the end of the war. Although it was forbidden, many listened to Allied radio broadcasts and wished for an Allied victory. After the landings in North Africa the words "separate peace" were heard persistently. The most outspoken of Mussolini's collaborators bluntly told him that the country could not fight any longer and he should insist that Hitler release Italy from her military obligations. Every time Mussolini made a speech or a public announcement, people waited for mention of an imminent "unfastening" from Germany. As this mention never was made, discontent increased, even in the higher echelons of the Fascist hierarchy.

Yet, after twenty years of dictatorship, the Italians were passive and appeared resigned to their fate, incapable of concerted action to shake off the yoke. Nothing seemed to happen. Nothing, that is, until after the Allied landing in Sicily in July, 1943.

23

THE WILL SURRENDERED

"Only God can bend the fascist will. Men and things, never."

MUSSOLINI, December, 1934

THE hall where the Grand Council met adjoined the Sala del Mappamondo; although not as deep as Mussolini's office, it was equally impressive. Its high ceiling was lavishly ornamented with costly woods, with the same heavy wheel-like lamp of wrought iron hanging from it. The same tall windows, each cut by a big stone cross, opened in the outside wall; on the other walls, lined with blue velvet, were huge paintings in elaborate gilt frames. Letters inlaid in the colored marble floor spelled out the date of its completion: Anno VII.

At 5:15 on the afternoon of July 24, 1943, Mussolini emerged from the Sala del Mappamondo and made for his "throne," an imposing chair decorated with laurel wreaths and golden *fasci* and raised on a dais covered in red plush. "Salute the duce," called the secretary of the party. The members, in pitch-black uniforms, were already at their places around a long and narrow U-shaped table that extended at the sides of Mussolini's dais. They replied: "*A noi!* [To us!]" and gave the Roman salute with outstretched hands.

All twenty-eight members of the Grand Council were present: among them were the two surviving quadrumviri of the March on Rome, eighty-year-old General de Bono and the insignificant De Vecchi. There was Ciano, now ambassador to the Holy See; Mussolini had "resigned him" from his cabinet post because of his too-independent and too anti-German stand in foreign policy; there were, among the ex-officio members, the cabinet ministers, the secretary of the Fascist Party, the head of the militia, the president of the *Tribunale Speciale* (the political court of justice), and the presidents of the senate and of the new "Chamber of *Fasci* and Corporations."

It was an unusual meeting, the first in three and a half years, called not because Mussolini had wanted it but because several members had requested it. Against the customary practice, no stenographer was present and no minutes were to be taken.* The *moschettieri* who had served as guard of honor at the previous meetings had been excused that day, but in the corridors and courtyard there were armed militiamen, and in the Piazza Venezia strange groups of civilians strolled about with that contrived casualness that marked them as plainclothesmen. Several members in the meeting hall were armed with pistols, and Ciano and Dino Grandi, the president of the new chamber, had each a couple of hand grenades concealed in their pockets.

After the roll call Mussolini began to speak: "The war has reached an extremely critical phase. What appeared, and everyone considered, an absurd hypothesis . . . has come true: the invasion of the metropolitan territory [British and American troops had landed in Sicily early in July]. . . . In a situation like this all official and unofficial, open and underground currents against the regime have united against us and have already caused symptoms of demoralization in the very ranks of fascism. . . . At this moment I am certainly the most detested, indeed hated, man in Italy. . . ."

He looked tired and unwell, of an unhealthy, grayish pallor. He sat slightly bent forward, knees somewhat raised, as if the pressure could ease the pains in his stomach. In the last year his health had grown much worse: a recrudescence of his old duodenal ulcer, or a severe gastritis — doctors did not agree on the diagnosis — had given him sharp, agonizing pains and forced him to frequent periods of rest or confine-

---

* There are, however, several accounts of the meeting by members of the Grand Council. The reconstruction here is based on Mussolini's own description, in the series of articles he wrote in 1944, and on an article by Dino Grandi, published in *Life* on February 26, 1945.

ment to his home, to the frequent use of morphine that dulled his eyes. In the fall of 1942 his condition was so grave that his chiefs of staff began to study ways of insuring a smooth transfer of power in the event of his demise. Later, Hitler offered to send German physicians of his choice, but Rachele refused the offer, feeling that her husband was already undergoing too many cures and receiving too much advice. And yet Mussolini remained in power, directing the nation in its tragic hours, holding in his weakened hands the fate of 40 million people.

To the Grand Council, on that stifling hot July afternoon, he talked for two straight hours, without interruption. He spoke of the supreme command that the king had delegated to him and, documents in hand, strove to prove that he had not sought it: "Be it said once and for all that I have not in the least solicited the delegation of the supreme command of the armed forces, given to me by the king on June 10. The initiative belongs to Marshal Badoglio." Then he examined the conduct of the war with great attention to detail, blaming all reverses on his generals, saying that he had never had the technical direction of battles — except once, and then won a victory. His account was a thin defense of himself, sought through a confused and disorderly exposition of vague facts and uncertain data, in cold aloofness, revealing once more his unlimited egocentrism.

The members of the Grand Council knew the facts well and were not expecting the report that Mussolini made. They did not expect this lame, ingenuous, pitiful attempt at self-justification, this passing of the buck, this condemnation of others for his own mistakes, which to them seemed more incriminating than his very errors. They had thought, if Mussolini insisted on giving a report on the military situation, that they would hear from him about his recent encounter with Hitler in northern Italy, the so-called Feltre meeting, their thirteenth. But of this the self-centered duce could not speak, for it had been as unlucky as the number thirteen itself and resulted in renewed humiliation.

For two hours, in one of his usual monologues, Hitler had coldly and cruelly reviled the Italians: a people unable to sustain military reverses with sufficient fortitude; troops and commanders who had performed poorly and were easily demoralized; civilian organizations unable to cope effectively with the population. He had gone on chiding and scolding, stressing Italian inefficiencies, advising, demanding. Mussolini sat mute under the shower of recriminations. He interrupted Hitler's monologue only once, to announce, after having read a telegram, that for the first time the enemy had bombed Rome. He sat ill at ease, unwell physically, worn out by the effort of listening to a tirade that he did not fully understand. As at all previous meetings, he had no interpreter, for he did not want it known that his mastery of German was not as total as he claimed. (Even his apologetic biographers, Pini and Susmel, reveal Mussolini's efforts to keep up his scanty knowledge of German: "Through the raging of war he continued his reading and study of the German language, as an exercise in which he translated passages from [Manzoni's classic novel] *I Promessi Sposi*.") Under these circumstances Mussolini even failed to mention what he intended to discuss: an honorable way for Italy to withdraw from the conflict. Instead, he had to be satisfied in that before parting Hitler agreed, or so Mussolini said, to send to Italy further, if limited, amounts of war materials.

Before the Grand Council, the duce was not willing to relive the humiliation, to admit that with Hitler he had kept the guilty silence of a schoolboy being reprimanded by his teacher; instead, he went on in his rambling, detached way, talking of the unpopularity of war and posing the rhetorical dilemma: unconditional surrender or fight to the finish? When at last he stopped talking some of the others spoke, more daringly than usual: they defended the army, they tried to clarify some of Mussolini's vague assertions, they criticized his choice of military leaders, they blamed him for destroying their last illusion of the possibility of defending Italy. "You believe you have the devotion of the people," said the president of the Chamber of *Fasci* and Corporations, Dino Grandi. "You lost it the day you tied Italy to Germany. You believe yourself a soldier — let me tell you Italy was lost the very day you put the gold braid of a marshal on your cap. . . .

In this war we have already a hundred thousand dead, and we have a hundred thousand mothers who cry: 'Mussolini has assassinated my son!'"

Only then did the council take up the matter for which it had been summoned: a motion that Dino Grandi had prepared and shown to the duce two days before. Grandi has been called "the most presentable" of the Fascist leaders, and indeed his easy elegance and his good manners gave him an air of aristocratic refinement that most other top Fascists lacked. As a young man he had played a key role in relations with the monarchy during the March on Rome, and later he had become a powerful *ras* (local leader) in Bologna. He was an opportunist, and although he often disagreed with Mussolini he always professed his loyalty and obtained responsible positions as reward. As foreign minister he achieved the Fascistization of the Ministry of Foreign Affairs; as ambassador to London he represented the Fascist government in its most favorable light and made many friends among the English. Summoned to Italy, he was Minister of Justice before being appointed president of the new chamber.

The essential part of Grandi's motion, which he read to the other members, consisted of a proposal whereby all national institutions, the crown, the Grand Council, the government, Parliament, and the corporations, resumed their original functions and responsibilities and the king assumed supreme command of the armed forces and the initiative for all decisions, according to his prerogatives. This proposal, tantamount to a motion of no confidence in Mussolini, caused a great stir and a heated discussion, which lasted late into the night. There was a brief interruption at midnight, when Mussolini went back to the Sala del Mappamondo to talk privately to a few members and sip a glass of milk, and the others were served light refreshments. Then the discussion was resumed. Mussolini did something that he had never done before: he mentioned his age: "I am sixty," he said. "I can look on these twenty years as a wonderful adventure that is now over. I might even, in such circumstances, contemplate ending the adventure — but I will not. The king, as well as the people, is on my side." Then he added: "Grandi's motion calls the crown on the scene; his is not so much an invitation to the government as to the king. Now, there are two alternatives: the king may tell me: 'Dear Mussolini, matters have actually not gone well recently, but after a difficult phase of the war a better one may follow; you began, you go on.' The king may also say, and it is the most probable, 'So, gentlemen of the regime, now that you feel you are sinking you remember that there is a Constitution, . . . that besides the Constitution there is a king; well, I, accused of having violated the Constitution of the kingdom for twenty years, come into the limelight, accept your invitation; but since I consider you responsible for the situation, I take advantage of your move to liquidate you at one stroke.'"

These were threatening words; they sounded like blackmail. Some members had signed Grandi's motion before coming to the meeting. Would they leave Palazzo Venezia alive? But the hand grenades carried by Grandi and Ciano were not produced. No violence followed, although the atmosphere remained tense. Other motions were introduced. Ciano spoke twice, firmly yet with deference, once against the Germans, then against a motion introduced by the secretary of the Fascist Party. Mussolini tried another bluff: he said that he had in his hands something that would soon turn the fortunes of war in favor of the axis, but he preferred not to reveal what this was for the moment. Finally Mussolini called for a vote on Grandi's motion: nineteen members voted in favor of it, including Ciano, De Bono, and De Vecchi; seven against it; two abstained. Heavily, slowly, Mussolini got up and in a bitter, harsh voice said: "You have caused the crisis of the Regime. The meeting is closed." Quietly they left the hall. It was 2:40 A.M., Sunday, July 25.

During the meeting of the Grand Council, Mussolini's attitude had been unusual, detached and unexplainably apathetic, as if his soul had left him and he had become a worn-out automaton. While the members were leaving the hall at the end of the meeting, one is reported to have said: "Now we shall

all be arrested." And, indeed, Mussolini had only to push a button and all doors and gates would close, imprisoning the men. But he did nothing of the sort. Instead, he went home for a few hours' rest and then returned to Palazzo Venezia, arriving before 9:00 A.M. and until mid-afternoon carrying out business as usual. Among other activities, he received the ambassador of Japan, to whom he stressed the need that Italy and Germany conclude a pact with Russia. He expressed the wish that Tokyo put pressure on Moscow to open negotiations. (The ambassador, who thought Mussolini's wish very reasonable, left in an amiable mood and said that the interview had been very interesting.) Mussolini also visited the *quartiere Tiburtino*, a section of Rome heavily damaged by the recent bombing. The people there, busy at their sorrowful task of digging among the ruins, saluted him mechanically: "Duce."

It has been reported that by this time Mussolini had begun to convince himself that the vote of the Grand Council had only a consultive value and that nothing much would happen. The king, who had always evinced confidence in him, would stand by him on this occasion; at most, he would resume supreme command. In that case, Mussolini is said to have told the secretary of the party, he would defer to the king, provided the king had the "traitors" arrested.

In this blissfully unrealistic state of mind, Mussolini went to see the king at his private residence, Villa Savoia, at 5:00 P.M. to report on the meeting the night before. There was nothing unusual in this except that it was Sunday: throughout his years in government, he had gone to see the king on Monday and Thursday mornings, usually at the Quirinal, to bring him laws and decrees for his signature and to report on governmental activities. The relations between king and prime minister had been according to protocol, polite and courteous but never warm. The king, somewhat dull and pedantic though well-read and informed, was always painfully aware of his diminutive size, his short legs, his anything but regal carriage; in the presence of Mussolini, with his broad, peasant frame, he felt more keenly his physical inferiority. He envied his prime minister's ability to work untiringly for many hours and fit exercise in his busy schedule, his outwardly great self-assurance, and his vivid way of talking. As if the king wished to compensate for his shortcomings, he called Mussolini "president," never "duce," and insisted that Mussolini wear civilian clothes, not the Fascist uniform, when on business at the royal residence. Mussolini, for his part, was awed by the centuries-old traditions of the monarchy, the aura of lasting nobility, the dull grandeur of the Quirinal, and the many portraits of ancestors, kings, princes, and dukes, hanging on the walls.

Mussolini himself, writing of his own relations with the king in one of his articles of 1944 (in which he speaks of himself in the third person) comments: "Their intercourse was always cordial but never friendly. Between the two there was always something that did not make for relations of true confidence." In the first years of Mussolini's government the king bestowed upon him the highest decoration, the Collar of the Annunciation, which made the prime minister the king's "cousin." After the conquest of the empire, the sovereign offered the duce a title of nobility, but Mussolini refused, saying that a title would not become his chosen style of life. Despite these recognitions, Mussolini was asked to court only once. The king, on the other hand, went on one pilgrimage to Romagna, where he visited the house where the duce was born and the graves of the duce's parents; on that occasion he was entertained at the Rocca delle Caminate and, according to Rachele, accepted a glass of orangeade.

Reason for dissent between king and prime minister was the law that legalized the Grand Council in 1928, making it the supreme organ of the state and giving it consultive power in the royal succession. The king was indignant, but having yielded to fascism at the time of the March on Rome, he could do nothing but yield again, and in a few months his resentment subsided. He went into a greater fit of rage ten years later when, on the initiative of the Chamber of Deputies, a law was passed which gave the king and Mussolini the same title, First Marshal of the Empire. The king, who, according to the Constitution, was the supreme chief of the armed forces, almost refused his signature. "This law," Mussolini reports him to have said, "is another mortal blow to my sovereign prerogatives, . . . this equality creates an unbearable situation for

me. . . . The chamber cannot take initiative of this kind."
"The king," Mussolini writes, "was pale with anger. His chin
was trembling." It was the spring of 1938; the international
scene was tense and darkening; and rather than create internal
difficulties the king submitted and signed the law. ("In other
times," he said, "I would have abdicated rather than undergo
this insult.")

In private Mussolini often spoke slightingly of the king,
whom he found useless and embarrassing, especially during
Hitler's visit to Rome. To Ciano the duce often said that he
was tired of the monarchy, which he compared to empty train
cars to be dragged along, and that at the first chance he would
get rid of it. But these were only words. The king also was
guilty of empty talk: he professed himself anti-German but
signed the Pact of Steel; he knew the sad state of the Italian
armed forces but put no pressure on his government to improve them; he spoke against the war, but when the time came
he did nothing to prevent or delay Italy's entry in the conflict.

There was certainly some grounds for Mussolini's belief
that his visit to the king would not drastically change matters.
In the last years, however, his intuition and animal flair had
betrayed him often. Before the meeting of the Grand Council,
Rachele had warned him repeatedly — as she herself relates
— that disloyal elements in his inner circle were plotting
against him; and now, on that stifling hot July afternoon,
she had forebodings of calamity and begged him not to go
to Villa Savoia. In this instance she seems to have had a better
knowledge of men than her husband, a greater intuition and
flair than that which remained to him, for it has been established that through the minister of the royal household, Duke
Piero Acquarone, the king had long kept in touch with Grandi,
Ciano, and other Fascists, with admirals and generals, including Badoglio, and with men who had been in government
before fascism. Although too old and weak to take the initiative, the king had planned to oust fascism at the first opportunity. The events of July 25 justified Rachele's presentiments.

Unmindful of his wife's entreaties, Mussolini left Villa
Torlonia for the king's residence. Villa Savoia, on Via
Salaria, on the outskirts of the city, is little more than a large

country house of rustic appearance, set in a vast and beautiful park where old oaks and umbrella pines grow in a natural setting, with no formal gardens or cultivation. The king was waiting on the doorstep, nervous, wearing the uniform of a marshal of the empire, which did not make him appear any more martial or regal.

There were no witnesses to the short interview that took place in the king's study. Mussolini's own description in his articles of 1944 is doubtless distorted. The king was in a state of extreme agitation, according to Mussolini; he was discomposed, and he spoke in broken sentences: "Dear Duce," he said, "things don't work any more. Italy has gone to pieces. The army is morally prostrated. The soldiers no longer want to fight. . . . The vote of the Grand Council is dreadful. . . . You certainly don't entertain any illusions about the Italians' state of mind. In this moment you are the most hated man in Italy. [These were the words that Mussolini himself, according to his testimony, had uttered at the meeting of the Grand Council.] You cannot trust a single friend. You have only one friend, myself. Therefore, I tell you that you need not worry about your personal safety, which I shall take care to protect. I think that the man for the [present] situation is Marshal Badoglio. He can begin by forming a cabinet of caretakers [who will manage] the administration and go on with the war. . . . Everybody expects a change."

According to Badoglio, who may have had a direct account of the interview from the king, this dismissal came as a tremendous blow to the duce, who only managed to say: "This means my complete collapse!" According to Mussolini, however, he calmly replied: "You are making a decision of extreme gravity," and launched into a tirade on the probable effects of this decision on the people and the army. "This crisis will be considered a victory of the binomial Churchill-Stalin, especially of the latter, who sees the withdrawal of an adversary who has fought for twenty years. I am aware of the hate of the people. . . . One does not rule for so long a time and demand so many sacrifices without causing resentments, either fleeting or lasting. . . ."

It is reported that the king and the former prime minister

looked grave as they appeared in the entrance hall. The king remarked on the heat of the day. "Indeed," Mussolini replied, "it is very hot." At the door they parted with a handshake.

Mussolini looked around for his car and driver, but both had vanished. Instead, a captain of the *carabinieri* motioned him to a Red Cross ambulance, saying that he was under the king's orders to assure Mussolini's safety — Mussolini's own car would be recognized and made a target of the populace. Thus, quietly, Mussolini was arrested without his realizing it; always willing to believe what he was told, he thought he was to be protected. Fascism collapsed, and with it a dictatorship that had lasted for nearly twenty-one years.

For two days Mussolini was kept in Rome, in a barracks of the *carabinieri*, while on the outside the people gave vent to their joy in wild demonstration and began to destroy Fascist symbols and insignia as well as portraits and statues of Mussolini. To the celebrations outside Mussolini paid no heed. Not always during those two days did his "protectors" remember his comforts and needs, his food, the fact that he had no change of clothing, no money. He did not object or protest, nor did he explode in those once-habitual fits of rage at the least contrariety, a custom which for years had held his collaborators in constant fear and furthered the disastrous practice of telling Mussolini what he wanted to be told.

Badoglio sent a telegram confirming that the action taken was solely out of concern for the duce's personal safety, as there had been indications of a plot against him. The new head of the Italian government also promised to send him safely to any place he chose. Mussolini chose Rocca delle Caminate. There he had gone in recent years when he felt the need for rest and tranquillity, and there he hoped to spend the rest of his days, relieved of all cares, in the friendly surroundings of his native land. But when he was taken instead to Gaeta and from there to the island of Ponza he did not protest. He had relinquished his will and initiative to the men who accompanied him and sank into a state of complete apathy.

The island of Ponza, the largest of the Pontine islands, which lie outside the gulf of Gaeta, was in Fascist times a place of banishment for political offenders. Many prominent anti-Fascists had spent or were spending time on the island. It is then not surprising that at the moment of Mussolini's arrival two men were there who had had significant roles in his earlier life: Tito Zaniboni, who in 1926 had attempted to kill him, and his once-good-friend Pietro Nenni. Nenni had gone to France after fascism became a strong dictatorship and after the fall of France was arrested there by the Germans, who deported him to Italy, where the *Tribunale Speciale* sentenced him to confinement on Ponza. (It is said that Mussolini interceded with the Germans in Nenni's favor and thus saved him from harsher punishment.)

Neither Zaniboni nor Nenni approached Mussolini during the ten days he was forced to spend on the island. But Nenni, who had preserved the lively interest of his youth, watched his fellow prisoner through binoculars and learned from the officers who had taken Mussolini to the island that he was "more dazed than resigned, as if he had not yet realized what was happening to him." In fact, only at about this time did it dawn on Mussolini that he was a prisoner, that the so-called protection had in effect been an arrest.

His custodians had two preoccupations: that the British might attempt to seize their prisoner, and that the Germans might want to rescue him. Mussolini could not bear the idea of falling into Allied hands, but it was fear of a German surprise that induced the Italian authorities to move him, on August 7, from Ponza to the island of Maddalena, near the northern tip of Sardinia. Maddalena, a naval base, seemed less vulnerable than Ponza, and Mussolini was made to settle in a moderately comfortable villa. Here, for his sixtieth birthday, he received a present from the fuehrer: a special edition of Nietzsche's works in twenty-four volumes, with Hitler's personal dedication. At once he began to read.

Mussolini's health was growing slowly but steadily worse. On Ponza he had a violent gastric attack which alarmed his custodians — not having seen previous attacks, they thought that he was going to die. On Maddalena he was unwell and under the treatment of an army doctor. He still yearned for Rocca delle Caminate. Instead, three weeks after his arrival on the island, the sighting of a German plane induced the authorities to remove him to the mainland.

For a few days he stayed at a villa on the slopes of the Gran Sasso d'Italia, the highest mountain in the Apennines. His guards did not deem the villa to be sufficiently safe, and they decided to take him to the highest inhabited place on the Gran Sasso, a winter-sports hotel at Campo Imperatore. Mussolini was not keen on moving once more, and even less on riding the cable car, the only available transportation to Campo Imperatore. "Is the funicular safe?" he asked, and added: "Not for my sake, because my life is over, but for those who accompany me." (That his life was over, that he was dead and defunct, was Mussolini's recurrent theme in the period of his imprisonment; he signed the dedication of a book "the late Benito Mussolini" and wrote to his sister: "I consider myself a man three-quarters dead.") The funicular, which had transported countless skiers, was perfectly safe, and Mussolini reached his new prison at about 7,000 feet, certainly the highest prison in Italy. In that grandiose setting, in view of rugged, craggy peaks and vast green pastures where flocks of sheep from the valley below came to graze, the prisoner had an almost pleasant time. The rigidity of his treatment softened, and he was allowed to write, read newspapers when they could be had in that remote spot, listen to the radio, take walks accompanied by a single guard, and play cards with the *carabinieri*.

From the radio he learned that on September 8 Italy had surrendered and signed an armistice with the Allies; that the Allies had landed in Calabria and Salerno, the king and Badoglio had fled Rome, and confusion reigned in the army. (The forty-five days between the fall of fascism and the armistice gave Hitler time to prepare. He felt strong at this juncture and could afford not to allow political vicissitudes to determine his relations with Mussolini. After the armistice, Hitler made a speech in which he called Mussolini "the greatest son of Italian soil since the collapse of the Roman Empire.") On September 10, Mussolini heard over the radio that one condition of the armistice was his delivery to the Allies. Immediately he announced that he would not allow himself be taken alive, and the commanding officer of the *carabinieri* who guarded him said that, should he get orders to surrender Mussolini, he would give his prisoner an hour's warning and let him escape. But Mussolini did not trust his fellow men and repaid the spontaneous demonstration of good will by writing that some of his keepers had "shifty and sinister looks" and the "interior and exterior aspects of cut-throats." As had happened before, he was unnerved but would not admit it.

On Sunday, September 12, at 2:00 P.M. Mussolini was sitting at an open window, arms crossed on his chest, basking in the mountain sun. There was the droning of planes overhead. A glider dropped from one of the planes and landed in a field near the hotel, some hundred yards from him. A group of German soldiers bearing machine guns stepped out. More gliders and more men appeared out of the sky. In the sudden commotion that ensued, the *carabinieri* rushed out, weapons in hand. Some forty German parachutists arrived (by cable car), and a column of six armored cars completed the expedition. In the group of men coming from the first glider, Mussolini recognized an Italian general and shouted to the *carabinieri* preparing to defend him: "What are you doing? Don't you see? There's an Italian general [among the Germans]. Don't shoot. Everything is all right." The *carabinieri* lowered their arms, and the Germans entered the hotel at the cry of "Du-ce, du-ce!"

Taking along an Italian general as a symbol of friendship and means of protection was the master stroke of Captain Otto Skorzeny, a Viennese commando leader, who had been ordered by Hitler to find and rescue the duce. Skorzeny missed Mussolini at Maddalena by one day and rediscovered him on the Gran Sasso. When he now introduced himself, saying that he was sent by Hitler, Mussolini replied: "From the beginning I was always convinced that the Fuehrer would give me this proof of his friendship."

Within an hour everything was ready for the departure: a "stork" — a small, slow reconnaissance plane — was waiting on the field by the hotel. The peaks of the Gran Sasso were rocky and forbidding. The plane looked frail. Mussolini hesitated to board it. Skorzeny covered the embarrassment of the moment under a flood of words about Hitler and his own promise to bring the duce safely to Germany. The stork taxied on the small strip that German soldiers had cleared of stones, neared a precipice, hit a rock with its landing gear, seemed about to crash, recovered its balance, and took off. The rest was easy. The stork landed on the seashore not far from Rome. A larger plane picked up the party and flew on to Vienna.

The next day Mussolini was flown to Munich. There his family awaited him: Rachele and their younger children, rescued by the Germans from the Rocca delle Caminate where the Italians had confined them — not Edda, who was busy doing all in her power, but unsuccessfully, to obtain from the Germans permission to go to South America with her husband Count Ciano and their children; not Vittorio, who was already at the fuehrer's headquarters; not Bruno, who had died in 1941 in a plane accident in the sky above Pisa, in a flight to which no glory was attached and which had nothing to do with war operations. To Rachele Benito said "I did not think that I would see you again."

The following day, September 14, Mussolini flew to the fuehrer's headquarters at Rastenburg, and to the embraces of his son Vittorio and of Hitler.

Mussolini was no longer his assured, vigorous, and wilful self but an emaciated man, ravaged by illness, to whom it had become habitual to press a hand to his stomach to lessen the pain; a man who looked wasted in his crumpled and ill-fitting civilian clothes, worn continuously throughout his days of imprisonment; a man shrunken physically and morally, who seemed to have given up his old ambitions, the commanding posture, the habit of play-acting for an audience, and his very will: a wreck of a man, and yet a man who having divested himself of his artificial shell had become more human.

He was altogether unrecognizable: a photograph published in Italy showed him with the rescuing party on the Gran Sasso, but many Italians refused to believe the man was Mussolini; on September 18 he spoke over the radio in a flat and tired voice, devoid of sonorous and vibrant tones, and the Italians said that it was not Mussolini who spoke. They came to be convinced that a double who bore a vague resemblance to Mussolini and who had the same burning eyes had been found to play the part of the duce. For some time they believed that the true Mussolini was dead.

There is another picture of the duce as he arrived in Rastenburg and shook hands with Hitler. It is a Mussolini who had nothing left of the Caesar, a Mussolini who had reverted to his humble origins and clumsily bowed in subservient fashion before the man he had once considered his pupil and imitator. He was to remain to the end subservient to Hitler, despite the uniform that again he took to wearing, despite the role of great man that he assumed once more. From the moment he arrived in Rastenburg he yielded to Hitler's will. Passively, he let himself be placed in the hands of Hitler's physicians.

The fuehrer had organized his friend's rescue because he wanted to restore Fascist dictatorship to Italy, but for this he needed a man in decent physical shape, not the near-invalid that Mussolini had become. He entrusted the ailing dictator to the care of his personal physician, the quack Theodor Morell. According to an account in Goebbels' *Diaries*, Morell did not find Mussolini as ill as he was thought to be. If he had ever been syphilitic he was completely cured, there were no symptoms of an acute or dangerous disease, and Dr. Morell believed that a complete recovery was possible. A less optimistic view is given by another German doctor, Georg Zachariae, who was dispatched to Mussolini shortly after his return to Italy and remained with him until his last days.

Zachariae later published a book on his experiences (a not entirely reliable book, for its portrait of the dictator is strongly idealized). In it he reports that a previous examination of his patient in Germany had revealed a large duodenal ulcer. He also describes the duce's appearance when he first saw him, less than a month after his rescue: "That face that I had seen in a hundred photos, that face of a Roman emperor, was pale, yellowish, extremely thin. . . ." He could sleep very little (he had cramps like a fist that pressed with all its might), and the doctor found acute constipation; a secondary anemia, which paled the inside of his eyes and was due to the fact that he ate very little; his blood pressure was low; his skin was dry and not elastic; his liver was enlarged and hardened. The doctor comments: "I was profoundly perturbed. . . . It was a wreck of a man who was evidently on the brink of the grave. . . . He had borne with fortitude atrocious pains for almost four years. . . . We must assume that he had not always been in full control of his physical equilibrium and of his total energies. . . ." Under treatment, Zachariae relates, the duce greatly improved, and within three months he appeared to be almost completely recovered. But it was a temporary recovery, and in the last months of his life Mussolini collapsed into a state of pain, depression, and apathy.

The mental and physical changes in Mussolini did not escape Hitler's notice and thoroughly disenchanted him. He was bitterly disappointed in the man who when needed to restore a strong Fascist government in Italy had suddenly shed his make-up as a superman and yearned not for political adventure but for the quiet of Romagna.

Mussolini's fall and Italy's surrender had been heavy blows to Hitler's prestige and constituted an especially dangerous example for his other allies. The fuehrer did not lose his head. He softened the news of Mussolini's arrest by announcing that the duce had resigned on account of poor health; he gauged the situation accurately and during the forty-five days of Badoglio's government prepared for the moment when

Italy would inevitably surrender. Yet the dealings between Badoglio and the Allies were kept strictly secret, and Hitler had no warning of the armistice. He reacted promptly, at once strengthened his forces in Italy, seized key positions, including control of Rome, and took over Italy's zones of occupation. Thus Hitler had all and Mussolini nothing when the two met at Rastenburg. Mussolini had once become furious upon hearing that he had been called the gauleiter of Italy. Now he could not even claim that position. Hitler was absolute master.

After their friendly reunion, duce and fuehrer had a long personal interview, without witnesses. What they said is at least in part known, because Mussolini spoke of it to the Italian newspaperman Carlo Silvestri and Hitler to his propaganda minister, Dr. Goebbels. Mussolini reportedly related to Hitler his adventures from the meeting of the Grand Council to his rescue on the Gran Sasso, revealing details unknown to Hitler, especially concerning his relations with the king. The fuehrer, on his part, urged the duce to return to power immediately and announce that the monarchy was deposed and the new Fascist state replaced it. Only by this move, by resuming all responsibilities, would Mussolini guarantee the full validity of the alliance between Germany and Italy. "The Italian betrayal," Hitler said, according to Silvestri, "could have caused the sudden collapse of Germany, had the Allies known how to take advantage of it. I should have given immediately a terrible example of punishment to intimidate those, among our allies, who might be tempted to imitate Italy. I suspended the execution of a plan that had been prepared in all its details only because I was sure that I would be able to free you. . . . But if you disappoint me I must order that the punitive plan be carried out."

An important point of disagreement between duce and fuehrer was how to deal with "the traitors of the Grand Council." Many of these, and Dino Grandi among them, had managed to flee Italy and find asylum in neutral countries. Ciano was a virtual prisoner of the Germans, and a few others were in the hands of trusted Fascist elements. Hitler demanded the death sentence. "Were I in your place, nothing would have kept me from taking justice into my own hands,"

Hitler is said to have told Mussolini. Mussolini had no such intention, as Goebbels commented in his *Diaries*: "The Fuehrer expected that the first thing the Duce would do would be to wreak full vengeance on his betrayers. But he gave no such indication and thereby showed his real limitations. He is not a revolutionary like the Fuehrer or Stalin." And further on: "But punishment of the Fascist traitors is the condition precedent to a resurgence of Fascism. . . . The Fuehrer was deeply disappointed at the Duce's attitude. . . . I have never before seen the Fuehrer so disappointed as he was at this time." And: "There was, of course, no actual quarrel between the Fuehrer and the Duce. . . . But even the Fuehrer's observation that the Duce had no great political future signifies a lot, considering his former admiration of him."

There was no truer assertion than that the duce had no political future, nor did he have to face a greater drama, before his death, than the punishment of the "traitors of the Grand Council."

There can be little doubt that even without Hitler's pressure and intimidation Mussolini would have soon yielded to the temptation to stage a comeback and resume his role as dictator. His physical and spiritual lassitude, it is true, had greatly reduced his drive and stilled his once tireless dynamism, but his enormous vanity and conceit remained. Perhaps, in his depressed state, he would not have been able to take the initiative in restoring fascism, but since the chance presented itself, all that remained of his old self impelled him to take it. Before his arrival in Rastenburg, members of the Fascist hierarchy who had taken refuge there (including his own son Vittorio) had proclaimed a new Fascist government. With them Mussolini began working toward the foundation of the "Italian Social Republic," and he announced its program in his radio talk of September 18.

"The state that we want to establish," he said, "will be national and social in the widest sense of the word; that is, it will be Fascist in the original sense. While we wait for the

movement to develop until it becomes irresistible, our postu-
lates are as follows: 1. to resume the fight at the side of Germany, Japan, and the other allies . . . ; 2. to prepare without
delay the organization of our armed forces around the militia
formations . . . ; 3. to eliminate the traitors . . . ; 4. to destroy the parasitarian [*sic*] plutocrats and make labor, at last,
the subject of economy and the infrangible basis of the state."

In reality the new republic was a weak, powerless organism,
little more than a Fascist façade hiding a houseful of Germans. It was decided that its capital would not be Rome but
on the shore of Lake Garda, in and near the town of Salò.
(Hence the name "Republic of Salò," by which Mussolini's
puppet state became known.) The Germans wanted the Fascist
government nearby, in northern Italy, and Mussolini nursed
a serious grievance against Rome. ("I would never go back to
Rome . . . ," he told his secretary. "It is the city that got
the most out of the regime. . . . It has shown its gratitude to
us by a record celebration of our fall. [The Romans] displayed their flags for fourteen days! Do you understand?
Fourteen consecutive days to celebrate the event.")

The shore of Lake Garda, especially the stretch between
Salò and Gargnano, is a well-known winter resort. The setting
is softly beautiful against the green foothills of the Alps,
which leave only a narrow strip of flat land and in places
extend to the water of the lake. The surprisingly mild climate
fosters a luxuriant vegetation in which citrus fruits, pome-
granates, and agaves abound.

The government of the Republic of Salò was scattered
along this strip of land, wherever buildings could be com-
mandeered, and Mussolini established his headquarters in
Gargnano. He did not like his new residence. He called lakes
"compromises between seas and rivers" and found them all
gloomy. But the sky over Salò and Gargnano is almost invariably blue, and the landscape is restfully sunny. Lake
Garda was not the true reason for Mussolini's gloom: this
was due to his loss of vigor, his fatalistic pessimism, and his
deep dissatisfaction in being a puppet in German hands. Germans surrounded him on all sides, gave him unsolicited
advice, checked on all his moves, interfered with his actions.

Germans watched him closely, as if he were their prisoner instead of the head of an allied state. When he flew to the Rocca delle Caminate to run away from his gloom in Gargnano, he was allowed to pilot his plane, as he still liked to do, but a German sat beside him, silent, cold, watchful. When he traveled by car he was accompanied by his own guards, but a German armored truck never failed to join the party. There were Germans at all switchboards, intercepting his conversations.

The German ambassador, Rudolf Rahn, and the commander of the German police and S.S. in Italy, Karl Wolff, had their way more often than did Mussolini (who referred to them as "the Viceroy of Italy" and "the Minister of Internal Affairs"). All appointments in the new government had to be approved by the Germans, with the result that key positions in the cabinet were given to men well known for fanatical inflexibility, corrupted cunning, or complete subservience to Nazi-Fascist rule. To each Italian official of any status a German counterpart was assigned, either in an advisory capacity or in charge of "German affairs." On the pretext that the war required it, the Germans took over Trieste and its territory, Istria, and the South Tyrol.

Mussolini tried to reorganize the army under Marshal Graziani, but many officers and soldiers did not respond to the call. Soon there were many defections among the eighteen-year-old recruits, many of whom were obliged to go to Germany for their training. On the other hand, many autonomous groups sprang up here and there on the pattern of the old *squadrismo*, and police formations of various kinds were organized in military fashion. Whatever war material was valuable and in good condition was requisitioned by the Germans, who did not care if chaos reigned in the Italian army; they did not trust it and preferred to defend the Italian soil with their own troops. What they needed were workers for the rear lines and for industry — in large cities German efforts to round up able-bodied men were dreaded.

Faced with a situation with which he was unable to cope, Mussolini spent much time grumbling and exploding in violent, short-lived, and unproductive fits of anger. He withdrew within himself, read Plato, played solitaire, and wrote a column, *"Corrispondenza repubblicana,"* for all the papers in the republic, commenting on news he intercepted on foreign broadcasts. His eyesight weakened, and to read the papers he wore glasses and flooded his room with light. A new character trait developed and became prominent: self-pity, manifested in his steady complaining, mostly against the Germans but also against the king who had betrayed him, his own credulity, his lack of friends, the unreliability of the Italians, and his own family.

In Gargnano relations with Rachele were strained to breaking point by the arrival of his mistress, Claretta Petacci. Mussolini first met Claretta in 1933, when she was a young girl engaged to be married and he a married man of fifty. He was at once captivated by her liveliness and prompt intelligence, and a few years later he made her his mistress; undoubtedly she was dazzled at the prospect of having an affair with the Caesar who had just conquered Abyssinia, and she agreed to abandon her husband. Her spontaneous, fresh passion relieved him in part of the burden that his lack of friends had begun to be and brought to his chilly life a warmth he had never experienced before. Soon it was her habit to visit daily his private apartment in Palazzo Venezia. At first Mussolini and Claretta were discreet and their relationship was not known, but by the time it was in full bloom at the beginning of World War II it had become a public scandal. Although there is no evidence that Claretta was anything but a young woman tremendously in love, her relatives, especially her brother, exploited the situation in the most obvious and scandalous way. The "Petacci clan" became famous for its shady financial dealings, the influence its members exerted on the duce to their own and their protégés' advantage, its meddling in government affairs. The duce, apathetic as he had become, made no effort to keep the clan in check.

After his fall and arrest, the Petaccis were sent to jail in northern Italy, and there Claretta kept a diary filled with passionate and hysterical invocations to her Benito, of whose whereabouts she had no inkling. After her release from prison she went to live on Lake Garda not far from Gargnano, despite the disapproval and hostility of the Fascists surrounding Mussolini. More hostile than the rest was Donna Rachele. Claretta's mere presence on the lake exacerbated her; incapable of containing her emotions, she made impulsive, noisy scenes that annoyed and irked the duce. In his old age and poor health, in his new state of self-pity, the duce felt entitled to Claretta's warm affection and refused to give it up even though it deeply distressed his wife.

¶

His daughter Edda was a problem of a different sort. When Mussolini arrived in Germany after his rescue from the Gran Sasso, he found Galeazzo Ciano, Edda, and their three children living in a villa near Munich, virtually prisoners. He learned that after the meeting of the Grand Council Ciano had been refused a passport to Spain because he was accused of, and to be tried for, the illicit accumulation of wealth during the regime (he claimed that his money and property came from his father). Ciano managed to avoid arrest at the hands of the Italian police by climbing a dividing wall into the yard of the next house while the *carabinieri* were guarding his home. The escape had been planned by Edda with the help of the German embassy: a German car whisked away Ciano, Edda, and the children, and they were soon flown to Germany; they hoped then to proceed to Spain and South America. But Ciano was naïve: after his open hostility toward the Germans, whom he knew to be deceitful, he should not have trusted them. As if the odds were not great enough, he foolishly mentioned that he had kept a diary and once abroad would have it published, so destroying the chance, if there had been any, that Hitler might let him go free.

In Germany Mussolini had a long interview with Edda and two conversations with Ciano, which the Germans interpreted as a reconciliation and did not like. Shortly afterward a threatening letter from Edda to her father was intercepted, which made the Germans suspect that Ciano was in a position to blackmail the duce. Upon the establishment of the new

Fascist government, Ciano was delivered to the Fascist police, who imprisoned him in an old castle in Verona.

If there had been a reconciliation between Mussolini and Ciano in Germany, it did not last long. One of the first acts of the Republic of Salò was to establish a special court in Verona to judge the "traitors of the Grand Council." A few of Mussolini's advisers, among them his Minister of Justice, told him that the accusation of "treason" had no legal basis, for the Grand Council had the right to introduce motions and vote upon them; there was no proof of previous collusion of the members with the monarchy and Marshal Badoglio; therefore, Grandi's action was within the law. Yet the new law regulating the Verona court was so drastic that, in the opinion of the Minister of Justice, the trial would undoubtedly result in capital punishment for all defendants. Upon hearing this analysis of the situation from the minister, Mussolini replied: "Of the trial you see only the juridical side. . . . I must see it in political perspective. Reasons of state take precedence over any other contrary considerations. Now we must get to the heart [of this matter]."

The president of the Verona court, faced with a responsibility which he felt to be excessive, sought the duce's directives and received precise instructions: "To proceed without regard for anyone, according to conscience and justice." Of the men who had voted in favor of Grandi's motion only five, including Ciano and General de Bono, were in Fascist hands and would bear the consequences of a sentence; the others had escaped to safety. It was then clear that the true issue, the very reason for going through with the trial (and the big question mark in the whole affair), was Ciano. Most Fascists believed that because Ciano was the husband of Mussolini's favorite daughter the trial would be a farce, and they did nothing to prevent it; the few who wanted to see "justice done" did nothing to dispel the optimism. In Mussolini's own family, Vittorio and Donna Rachele were incensed by the thought of Ciano, whom they considered a renegade and a traitor.

Only Edda fought desperately for her husband, feeling from the first that his life was doomed. She spoke to her father, threatened scandal, and stormed into Gargnano, fierce, determined, passionate, and enraged. But her violent scenes were of no avail. Mussolini advised her to retire to a nursing home and come to see him less often. And so the day arrived on which the five defendants were sentenced to death. It was January 10, 1944. In order not to upset the duce, pleas for mercy were withheld from him, and the next morning the five were shot. Mussolini's secretary reports that "the hypothesis of mercy was never advanced in Gargnano. Mussolini did not speak of it either in the days immediately preceding the trial, or during the debates, or in the twenty-one-hour pause between the sentence and its execution. Once he had reached the extreme decision, it appeared irrevocable to him."

A few hours before the execution Mussolini received a letter from Edda: she had managed to flee to Switzerland, taking along the famous diaries. She would have them published unless Ciano were released within three days. Upon receiving this letter Mussolini was thrown into a state of great agitation. To his secretary he is reported to have said: "The publication of this diary, tending to prove continued German wickedness toward us, even during the period of full alliance, might at this moment have irreparable consequences. In any case, of an exceptional gravity."

Mussolini's biographers have described him as somber, silent, and depressed during the days of the trial, and they have pitied him for his inner tragedy, which they interpreted as proof of his fortitude and sensitivity. But, one may ask, what sort of man orders the death of his son-in-law, the father of his own grandchildren, innocent by all decent standards? Surely the least he could feel was "depressed." It may well be that Mussolini's inexorability was due in part to Hitler's pressure and the German's desire for revenge. Perhaps, by showing that he could be as cold and tough as Hitler himself, Mussolini hoped to regain Hitler's trust and his own independence of action. If so, he was mistaken, for the trial did not change matters. The sacrificial offering of Ciano, if such his death had been, did not move the German demigod. Hitler did not send a word of praise or comment and affected to be entirely indifferent in the matter. Mussolini remained what he was, what he had begun to be called: "the prisoner of Gargnano."

The court in Verona had jurisdiction over the members of the Grand Council exclusively. Other special courts were established throughout the republic to try those who, in Mussolini's words, "had hidden their falsity behind a formal adherence [to the Fascist Party]; had held high posts, sometimes for years and years; had received honors and remuneration, and at the moment of the test, in the days of the coup d'état, passed to the enemy."

Mussolini's apologists have taken every opportunity to stress how lenient he had been to these "traitors." In many cases, they pointed out, he intervened in favor of the accused, accorded him pardon, reduced or even annulled a sentence. These apologists implicitly subscribed to a system in which the life and death of many remained at the discretion of one man, who made laws and applied them at his whim.

Typical of this arbitrariness was the trial of those military leaders, admirals and generals, who had ceased fighting on the day of the armistice and surrendered the territory they held to the Allies. Mussolini, according to one apologist, was "furious" because four admirals had delivered to the enemy small islands in the Mediterranean and the Aegean; he determined to make an example of them. The four were sentenced to death, but only two were executed; the others had been tried *in absentia*. Mussolini, who firmly rejected the plea of mercy for the two who were to be shot, was sorry only that one admiral against whom he nursed a special hatred was not at hand and could not be executed. The generals fared better, for against them Mussolini was less resentful. Three generals out of seven went unpunished; the others received prison sentences varying between ten and fifteen years.

24

THE INGLORIOUS END

"On my grave I want this epitaph: 'Here
lies one of the most intelligent animals ever
to appear on the surface of the earth.'"
MUSSOLINI, December, 1937

THE last two encounters between Mussolini and Hitler took
place in April and July, 1944. The first meeting, in a splendid
castle near Salzburg that had once housed a margrave's
court, was inconclusive and, except for its setting, colorless.
Mussolini complained to Hitler about the Germans' behavior
toward the Italians in the Republic of Salò and interference in
his government. He also tried to obtain better treatment for
Italian troops in German camps: upon Italy's surrender to the
Allies, numerous Italian units in southern France, Albania,
Greece, and elsewhere were abandoned to their fate by the
Badoglio government, which lacked the means to repatriate
them. Despite the stiff resistance that many put up, the Germans succeeded in rounding up a large number and by July,
1944, 700,000 Italian servicemen were interned. Mussolini,
aware that these Italians were being treated cruelly, with the
contempt reserved for traitors, pleaded in their behalf. But
Hitler paid little heed to the duce's complaints. He called the
internees Badoglians and Communists and said they were not
worthy of Mussolini's solicitude. Sternly, with no feeling for
his guest, he denounced the disintegration of fascism and
hinted that a treason comparable to the meeting of the Grand
Council could not have happened in Germany. As far as the
course of the war was concerned, Hitler alluded to German

secret weapons and made forecasts that Mussolini later considered "damnably optimistic." But, as always when Hitler spoke, Mussolini listened without interrupting, accepting what the fuehrer had to say at its face value, impressed, undoubtedly taken in by his prophetic tone.

The second of the final meetings between the two dictators was by far the most dramatic. It took place at Hitler's headquarters in Rastenburg on July 20. Mussolini and his party had reason to believe that something unusual had happened: at the last stop before their destination their train was ordered to proceed at a reduced pace, with windows closed and shades pulled down. In Rastenburg, Hitler was on the platform to meet them, as he had in the past, but his aspect was different: he was extremely pale and his right hand was bandaged. His first words were astounding: "Duce, a truly infernal machine was directed at me." To the duce, who showed his bewilderment, the fuehrer pointed out his scorched hair and said that both his eardrums had been hurt and his back was bruised. Only two hours before he had miraculously escaped death when a time bomb exploded and killed or mortally wounded four men in the hut where he was holding a conference with his generals. For one who had been through such an ordeal, the fuehrer was amazingly calm. He took Mussolini to see the shattered hut, the scorched walls, the fallen ceiling, and the uniform that he had been wearing at the time of the explosion, of which one trouser leg was in shreds.

Hitler and Mussolini, both believers in supernatural portents, interpreted Hitler's escape as a good omen. Hitler was more than ever convinced that it was his fate to bring their common enterprise to a successful conclusion, and Mussolini said that after what he had seen he was absolutely of Hitler's opinion: the miraculous escape was a sign from heaven. This was an incredibly optimistic point of view, for the Allies had already occupied Rome and landed in Normandy, and they were relentlessly pressing the retreating German armies.

After the visit to the hut Mussolini and his party were left alone for a while, seemingly forgotten, while Hitler and Nazi leaders were occupied with the aftermath of the plot. They conferred; ran around busily; gave orders; talked by telephone with Berlin to gather and relay information, to identify the main culprit — who turned out to be a certain Colonel von Stauffenberg — and have him arrested; to thwart the whole conspiracy, which proved more extensive than it was first thought. Then the Italian visitors and their German hosts gathered at a tea party. Hitler was calm at first, but when the purge of 1934 was mentioned and Roehm's death recalled he displayed a terrible rage, screamed shrilly for half an hour until his mouth was flecked with foam, and declared that he would take revenge on all traitors. Mussolini was silent and embarrassed; he had never seen his friend in this frenzied state, and he could not express what he secretly felt, a certain amount of satisfaction that, in spite of Hitler's assertions at their previous meeting, treason had proved possible in Germany. But when at last he had a chance to state briefly the matters he hoped to discuss at length, he found the fuehrer in a more conciliatory mood than ever before and obtained many concessions, for his government, for the Italian divisions being trained in Germany, and for the Italian internees. According to one report, these were Hitler's parting words to Mussolini: "I know I can count upon you, and, please, believe me when I say that I consider you my best and perhaps the only friend I have in this world."

On his way to visit the fuehrer Mussolini had stopped in Bavaria to review the four Italian divisions trained by the Germans and almost ready to come home. The "delirious enthusiasm" with which the homesick troops met him was a tonic to his spirit and improved his physical condition, according to his doctor. Upon his return to Gargnano, he wired the fuehrer: "Coming back to Italy in the hour in which Providence has wished to save you, for the love of the German people and a better future in Europe, I wish, Fuehrer, to restate that from the faith of the soldiers of the Italian Republic who are being trained in Germany and from your troops' indomitable valor I draw the most certain auspices for Nazi-Socialist Germany and Fascist Italy against the forces of reaction that have allied themselves with bolshevism.

Accept, Fuehrer, my sentiments of immutable, comradely friendship."

The two dictators were not to meet again.

¶

Mussolini's optimism was all on the surface. It was dictated by his pride that would not let him admit defeat. But deep inside him his pessimism was growing with his apathy and the realization that he was more and more powerless in the face of events. His few political acts were ineffectual. He decided to mobilize the republic, the better to resist the advancing enemy, and decreed that all men between the ages of eighteen and sixty not belonging to the armed forces would constitute an auxiliary corps of Blackshirts. But by this step he seemed to encourage a return to the old *squadrismo* that had signified illegality, violence, and abuse, and he did not obtain the strong support from his people which he had hoped to find.

In order to attract former anti-Fascists to the ranks of the new Socialist fascism, he promised freedom of the press and freedom of discussion; but when discussions took a turn he disliked, he suppressed those freedoms. He attempted to captivate the masses with social legislation, but when he nationalized several industries, the workers looked upon his reforms with undisguised suspicion. To them he was still the man who had abandoned socialism in 1914 and had then favored the propertied classes, neglecting the workers' interests, despite his many promises to them; who had denied them rights as basic as the right to strike and to organize free unions and had used his power to persecute leading Socialists. They did not recognize that his change of mind was in a sense sincere, for the introduction of new ideals was his only hope of salvaging the wreck of a regime that had fallen apart. Mussolini himself was at last obliged to admit that the socialization of industries had met with failure, a failure which he blamed on the social immaturity of the workers, giving him one more reason to despise the Italians.

The fact is that "faithful" Italians were rapidly decreasing in number as the size of the republic shrank under pressure from without and from within. From without, its territory was conquered by the Allied armies advancing slowly but steadily along the Italian peninsula. At each forward step the Allies were hindered by the stiff and aggressive resistance that the Germans put up, fighting alone, with little help from the reluctant Italians. (Mussolini would have liked his troops to fight alongside the Germans and made repeated requests to this effect, but the Germans sensed Italian hostility. Besides, they considered the Italians poor soldiers and preferred to use them as workers.) The Germans' main concern was not to save Mussolini's Italy but to spare Germany Italy's fate: a bitter war fought on her soil. Theirs were delaying tactics, pursued with thorough ruthlessness and with cold contempt for their onetime ally.

As the territory of the republic was invaded, anti-Fascists, encouraged by the Allies' success, formed groups of various political colors to attack the republic from within: the partisans, the Committees for National Liberation, the Squads for Patriotic Action, and several others. They were known collectively as the Resistance. Disorganized at first, these different groups united for the common cause as soon as they realized that the time of total liberation was approaching. Then the Resistance groups made contacts with the Allies, obtained help from them, and fought a stubborn guerrilla warfare, in the face of savage Nazi reprisals — entire Italian villages were razed and their populations machine-gunned. But the Resistance succeeded in clearing small zones of Fascists and Nazis.

In Gargnano Mussolini exploded in his now continual fits of rage against the Germans and their cold-blooded behavior. He presented his grievances to the German ambassador and was not heeded. Agitated but powerless, he saw the war proceed at the same steady, destructive pace and the Allies advance toward northern Italy, threatening even the seat of his government. Then events precipitated.

In March, 1945, General Karl Wolff, still serving as head of police in the Italian republic, opened secret negotiations with the Allies for the surrender of German troops in Italy and did not inform Mussolini of these dealings. At the same time Mussolini's government secretly negotiated through Ildefonso, Cardinal Schuster, archbishop of Milan, for the cessation of hostilities. The Allies replied that they had no intention of dealing with Mussolini and insisted in asking for his unconditional surrender. Cardinal Schuster thought it best not to forward this reply — perhaps he knew, as most people close to Mussolini did, that for many months the duce's chief fear had been to fall alive into Allied hands.

Wolff's negotiations were not yet conclusive and Mussolini was still without a reply when the people of northern Italy joined the Allied forces against Germans and Fascists.

On April 18, 1945, Mussolini abandoned Gargnano and moved to Milan, into a few rooms of Palazzo Monforte, the seat of provincial administration. He probably hoped to reorganize his government around his new residence. It is difficult to ascertain whether Mussolini himself made the decision to move or whether he was advised by others, and the same doubt arises about his subsequent actions. His German doctor, Zachariae, writes that when the Allies began advancing more rapidly and defeat appeared inevitable, the duce's health deteriorated; he had a relapse and lost whatever will power he had regained in the quieter period of the Republic of Salò. One must therefore conclude that in this last period Mussolini was seldom in a condition to make well-considered decisions. His actions appeared chaotic, and he seemed to drift like a leaf in a storm.

In Milan Mussolini acted at first as if he had a long time before him. Since he had not been informed that General Wolff was dealing with the Allies, the duce had no impelling reason to believe that the Allied victory was close at hand. On April 20 he called a meeting of the cabinet to discuss a plan, previously proposed in Gargnano, for a last-ditch stand in Valtellina, in the mountains north of Milan. No one but himself had faith in this plan.

Two days later he received a long telegram from Hitler.

From the bunker beneath the Reich chancellery, fifty feet below the ground, which he had made his headquarters, the visionary fuehrer said that bolshevism and Judaism had brought to German soil "their destructive forces with the aim to precipitate our continent into chaos"; but he also reaffirmed his conviction that the German people "with their unparalleled heroism" would change the course of the war.

On the afternoon of April 25, while the first motorized partisan formations entered Milan to the acclaim of thousands, Mussolini allowed himself to be persuaded to seek accord with the leaders of the Resistance in Cardinal Schuster's presence. In the midst of their discussion, news arrived that the Germans had surrendered. Prey to great irritation, sure that he had been dragged into a trap, Mussolini left the archbishop's palace and returned to Palazzo Monforte. Dr. Zachariae noted that "his face was extremely contracted and as pale as death." Not only was he under the shock of the Germans' treason — they had surrendered without taking the pains to warn him — but he was also angered because Cardinal Schuster, from whom he had expected help and support, had had little more to say than "Repent of your sins."

It was decided that Mussolini should at once leave Milan for Como, accompanied by a small body of German and Fascist troops, and that an army column should join him soon for the last stand in Valtellina. Thus Mussolini's ultimate odyssey began. A submachine gun hung from his shoulder as he entered his car, as if he, an actor to the end, wanted to dress for the occasion: it is likely that he had not fired a gun since World War I, and in his depressed, fatalistically resigned state he would not have been able to fire one.

They stopped in Como for the night. Rachele with the younger children was also in Como where she had taken refuge after leaving Gargnano. But Mussolini did not see his family. Nor is there evidence that he tried to see them. Rachele managed to put through a telephone call to him, and in her account of the last hours she describes their conversation in pathetic terms. Earlier in the evening she had received a letter from him in which he said that his end was nearing and probably they would not get together again. On the phone, to

Rachele who tried to comfort him by saying that there were still many ready to die for him, he replied: "There is no one any more. I am alone, Rachele, and I see that this is the end of everything." He was right: he was alone, and this historic moment marked the end of all that he had thought he had so sturdily built.

He should not have reviled Cardinal Schuster's exhortation to repentance: retributive Justice was confronting him. He had never permitted warmth to flow from him to his fellow men, and now he was immersed in the chill that he had fostered. He had ignored human dignity and human rights, had treated men with contempt, had used them as tools to satisfy his ambitions and his lust for power, and he had encouraged the development not of their virtues but of their least attractive traits. Now he suffered the consequences and saw defection all around him. When the armies of his enemies entered Italian cities, the people he had believed to be solidly Fascist welcomed and acclaimed them as liberators. Even Milan exulted, Milan where fascism was born and in whose loyalty he had always believed. His own armed forces collapsed, seemed never to have existed; no body of troops came to fight for him, and the column that was to join him never appeared. His own personal guard vanished: the magnificent youths who had promised to defend him to the last were nowhere in sight. His close collaborators, afraid of falling into partisan hands, left him one by one, seeking safety for themselves and their families, oblivious to their vows of allegiance. His own son Vittorio was soon to participate in negotiations for the surrender of the Fascist hierarchy and then save himself by going into hiding. And Rachele, who would have followed her husband, was left to fend for herself and her two younger children — eventually she was taken into custody and interned by the Americans. Only Claretta Petacci was doing all in her power to join him.

Very early on the morning of April 26 Mussolini and his ever-slimmer group left Como headed toward Valtellina. They followed the road on the west shore of Lake Como and stopped in Menaggio to await the arrival of the column which they still believed would escort them. But the column that had formed in Milan went only as far as Como, where it disintegrated, whatever remained of it surrendering to the Committee for National Liberation. Mussolini spent the entire day in Menaggio and its immediate surroundings. News that the partisans were killing many Fascists in neighboring regions, the arrival of wounded men, and the sight of the dead increased the panic among Mussolini's companions. A few of them went to inspect the road to Switzerland and were captured by frontier guards who had joined the partisans. Only one man escaped and hastened to Menaggio where his report of the incident further discouraged the small group of Fascists: some of them had placed their last hope in an escape to Switzerland, but now they knew that Swiss doors were closed to them.

At dawn on April 27, Mussolini and a few other Italians — among them Claretta Petacci, who had reached Menaggio — joined a German motorized column retreating to the north. They left Menaggio and had driven little more than ten miles when they discovered that the road, narrow at that point and squeezed between a wall of rock and the lake, had been blocked with a felled tree and a heap of stones. As the whole column came to a halt, a few partisans appeared. After several hours, during which the German commanding officer was taken for negotiations to partisan headquarters miles away, the Germans obtained permission to proceed on the condition that they take no Italians along. They were warned that all vehicles would be inspected on their passage through Dongo, a village a few miles farther on.

While the other Italians were compelled to stay behind and were taken prisoner by the partisans, Mussolini went on with the Germans: he wore one of their topcoats as a disguise. At about 3:00 p.m., in Dongo, the inspection of the German column began. Mussolini sat hunched in his German coat, with hat pulled down to hide his face, pretending to sleep. But on the second round of inspection he was recognized and taken prisoner by a small group of partisans. He did not struggle or offer resistance of any sort. One of the captors, a certain "Bill" — all partisans had assumed fictitious first names and used no other — later wrote: "His glance is absent. . . . His face is waxy. . . . His beard makes his chin look darker and increases the pallor of his cheeks. The cornea [of his eyes] is yellowish. . . . Spiritually [he is] dead. . . ."

After the halt in Dongo, Mussolini was taken to a frontier post in the mountains above that village. There he talked for a while with the young partisans who held him prisoner before retiring for the night to a small room that served as a cell. But after a few hours he was awakened and told that he was going to be moved elsewhere: "Pedro," the commander of the partisan brigade stationed in Dongo, felt that the mountain post was not sufficiently safe. The partisans were afraid to lose their quarry, for the Allies were looking for the former duce; but the general command of the Italian liberation forces had decided that the chief Fascists, those responsible for the long years of moral slavery (and for the defeat of their country), should be captured, held, and judged by Italians.

Accordingly, they took the precaution of bandaging Mussolini's head to make him look like a wounded partisan so that he would not be easily recognized on the way. He raised no objections. "Pedro" and two other Partisans — one of them a girl dressed as a nurse — escorted him to a car. It was raining, and the night was chilly. They drove out of the mountains, toward the road along the shore of the lake, the way Mussolini had come the day before. Soon they encountered another car. Both cars stopped, and everyone got out into the darkness. A woman walked toward Mussolini, and he recognized Claretta Petacci. He said: "You here, too, *signora*?" Claretta, with the other Italians, had been taken to Dongo. There, in late afternoon, she had met "Pedro," who gave her news of the prisoner. Claretta had at once implored "Pedro" to let her rejoin her lover.

In the very early hours of April 28 the two cars resumed their drive southward through the rain, in the direction of Menaggio and Como. At 3:30 A.M. the party reached a small house owned by a peasant family known to the partisans and accustomed to guests arriving in the middle of the night. The peasant's wife, who did not recognize Mussolini and his mistress, agreed to let them stay and hurriedly made beds for them in an upstairs room. The room was plain, almost squalid, and in its bareness, in the poverty of its furnishing, it called to mind the room in which Benito had been born over sixty years before. It was as if Fate were announcing that the cycle of Mussolini's life was at a close. Two partisans stood guard outside the room.

The two prisoners got up late in the morning, about 11:00 A.M., and ate a meal of mush, milk, bread, and salami in their room. At 4:00 P.M. a partisan officer, "Colonel Valerio," came into their room — his true name was Walter Audisio, and in peacetime he was an accountant. Before coming to the country house, "Valerio" had convened a military court in Dongo. The court had swiftly tried Mussolini *in absentia* and sentenced him to death. (Also sentenced to die were seventeen of the high Fascists captured by the partisans and brought to Dongo.)

Now "Colonel Valerio" led Mussolini and Claretta Petacci outside and down a steep path to a car. Several partisans accompanied them. The car was driven along a country road and stopped at a place called Giulino di Mezzegra, near the solitary gate of a villa hidden in a cluster of trees. The two prisoners were made to stand against a low wall a few feet from one another. According to one report, Claretta whispered to her lover, "Aren't you glad that I followed you to the end?" "Valerio" read the death sentence to Mussolini, and then he and the other partisans fired. The next day in Milan the two bodies were exposed in Piazzale Loreto, with those of other Fascists executed in Dongo.

Thus ended the long dictatorship of the man who gagged liberty, smothered independent thinking, and led his country into a fateful war. He left behind little regret, for that love of himself which he had thought so strong in his people was stilled. Few mourned him; many more rejoiced over the regained freedom and the new hopefulness rising from his death. His creature, fascism, had grown out of the chaotic conditions after World War I: a wrecked economy aggravated by the improvidence of the government; a frustrated idealism fostering blind nationalism and misplaced hero worship; a strong resistance to spiritual demobilization; and a disproportionate fear of communism. In several respects World War II left Italy in an even more serious state, a vanquished country torn apart by the consequences of civil war, bitter and disoriented, half-starved, prostrated after the long years of suffering. The pattern in the aftermath of war could have repeated itself. But it did not. The people had learned their lesson and did not let Italy plunge again into chaos. They had a purpose now, an aim to attain: to rebuild what fascism had destroyed, to wipe out the memory of the dictator and cleanse themselves of his sins. Industriously, with determination and zeal, they set to the task — and succeeded. Today Mussolini is the skeleton in the cupboard, a shameful incident in the history of a people.

SELECTED BIBLIOGRAPHY

The literature relating to Mussolini's life and times is vast, and a full bibliography would be beyond the scope of this book. The reader who wishes to read more about this subject is referred to CHARLES F. DELZELL, "Benito Mussolini: A Guide to the Biographical Literature," in the *Journal of Modern History*, XXXV (December, 1963), 339–53. The limited selection offered here includes only books in English and Italian. When a foreign-language book is known to have been translated into English, the translation is listed in place of the original.

MUSSOLINI'S WORKS

Opera Omnia di Benito Mussolini. Edited by EDOARDO AND DUILIO SUSMEL. 36 vols. Florence: La Fenice, 1951–63.
The Cardinal's Mistress. Translated by HYRAM MOTHERWELL. New York: A. & C. Boni, 1928.
Carteggio Arnaldo-Benito Mussolini. Edited by DUILIO SUSMEL. Florence: La Fenice, 1954.
Dizionario Mussoliniano. Edited by BRUNO BIANCINI, Milan: Hoepli, 1942.
Hitler e Mussolini, lettere e documenti. Edited by VITTORIO ZINCONE. Milan: Rizzoli, 1946.
John Huss. Translated by CLIFFORD PARKER. New York: A. &. C. Boni, 1929.
Memoirs, 1942–1943. (With documents relating to the period.) Translated by FRANCES LOBB. Edited by RAYMOND KLIBANSKY. London: Weidenfeld & Nicolson, 1949.
My Autobiography. Translated by RICHARD WASHBURN CHILD. New York: Charles Scribner's Sons, 1928.
Vomere e Spada (Thoughts and Maxims). Edited by LENA TRIVULZIO DELLA SOMAGLIA. Milan: Hoepli, 1936.
BALABANOFF, ANGELICA. *Il traditore Mussolini*. Rome: *Avanti!*, 1945.
BEDESCHI, SANTE, AND ALESSI, RINO. *Anni giovanili di Mussolini*. Milan: Mondadori, 1939.
BONAVITA, FRANCESCO. *Il padre del Duce*. Rome: Pinciana, 1933.

BORGHI, ARMANDO. *Mussolini Red and Black.* (With an Epilogue, *Hitler: Mussolini's Disciple.*) London: Wishart, 1935.

DE BEGNAC, YVON. *Vita di Benito Mussolini.* (From the origins to May 24, 1915.) Milan: Mondadori, 1936.

DINALE, OTTAVIO. *Quarant' anni di colloqui con lui.* Milan: Ciarrocca, 1953.

DOMBROWSKI, ROMAN. *Mussolini: Twilight and Fall.* Translated and with a preface by H. C. STEVENS. New York: Roy Publishers, 1956.

BIOGRAPHICAL WORKS ON MUSSOLINI

DORSO, GUIDO. *Mussolini alla conquista del potere.* Turin: Einaudi, 1949.

FUSTI CAROFIGLIO, MARIO. *Vita di Mussolini e storia del fascismo.* Turin: Società editrice torinese, 1950.

HALPERIN, SAMUEL WILLIAM. *Mussolini and Italian Fascism.* Princeton, N.J.: Van Nostrand, 1964.

HIBBERT, CHRISTOPHER. *Benito Mussolini, a Biography.* London: Longmans, 1962.

KIRKPATRICK, SIR IVONE AUGUSTINE. *Mussolini, a Study in Power.* New York: Hawthorn Books, 1964.

LUDWIG, EMIL. *Talks with Mussolini.* Translated from the German by EDEN AND CEDAR PAUL. Boston: Little, Brown & Co., 1933.

MACGREGOR-HASTIE, ROY. *The Day of the Lion: The Life and Death of Fascist Italy — 1922–45.* London: MacDonald, 1963.

MEGARO, GAUDENS. *Mussolini in the Making.* Boston: Houghton Mifflin Co., 1938.

MONELLI, PAOLO. *Mussolini, An Intimate Life.* Translated by Brigid Maxwell. London: Thames & Hudson, 1953.

MUSSOLINI, EDVIGE. *Mio fratello Benito.* (Memoirs, collected by her daughter, ROSETTA RICCI CRISOLINI.) Florence: La Fenice, 1957.

MUSSOLINI, RACHELE. *Benito il mio uomo.* (As told to ANITA PENSOTTI.) Milan: Rizzoli, 1958.

―――. *La mia vita con Benito.* Milan: Mondadori, 1948.

―――. *My Life with Mussolini.* (In collaboration with MICHEL CHINIGO.) London: R. Hale, 1959.

MUSSOLINI, VITTORIO. *Vita con mio padre.* Milan: Mondadori, 1957.

NANNI, TORQUATO. *Bolscevismo e fascismo al lume della critica marxista: Benito Mussolini.* Bologna: Cappelli, 1924.

PINI, GIORGIO, AND SUSMEL, DUILIO. *Mussolini, l'uomo e l'opera.* 4 vols. Florence: La Fenice, 1953–55.

RAFANELLI, LEDA. *Una donna e Mussolini.* Milan: Rizzoli, 1946.

SARFATTI, MARGHERITA G. *The Life of Benito Mussolini.* Translated by FREDERIC WHYTE. New York: Frederick A. Stokes Co., 1925.

SELDES, GEORGE. *Sawdust Caesar*. New York and London: Harper & Bros., 1935.
ZACHARIAE, GEORG. *Mussolini si confessa*. Milan: Garzanti, 1950.

HISTORIES OF MODERN ITALY

ALBRECHT-CARRIE, RENE. *Italy from Napoleon to Mussolini*. New York: Columbia University Press, 1950.
CROCE, BENEDETTO. *Storia dell'Italia dal 1871 al 1915*. Bari: Laterza, 1928.
HUGHES, HENRY STUART. *The United States and Italy*. Cambridge, Mass.: Harvard University Press, 1953.
JEMOLO, ARTURO CARLO. *Chiesa e stato in Italia negli ultimi cento anni*. Turin: Einaudi, 1948.
MACK SMITH, DENIS. *Italy*. Ann Arbor: University of Michigan Press, 1959.
SALVATORELLI, LUIGI, AND MIRA, GIOVANNI. *Storia dell'Italia nel periodo fascista*. Turin: Einaudi, 1956.
SFORZA, CARLO. *L'Italia dal 1914 al 1944 quale io la vidi*. Milan: Mondadori, 1944.
————. *Contemporary Italy: Its Intellectual and Moral Origins*. Translated by DRAKE AND DENISE DE KAY. London: Muller, 1941.
SPRIGGE, CECIL J. S. *The Development of Modern Italy*. London: Duckworth, 1943.
TAMARO, ATTILIO. *Venti anni di storia (1922–1943)*. 3 vols. Rome: Tiber, 1954.
VOLPE, GIOACCHINO. *L'Italia in cammino: l'ultimo cinquantennio*. Milan: Treves, 1931.
YOUNG, WAYLAND HILTON. *The Italian Left: A Short History of Political Socialism in Italy*. New York: Longmans, Green & Co., 1949.

OTHER WORKS

THROUGH THE MARCH ON ROME

ALATRI, PAOLO. *Le origini del fascismo*. Rome: Editori riuniti, 1956.
ALBRECHT-CARRIE, RENE. *Italy at the Paris Peace Conference*. New York: Columbia University Press, 1938.
ANGIOLINI, ALFREDO, AND CIACCHI, EUGENIO. *Socialismo e socialisti in Italia*. Florence: Nerbini, 1921.
ANTONGINI, TOM. *Vita segreta di Gabriele D'Annunzio*. Milan: Mondadori, 1938.
ARFE, GAETANO. *Storia dell'Avanti!* 2 vols. Rome: *Avanti!*, 1956.
BALABANOFF, ANGELICA. *My Life as a Rebel*. New York: Harper & Bros., 1938.
BALBO, ITALO. *Diario 1922*. Milan: Mondadori, 1932.

BONOMI, IVANOE. *From Socialism to Fascism: A Study of Contemporary Italy.* Translated by J. MURRAY. London: Hopkins, 1924.
———. *Leonida Bissolati e il movimento socialista in Italia.* Milan: Cogliati, 1929.
BORGESE, GIUSEPPE ANTONIO. *Goliath: The March of Fascism.* New York: Viking Press, Inc., 1937.
BRENNA, PAULA G. *Storia dell'emigrazione italiana.* Rome: Mantegazza, 1928.
CAVIGLIA, ENRICO. *Il conflitto di Fiume.* Milan: Garzanti, 1940.
CHIURCO, GIORGIO ALBERTO. *Storia della rivoluzione fascista.* 5 vols. Florence: Vallecchi, 1929.
CORRADINI, ENRICO. *Il nazionalismo italiano.* Milan: Treves, 1914.
FARINACCI, ROBERTO. *Storia della rivoluzione fascista.* 2 vols. Cremona: Cremona nuova, 1937.
FERRARIS, EFREM. *La marcia su Roma veduta dal Viminale.* Rome: Leonardo, 1946.
GIOLITTI, GIOVANNI. *Memoirs of My Life.* Translated by E. STORER. London: Chapman & Dodd, 1923.
HARDING, BERTITA. *Age Cannot Wither: The Story of Duse and D'Annunzio.* Philadelphia: J. B. Lippincott Co., 1947.
MEISEL, JAMES H. *The Genesis of Georges Sorel.* (An account of his formative years followed by a study of his influence.) Ann Arbor: George Wahr Co., 1951.
MICHELS, ROBERT. *Storia critica del movimento socialista italiano.* Florence: La Voce, 1926.
NATALE, GAETANO. *Giolitti e gli italiani.* Milan: Garzanti, 1949.
NENNI, PIETRO. *Ten Years of Tyranny in Italy.* Translated by ANNE STEELE. London: Allen & Unwin, 1932.
RHODES, ANTHONY R. E. *The Poet as Superman: A Life of Gabriele D'Annunzio.* London: Weidenfeld & Nicolson, 1959.
ROCCA, MASSIMO. *Come il fascismo divenne una dittatura.* Milan: Edizioni librarie italiane, 1952.
ROSSI [TASCA], ANGELO. *The Rise of Italian Fascism.* Translated by PETER AND DOROTHY WAIT. London: Meuthen, 1938.
SCHNEIDER, HERBERT W. *Making the Fascist State.* New York: Oxford University Press, 1928.
SOREL, GEORGES. *Reflections on Violence.* Translated by T. E. HULME. New York: Huebsch, 1914.
STIRNER, MAX [SCHMIDT, JOHANN KASPAR]. *The Ego and His Own.* Translated by STEVEN T. BYINGTON. London: Fifield, 1907.
STURZO, LUIGI. *Italy and Fascismo.* Translated by BARBARA B. CARTER. London: Faber & Gwyer, 1926.
VALERI, NINO. *Da Giolitti a Mussolini: momenti della crisi del liberalismo.* Florence: Parenti, 1957.
VOLPE, GIOACCHINO. *Guerra, dopoguerra, fascismo.* Venice: Nuova Italia, 1928.

FROM THE MARCH ON ROME
TO THE CREATION OF THE AXIS

ALBERTINI, ALBERTO. *Vita di Luigi Albertini.* Milan: Mondadori, 1945.

ASCOLI, MAX, AND FEILER, ARTHUR. *Fascism for Whom?* New York: W. W. Norton & Co., 1938.

BADOGLIO, PIETRO. *La guerra d'Etiopia.* Milan: Mondadori. 1936.

BARTOLI, DOMENICO. *La fine della monarchia.* Milan: Mondadori, 1946.

BIGGINI, CARLO ALBERTO. *Storia inedita della Conciliazione.* Milan: Garzanti, 1942.

BINCHY, DANIEL A. *Church and State in Fascist Italy.* London: Oxford University Press, 1941.

BOTTAI, GIUSEPPE. *Vent'anni e un giorno (24 luglio 1943).* Milan: Garzanti, 1949.

BRAUNTHAL, JULIUS. *The Tragedy of Austria.* (Appendix: *Mussolini and Dolfuss: An Episode in Fascist Diplomacy,* by PAUL R. SWEET.) London: Gollancz, 1948.

CANTALUPO, ROBERTO. *Fu la Spagna.* Milan: Mondadori, 1948.

CAVIGLIA, ENRICO. *Diario (1925–1945).* Rome: Casini, 1952.

D'ANDREA, UGO. *La fine del regno: grandezza e decadenza di Vittorio Emanuele III.* Turin: Società editrice torinese, 1951.

DE BEGNAC, YVON. *Palazzo Venezia, storia di un regime.* Rome: La Rocca, 1950.

DE BONO, EMILIO. *Anno XIII: The Conquest of an Empire.* Translated by BERNARD MIALL. London: Cresset Press, 1937.

DE FELICE, RENZO. *Storia degli Ebrei italiani sotto il fascismo.* Torino: Einaudi, 1961.

DELZELL, CHARLES F. *Mussolini's Enemies: The Italian Anti-Fascist Resistance.* Princeton, N.J.: Princeton University Press, 1961.

DONOSTI [LUCIOLLI], MARIO. *Mussolini e l'Europa, la politica estera fascista.* Rome: Leonardo, 1945.

FINER, HERMAN. *Mussolini's Italy.* London: Gollancz, 1935.

FLORA, FRANCESCO. *Ritratto di un ventennio.* Naples: Macchiaroli, 1944.

———. *Stampa dell'era facista.* Milan: Mondadori. 1945.

FRANCOIS-PONCET, ANDRE. *The Fateful Years: Memoirs of a French Ambassador in Berlin, 1931–1938.* Translated by JACQUES LE CLERQ. New York: Harcourt Brace & Co., 1949.

GAROSCI, ALDO. *Storia dei Fuorusciti:* Bari: Laterza, 1955.

GARRATT, GEOFFREY T. *Mussolini's Roman Empire.* Harmondsworth, Middlesex: Penguin, 1938.

GUARIGLIA, RAFFAELE. *Ricordi (1922–1946).* Naples: Edizioni scientifiche italiane, 1949.

HOLLIS, CHRISTOPHER. *Italy in Africa.* London: Hamish Hamilton, 1941.

LETO, GUIDO. *Ovra: fascismo, antifascismo.* Bologna: Cappelli, 1952.

LUSSU, EMILIO. *Road to Exile: The Story of a Sardinian Patriot.* Translated by MRS. GRAHAM RAWSON. New York: Covici Friede, Inc., 1936.

McCORMICK, ANNE (O'HARE). *Vatican Journal, 1921–1954.* Edited by MARION TURNER SHEEHAN. New York: Farrar, Strauss & Cudahy, Inc., 1957.

NAVARRA, QUINTO. *Memorie del cameriere di Mussolini.* Milan: Longanesi, 1946.

OJETTI, UGO. *I taccuini (1914–1943)* Florence: Sansoni, 1954.

PHILLIPS, WILLIAM. *Ventures in Diplomacy.* Boston: Beacon Press, 1953.

PINI, GIORGIO. *Filo diretto con palazzo Venezia.* Bologna: Cappelli, 1950.

ROSSI, CESARE. *Il tribunale speciale.* Milan: Ceschina, 1952.

ROSSI, ERNESTO. *I padroni del vapore.* Bari: Laterza, 1955.

SALVEMINI, GAETANO. *Italian Fascism.* London: Gollancz, 1938.

——. *Mussolini diplomatico (1922–1932).* Bari: Laterza, 1952.

——. *Under the Axe of Fascism.* New York: Viking Press, Inc., 1936.

SCHNEIDER, HERBERT W. *The Fascist Government in Italy.* New York: D. Van Nostrand Co., Inc., 1936.

SILVESTRI, CARLO. *Matteotti, Mussolini e il dramma italiano.* Rome: Ruffolo, 1947.

SPAGNOLO, GIOVANNI. *"Ceka fascista" e "delitto Matteotti" nella requisitoria del Procuratore generale.* Rome: Ruffolo, 1947.

STARHEMBERG, ERNEST R., VON. *Between Hitler and Mussolini.* New York: Harper & Bros., 1942.

STEER, GEORGE L. *Caesar in Abyssinia.* Boston: Little, Brown & Co., 1937.

TEELING, WILLIAM. *Pope Pius XI and World Affairs.* New York: Frederick A. Stokes Co., 1937.

TOYNBEE, ARNOLD J. *Survey of International Affairs, 1935.* Vol. II, *Abyssinia and Italy.* London: Oxford University Press, 1935.

VILLARI, LUIGI. *Italian Foreign Policy under Mussolini.* New York: Devin-Adair, 1956.

VOLPE, GIOACCHINO. *Storia del movimento fascista.* Milan: ISP, 1939.

FROM THE AXIS TO MUSSOLINI'S DEATH

ALFIERI, DINO. *Due dittatori di fronte.* Milan: Rizzoli, 1948.

ANFUSO, FILIPPO. *Da palazzo Venezia al lago di Garda (1936–1945).* Bologna: Cappelli, 1957.

BADOGLIO, PIETRO. *Italy in the Second World War: Memories and Documents.* Translated by MURIEL CURREY. London: Oxford University Press, 1948.

BELLOTTI, FELICE. *La republica di Mussolini, 26 luglio 1943—25 Aprile 1945.* Milan: Zagara, 1947.

BULLOCK, ALAN L. C. *Hitler: A Study in Tyranny.* London: Odhams, 1952.

CHURCHILL, WINSTON L. S. *The Gathering Storm (The Second World War,* Vol. I. London: Cassell, 1948.

CIANO, GALEAZZO. *Diary, 1937–1938.* Translation and notes by ANDREAS MAYOR. London: Methuen, 1952.

———. *The Ciano Diaries, 1939–1943.* Edited by HUGH GIBSON. Garden City, N.Y.: Doubleday & Co., 1946.

———. *Ciano's Diplomatic Papers.* Edited by MALCOLM MUGGERIDGE. Translated by STUART HOOD. London: Odhams, 1948.

CIONE, EDMONDO. *Storia della repubblica sociale italiana.* Caserta: Cenacolo, 1948.

DEAKIN, F. W. *The Brutal Friendship: Mussolini, Hitler, and the Fall of Italian Fascism.* New York: Harper & Row, 1962.

DOLFIN, GIOVANNI. *Con Mussolini nella tragedia: diario del capo della segreteria particolare del Duce 1943–1944.* Milan: Garzanti, 1950.

FAVAGROSSA, CARLO. *Perchè perdemmo la guerra: Mussolini e la produzione bellica.* Milan: Rizzoli, 1946.

GOEBBELS, JOSEPH. *The Goebbels Diaries, 1942–1943.* Edited and translated by LOUIS P. LOCHNER. Garden City, N.Y.: Doubleday & Co., 1948.

GORLA, GIUSEPPE. *L'Italia nella seconda guerra mondiale.* Milan: Baldini & Castoldi, 1959.

MAGISTRATI, MASSIMO. *L'Italia a Berlino, 1937–1939.* Milan: Mondadori, 1956.

MONELLI, PAOLO. *Roma 1943.* Rome: Migliaresi, 1946.

MONTAGNA, RENZO. *Mussolini e il processo di Verona.* Milan: Edizioni Omnia, 1949.

NENNI, PIETRO. *Pagine di diario.* Milan: Garzanti, 1947.

PAPEN, FRANZ VON. *Memoirs.* Translated by BRIAN CONNELL. London: Deutsch, 1952.

ROATTA, MARIO. *Otto milioni di baionette: L'Esercito italiano dal 1940 al 1944.* Milan: Mondadori, 1946.

SALVADORI, MASSIMO. *Storia della resistenza italiana.* Venice: Neri Pozza, 1955.

SCHMIDT, PAUL. *Hitler's Interpreter.* Edited by R. H. C. STEED. London: Heinemann, 1951.

SCHUSCHNIGG, KURT. *Austrian Requiem.* Translated by FRANZ VON HILDEBRAND. New York: G. P. Putnam's Sons, 1946.

SENISE, CARMINE. *Quando ero capo della polizia.* Rome: Ruffolo, 1946.

SIMONI, LEONARDO [LANZA, MARIO]. *Berlino — ambasciata d'Italia, 1939–1943.* Rome: Migliaresi, 1946.

SKORZENY, OTTO. *Secret Missions: War Memories of the Most Dangerous Man in Europe.* Translated by JACQUES LE CLERQ. New York: E. P. Dutton & Co., Inc., 1950.

TAMARO, ATTILIO. *Due anni di storia (1943–1945).* 3 vols. Rome: Tosi, 1948–50.

TOSCANO, MARIO. *Le origini diplomatiche del patto di acciaio.* Florence: Sansoni, 1956.

WELLES, SUMNER. *The Time for Decision.* New York: Harper & Bros., 1944.

WISKEMANN, ELIZABETH. *The Rome-Berlin Axis: A History of the Relations between Hitler and Mussolini.* New York: Oxford University Press, 1949.

INDEX